HD 5707 RUB

D0263251

The organization of employment

An international perspective

MAIN LIBRARY
QUEEN M'

WITHDRAWN
FROM STOCK
QMUL LIBRARY

MANAGEMENT, WORK AND ORGANISATIONS

Series editors: **Gibson Burrell**, Warwick Business School
Mick Marchington, Manchester School of Management, UMIST
Paul Thompson, Department of Human Resource Management,
University of Strathclyde

This series of new textbooks covers the areas of human resource management, employee relations, organisational behaviour and related business and management fields. Each text has been specially commissioned to be written by leading experts in a clear and accessible way. The books contain serious and challenging material, take an analytical rather than prescriptive approach and are particularly suitable for use by students with no prior specialist knowledge.

The series is relevant for many business and management courses, including MBA and post-experience courses, specialist Masters and postgraduate diplomas, professional courses and final-year undergraduate courses. These texts have become essential reading at business and management schools worldwide.

Published

Paul Blyton and Peter Turnbull **The Dynamics of Employee Relations** (2nd edn)
Peter Boxall and John Purcell **Strategy and Human Resource Management**
J. Martin Corbett **Critical Cases in Organisational Behaviour**
Marek Korczynski **Human Resource Management in Service Work**
Sue Ledwith and Fiona Colgan (eds) **Women in Organisations**
Karen Legge **Human Resource Management**
Stephen Procter and Frank Mueller (eds) **Teamworking**
Helen Rainbird (ed.) **Training in the Workplace**
Michael Rowlinson **Organisations and Institutions**
Jill Rubery and Damian Grimshaw **The Organization of Employment**
Harry Scarbrough (ed.) **The Management of Expertise**
Adrian Wilkinson, Mick Marchington, Tom Redman and Ed Snape
   Managing with Total Quality Management
Diana Winstanley and Jean Woodall (eds) **Ethical Issues in Contemporary**
   Human Resource Management

Forthcoming

Richard Badham **The Management of Change**
Pippa Carter and Norman Jackson **Critical Issues in Organisational Behaviour**
Keith Grint **Leadership**
Irena Grugulis **The Learning Organisation**
Karen Legge **Critical Perspectives on Organisational Change**
Hugh Scullion and Margaret Lineham **International Human Resource Management**
Graham Sewell **Demystifying Management**

Series Standing Order

If you would like to receive future titles in this series as they are published, you can make use of our standing order facility. To place a standing order please contact your bookseller or, in case of difficulty, write to us at the address below with your name and address and the name of the series. Please state with which title you wish to begin your standing order. (If you live outside the United Kingdom we may not have the rights for your area, in which case we will forward your order to the publisher concerned.)

Customer Services Department, Macmillan Distribution Ltd
Houndmills, Basingstoke, Hampshire RG21 6XS, England

The organization of employment

An international perspective

Jill Rubery and Damian Grimshaw

QM LIBRARY
(MILE END)

© Jill Rubery and Damian Grimshaw 2003

All rights reserved. No reproduction, copy or transmission of this
publication may be made without written permission.

No paragraph of this publication may be reproduced, copied or transmitted
save with written permission or in accordance with the provisions of the
Copyright, Designs and Patents Act 1988, or under the terms of any licence
permitting limited copying issued by the Copyright Licensing Agency, 90
Tottenham Court Road, London W1T 4LP.

Any person who does any unauthorized act in relation to this publication
may be liable to criminal prosecution and civil claims for damages.

The authors have asserted their rights to be identified as
the authors of this work in accordance with the Copyright, Designs and
Patents Act 1988.

First published 2003 by
PALGRAVE MACMILLAN
Houndmills, Basingstoke, Hampshire RG21 6XS and
175 Fifth Avenue, New York, N.Y. 10010
Companies and representatives throughout the world

PALGRAVE MACMILLAN is the global academic imprint of the Palgrave
Macmillan division of St. Martin's Press, LLC and of Palgrave Macmillan Ltd.
Macmillan® is a registered trademark in the United States, United Kingdom
and other countries. Palgrave is a registered trademark in the European
Union and other countries.

ISBN 0–333–80236–5 paperback

This book is printed on paper suitable for recycling and made from fully
managed and sustained forest sources.

A catalogue record for this book is available from the British Library.

Library of Congress Cataloging-in-Publication Data
Rubery, Jill.
      The organization of employment: an international perspective/Jill Rubery and
      Damian Grimshaw.
         p. cm. — (Management, work and organisations)
      ISBN 0–333–80236–5 (paper)
         1. Labor. 2. Labor—Statistics. 3. Employment (Economic theory). 4. Labor
economics. 5. International division of labor. 6. Labor market. 7. Manpower policy.
8. Personnel management. 9. Industrial relations. 10. Labor unions. I. Rubery,
Jill. II. Grimshaw, Damian. III. Title. IV. Series.
      HD4854.R76 2002
      331—dc21

10   9   8   7   6   5   4   3   2   1
12 11 10 09 08 07 06 05 04 03

Printed and bound in Great Britain by
Creative Print & Design (Ebbw Vale), Wales

Contents

List of boxes, figures and tables

Boxes

Figures

Tables

Abbreviations

CEC	Commission of the European Communities
ETUC	European Trades Union Confederation
EU	European Union
GDP	Gross domestic product
ILM	Internal labour market
ILO	International Labour Organization
IMF	International Monetary Fund
JAM	Job classification, adversarial relations and minimal training
MNC	Multinational corporation
NAFTA	North Atlantic Free Trade Association
OECD	Organization for Economic Cooperation and Development
OLM	Occupational labour market
SET	Security, employee involvement and training
UNICE	Union of Industrial and Employers' Confederations of Europe

Acknowledgements

In the course of writing this book we have had help and encouragement from a number of sources. Mick Marchington, a colleague and a series editor put the idea of writing such a book with Palgrave Macmillan into our heads and has provided strong encouragement along the way. Sarah Brown at Palgrave was also helpful and supportive until leaving the organization shortly before we finished the manuscript. Direct assistance with the production of the book has been ably and willingly provided by our secretary Mary O'Brien. Further assistance was provided by research assistants and students: Hugo Figueiredo, Peter Fröbel, Rory Donnelly and David Gastearena. Helpful comments and suggestions on the draft manuscript were provided by the series editors.

Our intellectual debts are difficult to identify in a book of this nature as it spans the whole field of employment issues on which we have worked separately or collectively. Immediate debts are to those whom we have worked with closely in Manchester on comparative issues, including Mark Smith and Colette Fagan. Jeremy Waddington and Mick Marchington at UMIST also offered comments on parts of the book. Much of our approach to comparative research and our knowledge of comparative employment systems has come through our involvement in the International Working Party on Labour Market Segmentation, Jill since 1979 and Damian since 1994. We have also benefited enormously from the comparative work we have carried out in the context of coordinating the European Commission's gender and employment expert group and we are grateful to the experts who have helped us in our understanding of the fifteen member states of the European Union. Consultancy work with the International Labour Organization and discussions with friends and colleagues on the staff there have also helped our understanding of the issues related to international labour standards. Finally, we are indebted to our students who have taken the course in increasing numbers despite the lack of a handy text and who have helped us develop ways of covering this range of material even within the space of a 12 week course.

The authors and publishers wish to thank the following for permission to reproduce copyright material. Every effort has been made to trace all copyright holders, but if any have been inadvertently overlooked the publishers will make the necessary arrangements at the first opportunity.

Francesca Bettio, Colette Fagan, Frederike Maier, Sigrid Quack and Paula Villa for an extract from J. Rubery, F. Bettio, C. Fagan, F. Maier, S. Quack and P. Villa, 'Payment systems and gender pay differentials: some societal effects', in J. Rubery *et al.* (eds), *Equal Pay in Europe?* (Basingstoke: Macmillan (now Palgrave Macmillan)/ILO, 1998), pp. 13–16.

Clair Brown, Yoshifumi Nakata, Michael Reich and Lloyd Ulman for an extract from C. Brown, Y. Nakata, M. Reich and L. Ulman, *Work and Pay in the United States and Japan* (New York and Oxford: Oxford University Press, 1997), pp. 130–2.

Howard Gospel for an extract from 'The revival of apprenticeship training in Britain?', *British Journal of Industrial Relations*, 36 (1998): 451–3.

Klaus Jacobs and Martin Rein for an extract from 'Early retirement: stability, reversal or redefinition', in F. Naschold and B. de Vroom (eds), *Regulating Employment and Welfare* (Berlin: de Gruyter, 1993), pp. 33–6.

Alice Lam for an extract from 'Work organisation, skills development and utilisation of engineers', in R. Crompton, D. Gallie and K. Purcell (eds), *Changing Forms of Employment* (London: Routledge, 1996), pp. 190–2.

Marc Maurice for extracts from: M. Maurice, F. Sellier and J-J. Silvestre, 'The search for a societal effect in the production of company hierarchy: a comparison of France and Germany', in P. Osterman (ed.), *Internal Labor Markets* (Cambridge, MA: MIT Press, 1984), pp. 251–4; M. Maurice, F. Sellier and J-J. Silvestre, *The Social Foundations of Industrial Power* (Cambridge, MA: MIT Press, 1986), pp. 35–6; 'The paradoxes of societal analysis: a review of the past and prospects for the future', in M. Maurice and A. Sorge (eds), *Embedding Organizations* (Amsterdam: John Benjamins, 2000), pp. 22, 24.

Paul Osterman for an extract from P. Osterman, *Employment Futures* (New York: Oxford University Press, 1988), pp. 119–121.

Birgit Pfau-Effinger for an extract from 'Culture or structure as explanations for differences in part-time work in Germany, Finland and the Netherlands', in J. O'Reilly and C. Fagan (eds), *Part-Time Prospects* (London: Routledge, 1998), p. 192.

Colette Fagan and Janneke Plantenga for an extract from C. Fagan, J. Plantenga and J. Rubery, 'Part-time work and inequality? Lessons from the Netherlands and the UK', in *A Time for Working, A Time for Living* (Brussels: ETUC and ETUI, 1995), pp. 139–41.

John Storey for extracts from P. Garnjost and K. Blettner, 'Volkswagen', in J. Storey (ed.), *Blackwell Cases In Human Resource and Change Management* (Oxford: Blackwell, 1996), pp. 86, 87, 89–90, 91–2, 95, 96, 97.

Lowell Turner and The Brookings Institution for an extract from L. Turner, 'Prospects for worker participation in management in the single market', in L. Ulman, B. Eichengreen and W. Dickens (eds), *Labor and An Integrated Europe* (Washington, D.C.: The Brookings Institution, 1993), pp. 63–9.

Preface

This book explores the organization of employment from an international perspective, taking as our main field of vision advanced countries, as defined by membership of the OECD. There are three main reasons for taking an international approach to a book on employment and labour markets.

The first relates to our intellectual background and perspective. We take labour markets to be social constructs, shaped and influenced by institutions and by social actors. Comparison of labour markets among nation states, where the institutional arrangements, the social conditions, the forms of economic organization and the role and attitudes of social actors all vary, provides a very rich field for developing these concepts and alerting students to the variety of ways in which employment can be and is organized. Our exploration of these forms of diversity is primarily focused on comparison between nation states. It is at this level that many of the important institutions and social arrangements that impact on employment are constituted, from the welfare state, the education and training system to the legal system. The purpose is not, however, simply to describe different institutional arrangements but to understand how these lock together to generate a particular societal logic or path of development, and to impart different meanings and significance to apparently similar employment policies and practices in different nations or social environments. While we take the nation state as the starting point for our comparative analyses, we are conscious that national employment systems should not be seen as stand-alone entities but analyzed as part of the increasingly integrated world economic system. The objective is therefore not to provide a static and stylized account of comparative employment systems, but to identify the dynamics of change at both the national and the more global levels.

The second reason for writing this text is to expand the scope of texts available for courses on international aspects of employment, by bringing together literatures from a range of social science disciplines that are rarely integrated into one text. Our particular frustration in this regard has been with the subject of international human resource management; texts in this area often define their topic very narrowly, focusing on the management of employment — and primarily managerial employment — within multinationals. The issue of diversity in employment systems is neatly dealt with by the rather abstract but contentious notion of differences in national culture, which absolves students and textbook writers alike from being required to know too much about the actual social and institutional context in which the subsidiaries of multinationals are located. This institution-free approach to human resource management cannot be justified in the light of the now prolific literature on diversity in employment systems. Comparative texts tend to fall into two categories: either they provide a series of single country studies, leaving it up to students to do the hard work of comparison, or they take a relatively narrow focus such as the industrial relations system or the training system. The task of integrating information provided by either topic or country is, for many university courses, particularly those like ours based on a single semester, too ambitious. Our own students have had to struggle with this task for several years. In many ways this was no bad thing; it encouraged the students to read journal articles and to dip in and out of material rather than expecting a ready-made synthesis. Nevertheless we felt that for the benefit of our students and others it would be valuable to draw this material together into a single volume. The text draws on literature from most of the social science disciplines, industrial relations, organizational behaviour, sociology, social policy, economics, political science, management and international business and human geography and integrates the more academic with the more policy-oriented comparative material produced by the OECD, the EU and the ILO.

Our third motivation for writing the text was our belief that the integration of the world economy at an economic and political level is reducing the validity of courses on production and employment systems that focus solely on the national context. Increased mobility of capital and labour requires students taking courses on employment issues to develop some knowledge and understanding of the new international division of labour and the growth of multinationals and their consequences for employment policy and practice. A perspective on these issues is needed whether or not our students in their future lives will be mainly attempting as citizens to understand political debates or seeking to operate as effective practitioners in the employment area. All educated citizens need to be able to weigh up the arguments and the balance of the evidence when confronted with policy agendas that politicians assert are the only valid response to the inevitable and unstoppable process of globalization. Such issues not only concern protesters at the World Trade Organization summits but also lie at the heart of the debates within the European Union, over whether the so-called European social model can be considered a contributor to European prosperity or a hindrance to the more rapid development of the European economy.

International employment issues have also increased in salience for practitioners concerned with issues of employment at the workplace. In the new globalized world, according to much of the management literature, managers are expected to be able to identify and implement the employment system that represents new global best practice. Managers therefore need to be informed about the debates that question whether such a thing as global best practice even exists. Similarly trade unionists often find themselves under increasing pressure to develop new local partnership arrangements with management; but in order for a proper partnership to develop the trade unions also need to understand how the particular plant or organization fits within the wider international company or the international supply chain.

It is with these three motivations in mind that we have developed this text, designed for final year undergraduate and graduate students studying issues related to work and employment on a range of social science and management courses. The book starts with an opening chapter designed to achieve two objectives: to make clear to the reader why employment issues are interesting and important in both a national and international context, and to introduce the reader to some of the rich and interesting literature on comparative employment systems. We do this by relying on the research to speak for itself, by including extracts from some of the key writings covering a range of employment topics. Chapter Two describes and critiques the different methodological approaches that have been developed towards comparative analysis and sets out the theoretical or analytical framework that we adopt through the book. This framework draws on an institutionalist rather than a cultural approach to diversity in employment systems, but develops the approach to focus on the dynamics of change within societal employment systems, in response to global and international pressures. The next two chapters focus on how and why the employment systems in apparently similar advanced countries have taken on different forms. Here we draw on the debate on the varieties of capitalism, focusing on the reasons for and the consequences of the emergence and sustainability of variety in the organization of production and employment. Chapter Three, informed by debates in organization analysis, the labour process and political science, discusses the move from Fordist to a variety of post-Fordist production regimes. The chapter identifies the role of societal factors in giving rise to a range of alternative models compatible with the new competitive requirements. These societal factors inhibit the extent to which models may be copied or transferred. Nevertheless there are forces promoting the spread and diffusion of new production techniques and employment systems, sometimes known as best practice. However, the process of diffusion is shown not necessarily to be leading to convergence as the integration of the new approaches may be only partial or selective, influenced by national conditions and by the particular societal logic. Chapter Four introduces a parallel literature on varieties of capitalism, found mainly in sociology and social policy, on the different patterns of welfare state development or welfare regimes. The chapter explores the impact of these welfare regimes on employment, identifying their influence on the level of employment, patterns of participation, the role of public employment and, above all, on gender relations inside and outside the labour market. The chapter draws together the work on welfare regimes with comparative research on women's integration into the labour market. The expansion of women's employment is one of the most sustained and universal features of OECD labour markets, but the pattern of integration has taken different forms, with implications for example for the growth of flexible employment forms or for the level of wage inequality within labour markets.

Chapter Five takes up the issue of how nation states have developed different ways of skilling the labour force. One set of institutions that has been particularly well studied as a result of this interest in varieties of capitalism is that of education and training systems, often believed to hold the key to better economic performance. These claims and the possibilities of transferring the apparently more successful systems to other nation states are critically explored. The chapter concludes by considering the extent to which training and education systems are capable of adjusting to new needs for training and development.

In Chapter Six the focus is on the system of labour market regulation and its implications for labour market flexibility and rigidity. The meaning of the term flexibility and the role of regulation in creating or promoting flexibility are critically examined. Here we draw on two main sources of material: on the rich tradition of comparative research within industrial relations that has demonstrated the variety of forms and meaning to be attached to collective bargaining systems, trade union structures and even systems of labour law; and on the ever expanding research by policymakers and economists seeking to find the relationship, if any, between different ways of organizing and regulating employment and economic outcomes. This focus on the role of labour market institutions in economic performance has been driven to a large extent by the OECD, the policy think tank for advanced countries operating within the UN system, and also by the European Union as it strives both to defend the European social model and to develop a new employment strategy for Europe. The chapter suggests that the need now is to move the debate forward, beyond the question of whether regulation is desirable or undesirable and instead towards the analysis of what constitutes an appropriate mix of policies, taking into account the regulatory traditions and institutions within a given society.

The implications of these different approaches to employment policy and practice identified at the national level for the experience of work and employment at the workplace level are the subject of Chapter Seven. Here we explore the employment policies and practices in a number of major OECD economies with respect to work organization, pay, redundancy and working time.

The final three chapters of the book address, each in a different way, the impact of increasing international integration on employment systems. Chapter Eight explores the factors influencing employment policy and practice within multinationals and considers the role of multinationals in the diffusion of employment practices across international boundaries. The consequences for national employment systems are also considered. Here we draw on the typologies of multinationals developed by international business experts and the now expanding literature on the management of employment within multinationals found both in the industrial relations and the international business literature.

In Chapter Nine the focus is on globalization and the implications of globalization for the survival of national employment regimes. This theme is addressed throughout the book but in this penultimate chapter we explore in more detail the different perspectives on globalization found in political science literature and elsewhere, and identify the pressures for change upon employment regimes. However, although there are problems in sustaining some of the key features of the labour market models — for example the job-for-life system in Japan and the dual training system in Germany — there is also evidence of adaptation and change within these models which may secure their survival, albeit in a modified form. Chapter Ten completes the volume by taking up the issue of the role of international labour standards. This complements the analysis of the role of labour market regulation at a national level found in Chapter Six. Here we describe the current initiatives taken at both an international and regional level (for example the EU and NAFTA) to promote and regulate labour standards. The argument is made that the promotion of decent work must become a major part of the policy agenda to regulate and develop the international economy. To achieve this objective we need not only to promote international labour standards but also to integrate employment objectives and considerations into general economic and development policy.

1

Diversity in the organization of employment: an introduction to the subject

The subject of this book is employment; and employment matters — not only to those who provide the labour or those who provide the jobs, but also to all of us who have a stake in the well-being of our economies and societies. Most books about employment focus on what happens within a particular country or locality. This is because the organization of employment is influenced by a whole variety of institutions — the law, the collective bargaining system, the training and education system, the family and household organization, and gender relations — and these institutions are often local or national in character. Yet if the way in which employment is organized is crucial to people's lives and livelihoods, to the economic success of companies or nation states and to the creation of social cohesion or division, then it is also crucial to understand how and why the organization of employment differs outside the local or national context. Knowledge of alternative ways of organizing employment expands the range of options that may be considered in shaping employment in the national context. Moreover, as economies become more integrated on a global or regional basis, there is increasing competition between economies based, in part, on different modes of organizing employment. These pressures have been calling into question traditional ways of organizing employment within nation states, and generating debate about whether there is one best way of managing employment that all nation states and all organizations should try to emulate. To evaluate these debates and to understand more about the possibilities or scope for organizing employment in different ways, we need both more knowledge about how and why employment organization currently varies, even within advanced countries, and more understanding of the forces that drive and limit the pressure for globalization and homogenization. The purpose of this book is to contribute to increasing knowledge and understanding of these two issues. First, however, we need to explore a little more why employment matters and to whom.

1

Why employment matters

Employment is of central concern to all individuals and to all the major social actors in society. For individuals, the interest in employment is clear: it provides their main source of economic livelihood and often their source of social identity. Working under an employment contract defines the daily activity of most people in their prime years. Their interest in both the rewards from working and the conditions and constraints under which they work is direct and considerable. Both private and public sector employers are equally concerned with employment issues: the skills their employees use and the effort that they expend define these organizations' ability to provide goods and services. Employers have just as strong an interest, however, in how much employment costs and how much risk they incur from employment contracts that provide some employment and income security to employees, and thus involve fixed as well as variable costs.

Employment is also a political issue. Governments are expected to take some responsibility for generating economic growth and for providing reasonable employment opportunities for citizens. Failure in these respects may lead to a change of government or to more serious political unrest. Governments feel obliged to intervene but there are mixed views on what forms of intervention are appropriate. Is it better to try to attract capital to enter or to remain within the economy by offering opportunities to companies to employ labour at low costs and with low economic risks? Or should the government foster the development of a highly skilled workforce and an atmosphere of high mutual trust between employers and employees, bolstered by a strong system of employment protection?

A book on the organization of employment, therefore, addresses a wide number of audiences. Its function first and foremost must be to explain and illustrate why employment is not only important but also complex. The term 'labour market' often gives the impression that employment can be analysed in the same way as the market for any other type of commodity. However, labour is not a commodity as it is provided by human beings, who must be treated with respect and dignity and who only sell their labour and not their souls on the labour market. This distinction has fundamental consequences for the nature of the market, not least because the exercise of labour remains under the control of the persons supplying the labour, not the purchaser. Issues of motivation are as important in determining outcomes as the original transaction, based on an exchange of hours of work for a wage. Employers in fact do not usually seek to purchase a predetermined level of effort, as they wish to engage the creative and problem-solving capacities of labour in furthering the interests of the organization. These capacities are needed in a whole spectrum of activities, including some often considered low skilled or low discretion jobs.

The first element of complexity in employment analysis, therefore, emerges out of the nature of the employment relationship and the distinctive form of the

Box 1.1   The nature of the employment contract

The employment contract is an example of what is now sometimes called an 'incomplete contract'; that is to say, some of its terms are unspecified. Employees agree to do, over the life of the contract, what they are ordered to do; but the orders will not be issued until some time after the contract is negotiated. The usual argument (within the neoclassical framework) for the existence of incomplete contracts is that in a world of uncertainty actions will have to be taken as the situation calls for them, without time for negotiation ... An employment contract contains all sorts of implicit (and explicit) limitations that set boundaries to the range of actions the employee will be directed to perform. These boundaries define the 'zone of acceptance' within which employees can be expected to obey orders ... Authority in organisations is not used exclusively, or even mainly to command specific actions ... most often, the command takes the form of a result to be produced ('repair this hinge'), or a principle to be applied ('all purchases must be made through the purchasing department'), or goal constraints ('manufacture as cheaply as possible consistent with quality'). Only the end goal has been supplied by the command, not the method of reaching it ... Doing the job well is not mainly a matter of responding to commands, it is much more a matter of taking initiative to advance organisational objectives ... For organisations to work well, it is not enough for employees to accept commands literally. In fact, obeying operating rules literally is a favourite method of work slowdown during labor-management disputes, as visitors to airports when controllers are unhappy can attest. What is required is that employees take initiative and apply all their skill and knowledge to advance the achievement of the organisation's objectives.

Extract from H. Simon, 'Organizations and markets', *Journal of Economic Perspectives*, 5 (1991): 30–2.

employment contract (see Box 1.1). A second level of complexity arises out of the divergences in interests and objectives of employment from the perspective of the various actors. These divergent interests can clearly be found between the main actors — namely labour, capital and the state. However, even the individual actors may be seeking potentially contradictory objectives in their employment strategies (see Figure 1.1). Can organizations have both cheap labour and high productivity and performance, or do they have to accept a trade-off? Can wages provide both a fair standard of living for all and still provide a fair reward for effort, performance and skill? Can governments both build up the skill base of the economy and respond to problems of high levels of unemployment?

The range of objectives pursued under the heading of employment provides also the scope for finding mutually beneficial solutions between actors with different interests. For example, employees interested in increasing their job security may be willing to cooperate with and facilitate a process of change and innovation within an organization. However, there is always a risk of divergent interests re-emerging and undermining such a coalition of interests if, for example, employees come to fear that the restructuring may eventually lead to job losses or to further work intensification. There tend to be, therefore, no simple solutions to employment

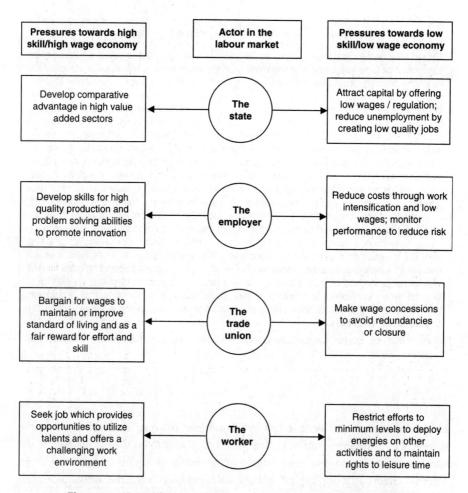

Pressures towards high skill/high wage economy	Actor in the labour market	Pressures towards low skill/low wage economy
Develop comparative advantage in high value added sectors	The state	Attract capital by offering low wages / regulation; reduce unemployment by creating low quality jobs
Develop skills for high quality production and problem solving abilities to promote innovation	The employer	Reduce costs through work intensification and low wages; monitor performance to reduce risk
Bargain for wages to maintain or improve standard of living and as a fair reward for effort and skill	The trade union	Make wage concessions to avoid redundancies or closure
Seek job which provides opportunities to utilize talents and offers a challenging work environment	The worker	Restrict efforts to minimum levels to deploy energies on other activities and to maintain rights to leisure time

Figure 1.1 Contradictory pressures on employment policy and practice

problems, only compromises and second best solutions, which are constantly subject to renegotiation and change.

Given this complexity even at national level, it is reasonable to ask if there are strong grounds for extending this complexity further by looking at these practices from an international perspective. The answer depends on two issues. First, how much do employment policies and practices actually vary in practice between countries? And second, if we find evidence of difference, is that discovery interesting and important?

The answer to both questions is in the affirmative. Our argument will be that employment practices do indeed differ significantly between countries and that these differences are likely to persist. Knowledge of these differences is not only important for anyone who has direct concern with, or responsibility for, employment spanning more than one country — for example those employed in the human resource functions of multinationals or in the international branches of unions — but also for anyone concerned with employment issues within their own country. In each society there are different ways of organizing employment, reflecting the various institutional arrangements in place to generate skills, regulate the employment relationship and shape the wage structure. Recognition that there is not only one way of doing things, that alternative methods, for better or for worse, are available and in use, can be extremely illuminating in opening up debate and discussion even over a very local employment issue.

At one extreme, there is a predisposition to take local arrangements and ways of doing things as representing the only way or the commonsense way of organizing and managing complex issues such as employment. At the other extreme, systems deployed in other countries may be seen as offering simple solutions. Under this latter approach, it is tempting to blame government myopia or the vested interests of employers or workers for the apparent failure to learn from a 'best practice' example in another country.

The approach taken here is not to regard examples from different nation states as providing models that can be simply emulated in other environments. Employment policies and practices are necessarily embedded in a social environment and do not operate independently of other aspects of social and economic life. Analysis of other ways of doing things requires a full assessment of both the pluses and minuses of particular arrangements or systems of employment organization. This evaluation requires an understanding of how the arrangement operates within its own social context and an understanding of how the interactions with the immediate environment influence the effectiveness of that particular way of organizing employment.

The first task of this book is, therefore, to explore the different approaches to employment in order to open up the range of options considered in the organization of employment. At the same time care will be taken to warn against notions of easy transfer or learning from best practice. A second and equally important task is to try to understand the likely developments in employment policies and practices in the light of current trends towards an increasingly integrated world economy. To what extent will nation states, or indeed individual organizations, be able to retain their distinctive approach to employment? Would a move towards a more homogeneous approach to employment organization be beneficial, and if so to whom? What types of protections and institutional arrangements are needed in a world where capital is relatively free to travel and labour remains the factor of production most tied to the fate of a particular society or even region?

Introducing national differences

There is now a wealth of empirical material, including detailed statistical information, to inform our analysis of employment organization between countries.

However, understanding of the importance of the statistical variations cannot be achieved without locating these differences within the whole set of institutions found within a particular country. For example, if we want to assess the significance of differences in training systems we need to be interested in much more than differences in numbers receiving training. In assessing the significance of these different systems, it is essential to understand their implications for how work is organized, for the development of capacities for innovation and for career patterns and inter-job mobility.

To focus on interpreting the significance of differences in employment policies and practices, we present a number of examples, in the form of case studies of usually two or three countries where there are clear differences in the nature and significance of a particular employment form or employment practice, based on detailed research carried out by a variety of employment analysts. We call these examples case studies, in line with the traditional terminology applied to the study of individual organizations, as we are not claiming to pick representative or average country cases. Moreover, even if a country seems to be 'average' or 'typical' in one employment area, it may be at the opposite end of the spectrum on another dimension. However, it is in the nature of comparative research that opposites tend to attract; that is, countries are selected for study around a particular employment practice precisely because they are known to, or are strongly expected to, display major differences. The differences may therefore be considered overdrawn relative to the differences one might expect to find between any two or three randomly selected countries. Often the selection is in fact deliberate, to represent a category or type of employment regime. In later chapters of the book, we discuss whether it is possible or desirable to develop typologies of employment systems, with respect to the system of work organization (see Chapter Three); the welfare state system or the gender relations regime (see Chapter Four); the training and education system (see Chapter Five); or the regulatory and collective bargaining system (see Chapter Six). For the moment, however, the selections are used to give some flavour of the richness of diversity in employment systems and to begin to establish why employment policies and practices may differ in significant ways between societies.

The organization of employment: some national comparative case studies

To provide examples of differences in employment organization we have to be selective over both the choice of countries and the choice of aspects of employment to be considered. Here we focus on five areas, all of which feed in important ways into either the cost and/or the productivity side of the wage-effort bargain at the heart of the employment relationship. As such they are significant in shaping comparative advantage for both individual organizations and whole economies.

They also each have considerable importance for how individuals experience employment in their working lives. The five dimensions selected are:

- skills and work organization;
- pay systems;
- working time arrangements;
- downsizing and retirement;
- employee involvement or voice.

We also return to these dimensions at various points in later chapters of the book. In particular we look in Chapter Three at the significance of skills and work organization for comparative advantage; and in Chapter Five we explore how the education and training systems in advanced countries help to shape these different systems of work organization. Working time arrangements are looked at from a supply-side and, in particular, from a gender or household perspective in Chapter Four. In Chapter Six we look at the influence on working time practices of regulations, deriving both from legislation and collective bargaining. Downsizing and retirement policies again feature in Chapter Four, where we consider the influence of welfare regimes on labour supply, and again in Chapter Seven where we look at how employment policies and practices operate at the workplace or organization level. Employee involvement or voice is another issue considered in Chapter Seven, and provides an underlying theme in our discussion of the development of high trust versus low trust production regimes in Chapter Three.

The aim here is not to provide a comprehensive analysis of these dimensions of employment but rather to introduce some of the key issues in comparative analysis, around these five dimensions. The research-based studies that we draw upon fit within these broad areas, but each study has a narrower specific orientation or focus, on particular occupational groups, particular sectors or indeed particular employment arrangements within the broader area. Moreover, these studies are drawn from different time periods and have used divergent methodologies; their findings may have significance at different levels of generality. Some may only be relevant for the particular firms or sectors or occupations studied; but for the most part they have been chosen because of their salience for understanding how the employment system operates in those particular countries. Limitations of space, and indeed limitations of available research, prevent a full discussion or defence of the validity of these arguments. However, the reader will find much supportive evidence in the other chapters of this book.

It should still be noted that in some cases recent developments in employment organization in the countries concerned may have changed the state of play since the research was conducted or the article written. For the moment we take the differences as revealed at the time of the research and do not attempt to update this research or comment on the continuing significance of the differences revealed.

Skills and work organization

Much comparative research has focused on the ways in which work is organized, and in particular on differences in the opportunities that these systems offer for workers to exercise skill and discretion or to contribute to organizational learning, development and innovation. To some extent these differences are related to trends in the management of employment which transcend national boundaries. Over recent years the post-war interest in a mass production work organization system allowing minimum discretion to workers — sometimes referred to as the Taylorist or Fordist production system (see Chapter Three) — has given way to an interest in work organization systems more geared to flexible and variable production. Here the focus has been more on harnessing the problem-solving and innovatory capacities of the workforce as a means of improving competitiveness in an era character-ized by niche markets and competition based on fashion, design and variety. However, although research has revealed that there may have been some general tendencies towards Taylorist techniques in the earlier period, and more recently a relatively widespread interest in more flexible systems, these broad or general trends in work organization are not capable of accounting for the variety of systems of work organization found over time and space (see Chapters Two and Three). There were significant variations in the extent to which production systems within specific countries or sectors emulated the Taylorist model in the first place, and there remain equally major differences in the extent to which there has been a systematic move away from low discretion systems to post-Fordist systems or high trust forms of work organization. Further variations are found in the form of post-Fordist/non-Taylorist system that has been adopted and developed (see Chapters Two and Three). The capacity of organizations within a particular societal context to adapt and respond to product and technological changes has been found to be dependent upon the specific cultural and societal context in which they are located and indeed embedded.

The organization of work is influenced not only by competitive requirements, but also by how work organization relates to other major features of the societal system. Here two areas can be focused on in particular. The first is that of career structures and career expectations; the second is the role of the education and training system in shaping employment. In our first extract from a comparative study on work organization (Box 1.2), we find that the greater separation of managerial from technical work in British compared to Japanese companies is related to a large extent to differences in career structures. In the UK managerial careers are structured independently of technical careers, while in Japan technical expertise provides the legitimacy for exercising authority within the organizational hierarchy.

Box 1.2 Player manager or coordinator: engineers in Japan and the UK

Successful product development requires effective integration across different engineering activities and functional groups ... The more uncertain the market environment, the greater the need for efficient communication, and elaboration of knowledge and information across the product development cycle.

Organisations operating on the principle of functional specialisation create a heavy demand for an administrative hierarchy specialising in coordination and integration. The more sub-divided the organisation into individual tasks and functional disciplines, the greater the need for coordinators to act as focal points of communication and information flow. In the British firms, this specialist coordinating role is carried out predominantly by project managers. In our interviews, all the British project managers emphasised the importance of their coordinating function. The following examples of how these people described their 'typical day's work' are illustrative:

As deputy engineering manager on the systems my prime task is liaison among engineering groups in three different divisions of the company. So I spend a lot of time on the phone, at meetings, reading papers generated by engineers in their groups, because the systems function is to really make sure that all the different engineers working in the company on this project are tied into the contract ... It's a technical liaison job and you have to trace people for information, go to meetings, help engineering meeting and project meeting ... It's basically liaison and coordinating. I am not designing any equipment.

I headed up a team of five, and they did the technical work of producing the workbenches and specs and things, and I had to make sure it all held together ... I spend quite a lot of time on the phone ... If I have an overriding function it's that of coordination. So, yes, I do lots and lots of coordination. I actually produce very little.

Most of the British engineers promoted to project leader positions often become preoccupied with their coordinating role and find themselves having to disengage from their design and development role very early on in their supervisory roles. The separation between managerial and technical work is distinct in the British firms.

In the Japanese firms, the relationship between technical and managerial work is quite different. Although Japanese project managers also have an important coordinating role, they are not 'specialist coordinators' like their British counterparts. The overlapping nature of the Japanese approach to product development means that a great deal of the coordinating functions are carried out by engineers at the working level. Information necessary for the coordinated adjustments in the product cycle tends to flow laterally across the functions through direct communication among the project team members rather than necessarily passing up and down the hierarchy via the project manager. In the Japanese firms, the product development cycle is coordinated by a decentralised network structure of communication and information sharing rather than a centralised hierarchical information system. As a result, Japanese project managers tend to devote more time and effort to product planning and strategic decision-making rather than specialising in operating coordination. They emphasise their technical leadership role and act as product champions in integrating technical development with corporate objectives. A project manager (*kacho*) at an R&D laboratory described his key role as follows:

In my case, there is of course, the overall policy of the company. The primary concern is to follow the policy, and then deciding how to translate it into concrete details. The top management only provides very broad guidelines and it is really up to the project managers (*kacho*) and team leaders (*kakaricho*) to come up with concrete strategies, for example, how we can double the sales figure next year. In order to achieve the objective, I have to carry out detailed analysis in a wide range of areas, including marketing, costing

Box 1.2 Continued

and then consider how to incorporate the technical aspects in order to achieve the overall objective. On the technical side, we know what level of technical performance we want to achieve but it is important to work out how to translate it into actual development work. I have to ensure that my subordinates understand all these.

In the Japanese firms, a project manager effectively functions as a general manager of a product. Their role is 'strategic' in that they are responsible for product planning and concept development; it also contains a strong technical dimension in the sense that they are ultimately responsible for translating the product concept into technical details.

While most of the British engineers promoted to project managers often find themselves having to disengage from their technical work very early on in their supervisory roles, Japanese project managers often remain technically involved — many of them described themselves as 'player managers'. There are two main reasons why Japanese project managers tend to maintain a closer involvement in technical work. First, unlike their British counterparts whose role is to liaise with local representatives from different functions within a vertical administrative hierarchy, Japanese project managers often directly lead a project execution team — members who leave their functions and report directly to the project manager. They have direct contact and stronger influence over the working level engineers. They are responsible not just for coordination but also for product planning and translating product concepts into detailed technical work. It is a technical leadership role and thus knowing the technical details of their subordinates' work and providing on-the-job training is all part of the job. Second, it is important for Japanese project managers to remain technically competent in order to justify their authority and control within the project team. Unlike their British counterparts, they are not specialist coordinators and they do not have monopoly access to organisational information. Japanese project teams have a high degree of integrative autonomy and lateral information processing capacity. The coordinating role of a manager can easily be made redundant and bypassed. Thus, remaining technically active and involved is a good way of ensuring authority and gaining 'competence trust' among the engineers.

Extract from A. Lam, 'Work organisation, skills development and utilisation of engineers', in R. Crompton, D. Gallie and K. Purcell (eds), *Changing Forms of Employment* (London: Routledge, 1996), pp. 190–2.

The second extract (Box 1.3) is drawn from the study that to a very large extent was responsible for sparking off the debate about international differences in employment policies and practice. The research was based on case studies of plants in Germany and France, carefully matched according to size, nature of production and technology (Maurice *et al.*, 1984, 1986). The study found major differences in the occupational structure, authority systems and inter-occupational relationships, such that the French system was based on a much longer hierarchy of jobs, determined both by status and pay, and with the system of work organization based much less on a cooperative and multi-skilled basis than in the German case. The more hierarchical French structure was found to reflect the more elitist French system of education, and the more cooperative approach in Germany, based around a higher average skill level, reflected the strong vocational training system there. This particular extract focuses on the different organization of the management function in France and Germany, from foremen to top managers.

Box 1.3 The basis for authority of the foreman: technical competence or ability to give orders?

The German *Meister* is a case in point: his technical competence is sanctioned by a socially recognized diploma, which puts him in the same qualification space as the skilled worker, though at a higher level, and with a broad span of control. German foremen are less numerous than their French counterparts and have more men under them... This is the concept of *Arbeiterschaft* which, according to Popitz, covers the worker–foreman relationship: there is only a slight difference between workers and technical management which is comprised of graduated engineers, for they fall into the same qualificational space. Graduated engineers receive an education that is oriented more toward applied technology than a university-trained engineer, and their social background is more modest. All this makes them feel closer to the workers than to university graduates.

The middle-management characteristics observed here apply equally well to all levels of management: promotion into management corresponds more to increased technical competence recognized by the company than to a change of status decided on by management... there is a strong tendency to link the level of training with the job level. The result is a relatively homogeneous management, and a degree of continuity between management and nonmanagement... this homogeneity is related to a technical competence whose basic point of reference is the manual apprenticeship. Among top management in industry only 19.4 percent have university degrees (as opposed to 41 percent in France). The majority have nonuniversity occupational education, that is, further education after apprenticeships but on a fairly high level (*Technikschule-ingenieurschule*). Only a minority of top management is hired on the basis of diplomas to exercise executive functions (*Leitende Angestellte*). The relative continuity between management and other categories reflects both occupational mobility based on a progressive development of qualifications and on less sharp social and occupational distinctions made between management and nonmanagement. This holds true particularly for technical middle management, but it often applies to top management (those who hold an *L.A.* function) as well, for many start out as workers or apprentices.

The dividing line between managers and nonmanagers in French companies is drawn more often according to organizational rather than to professional criteria. In this respect the movement into management represents a discontinuity. Whereas in Germany managers and nonmanagers have relatively similar types of education and a continuity of qualification, in France one finds a greater professional diversity among management even though their presence in the organizational hierarchy might provide a symbolic unity. The case of production supervisors (foremen) is particularly revealing. Although the French foreman usually starts off as a worker, like his German counterpart, conditions for promotion are not the same. His position is not supported by an occupational diploma; it is given to him by the company, which bases its choice on his capacity to lead men and give orders... it means that he is entering management (albeit at the lowest level) rather than developing a higher level of training. The French foreman's functions are also different from those of the German *Meister*, for he does not play the same role in the work system. Production norms are more precisely laid down by the technical departments, and the foreman has to ensure they are met... His authority, which has only weak professional justification, is based on rank; as he is at the lowest level of the hierarchy, he has little scope for decision making... The foreman may exercise authority, but he has no power...

Though one cannot make broad generalizations for all of French management, these traits are nonetheless the most basic: becoming a manager corresponds to a promotion up the status hierarchy rather than the attainment of greater technical ability. Therefore access to a management position and internal mobility within the category will generally result from the way the company functions and from socialization in accordance with its organizational norms... all the managers, including those who were graduated from a *Grande Ecole*, are

Box 1.3 Continued

considered by the company to be 'self-taught': success in the company depends on their degree of integration. Though socialization is similar for all managers, there are in fact significant discontinuities within the category. These are the result of the importance given to managers who have graduated from higher education institutions (usually the *Grandes Ecoles*) over others whom the company calls 'self-taught men' (a category which to all intents and purposes does not exist in Germany) ... The 'self-taught men' ... reach their ceiling much more quickly at an intermediate level, having made their career in the production or technical divisions, or more often in the administrative or sales departments.

Extract from M. Maurice, F. Sellier and J-J. Silvestre, 'The search for a societal effect in the production of company hierarchy: a comparison of France and Germany', in P. Osterman (ed.), *Internal Labor Markets* (Cambridge, MA: MIT Press, 1984), pp. 251–4.

Reference in text:
H. Popitz, H. P. Bahrdt, E. A. Jüres and H. Kesting, *Das Gesellschaftsbild des Arbeiters*, (Tübingen: Mohr, 1957).

Pay systems

Payment systems are at the core of the employment relationship. Work under an employment relationship is undertaken in return for pay; in order to motivate people to work there needs to be some agreement among employees that the reward they will receive is in some sense fair. Notions of fairness, however, vary between societies as well as between occupational groups. The size of acceptable differentials between, for example, chief executive officer and manual worker pay appears to vary dramatically between societies; in the US the ratio is over 27 to one, while in Sweden the ratio is only eight to one (Figure 1.2). While not everyone in the US accepts these differentials in pay as fair, their existence certainly excites less comment there than if similar differentials were revealed in most European societies.

There is a range of different principles upon which pay differentials can be based. Should they reflect differences in status or in educational qualifications? Or differences in the productivity or profitability of the organization? How far should pay reflect differences in individual performance or differences in job category? What account, if any, should be taken of differences in age, seniority or gender?

Two countries which exemplify the possible range of different principles are the US and Japan. The extract in Box 1.4 summarizes the differences in principles

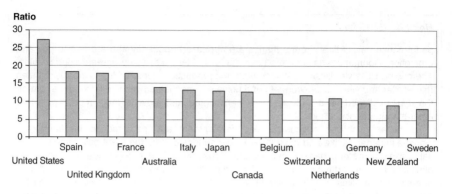

Ratio

Source: Adapted from L. Mishel *et al.* (1997): Table 3.53

Figure 1.2 Ratio of chief executive pay to manufacturing workers' pay in advanced countries

between the prevailing systems in the two countries, which have implications not only for how work is organized within organizations, but also for inter-occupational and intergenerational variations in income and standards of living. The extract uses the terminologies *JAM pay systems* (that is, based on job classification, adversarial relations and minimal training) and *SET pay systems* (that is, based on security, employee involvement and training). In the US there is more variation between companies and occupational groups according to whether the pay system is more of the JAM variety — focused on the job grade — or the SET variety, where the focus is more on the individual employee. In Japan, as the extract explains, payment systems in large organizations are usually more related to SET, where the pay reflects the age, seniority and skills of the employee and not the job grade.

Box 1.4   Pay variations by lifecycle or by job category?

The pay systems in the United States and Japan are both highly segmented, but the divisions occur along different lines in the two countries. In the United States, JAM and SET pay systems for production and clerical workers are usually highly compressed, with small wage differentials determined mainly by seniority, within a context of interfirm mobility and interindustry wage differentials. Job ladders for blue-collar workers are relatively short, and while most companies have evaluation systems, appraisals are tied only loosely to pay. Blue-collar and clerical workers in large nonunion companies tend to have somewhat broader differentials than in union companies, but they still typically face relatively flat age-earnings profiles. College-educated workers are in professional and managerial occupations, with different pay tracks and steeper age-earnings profiles from those of production and craft workers. Gender differences in pay and promotion, while still important, have been diminishing.

The pay system in Japan is segmented along the dimensions of age, employer size, gender, and, to a lesser degree, education. The components of pay in large Japanese companies are life cycle (or age, with housing and family allowances), job-grade, and

Box 1.4 Continued

performance pay. Skill and performance are appraised frequently and are tied to pay and promotion. Nonmanagerial workers have career ladders with steep age-earnings profiles. There is no US-style division between craft and production workers. High school graduates (blue-collar and white-collar workers) and university graduates (white-collar workers) are on the same published pay schedules, but university graduates move up much more rapidly and enter management sooner.

Individual incentives encourage skill development and performance for blue-collar workers in Japan. Koike and Inoki (1990) have suggested that the merit pay component of Japanese pay systems has grown since the 1970s and that, as a result, age-based pay has diminished in importance. This view is supported by several studies that found that age-earnings profiles were flattening in Japan in the 1980s. Our findings provide only partial support for Koike's hypothesis. We argue that the long career ladders reflect management's response to a system of lifetime employment with age-based pay by ensuring worker's productivity and increasing their responsibilities as they gain experience. The SET pay system in Japan rewards and supports security, employee involvement, and training in a system that produces less overall inequality than exists in the United States.

Extract from C. Brown, Y. Nakata, M. Reich and L. Ulman, *Work and Pay in the United States and Japan* (New York: Oxford University Press, 1997), pp. 130–2.

Reference in text:
K. Koike and T. Inoki, *Skill Formation in Japan and Southeast Asia* (Tokyo: University of Tokyo Press, 1990).

The second extract (Box 1.5) explores the different principles and practices of job grading in Germany, Italy and the UK. The implications of these different systems lead to differences in the form and extent of gender inequality. As a consequence, policies to reduce gender pay inequality need to take into account the different ways in which these inequalities are embedded within payment systems.

Box 1.5 Different job grading principles affect the structure and form of the gender pay gap

Very different systems and principles of job grading prevail in the three countries under consideration. Italy provides the most straightforward case: there are four legally recognized categories of employees (blue-collar workers, white-collar workers, senior white-collar workers, and managers), but a single unified grading system applies to the first three categories of workers in almost all industries. The allocation of jobs to grades is specifically not established through job evaluation. Job grading is not regarded as reflecting any objective measure of job content or qualifications, but instead is recognized as the result of collective bargaining.

In Germany there is also a formal distinction between white-collar workers and blue-collar workers, linked to differences in social security arrangements. In practice, however, these groups tend to be covered by separate collective agreements. However, there are further important divisions or cleavages within these occupational groups — between those jobs that require and those jobs that do not require a vocational training qualification. The existence of apprenticeships in both blue- and white-collar sectors provides in fact a form of linkage between the two groups, such that a job requiring apprenticeship training for white-collar workers would not normally be graded below a blue-collar job not requiring such training, or vice versa. The importance of vocational training for job grading in Germany is illustrated by the tendency to use vocational qualifications as job titles (Méhaut, 1992). Thus although job grading in Germany is also the result of collective bargaining and not job evaluation, there is

Box 1.5 Continued

a general perception that the job grading system does reflect skill and job content, a perception that is not shared in the Italian case. In Germany the measure of skill is strongly tied to vocational training requirements, and the collective bargaining process is constrained by these strongly held perceptions.

Nevertheless, the emphasis on vocational qualifications is greater among blue-collar workers. This is also the area where women are less likely to be qualified, and thus this form of grading serves to establish gender differentials. Among white-collar workers there is little difference in the share of qualified male and female workers. Here the emphasis for job grading is on job content, and many female skills and responsibilities are not recognized in the traditional grading structures. Thus possession of qualifications is not sufficient to guarantee women a favourable place in the grading scheme. It can be argued that where qualifications do not adequately differentiate between men and women, other criteria may be added.

Practices in the UK diverge from both the German and the Italian system, and in fact can be characterized as demonstrating the absence of any national system of job grading. There is no formal or legal distinction between blue- and white-collar work, although both groups of workers have tended to be covered by different wage agreements or systems of pay determination (with white-collar workers much less likely to be covered by collective bargaining arrangements). In practice, organizations tend to divide their jobs into a number of job clusters for grading purposes, and research has found no coherent pattern to this division other than that job clusters tend to consist of either male-dominated or female-dominated jobs (IRS, 1991). As comparisons tend not to be made across job clusters, female- and male-dominated job groups are often graded and paid according to completely separate systems. There is no national system of vocational qualifications spanning occupational groups to provide some basis for comparing jobs in, for example, blue- and white-collar areas, unlike in Germany. There is thus much greater freedom in the UK for firms to create job grading systems which vary between and within firms and which certainly do not conform to any national system of conventional hierarchies. Analytical job evaluation is made greater use of in the UK than in Germany and Italy but is often used only for specific groups of jobs, or different systems are applied to different job clusters. It does not normally result in integrated job grading systems.

...

Grading in the public sector also conforms to these national systems, with Germany retaining the emphasis on vocational qualifications and distinctions between blue- and white-collar work, while Italy has an integrated single graded system. In the UK the situation is somewhat different because of the continued influence of national-level agreements in the public sector, compared with the private sector where they have largely disappeared. However, most national agreements cover only specific occupational groups, and as a result there is no integrated grading structure covering all groups at the organizational level. One of the incentives for decentralization in the public sector is in fact to provide the opportunity to establish integrated grading and pay structures at the organizational level.

Many different issues are raised by these grading practices for the establishment of equal pay for work of equal value. There is perhaps a paradoxical situation in which the UK makes most use of analytical job evaluation, the often preferred method for the application of the principle of equal value, but has probably the least integrated grading structure, such that the comparisons between jobs tend to be made across a relatively narrow field. Italy probably pays the least attention to actual job content but has the most integrated system of job grading whereby white-collar and manual jobs are placed in grades alongside each other, while in Germany the common system of vocational training provides at least some form of integration between the structures. However, there is still no strong tendency in Germany within the trade union movement, let alone within the employers' associations, to question whether the traditional job gradings reflect principles of equal value

Box 1.5 Continued

(Jochmann Döll, 1990). Nevertheless … in Italy as well as in Germany it would be difficult for a skilled clerical worker, for example, to have a lower salary than a semi-skilled production worker in the same factory, but this is a normal and possible outcome in the UK.

Extract from J. Rubery, F. Bettio, C. Fagan, F. Maier, S. Quack and P. Villa, 'Payment systems and gender pay differentials: some societal effects', in J. Rubery *et al.* (eds), *Equal Pay in Europe?* (Basingstoke: Macmillan/ILO, 1998), pp. 13–16.

References in text:
IRS (Industrial Relations Services), *Pay and Gender in Britain* (London: Equal Opportunities Commission and IRS, 1991).
A. Jochmann-Döll 'Gleicher Lohn für gleichwertige Arbeit: ausländische und deutsche Konzepte und Erfahrungen', doctoral dissertation (University of Trier, 1990).
P. Méhaut, 'Further education, vocational training and the labour market: the French and German systems compared', in A. Castro, P. Méhaut and J. Rubery (eds), *International Integration and Labour Market Organization* (London: Academic Press, 1992).

Working time

There is a range of variations in working time patterns across countries, including differences in standard weekly hours, differences in the incidence of overtime working, and of working over the weekend; and strong national differences in when and how much holiday is taken. The extracts chosen here relate to one form of working time arrangement which shows particular variability across countries, namely part-time working. Part-time work is one of the major areas of employment growth in advanced countries. It is associated in part with the expansion of female employment and also with the growth of the service economy. However, there is no universal relationship between the availability of part-time work and the integration of women into the labour market (Rubery *et al.*, 1998b) as the extract in Box 1.6 from Birgit Pfau-Effinger's (1998) comparison of part-time work in the Netherlands, Germany and Finland outlines.

Box 1.6   The role of part-time work in the integration of women into employment depends on the gender order

In the postwar period, the basic characteristics of the gender culture already differed significantly between the countries examined here (the Netherlands, Germany and Finland) exemplified by the rates of female activity. In the following decades, in all three countries, processes of renegotiation of the gender arrangements between societal actors and a change in cultural ideals took place which was primarily initiated by women and in which men participated to a different degree. The new ideals are, more than before, based on the cultural construction of the 'employed mother'. Differences in the degree and forms in which women were integrated into the labour market can be primarily explained by the fact that cultural change was based on different cultural traditions, proceeding under different dynamics of change which resulted in diverging paths. In those countries where the tradition of the male breadwinner/female carer family prevailed, the idea of privatised childhood survived in part. As a consequence, part-time work was a substantial element of the modernisation of the male breadwinner family model. Though in parts precarious, part-time work turned out to be a new form of employment for women in the biographical phases of active motherhood. This is even more true for the Netherlands than for West Germany. These differences can be explained by the fact that the tradition of the 'home caring society' and the housewife marriage was more deep-rooted in the Netherlands. Institutional regulation has in part reinforced the orientation of women towards part-time work in these countries. In contrast, in Finland, where the male breadwinner/female carer model was never dominant, the tradition of women's full-time participation in the production sphere was maintained during the modernisation process and change in the gender arrangement.

Extract from B. Pfau-Effinger, 'Culture or structure as explanations for differences in part-time work in Germany, Finland and the Netherlands?', in J. O'Reilly and C. Fagan (eds), *Part-Time Prospects* (London: Routledge, 1998), p. 192.

Part-time work has implications for terms and conditions of employment, and also, because of the concentration of women in part-time work in many countries, for gender equality in the labour market. However, as the comparison in Box 1.7 of the Netherlands and the UK illustrates, the consequences for earnings and employment opportunities of working part-time do vary significantly, even between two of the countries with the highest use of part-time work in the EU.

Box 1.7   Part-time work is women's work in both the Netherlands and Britain, but the penalties for working part-time are higher in Britain

Part-time employment is segregated in both countries, but the wage conditions which result are quite different. In the Netherlands the average hourly wage of women part timers is equal to that for women full timers and in 1988 both groups of women earned 73% of men's average hourly earnings (Plantenga and van Velzen, 1993: 5). In the same year women full timers did slightly better in the UK, earning 75% of male full-time hourly earnings, and this rose to 79% by 1992. However, women part timers only receive 75% of the earnings of full timers of their own sex and only 58% of male full-time earnings (Rubery, 1993: Figures 2 and 3).

When part timers are working alongside a full timer doing a job with the same job title they usually receive the same basic hourly rate of pay, even within deregulated sectors of deregulated labour markets such as the UK (IRS, 1991). However, the segregated pattern of part-time jobs means that most part timers work in female-dominated areas of the economy.

Box 1.7 Continued

Across the European Union employment in female-dominated sectors has some association with low pay, both within manufacturing and in service sectors for which earnings data are available. In both the Netherlands and the UK (and for other member states where data are available) retail ranks as the lowest paying service sector by total average earnings, followed by hotels and catering, which falls within 'other services'. Retail also pays lower than the lowest paying manufacturing industries, based on total average male non-manual earnings in industry (Rubery and Fagan, 1994, pp. 167–70 and appendix tables).

We have already noted that three quarters of female part timers in the Netherlands and the UK are found in other services and distribution, the two lowest-paying service sectors in both countries. In the UK it is intra-industry differentials between full timers and part timers, but more importantly the high concentration of part timers in service and retail activities, which accounts for the lower hourly earnings of part timers (Rubery, 1993: 79). In contrast, the absence of a pay gap between women full timers and part timers in the Netherlands arises from two factors. First, the wage floor set by established minimum rates acts to narrow the earnings gap between high and low paying sectors and occupations (Rubery and Fagan, 1994a). Second, while similar shares of part timers in both countries hold service jobs, fewer are concentrated into retail jobs in the Netherlands (see above).

Although a large share of part timers in both countries are concentrated in two low paying sectors, the implications for their earnings differ because of the different wage systems. Indeed, the CERC (1991) report provides a comparison of low pay among part timers based on hourly earnings which shows that part timers are less at risk of low pay in the Netherlands than in the UK. On this comparison, 17% of all full timers and 60% of all part timers are low paid in the UK, while in the Netherlands 11% of full timers and 23% of part timers were low paid. And it is estimated that in the UK close to half (46%) of all workers paid below two thirds of the full-time median hourly wage are female part timers, while 23% are women full timers and the remaining 30% are men (Rubery, 1993: Table 1.2.3).

Extract from C. Fagan, J. Plantenga and J. Rubery, 'Part-time work and inequality? Lessons from the Netherlands and the UK', in *A Time for Working, A Time for Living* (Brussels: ETUC and ETUI, 1995), pp. 139–41.

References in text:
CERC, *Les Bas Salaires dans les Pays de la CEE*. V/20024/91-FR (Brussels: European Commission, 1991).
IRS (Industrial Relations Services), *Pay and Gender in Britain* (London: Equal Opportunities Commission/IRS, 1991).
J. Plantenga and S. van Velzen, *Wage Determination and Sex Segregation in Employment: the Case of the Netherlands*, Report to the European Commission (DGV–Equal Opportunities Unit, Brussels, 1993).
J. Rubery, *Wage Determination and Sex Segregation in Employment: Report for the UK*, Report to the European Commission (Brussels: DGV–Equal Opportunities Unit, 1993).
J. Rubery and C. Fagan, *Wage Determination and Sex Segregation in Employment in the European Community*, Social Europe Supplement 4/94 (Luxembourg: Office for Official Publications of the European Communities, 1994).

Downsizing and retirement

Patterns of exit from employment also vary according to societal arrangements, institutions and values. Restrictions on layoffs and redundancies vary from, at one extreme, the USA, where there are no statutory requirements for advance notice or compensation for plant closures and redundancies, to societies such as Spain, where employers who wish to dismiss permanent staff have to engage in a lengthy legal process and pay significant compensation (although these conditions have been relaxed over recent years). These differences in approaches to layoffs and redundancy are by no means entirely explained by legal regulations; in particular the well-known job-for-life system in Japan is based on trust rather than legal entitlements to a job for life. Moreover, differences in approaches cannot be regarded as simply leading to delays or frustrations for management; they may also encourage a different approach to the internal organization of the labour market, with greater emphasis placed on redeployment and retraining rather than redundancy in societies where employers' prerogative to fire workers is constrained by legal and voluntary systems of job protection. Osterman's (1988) account of the differences in approach to the regulation of layoffs between Germany, Sweden and the USA recognizes that the systems prevailing in the first two countries do not prevent layoffs but raise their costs relative to the situation in the USA (Box 1.8).

Box 1.8 Employers face different restrictions on their rights to lay off workers without consultation

The (German) law provides that works councils be consulted with and be provided with information on a range of manpower topics including the number and procedures for layoffs, promotion criteria, changes in working conditions, the use of overtime and of 'short time', and the introduction of new technologies. Although management in principle need only consult, in practice on at least some of these topics the consent of the works council is necessary. The nature of works council agreement varies according to topic. For example, on the key issue of layoffs if, through negotiations, management is unable to reach agreement with the works council (which takes the form of a 'social agreement' [*Sozialplan*]), the council can submit the plan to an arbitration committee (*Einigungstelle*) whose binding decision must take the social situation of the employees into account along with purely economic considerations of the firm. In addition, individual workers may take legal action in an industrial court in order to obtain severance pay. The consequence is not to render layoffs impossible but to raise their cost substantially ...

Swedish labour contracts do not generally contain the extensive prescription of work rules and job classifications found in American contracts. However, in the 1970s legislation was passed that is potentially more prescriptive concerning internal labor market rules. The two key laws are the Law on Codetermination (1997) and the Employment Security Legislation (1974).

The important characteristic of these laws, for our purposes, is that the codetermination legislation requires that firms inform and consult with unions on all matters concerning job design, work organisation, technological innovation, and promotion procedures. The employment security legislation requires that firms provide lengthy notification prior to layoffs and that layoffs proceed in the order dictated by (reverse) seniority.

As is apparent, the Swedish and German arrangements show a good deal in common. In both countries unions are stronger than in the United States, although the Swedish unions are far more powerful than their German counterparts. Both nations have passed national legislation that establishes workplace-based councils and restricts employer freedom to lay off employees. At the same time, there are important differences between the two countries, in particular that the German restrictions concerning employer freedom in establishing work

Box 1.8 Continued

rules and in laying off employees are considerably more stringent. In addition, social policy is much more tied to a specific work site in Germany than in Sweden.

Extract from P. Osterman, *Employment Futures* (New York: Oxford University Press, 1988), pp. 119–21.

The age at which people leave the labour market has tended to decline, particularly over the past two decades. However, the actual age at which the departure takes place, the conditions under which it occurs, and the extent to which there is a gradual and multi-phased departure or an abrupt clean break vary significantly between advanced societies. However, there have been relatively few comparative studies of retirement systems and in particular so-called early retirement systems. Naschold and Vroom's (1993) study of seven countries (the Netherlands, UK, USA, Sweden, Japan and the former West and East Germany) is a major exception, providing both analysis at the inter-country level (based on comparative statistics of participation rates), at the national level (based on comparative analyses of the societal systems of labour market organization and social security funding), and at the organization level (based on case studies of how organizations treat their older workers and why). Here we draw on Jacobs' and Rein's (1993) contribution to the study in their analysis of 'patterns of early retirement' to provide some examples not only of the different working patterns of older men across the seven countries, but also of the differences in the distribution of responsibilities towards older workers found in advanced countries (Box 1.9). Note that early retirement has so far been considered primarily an issue affecting men, as the involvement of older women in the labour market has up until recent years been much lower than that of men. These issues are likely to be significant for more women than men in the future as more women become continuous participants in the labour market.

Box 1.9 Exit means exit in some societies; in others work and partial retirement are combined

When we limit our analysis only to employed wage and salary workers, we find two quite distinct patterns. In the Continental countries of Germany, France and the Netherlands, men move from full-time work to full-time retirement. This means that there is, by and large, no partial exit or re-entry into employment at some later period of time. We call this pattern 'exit is exit' because it graphically illustrates that once a man leaves work, his opportunity to re-enter work is virtually non-existent.

What about the remaining countries where there is a much higher employment activity rate among wage and salary workers? What these countries share in common is that at least a substantial minority of older men combine work and retirement, or have their work redefined so that the job itself signals the beginning of a retirement process. But the different

Box 1.9 Continued

methods of how work and retirement are combined are quite varied. Here we want to call attention to the different processes that produce a similar outcome ...

Sweden: partial retirement

In Sweden, the relatively high proportion of employment for older workers in wage and salary positions is created by a system of partial pension arrangements which permits an individual to get roughly about 75 percent or more of his previous earnings while working only half the number of hours ... But the system apparently seems to work only in Sweden where one finds a very strong commitment to the right to work which extends also to older men and even to those who are partially disabled and cannot find a job because of labor market conditions. There have been some changes, however, in this regard since the elimination of partial disability due to work-related conditions in 1990. What is distinctive in the Swedish system of partial pensions is that individuals stay on their same job, and the employer reconstitutes it from a full-time to a part-time position. In this scheme there is an institutional commitment on the part of the employer to continue hiring the older worker and on the part of the state to create a special program to buffer the loss of income from a reduction in hours worked and earnings. As a result, we find that almost a third of all men 60 to 64 work part-time in Sweden. While part-time employment for men 60 to 62 is high in the United States, there is no institutional commitment to find partial work. The responsibility to find part-time work falls on the individual and is not an obligation of the firm ...

Japan: re-employment

What distinguishes the Japanese pattern? Whereas the Swedish system emphasizes a change in the hours of work but a continuity of type of work, the Japanese system emphasizes a change in the status of work and a change in earnings. At a given age of termination of employment called the '*teinen*' age, at one time age 55 and later raised to age 60, virtually all wage and salary workers are expected to terminate their contracts with the firm. Rebick has shown that the '*teinen*' age arrangements increasingly apply to small as well as large firms. We conclude that most workers are covered by this arrangement. Workers are either reemployed by the firm, or are placed out to another affiliate or daughter firm. There are a variety of different levels that the parent firm can be involved in arranging for this placement. In general, the more the parent firm is involved, the better off the worker is economically ... The core idea underpinning the Japanese system is the obligation of the firm to continue employment of workers on a full-time basis, but at lower earnings which can be supplemented with a public or private pension arrangement. In this sense the Japanese approach is similar to that of Sweden where firms have a social obligation to reemploy individuals, so the transition is an institutionally established principle and not merely an ad hoc arrangement where the initiative falls on the individual alone ...

The United States: multiple options

The distinguishing characteristic of the American system is to support a variety of options that individuals can pursue on their own. There are at least two institutions which reinforce the support of these options. First, there is the public social security system which by its nature is designed to provide only a floor of social protection to prevent poverty and hardship. Unlike the European system, it is not designed by itself to promote for middle and higher income groups the continuity of lifestyles achieved before retirement ...

The second institutional arrangement arises from legislation which eliminates mandatory retirement age and seeks to implement anti-age discrimination practice in firms. Of course, the legislation does not end age-linked hiring and firing, although it certainly reduces the extent to which age plays a role in this process. The point we want to stress here is that the

Box 1.9 Continued

existence of anti-age discrimination legislation works institutionally to support the range of individually chosen options.

The American system might, therefore, be described as follows. A majority of individuals follow the European pattern of exit is exit... There is, however, a substantial minority of individuals who create ad hoc arrangements which work in different ways depending on the individual's situation. This generates a range of patterns rather than a definite national norm. The following variations are identifiable:

(a) Men move into other jobs that pay less and demand less of them. These are jobs characterized by easy entry and easy exit...

(b) Men remain in the same line of work or in the same field, but diminish their investment in their career job. Of course, this can occur at any age; for example, the professor who stops writing after receiving tenure.

(c) Men gradually retire from work by acquiring a part-time position, which may be in heir own field or, more typically, in a different industry or occupation

(d) Men may reenter work after a period of retirement because the public and private pensions they receive turn out to be inadequate to maintain the lifestyle they seek to maintain, or perhaps because the lack of work undermines their ability to realize a meaningful life, or for some combination of both financial and personal reasons.

Extract from K. Jacobs and M. Rein, 'Early retirement: stability, reversal or redefinition', in F. Naschold and B. de Vroom (eds), *Regulating Employment and Welfare* (Berlin: de Gruyter, 1993), pp. 33–6.

Employee involvement

Various European countries provide rights for worker participation in management at the workplace level. These rights have also been extended across the whole of the European Union for those workers in companies which have plants in more than one European country (see Gill and Krieger, 2000; Hancké, 2000; Marginson, 2000; Whittall, 2000; Wills, 2000). However, as the extract in Box 1.10 from Turner (1993) explores, the existence of legislative rights does not say very much about how worker participation schemes work in practice. In this comparison of Germany and France we find that the trade union system, the political culture and the form of legislation play a major role.

Box 1.10 Is worker participation a means to pursue common interests or does it compromise the class struggle?

Germany

The German version of WPM (Worker Participation in Management), known as codetermination (*Mitbestimmung*), is an integral part of an industrial relations system that has been widely recognized for its success. There are two poles to codetermination: employee participation on company supervisory boards and elected works councils at the plant and firm levels.

Board representation, although not insignificant, is the least important of the two poles of codetermination. Supervisory boards meet only a few times a year, with day-to-day

Box 1.10 Continued

decisions made by a separate management board, which is, however, elected by the supervisory board. For the worker representatives on these boards (usually works councillors and union representatives), these meetings afford occasions to learn of company financial and strategic planning. The access to information and the ability to speak out at top levels has sometimes served works council and union interests and smoothed labor-management negotiations. Yet except in the iron, steel and coal industries, which have parity representation on the boards, labor's minority position on the supervisory boards has given codetermination at this level a minor role compared to the daily activities of the works councils.

Works councils are legally independent of both union and management, and they are democratically elected by the entire work force, blue and white collar employees.

Work councils are empowered by law, precedent and plant- and firm-level agreements to receive full information and consult with management prior to the implementation of decisions affecting personnel. In specified areas, works councils have veto rights, giving true meaning to the term 'codetermination'.

How does this works council system work in practice? From a management point of view, there are many actions a firm cannot take without first consulting the works council. In such areas as the introduction of new technology and job design, management is required to inform the works council and listen to comments and suggestions prior to implementation. In these areas, management often ignores the wishes of the works council once the consultation obligation is fulfilled. But in other areas, management must either gain the assent of the works council or, in the event of stalemate, submit the matter to binding arbitration. Under the Works Constitution Act, works councils have codetermination rights in the areas of working hours, piecework rates and bonuses, and performance monitoring (Article 87); working conditions in cases where employers have violated accepted principles of suitable job design (Article 91); hiring, firing, transfers, assignment to pay groupings, or job classifications (Articles 95 and 99); and training and retraining (Article 98).

In spite of West German industry's often cited shop-floor flexibility, given the myriad personnel issues involved, management is not free to reorganize work without extensive discussion with the works council. While decisionmaking may be slowed in this consensus-building process (and the outcome may be altered), once agreement is reached management has an important ally in the works council for winning work force acceptance and smoothing implementation.

Germany also has a strong and fairly cohesive labor movement organized into one principal labor federation (the DGB), itself composed of sixteen industrial unions. From 1978 until unification, union membership density of the employed work force in West Germany was stable at around 40 percent. Relations between unions and works councils are typically close: works councils, especially in the larger firms, are usually dominated by union activists who work closely with the local union office.

At the regional level, fairly centralized unions and employer associations conduct nationally coordinated collective bargaining for entire sectors, establishing the framework for wages, working conditions and hours within which works councils and managers operate. The unions, with substantial resources at the national level, are in a position to offer works councils important advice on strategy, bargaining, key issues and daily operations. This is especially true of the larger unions such as IG Metall and works councils at the larger firms.

France

Although less developed and more limited, WPM is nonetheless widespread in France. At plant and firm levels, workers are represented through staff delegations (*délégations du personnel*), trade union sections (*sections syndicaux*) and works committees (*comités d'entreprise*). The staff delegations monitor company rules and present grievances, but they have no bargaining power. The union representatives can engage in collective bargaining

Box 1.10 Continued

and represent worker interests in other ways. They also put up slates of candidates for election to the works committee, itself designated to play a limited role in WPM. Established by law in 1946, works committees are elected bodies at firms with 50 or more employees, with rights to information and consultation. Through the works committees, workers and unionists receive advance information regarding company plans, giving them the opportunity to mobilize if necessary. But the committees themselves are chaired by the plant manager and have no formal joint decisionmaking rights except in managing recreational facilities and activities. In most cases this latter area is the major preoccupation of the works committees; on the average they derive two-thirds of their budgets from revenues generated in the recreational programs, with the remaining third provided by the company.

At some large firms such as EDF (the national electric company), the works committees are powerful bodies. Their activities often overlap with union representatives' work. Most of the elected committee members are unionists; at large firms they are often freed from normal work duties by virtue of their positions on the committees. Yet even in these cases, works committees generally have not advanced beyond information rights into more extensive WPM for a number of reasons: employers are opposed; French unions have rejected in principle participation in management decisionmaking although one of the principal labor federations, the CFDT, supports worker decisionmaking or 'autogestion'; and plant representation is typically fragmented into several contending union sections who may carry their rivalry into their works committee efforts.

The French labor movement is divided into six principal, often contentious union federations (CGT, CFDT, FO, CFTC, CGC and FEN). The three largest, the CGT, CFDT and FO, are all on the left (the CFDT and FO are socialist, but bitter rivals; the CGT is communist and still the largest). Ideological divisions and organizational rivalries among them are intense. Ever since the breakdown of efforts to form a coalition between the socialist and communist parties in 1977, and between the CFDT and CGT in 1980, the French labor movement has been in decline. This has persisted, especially for the CGT, even under socialist governments. France is the only industrial democracy with a lower union membership density (12 percent or less) than the United States. Divided and in decline, the unions have hardly been in a position to promote expanded WPM through the works committees or in other ways, even if they were inclined to go in that direction. In fact, in the 1989 works committee elections, nonunion candidates for the first time won the largest number of elected committee positions for France as a whole. The expansion of WPM in France in the past decade has been significantly employer led. Managers have promoted various forms of direct participation, including quality circles and expression groups. Such programs aim at complementing the works committees on the shop floor; they also appear to have had the effect of further undermining the unions.

As for Europe, the socialist party and the government support worker protections embodied in the Social Charter and its action program, including expanded information and consultation rights. But the French perspective, even the socialist and union views, are decidedly different from the German union perspective. As Jansen and Kissler [1987] put it: 'Radical democratic traditions, overlapping an individualism which has a definite existence in France, give rise to the fact that common interests hardly ever arise in the area of industrial relations ... The co-determination model favoured by Germany is rejected virtually universally in France. Political groups and trade unions object that co-determination presumes harmony to exist where, in reality, conflict rules.'

Extract from L. Turner, 'Prospects for worker participation in management in the single market', in L. Ulman, B. Eichengreen and W. Dickens (eds), *Labor and an Integrated Europe* (Washington, D.C.: The Brookings Institution, 1993: 63–9).

Reference in text:
P. Jansen and L. Kissler, 'Organization of work by participation? A French-German comparison', *Economic and Industrial Democracy*, 8 (1987): 379–409.

Conclusions

This introductory chapter has sought to do three things. First it has set out some of the reasons why employment is a topic of key importance to a whole series of agents or actors in society, from individual citizens, to corporations, through to governments and political bodies. Second, it has identified five key aspects of employment and indicated how differences between societies may be important factors to take into account in looking at some of the key debates in these areas. The questions whether labour markets are tending to deskill work, to move to individualized pay, to introduce flexible and part-time work, to increase downsizing and early retirement or to provide an increased role for employee voice cannot be answered without reference to the experience of particular societies. Third, the chapter has introduced the reader to a sample of some of the rich qualitative material now available on comparative employment systems. We hope this has whetted the appetite for further reading and in-depth country comparisons. This now significant literature will be pointed to throughout the rest of the book, to provide ample opportunities for following up specific country cases and interesting comparative analyses.

Making sense of international differences: some methodological approaches

The variety of employment policies and practices that we saw in Chapter One challenges any notion that there is only one way of organizing employment. To understand the significance of this rich variety of employment arrangements, we need to go on to ask a series of questions:

- How are we to account for and make sense of these differences in employment forms?
- Do the imperatives of competition and global capitalism impose limits on the varieties of employment policies and practices?
- Do some systems transfer readily between societies, or is their effectiveness always dependent upon the social and cultural environment in which the employing organization is located?
- And what are the grounds for expecting trends towards convergence or divergence in employment policies and practices over time?

To answer these questions we need to develop some theoretical tools and analytical frameworks that can be deployed to make sense of these differences.

Explaining international differences in the organization of employment

There is a range of theoretical frameworks, or ways of seeing the world, which have been used by researchers both to explain observed differences and to assess the relative importance, significance and longevity of variations in employment practice. Three main schools of thought on this subject can be identified. We name these the universalists; the culturalists; and the institutionalists (see Table 2.1 and Lane (1989)). This division into different approaches is necessarily somewhat arbitrary and individual scholars may not fall easily into one category or another. Moreover, none of the approaches, taken on its own, is entirely satisfactory, as we make clear in

Table 2.1 Frameworks for comparative research: universalists, culturalists, institutionalists and related schools of thought

School of thought	Explanations of variations	Dynamic developments	Impact of globalization and international competition
Universalists: market forces	*Economic theory*: Institutions as imperfections/ obstacles to market forces Variations due to stage of development	Towards convergence based on universal best practice	Globalization undermines capacity of national economies to maintain divergent systems
Universalists: contingency	*Organization theory*: Variations related to organizational factors, such as size, technology, scale of production	Sectoral rather than national differences dominate	Technological conditions lead to convergence Multinationals tend to establish similar systems in each location
Culturalists	*Psychological theory*: Variations due to ideational systems: ideas, values, norms Culture is embedded in institutional structures such as organizations	No expectation of convergence; no real theory of dynamic development of culture as focuses on individual	Variations in culture may correlate with differences in comparative advantage — e.g. Japanese culture seen as compatible with development of quality production systems
Institutionalists: societal effect	*Institutional/ interdisciplinary perspective*: Interlocking set of institutions lead to nationally-specific employment and production systems Variations among countries in organizations reflect embeddedness of societal system	Societal systems develop according to a path-specific trajectory, reflecting interlocking institutions and comparative advantage	Globalization places pressure on societal systems, leading to transformation, but not convergence Globalization also implies opportunities to exploit and develop societal differences/ comparative advantage
Institutionalists: dominant country	*Political science/ international relations*: In every era there is a dominant model/ dominant country which others try to imitate	Dominance followed by decline; American Taylorist model giving way in 1980s to Japanese/German/ East Asian — future may involve more than one dominant model	Countries compete in different part of the market dependent upon whether they are leaders (dominant countries), followers or innovators

the last section of this chapter. There we propose the adoption of a modified and more dynamic institutionalist perspective. Such an approach also provides a means of synthesizing some of these apparently opposing tendencies and perspectives. We need first of all to introduce these three approaches and to identify the main strands of social science thought with which they are associated.

The universalists

Universalists stress the general applicability of common models of social and economic organization. The best way of organizing a factory or a supermarket and the best way of managing labour or establishing an employment contract are not dependent on the social context. There may be variations observed between countries but these are not due to fundamental differences in what constitutes the best way. Instead they may reflect 'objective' economic or technological differences between societies or sectors. Alternatively there may be political or institutional barriers to the implementation of best practice. Changes over time in employment organization can be attributed to changes in either of these factors — to the advance of technological and organizational knowledge and adjustment to new market conditions, or to changes in institutional barriers to the adoption of best practice techniques. This universalist approach is pursued particularly by mainstream economists, as Pfeffer explains:

> The focus on equilibrium conditions and the assumptions of market competition tend to assure a more deterministic outcome from the analysis. In emphasizing equilibrium conditions, modern economics demonstrates less concern with 'path-dependence' or the idea that what has happened in the past is important for understanding the present and predicting the future. Both history and process are less important in this form of theorizing, which Jacoby has called 'timeless and placeless' (1990: 32), with no emphasis on how the economy acquired these features and how these vary. (Pfeffer, 1997: 45)

Economists do recognize that differences in a country's factor endowments — the amount and quality of land, the climate, the quantity of capital, the quantity and quality of the labour force — will exert a legitimate influence on modes of operation and therefore on employment organization. The logic of this approach, however, is to expect some degree of convergence in the organization of employment among countries at similar stages of development with similar factor endowments. As this book is mainly concerned with employment practices within advanced industrial societies, the 'choice of technique' approach offers little scope for understanding observed variations. However, even in considering differences between advanced and less developed countries, the notion of choice of technique has become less relevant. Capital and technology have become more mobile and economists have increasingly recognized that the advantage of adopting a new technology may outweigh those of choosing a technique, apparently better suited to the country's current capital endowments but less efficient in absolute terms. These factors tend to reduce the spectrum of technologies and employment systems that might be observed when comparing advanced and developing economies.

Where wide divergences in employment organization are evident, economists attribute the variation to distortions or imperfections in labour markets. This argument has been made particularly strongly over recent years in debates over the differences observed between Western Europe and the US. It has been argued that the more regulated European labour markets, coupled with the more developed social welfare systems there, are a source of imperfection that has caused Europe to fall behind in generating employment and competing with the US. The so-called European social model is contrasted with the more laissez-faire US labour market model, with the latter taken as representing the universalist best practice model.

> Among economists who study Europe, it seems clear that the most popular explanation of economic problems is that it is the fault of governments. Herbert Giersch*, who coined the term 'Eurosclerosis,' argues that the welfare state inhibits economic adjustment in a variety of ways. Generous unemployment compensation removes the incentive for discharged workers to seek new employment and removes pressure on still-employed workers to moderate their demands. Restrictions on hiring and firing prevent adjustment and ... reduce employment. Industrial change is blocked by protection and industrial policy. Heavy charges for social insurance raise employment costs relative to take-home pay. Legal restrictions on wage competition reinforce the market power of trade unions. All these factors together prevent market forces from working and thus lead to the European problems of low employment and slow growth. (Krugman, 1987: 67; *Giersch, 1985)

Another variation of the universalist approach from an economics perspective can be found in Marxist analyses of the development of the world economy. For Marxists there is a constant tension between the needs of capital and those of workers. The interests of capital are not bounded by nation state but have long been international.

> Radical theorists and political economists also identify cross-national contextual similarities in the evolution of capitalist societies, associated with a common location in the capitalist 'world system'. The attributes of capitalism are regarded as comparable across national boundaries and as of significance for the nature of organizations. For example, the pressures and contradictions of capitalism are seen to generate broadly similar trends in the management and structuring of the labour process ... This perspective, of course, also implies a contrast between capitalist and socialist societies. (Child and Tayeb, 1983: 25)

National differences in systems of welfare provision and employment relations are interpreted in different ways by different schools of Marxist thought. The dilemmas for Marxists over how to interpret the role of social policies and trade union 'victories' is summarized by Hyman:

> The question thus arises: in what contexts do material improvements serve as palliatives, and in what context do they act as stimulants? What gains represent inroads into capitalist control of production, and what gains lead rather to the incorporation of workers and

their organizations within capitalist hegemony? (Hyman, 1971, reprinted in Clarke and Clements, 1977: 397)

Those who believe in the possibility of making inroads into capitalist control will tend to stress the possibilities for varieties of capitalism. Others believe welfare capitalism was developed to make capitalism acceptable to workers. It is functional for capital as it reduces and minimizes social unrest and political opposition. These writers tend therefore to minimize the differences between varieties of capitalism and to focus on how nation states are all part of the world capitalist system, even if in different relationships to the centres of power (Hopkins and Wallerstein, 1982). Recent trends in welfare state provision can be interpreted using a class struggle perspective: for example the current advocacy of the US model and the pressure to reduce welfare provision in Europe could be interpreted as attempts by international capital to rid itself of the need to provide the relatively high welfare benefits enjoyed by Europeans in the post Second World War period. The timing of this pressure may be related to the collapse of the Communist bloc. While an alternative economic system appeared viable, there was pressure to reach some compromise with labour (Streeck, 1993); once it had crumbled, the need to maintain a welfare state system or to provide protection against competition in the labour market was reduced. This perspective allows for much more limited freedom of manoeuvre for nation states and trade unions and sees capital firmly in control even of the provision of worker rights.

> ... the market seems to be triumphing all across developed capitalist economies. Such an unexpected success would have been much less widespread, had not the Eastern bloc economies totally collapsed at the end of the eighties. (Boyer, 1997: 57)

While both free-market and Marxist economic approaches tend to focus on the macro or nation state level, there are other approaches which operate more at the organizational or sectoral level yet which could still be said to fall under the universalist umbrella. The dominant organizational theory of work organization in the 1960s and 1970s was the so-called contingency approach, associated with the Aston School. Under this approach, the employment system adopted depends upon the characteristics of the organizations and the sector of activity in which it is located; variations between countries are expected to be much less salient than variations between organizations, with factors such as size and internal organizational structure, technology, capital intensity, and batch size shaping employment organization. Employment systems are thus contingent on organizational characteristics.

> Hickson and co-workers (1979) have argued that that the contingency approach provides the basis for a 'supranational' theory of organizations; they point to a 'remarkable stability' in the relationships that have been found across national samples between variables of a contingency type (such as the size of organizations, and their dependence on other organisations) and certain dimensions of organisational structure. (Child and Tayeb, 1983: 25)

These organizational approaches can thus be categorized as universalist; even though they stress the scope for variations between types of organizations they deny a positive role for social organization in the shaping of systems of work organization. This organizational contingency approach also built upon the work of Clark Kerr, who foresaw a convergence of industrial societies driven on by technological change.

The contingency theorists of the 1960s and 1970s were the subject of a wide range of theoretical and empirical critiques (Child, 1972; Morgan, 1990; Silverman, 1970). It was pointed out that there was little empirical evidence to support the notion of contingencies as imperatives (Child and Tayeb, 1983). Instead there was scope both for strategic action by organizations and for culture-specific or country-specific ways of organizing (Gallie, 1978; Maurice *et al.*, 1984, 1986) to be sustained over the long term. Issues of organizational power relations were not given sufficient attention within contingency theories, which focused on the set of tasks to be carried out rather than on the set of social relations to be managed and sustained within an organization. Nevertheless, new variations on the universalist contingency theme have emerged to influence today's debates on employment policy and practice. These include, on the one hand, the advocates of the Japanese lean production model and, on the other, the promoters of the notion of human resource best practice techniques.

In their influential book *The Machine that Changed the World*, Womack *et al.* (1990) conclude with an unequivocal espousal of the notion of a new universalist best practice technique, based on the lean production model developed within the Japanese car industry.

> ... in the end, we believe, lean production will supplant both mass production and the remaining outposts of craft production in all areas of industrial endeavour to become the standard global production system of the twenty-first century. That world will be a very different, and a much better place. (*op. cit.*, p. 278)

Womack *et al.*'s (1990) approach fits within the standard economists' approach, according to which the most technically efficient system will prevail. However, as we discuss further in Chapter Three, the likely rate of diffusion of lean production throughout the world economy may depend not only on its technical superiority, but also on the fact that this production system is associated with a dominant country. Japan may have been able to spread its employment practices through its role as a leading source of foreign direct investment in the 1980s (Elger and Smith, 1994). Diffusion of the dominant country approach to production takes on a momentum of its own which may cause the technical superiority of the organizational form to be overestimated. These arguments can and have been made with respect to the spread of Taylorism in a period of American dominance of production systems (see Chapter Three) and may apply equally to the so-called process of global Japanization.

The 'best practice' human resource management approach fits perhaps more conventionally within the traditional contingency approach. Here the focus is on the interrelationships between different elements of a human resource package (see Table 2.2)

Table 2.2 Bundles of high performance
management practices

High performance management practices
Employment security
Selective hiring
Self-managed teams and decentralization
Extensive training
Reduction of status differentials
Sharing information
High and contingent compensation

Source: Pfeffer (1998), Chapter Ten.

which, if bundled as a package should, apparently, provide 'sustained profitability', as long as the model is not too easily imitated. The context is implicitly the US, which is taken as a universal model for all advanced countries. Other countries' human resource policies are then assessed according to their convergence with or divergence from the apparent best practice model.[1]

The culturalists

'Culture' is the shorthand term used by lay people and many academics alike to account for observed differences between societies. Specifically with respect to employment issues, differences in culture can and have been used to explain differences in organizational and management forms, differences in employment policies and practices and, perhaps most importantly within the study of international human resource management, differences within multinational companies in the responses to similar employment policies and practices, dependent upon location. The gradual acceptance that the transfer of apparent best practices from one country to another may lead to different outcomes within different cultures has prompted multinational companies to take cultural issues more seriously. If employment techniques were easily transferable, these multinational companies could decide not to concern themselves with differences in the ways business is done outside the multi or transnational companies. For international managers socialized, for example, in the individualistic, self-reliant culture of the US, there may be a reluctance to accept that these are not prized values in other societies where the focus may be more, for example, on collective not individual achievement, on social networks not individual space. The impingement of cultural values on the operation of multinationals has led to a growing interest in culture within international business and international human resource management.

As much of the interest relates to the specific employment problems of multinational companies, the approach to culture adopted has reflected the disciplines and concerns of management sciences, in particular that of psychology. The study of culture has a long history within a range of academic disciplines from anthropology, sociology, psychology, history and humanities, but this broader approach to the origins and functions of culture tends, within the management literature, to be assumed to be a given. Workers enter an organization already socialized into a range of norms, beliefs and values that together can be considered to constitute a culture; the specific conditions that have generated these norms and values lie outside the remit of management theorists, whose focus is primarily on what happens within the walls of the individual business enterprise. The emphasis is on identifying differences in the 'mental maps' (Hofstede, 1980b, 1991) of the individuals employed within an organization and not on how these differences in mental maps evolved in the past or will continue to evolve in the future. Individuals' mental maps are assumed to be congruent with, and to have been generated by, differences in a range of social practices and arrangements; however, the interrelations and interactions between these structures and the development of norms, values and ideas are not explicitly theorized or focused upon.

The best known study of culture is that of Hofstede (1980b, 1991). He identified four dimensions to culture — symbols, heroes, ritual and values — but focused on the final dimension: values. Investigation of values is in itself problematical and the definition or description of values may reflect the researcher's own socialization and values. Hofstede sought to overcome this problem by conceptualizing values at a relatively high level of abstraction (see Lane, 1989). The conceptualization involves four elements:

- power distance, that is the acceptability of an unequal distribution of power;
- uncertainty avoidance, that is the extent to which uncertainly, ambiguity or deviance is tolerated or minimized through the development of strongly codified rules;
- individualist versus collectivist values, that is the extent to which agents act individually or as part of cohesive social groups;
- and finally masculinity versus femininity, where masculine social values attach importance to acquisition of money, high achievement and recognition while feminine values involve concern for people and for the quality of life.

Hofstede found significant differences between countries on these four variables, and was thereby able to suggest a clustering of countries according to this definition of culture. One criticism of this approach is that the identification of differences in norms and values does not in itself provide proof that these norms and values actually affect behaviour within organizations. It may still be possible for countries to generate different cultures, but for organizations to act as if there was a common shared culture if norms and values are not always translated into actions. Exactly how differences in cultures lead to differences in behaviour has not been widely studied; instead, observed differences in norms and values have been used as indirect explanations of apparent differences in organizational forms and performance across countries.

The culture perspective has, in fact, been used both to explain some observed differences between societies and to cast doubt on some 'universal' theories of management practice. In the first place, the culture approach is used to explain both why certain approaches to employment organization may be more successful in one country than another, and why certain organizational forms may develop more in one society than another. For example, large bureaucratic employment systems may require a high tolerance of unequal power relations to thrive; similarly, the notion of stakeholder companies, in which all involved in the company, including the workforce, are recognized to have a stake in the survival and development of the company, may be an idea more likely both to find favour and have a chance of working effectively in societies where there is a long established culture of cooperation, consensus and power sharing. Hofstede (1993 reprinted 1996, p. 430) describes the approach to management in the Netherlands as based on consensus 'involving an open-ended exchange of views and a balancing of interests ... The organization in Holland is more *ménage* (running a household) while in the US it is more *manège* (horse drill)'.

Box 2.1 gives further examples of how different forms of market organization can be related to different cultures, as defined using Hofstede's scale.

Recognition of cultural differences calls into question the validity of universal theories, for example those relating to satisfaction at work, such as Maslow's hierarchy of

---

Box 2.1 Hofstede's analysis of culture

Motivation

Hofstede divides countries into four groups using two of the dimensions of culture — uncertainty avoidance, and masculinity. These give the following orientations/characteristics:

1 Performance plus risk (weak uncertainty avoidance, masculine), for example the US
2 Performance plus security (strong uncertainty avoidance, masculine), for example Japan
3 Social needs plus security (strong uncertainty avoidance, feminine), for example Korea
4 Social needs plus risk (weak uncertainty avoidance, feminine), for example Sweden

Organizational design

Hofstede identifies four implied types of organizational design using two of the dimensions of culture — uncertainty avoidance and power distance. These give the following organizational forms:

Pyramid of people (large power distance, strong uncertainty avoidance)
• Control from the top, for example France, Italy
Well-oiled machine (small power distance, strong uncertainty avoidance)
• Focus on rules but without centralization, for example Germany
Village market (small power distance, weak uncertainty avoidance)
• No decisive hierarchy, flexible rules, for example the UK
Family (small power distance, weak uncertainty avoidance)
• Strong personal authority, few formal rules, for example Asian countries

Sources: Hofstede (1980a, 1991); Olie (1995)

---

needs (Olie, 1995). In Maslow's theory the need for intrinsic job satisfaction is assumed to come to the fore once basic needs in the form of a reasonable wage and living standard have been met. However, the notion of culture casts doubt on whether there is a stable and ordered hierarchy of needs that is universal over time and space. As Olie points out 'putting self-actualization plus esteem above social needs and security reflects the dominant North American value system characterized by weak uncertainty avoidance, strong masculinity and very strong individualism' (p. 138). Current management fashions such as teamworking or performance management (Lane, 1989) may also be considered to be culturally contingent in their organizational effectiveness.

Similarly the culture perspective can be used to criticize the work of contingency theorists (Lane, 1989; Horvath *et al.*, 1981). Business policy and practice will reflect not only the objective measurable characteristics of the organization but also the goals that the organization is seeking to achieve, and these may differ between societies. For example, even at the level of the organization, culture may influence whether greatest importance is attached to uncertainty avoidance or survival of the company or whether the focus is on short-term returns and risk taking.

While culture theories provide a useful critique of the value-free universalist approaches, there are still a number of problems with these approaches from an analytical perspective. First of all, these culture theories can perhaps better be regarded as typologies or classification systems rather than fully developed social science theories. No analytical framework is provided to explain how these differences in values and norms have developed and why a particular constellation of countries by culture is detected. No explanations, for example, are offered for why France apparently shares similar cultural values to East Asia (Lane, 1989: 31). Most importantly, there is no theoretical framework for understanding the dynamic development of culture. These classifications are stuck in a particular time and place with no theory as to whether they will remain constant or change. The focus on values and norms and the socialized behaviour of the individualized actor has resonances with much of recent social science theory, where individuals are regarded as active agents, both reproducing and restructuring their own environments, and not as passive ciphers, simply moulded and shaped by their environments (Sorge, 1995). However, it is in the interactions between environment and institutional frameworks and the norms and values of actors that we have to seek an explanation of both the reproduction and the transformation of norms and values. Without situating culture in a social framework, the approach cannot contribute to the analysis of change over time. As McSweeney (2002) points out, from the cultural perspective, 'the social and the institutional are defined as consequences of the national culture. Hofstede's model is closed to the idea that values might be, or might also be, the consequences of the social/institutional' (2002: 99). National culture is taken as a given so that, by implication, the social and the institutional also remains static.

This absence of a dynamic framework can be seen to lead to some more specific problems. First of all, the culture approach runs the danger of developing and perpetuating national stereotypes that may prove to be increasingly outdated but still persistent.

> Culture tended to be employed as little more than a synonym for 'nation'; and so, in effect, differences about the national samples were simply ascribed to nationality in a circular and vacuous manner … Indeed, the operationalisation of culture was typically confined to attitudes and opinions that abstracted from, and discouraged attention to, national institutions and the sociopolitical systems. (Child and Tayeb, 1983: 23)

The recent critique by McSweeney (2002) of Hofstede's methodology raises major questions over the validity of both the sample and the methods through which national cultures were identified. The sample was based on only one multinational company, IBM, and McSweeney questions the assumption made that statistical variations between the samples, stratified by the nation state in which the employees were located, could be attributed to national cultures. First of all, the employees of IBM are not representative or not equally representative of the national populations; and second, belonging to the same organization does not rule out influences from organizational and occupational cultures, as Hofstede assumes. Indeed, the focus on differences in cultures between countries makes little allowance for differences in cultures within countries, linked, for example, to class, gender, religion, ethnicity or region. Much of the international human resource management literature is concerned with matching the organizational culture and the national culture, but it is the coexistence of different norms and value systems within an organization which can be said to be one of the main challenges to the development of an organizational culture. Because there is not just one set of cultural norms or values in a society, what matters for an individual organization is not the national stereotypical set of values but the range of norms and values to which its own workforce subscribes. Over time there may be an apparent change in dominant norms and values, but this may reflect changes in the composition of the workforce or in the dominance of particular groups in society. Norms and values also have to affect the actual operation of an organization for these to be relevant. Organizations may be able to change employment policies and practices, not because of a change in values and norms but because of a change in the relative bargaining power of particular groups; if such groups' bargaining power is weak their norms and values may perhaps be safely ignored by employers.

All these problems suggest that no one set of norms or values can represent societal differences. Instead these variations by society have to be understood within a social and political context, in which the power of particular groups to impose their norms and values on the employment relationship also has to be taken into account. Furthermore this focus on the social and institutional context in which norms and values emerge and take on relevance for social processes also provides a framework for understanding dynamic developments, both in respect of culture on the one hand and employment practices on the other. We therefore need at this stage to introduce the institutionalists.

The institutionalists

The main focus of the third school of thought, the institutionalists, is on how the set of institutional arrangements and societal structures in which an organization is located and embedded may account for and explain differences between societies. In contrast to the universalists, they do not regard institutions as sources of potential distortion or barriers to adaptation to market forces and the adoption of universal best practice techniques; instead, institutionalists regard institutions as an essential and integral part of social and economic organization. Indeed many would go further and argue that markets cannot be considered as working in opposition to institutions. Instead markets are themselves institutions; that is, they are socially constructed, according to legal and social rules, both formal and informal. Prices are not pure economic or market variables but reflect a whole raft of institutional arrangements. At the very least, prices will be structured by the laws of property, laws of competition and consumer protection, laws of intellectual property rights and arrangements for international trade, international capital flows and currency conversion. The term 'institutionalist' covers a great many of the writers and researchers whose work will be referred to throughout this volume (see Christiansen *et al.* (1999); Hollingsworth and Boyer (1997); and Maurice and Sorge (2000) for recent collections of work from an institutionalist perspective).

The labour market is the clearest example of an institutionally and socially constructed market. It is, for this group of theorists, impossible to consider the labour market and the price of labour as determined by some abstract universal force of supply and demand. Social and institutional arrangements are critical in structuring the supply of labour to the labour market. For example, which groups seek employment in the wage labour market and which groups remain outside is analysed by mainstream economists according to the opportunity cost of working, with the institutional arrangements regarded as a given. For institutionalists it is these factors, including the organization of family and community support networks, the system of state welfare support, and the possibilities of generating income outside the formal wage economy (for example through family-owned farms, business, the informal or illegal economy, landholding and so on) that provide the most interesting variations over time and space. Institutional and social arrangements also shape the quality of labour through family, education and training arrangements and through arrangements for the provision of health care, the protection of the environment (including housing, air pollution and so forth). Institutions from this perspective are not hindering progress but may instead act to facilitate or enable the development and operation of effective markets.

An institutionalist approach provides a very different perspective on national economies to that of a universalist approach, for two reasons. First, it suggests there is a wider range of possibilities for organizing social and economic life than is indicated by a narrow focus on market forces. Second, it also suggests that there are more difficult problems to be overcome in borrowing or learning from another society. Institutions matter, but for this reason they cannot be easily or readily transformed or indeed transferred to other societies. Societies make choices at particular points of time as to how to structure the institutions of their economic and social life, but once these institutions are in place they have long lasting consequences. These decisions not only help to structure the norms and values of the society, as we discussed in the previous section, but also serve to create vested interests, foster specific expectations and attitudes, and build up or run down specific national endowments. As a result, a country tends to become locked into a particular path of development or a specific national trajectory. If institutions matter, so does the history of the establishment of institutions; and future developments will also be conditioned by past arrangements and developments.

These barriers to diffusion and transfer of institutional arrangements are that much greater if each society not only has different institutional and social arrangements, but also if these social and institutional arrangements have interlocking and inseparable effects which thereby generate a specific societal logic or societal effect. This notion of interlocking arrangements was developed through the work of scholars who set out to study similar plants in France and Germany, with the aim of applying and critiquing the contingency approach to employment organization (Lutz, 1981; Maurice et al., 1986; Sorge and Warner, 1980). Despite selecting organizations that scored similarly on most of the variables used by contingency theorists to predict organizational and employment arrangements, the researchers found the plants to have widely different systems of work organization. These differences were ascribed by the theorists to the institutional and social systems in which the organizations were embedded (see Chapter One, Box 1.3). These arrangements were not considered to be barriers to organizations making efficient choices, as would be the implied interpretation under contingency theory. Instead the societal system permeated the whole way in which the organizations operated, including the mind-sets of the actors involved in structuring the organizations. Thus French plants had more hierarchically-based authority and employment structures than the German plants, not because these arrangements were imposed on the organizations but because this was the expected form of organization, reflecting in particular the much more hierarchical education and status system in France, the society in which the organizations were embedded.

This research extended the analysis of the organization embedded in its social environment to develop a theory of the interlocking nature of the whole societal system. These interlocking characteristics generate a specific societal logic and path of development. This argument has been developed particularly with respect to whether societies have developed high skill or low skill employment systems, or high value-added or low value-added production systems. The notion of low and high skill equilibrium societies (Ashton and Green, 1996; Finegold and Soskice, 1988) has been put forward to suggest that countries may become locked into a low level of

Box 2.2 On redundant capacities

Where accountants, as organizational representatives of economic rationality, are allowed to enforce rational return-on-investment calculations on investment decisions, ranging from worker training to the acquisition of new technology, investment will often fall short of the economically optimal. This holds in particular where high economic performance requires *redundant capacities*, i.e., excess production resources that are kept in reserve for coping with as yet unknown future contingencies. An example is a broadly based vocational training regime, like the German one, that generates skills, including the skill to acquire more skills, far in excess of present needs. Excess skills make possible an organization of work capable of flexibly restructuring itself in response to fast-changing, highly uncertain environmental conditions. Such capacity, which tends to be costly to build and whose productive contribution is difficult to measure directly at any given point in time — because it contributes only indirectly to production and remains unused most of the time — is always in danger of being rationalized away under pressures for detailed cost accounting, even though such rationalization may deprive the organization of crucial capacities for flexible adjustment.

Source: Streeck (1997), pp. 205–6

training and skill provision, a system reinforced by an orientation within the industrial sector towards low quality mass production, and by the organization of work to minimize the share of skilled workers. In contrast a high skill system supports a dynamic specialist production system based on 'redundant capacities', that is the building of skills in excess of normal production needs into the system of work organization to facilitate problem solving and innovation (see Box 2.2).

From the societal effect perspective, differences in employment policies and practices are an inevitable consequence of differences in societal logics and societal trajectories. All societies may be facing similar pressures for change, in part as a consequence of greater international integration and globalization, but these common pressures may not lead to a process of convergence. Instead these pressures will lead to modification and change of societal institutions, but the particular form of the response will reflect each country's own societal logic. From this perspective, for example, the notion of lean production will be incorporated in different ways within each society's system according to the differing opportunities for adaptation and adoption (see Chapter Three).

Developing the societal effect approach

The societal effect school has demonstrated not only the range of societal differences but has also gone some way towards providing an explanation of the persistence of difference. The analysis has moved beyond description of institutional differences to explore how institutional arrangements affect the whole operation of a societal system. However, the approach remains rather focused on an individual society and fails to situate the society within the broader field of international economic and political relations. Another development of the institutionalist perspective — the dominant country theory (see Table 2.1) — already suggests that not all societal systems are equally valued within the economic and political arena, and that some societal systems will be considered dominant and worthy of emulation (Smith and Meiksins, 1995). The emergence of a societal system as a dominant world model will reflect not only superiority measured in technical or efficiency terms but also superiority measured in political power. The relative importance of the political over the efficiency factors is a matter of debate (for further discussion of this approach see final section of this chapter). The societal effect school has thus begun to provide answers to issues which are not satisfactorily addressed by the universalists or the culturalists. At the same time, it has also generated new criticisms and raised new questions which need to be addressed, particularly in a period of rapid change and pressure for deregulation or de-institutionalization of societal systems. Three questions in particular can be identified:

- What are the implications of societal effect theory for the role of individual nation states in the world economy?
- Is the nation state the appropriate level of analysis?
- Does the societal effect approach lead to an overemphasis on coherence and consensus and fail to recognize sources of conflict and inconsistency?

Societal effect theory and the role of individual nation states in the world economy

There are two alternative ways of interpreting the implications of the societal effect school's thinking. On the one hand, it could be argued that societies simply find different ways of organizing the same economic and social activities. On the other hand, it may imply that societies are and indeed should be selective in the economic and social activities in which they specialize. Can, in fact, the societal system approach, in a similar way to the notion of comparative advantage in international trade theory, help to explain the process of specialization and trade between states (Sorge, 1991)?

Under the latter approach some societies are likely to be in a better position within the world economy at a particular point in time than others, as some activities offer more scope for growth and productivity gains than others. Whitley has developed the concept of 'distinctive business systems' as 'particular arrangements of hierarchy-market relations which become institutionalized and relatively successful in particular contexts' (Whitley, 1992: 6). He thereby integrates some notion of economic performance into the concept of path-specific development. However, this does not mean that all institutional arrangements at all times can simply be deemed to be relatively successful simply because they exist (Almond, 1999). Indeed as Streeck

(1997) notes in relation to the success of industrial districts in Northern Italy:

> Social arrangements that may be economically irrelevant or counterproductive under given conditions may unexpectedly turn out to be beneficial as conditions change. In the 1960s the predominance of small artisan or family firms in Northern Italy was widely deplored as a sign of economic backwardness. When the technological and market environment changed in the 1970s and 1980s, favouring flexible producers of semi-customised high quality products, the embeddedness of the economy of the Third Italy [a name sometimes given to this region] in dense family ties and local networks of parties, unions and employers' associations came to be regarded as a principal source of the region's suddenly impressive competitive performance in national and international markets. Hardly any of the social structures that were now found to be economically beneficial had originally been devised for economic purposes; the solidarity between Communist Party members in the various interconnected spheres of Bologna's civil society was not based on a shared desire to get rich. (1997: 211)

Similar arguments can be made that the apparently successful Japanese and German employment systems came about as unintended consequences of institutional developments designed to meet objectives other than promoting the competitive strength of private capital. The development of comparative advantage was thus more an unintended consequence than the objective of the institutional development. In Japan, the lifetime employment system has been attributed in origin to the development of Japan's military power and not, as is commonly assumed, in order to meet the perceived needs of the industrial system (Weiss, 1993). In Germany the co-determination system, on which its high trust industrial relations system is based, emerged out of efforts to contain class conflict (see Chapter Six) and not because employers spontaneously identified the benefits that might come from a policy of incorporating and consulting with the workforce.

While comparative advantage arises out of a specific path of development and may not be the objective of the development, it is not necessarily valid, as is implied at times within the societal effect school, that all methods and ways of operating are equally good and will be equally successful, provided a society is free to choose that method which best fits its particular societal logic. This approach tends to remove the societal effect debate from the analysis of how the processes of international trade and international integration necessarily involve some comparisons of the effectiveness or efficiency of different ways of doing things. Societies, unlike firms, cannot actually be forced out of business because they fail to adjust and adapt; but they may be forced out of a particular market and they may be forced into a downward economic spiral and lower performance in international trade, which in turn may create internal pressures for further adjustment and adaptation (Rubery, 1992; Wilkinson, 1983). In contrast to the mainstream economics approach, this critique of the societal effect school does not suggest that this adaptation will lead to convergence between societies; instead it may lead to continued instability and/or different forms of specialization. However, the links between the societal system and the position of the society in the world economic system have to be addressed directly and it cannot be assumed that all societal systems are in some sense functionally equivalent, or indeed that nation states operate as autonomous entities, not articulated with the world capitalist system.

Is the nation state the appropriate level or unit of analysis?

The second set of problems we can identify with societal effect theory relates to the implicit assumption that it is always useful and appropriate to discuss differences between countries. Some may argue that differences by region (Dunning, 2000), city (Sassen, 2001) or even by sector (Hollingsworth and Streeck, 1994) may be more appropriate. Increasingly there may be supra-national influences, for example a pan-European effect. The counter argument is that nation states are still important sources of uniformity in key institutional arrangements from the legal to the educational systems; and that although regional and other effects may also be present, the nation state remains dominant as the most important level at which to analyse interlocking institutional arrangements.

Does the societal effect approach place too much emphasis on coherence and consensus and too little on conflict and inconsistency?

The concern that the nation state is not always the appropriate focus feeds into the third set of issues: whether there is a danger of promoting national stereotyping by focusing on apparently coherent and systematic differences between societies. The ways of doing things within a society may be characterized as interlocking but they are also contested. Just as the cultural approach tends to overemphasize differences in norms and values between countries and underestimate the size and scope of differences within them, the societal effect approach tends to focus on internal coherence and to abstract from the sources of conflicts, tensions and differences within an organization and within the wider society. There have been attempts to make the societal effect school's thinking more sensitive to the norms and values of individual actors and less focused on all encompassing or deterministic institutional structures (Sorge 1995). In contrast to the culturalist approach, the norms and values of social actors are seen as produced and reproduced within a specific social and institutional context. It is the interactions between the framework and the actors' norms, values and behaviour that are actually responsible for differences in employment policies and practices. Sorge focuses on the need for a dialectical approach to the understanding of change — that is, societies must be viewed as evolving through creative tensions between actors with different values and interests. He thereby aims to avoid developing an overdeterministic approach to societal change which gives priority to institutional structures and neglects the interactions and behaviour of actors.

The three issues we have been outlining are taken up again in the next section, where we argue for a more dynamic and more open institutional or societal approach. The likelihood of divergent country trajectories is still central to the framework we develop, but more emphasis is placed on conflicts and tensions within specific societies in shaping the path of change. Societal systems are open to the influences of the international economy and the international transmission of political and social ideas. These international pressures may take on specific shapes and forms within a particular society; but the societal logic is not necessarily strong enough to resist pressures for change that may ultimately result in major transformation of the traditional institutional arrangements and even in the prevailing norms and values of the society. In making these arguments we are also developing a more hybrid approach in common with other theorists, as we illustrate in the final section of this chapter.

Towards a more dynamic framework

Under current conditions of change both in the organization of the world economy and in the micro-level organization of work, a crucial test for an appropriate theoretical framework must be its ability to deal with and explain processes of change. This poses particular problems for comparative analysis as a natural tendency is to focus on differences. Moreover, there is a temptation to try to regard such differences as static and unchanging characteristics of particular economies. This tendency can be found both in the cultural perspective and in some versions of the societal effect school. These approaches, therefore, focus on explaining why countries remain the same and not on how they adjust to change in the world economy. In contrast, the universalist approaches regard differences as temporary phenomena or aberrations, and tend to latch on to any evidence of change as proof of the disappearance of these manifestations of political interference and of the emergence of a true market form or of the diffusion of best practice.

This latter approach can be identified in recent surveys of international employment policy and practice conducted through the PriceWaterhouse/Cranfield survey of large organizations in European countries (Brewster *et al.*, 1994). The survey focuses on changes in employment practices and uses this analysis of trends to argue the case for convergence in European employment systems. However, identification of common trends is not sufficient to establish the case for convergence or the existence of a universal best practice approach. Without indicators of the intensity of trends or the extent to which the changes are actually leading to common outcomes, this approach can be very misleading. To illustrate this approach we quote from the conclusions of an overview of trends in flexible working practices:

> Several key facts emerge. The first, and perhaps most important, is that despite the different legal, cultural and labour traditions around Europe, there is a clear general trend amongst employers across the different sectors towards increasing their use of flexibility.

This trend varies by country, sector and size and has been slowed by the impact of the recession. It is, nevertheless, a clear and largely consistent development. (Brewster *et al.*, 1994, p. 189)

The trend towards more flexible employment, however, may also be consistent with a widening of the range of employment practices between countries. For example, the survey found that most countries had increased their use of part-time labour over the survey period, but in practice the most intensive rate of increase was found in those countries — the Netherlands, Germany and the UK — where the use of part-time work was already among the highest in Europe before the survey period began, while some countries such as Greece and Portugal, with already low levels of part-time working, had actually decreased usage over the same period. These trends towards divergence are not fully reflected in the above quoted summary of the development of flexibility in Europe.

The peculiarities or specificities of the labour market and the employment relationship, as outlined in the first part of this chapter, are to our mind sufficient reasons in themselves for rejecting any simplistic universalist approach to employment organization. The organization of the employment system plays a critical role in both the production and trading capabilities of an economy and in determining the nature of the society and the opportunities for citizens to lead productive and fulfilling lives. States are very unlikely to withdraw entirely from the role of shaping and organizing the employment relationship and therefore unlikely to give a clear run to international capital to shape the nation's future. However, the specificity of employment systems derives from more than the different policy decisions of governments, but also arises out of the nature of the employment relationship itself. This relationship is central to competitiveness but the outcome of entering into an employment relationship is, as we outlined in Box 1.1, ambiguous and uncertain, from the perspective of both the employer and the employee. The social context in which the employment relationship is constituted takes on a crucial importance precisely because of this ambiguity in form. Attention has to be paid to the psychological dimensions of the employment contract — to the commitment to the organization's goals and to the active use of human intelligence in the performance of tasks — and not just to the price of labour or the notion of standard performance measurements. This renders invalid the notion that employment can be reduced through international pressure to a predetermined set of contractual arrangements, conforming to best practice.

We therefore reject the universalist tradition as incompatible with our view of the employment relationship as socially constituted, but at the same time we recognize a need to move beyond the static versions of both the cultural and the societal effects schools. These approaches are not able, as we have seen, to deal adequately with the process of historical change. In part the solution is to draw upon the different approaches to develop a more dynamic institutionalist perspective, less bound by notions of the nation state as the main or only source of employment divergence.

Dore (1973) wrote the classic book comparing Japanese and British factories, and in doing so brought together the three approaches we have identified as the main 'schools of thought' on comparing international differences in the organization of employment. According to Lane (1989), Dore 'is able to show how an institution, such as the Japanese employment system, is partly an adaptation of earlier pre-industrial institutional patterns, partly an attempt to create new arrangements consonant with dominant cultural values, and partly the result of borrowing elements from other industrial nations' (*ibid.*, p. 375f). For Dore, the Japanese system should not be seen as having simply distinct and separate cultural origins, but instead as arising out of a fusion between Japan's own historical and cultural legacy and the dominant modes of production and employment organization outside of Japan. Diffusion of techniques does not lead to direct replication. The implementation of borrowed techniques within a specific societal system is itself a form of innovation which may lead to the development or the reinforcement of distinct societal models.

> I suggest that by this process of diffusion late-developing societies can 'get ahead' — can show in a 'more developed' form, patterns of social organisation which, in the countries which industrialized earlier are still emerging, still struggling to get out of the chrysalis of nineteenth century institutions. (Dore, 1973: 12)

The work of Elger and Smith (1994) and Smith and Meiksins (1995) has also been concerned with Japan, but with the focus on the diffusion of Japanese techniques to the rest of the world economy, rather than on the role of Western techniques in the development of the distinctive Japanese model. The starting point for their work has been the interpretation of the role of multinational companies in the process of convergence or divergence in employment forms, an issue rather side-stepped by the societal effect school which fails, by and large, to deal with the increasing multinational or transnational nature of capital (Smith and Elger, 2000). Smith and Meiksins (1995) set out an approach to comparative employment research which explicitly proposes a hybrid framework in which three effects could be identified: system imperatives, societal effects and dominance effects. Not only may these effects all be present but they may also interact with each other, as follows.

System imperatives relate to the impact of the changing nature of technology and capitalist competition and how these impinge on all forms of capitalism. These pressures for change on all societal systems are nevertheless, according to Smith and Meiksins, mediated through *societal effects*. These differences between societies 'are not confined to the environments of corporate enterprises, but penetrate powerfully into their internal operations' (Elger and Smith, 1994). However, the divergent trajectories of the nation state must not be studied only with respect to their internal logics of development; instead nation states must be analysed within a world system of international political and power relations. It is from the system of international relations that we find the *dominance effects*, and in particular the 'hegemonic' or overarching influence of America in shaping world production and consumption systems in the first part of the post Second World War period, to be replaced by a putative dominance of Japanese systems in the final decades of the 20th century (see Table 2.1). Pressures towards global Japanization, as addressed by Elger and Smith (1994), may not be founded solely or mainly on advances in technical know-how, that is system effects; but may also involve the international transmission of ideology both through direct means, such as foreign direct investment, and through more indirect means, such as the propagation of Japanization as the best practice techniques by governments, the press and business schools. Japanization has proved to be less 'dominant' than 'Americanization', particularly since the development of severe internal problems in the Japanese economy in the early 1990s. As a consequence Smith and Elger (2000) have called into question their use of the term 'dominance' to encompass all the effects of international power relations; the breakdown of American hegemony has been associated with the development of more complex inter-country relations and in particular with new pan-national organizations and arrangements, such as for example the European Union. From this framework, trends towards convergence need not be interpreted as evidence of superiority in technical performance but are also linked into the broader power relations between states and regional complexes.

This call for a more integrated approach, which includes the insights of political economy as well as the notion of cultural and societal difference, has resonances with other theoretical contributions, such as, for example, Child and Tayeb's (1983) critique of Sorge for prioritising cultural-specific action to the exclusion of all else. Lane (1989, 1995) has also called for fusion between the insights of institutionalists and those of Marxist political economy. There are also similarities with the more abstract theoretical framework proposed by Wilkinson (1983), that is the notion of productive systems (see Burchell *et al.* (2002) for further development of this approach). Wilkinson implicitly adopts the notion of interlocking social and institutional arrangements, but three factors distinguish his model from the societal effects school. First, the nation state is not prioritized as the relevant unit for analysing different productive systems; divisions by region or industry may be more salient. Second, the focus is not on equivalence of different productive systems but on the likelihood that international trading relations will cause some systems to be more or less successful than others, exerting pressures for adaptation and change within productive systems. Third, as with the societal effects school, the pressure for change does not necessarily lead to convergence and may under certain circumstances lead to deterioration rather than improvement in relative economic performance. Smooth adjustment is unlikely, as actors possess imperfect knowledge and receive contradictory signals; more importantly, there is a persistence of conflictual interests within productive systems. Thus Wilkinson avoids the trap of focusing on the coherence of distinct social systems by pointing to the constant pressure on all social arrangements arising out of diverging interests. Pressure from the international economy for change may provide an opportunity, not for coherent adaptation to new technologies, but for a reopening of conflicts between or within capital and labour and a new jockeying for position by the main actors.

In line with our own previous work in this area, the methodological approach we propose to follow in this book can be considered a further development of the Wilkinson productive systems approach, but applied more directly to the issue of societal differences in employment systems (Rubery, 1992, 1994). This approach also has close parallels to that proposed in the various writings of Elger, Meiksins and Smith, and of Lane. Figure 2.1 provides a schematic representation of the framework, where the external conditions are seen as exerting pressures on the social actors, whose behaviour is shaped both by the societal system and by these external pressures.

If we take the external pressures first, we have identified four types of forces. First, there are the systems effects, including changes in technologies and pressures related to changes in global market structures (for example, the whole market for telecommunications has changed as a result not only of technological change but also of product market deregulation and privatization of the telecommunications sector). Global market effects are not, in our view, independent of political processes, but an individual nation state may be faced with the need to respond to the accumulated impact of political changes on the ways in which markets are regulated and organized.

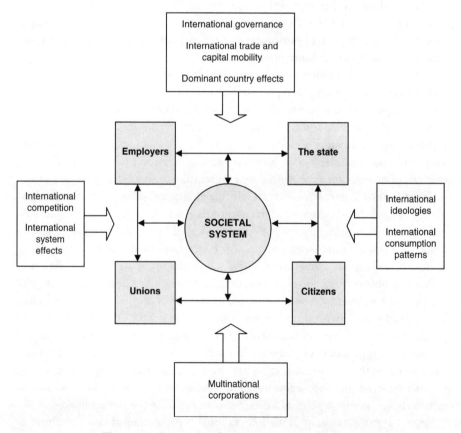

Figure 2.1   International pressures on societal systems

In this context it appears appropriate to include these alongside systems effects related to technological change. The second set of influences stem more directly from the international political system; these include the influence of international arrangements — organized on a world or regional level — on the organization of international trade, international capital flows and direct investment and the establishment of labour, environmental and other international standards. These international political arrangements are also shaped by the dominant country, in practice the United States, whose influence on world political arrangements is undisputed. International political arrangements also help to shape international markets and the system of global competition by setting the rules of the game for world trade (for example, the conditions under which import restrictions or tariffs are allowed). Thirdly, but no less importantly, there is the power of global or multinational capital. This power is exercised either directly, through negotiations with nation states over conditions for new investment or for agreeing to retain existing investment; or more indirectly, through exerting influence on the general international political arrangements for international trade, capital flows and environmental and labour standards. Global or multinational capital is strongly implicated in the diffusion of dominant country effects, for even when multinationals do not have parent companies in the dominant country or countries, they may still try to emulate and thereby diffuse the practices of the dominant country.

The fourth set of influences, the international transmission of ideologies, tastes and fashions, tends to have been given less prominence in debates over globalization and convergence or divergence of societal systems. These influences are not independent of the other three sets of forces; they are clearly dependent, for example, on international media industries and the international travel industry. The transmission of the political ideology of liberalism and deregulation is a particularly good example of how nation states with different traditions and modes of economic and social organization have been increasingly forced onto the defensive by the development of a global orthodoxy as to the appropriate way to organize social and economic life. This transmission is undoubtedly shaped by the political forces already discussed, including the dominant country effects, and by the lobbying powers of multinational capital. Some other global ideologies are, however, less obviously linked to global political forces. These include, for example, ideas of feminism and the rights of women to economic independence (see Chapter Four). These ideas have gained ground with women even in societies that have done little directly to promote them; and it is not necessarily in the immediate interests of global capital to promote this path of development (although some would argue that more women need to be in the labour market to help support the ageing population — see Chapter Four). It therefore seems useful to identify these transmission mechanisms separately from general political forces, while recognizing their interlinkages.

Similar arguments apply to the international transmission of tastes and preferences, even though again these are supported by global capital. It can in fact be argued that this transmission process has become *relatively autonomous* of the supporting political and economic institutions (Humphries and Rubery, 1984; Rubery, 1992). Once societies and groups become exposed to influences and ideas from outside the nation state there is unlikely to be a return to some notion of a closed culture. Politicians and other nationalists may hanker after a return to a society untouched by the influences of other nation states. Not only is this a misguided view of the past (as national characteristics have often been borrowed and imported from other countries in the past — such as English tea-drinking), but it is also an even more unrealistic view of the future. One possible outcome, however, of this international transmission of tastes and preferences is not a disappearance of distinctive national characteristics, such as cuisine and modes of dress and style, but an increasing diversity within nation states, as a consequence both of migration patterns and of wider awareness and appreciation of the varieties of such traditions across the globe.

These four sets of external pressures can then be seen as exerting pressures for change on societal systems. These pressures are mediated through the influence of social actors, identified in Figure 2.1 as employers, unions, the state and citizens. It is through social actors that the societal system is constructed and reproduced. The societal system is therefore represented as being encompassed within the set of social actors, to emphasize that the influence of external pressures on the societal system is indirect and contingent on the responses of social actors. The two way arrows between the social actors and the societal system emphasize that the social actors not only shape the evolution of the societal system but are themselves conditioned and shaped by the society in which they are operating. In that sense it would be just as appropriate to represent the social actors as embedded within the societal system. However, to emphasize the importance of agency on change, the alternative configuration seems in this case more appropriate.

The societal system must thus be considered to be a *relatively autonomous* system, where responses to the external influences depend on how 'individuals, organizations and governments perceive the changes and the consequent effects that these perceptions have on behaviour' (Rubery, 1992: 257). This approach thus takes seriously the influence of external pressures but also highlights the role of human agency in responding to those influences and pressures, following the dialectical approach of Sorge (see above). Actors within a societal system have to respond to external pressures, but their reasons for doing so and the mode of response will not necessarily be proportionate to the pressure. In some cases globalization will be a handy excuse to implement already planned changes, while in other cases the actors may choose to ignore global pressures, even if this has consequences for international trading positions. This point can be illustrated by the example of the role of the European Union in shaping European societies; where political parties, employers or trade unions decide to take up initiatives from Europe as a means of effecting change, the influence from the EU is likely to be much stronger than where the relevant agencies adopt a policy of either minimal compliance or even choose to ignore their obligations under European law. Thus these effects are not predetermined but filtered through the interests, priorities and political possibilities within the individual member state. Responses to similar pressures still take on a societal-specific form, although we would allow for the possibility of significant change and not argue, as have the main protagonists of the societal school, that emphasis should be placed on the stability of societal characteristics and the tendency towards the reproduction of these societal characteristics, even in a period of change. We would regard the responses to and outcomes of these external pressures as rather more open and politically contingent, an issue to which we will return in detail in Chapter Nine when we discuss the impact of globalization on the convergence or divergence of societal systems of employment.

This open and dynamic societal effect framework, as represented in Figure 2.1, will be used to inform and shape the analyses presented in the subsequent chapters of this book, where we turn our attention both to specific aspects or dimensions of societal systems, as in Chapters Three through Seven; and as we return to more global issues in Chapters Eight through Ten.

Note

1 There is an ongoing debate within the human resource management literature between those who promote notions of universal best practice systems and those who see the need to establish a 'best fit' between the employment strategy and the organization's business strategy (Purcell, 1999). This more sector- and organization-specific approach has also been developed to incorporate a less determinate analysis where the organization's own past history may shape future choices and close off alternative development paths; but the analysis is focused on the organization and not on how it is embedded in a specific social and national context.

3

The development of employment and production regimes

An economy's employment system is an integral part of its production system. Employment is not generated for its own sake but, in economists' jargon, is a derived demand, valued for what it can contribute to the production of goods and services. The production system cannot function, however, without the input of labour, from employees or the self-employed. An artificial separation is found in much of the economics and management literature between the discussion of industrial organization and that of employment organization. The result is that in industrial organization literature we find mainly stylized accounts of the labour process; and in the employment literature we find abstract analyses of labour markets, focused on the exchange of labour and distanced from any detailed account of labour's role in the production system. Our task here is to focus on the interrelations between employment systems and production regimes, with a primary focus on these issues within the manufacturing or traded sectors of the economy. Only a small share of wage employment is found within the internationally traded segment of an economy's activities. More important in quantitative terms is the employment that serves the domestic market, producing domestic goods and services, both public and private. Nevertheless, the organization of employment within the traded sector, primarily manufacturing, has particular significance for international competitiveness. This chapter explores the role of different systems of employment organization within competitive and traded sectors in the post Second World War period, and considers how critical these employment systems have been to the development of comparative advantage and the emergence of country-specific business systems. The significance of this historical legacy in the search for 'post-Fordist' or 'neo-Fordist' production solutions (Lane, 1995) is also explored.

Employment and production regimes

There is a two-way relationship between production regimes and employment regimes: on the one hand, the institutional, cultural and social organization of the

51

labour market will influence the likely success of a particular type of production and may therefore help to shape the nation's competitive strategy. For example, some countries may aim to become known for their strengths in producing already established or standardized products at a low price. Others may choose instead to compete on a reputation for quality[1] while yet others focus more on their capacity to develop and market new and innovative products and designs, to create new markets or transform old markets. These different competitive strategies are likely to be associated with different employment systems, and in particular with whether the system is based on high skills and high trust employment relations or on the minimization of labour costs and the control of effort levels.

On the other hand, the employment system prevailing in a particular country must reflect the dominant production regime. It is difficult, for example, to develop a highly skilled workforce in societies where organizations focus on deskilling and standardized products. As Sam Bowles (1991: 15) puts it: 'The labor market is also *constitutive*. How work is allocated and organized has a well-documented bearing on the development of our capacities, norms and preferences.'

The ways in which work and employment are organized can make positive contributions to the process of innovation and competitive development. Innovative competitive strategies rely not only on the goodwill of the workforce, but also on the harnessing of their intellectual, problem-solving and creative capacities. Even within standardized production systems the benefits of machines over the potentially more erratic and less pliable human productive factors may be overstated. In all production systems intervention by the intelligent human can act to solve problems not considered or anticipated in the design of the technology. Moreover, the role of labour within a production system is to do more than what is specified in the contract (see Box 1.1 in Chapter One).

Production processes are not only concerned with physical tasks or the manufacturing process narrowly defined but also with the development of effective communications with customers, suppliers and the internal workforce. In these processes, human capabilities or skills remain central. Production regimes cannot be reduced to the particular mode of production of a given piece of physical product, but must also include the whole set of activities, from purchasing and capital financing to marketing and debt collection, which are required to institute and to realize profits from a manufacturing process. Once production regimes are situated within complex organizations, the role of human agency in structuring competitive outcomes becomes ever more evident.

Employers and their agents, the workforce managers, have always been wary of this role of human agency, as it necessarily brings uncertainty and human discretion into the production systems for which they are responsible. There are constant tensions between, on the one hand, the desire to control the labour process and reduce uncertainty and, on the other, the desire to make full utilization of human capacities to develop and enhance the production system. The evolution of production regimes can be considered an outcome of these conflicting tensions. As such, it is hardly surprising that different societies and different historical periods have generated and promoted different 'solutions' as a means of resolving these fundamental dilemmas and conflicts.

From Fordist to post-Fordist production regimes

A significant example of how different time periods and phases of competition have favoured one type of production regime over another can be found in the decline of the Fordist production regime and its replacement by a range of post-Fordist systems. The rise and fall of Fordism has been attributed to changes in the nature of the dominant mode of competition.

The so-called Taylorist or Fordist production regime (see Box 3.1) appeared to fit competitive conditions when the focus was on the development of mass markets for relatively standardized consumer goods. The aim of the production system was to maximize work intensity and to reduce unit costs to create conditions under which the luxury goods markets could be converted to markets of mass consumption. The potentially negative impacts on work conditions and job satisfaction were to some degree offset by institutional employment arrangements which provided relatively high levels of job security and trend rises in real wage levels, conditions necessary to

---

Box 3.1 Taylorism and scientific management in America

For Taylor the design of the machine and of work were reducible to the same logic. Just as the principle of interchangeable parts had led to the decomposition of production into a series of precisely measured and endlessly repetitive movements, each of which could be done by a specialized machine, Taylor sought to decompose worker tasks into a series of precisely measured endlessly repetitive movements ... Taylor's mission was not to establish despotic managerial methods but 'scientific' methods ... his system called for an end to the foreman as general manager and the substitution of a planning department to administer the factory ... Although Taylor's ideal worker and management organizational recommendations were probably never carried out in a single factory, work organisation was reconstituted in the American factory with the arrival of mass production. The management quest for high rates of throughput was translated to the shopfloor as the need for a pliable labour force willing to operate the machines to full capacity. Labour responded by building trade unions that organized most of the mass production industries. Eventually a compromise was achieved that gave management its most fundamental demand — control over the processes and operations of work. Managers and staff alone would have responsibility for planning work along the lines of the Taylorist system. Workers' responsibilities were to obey instructions. The company had no responsibilities for upgrading worker skills and could freely lay workers off during business downturns. Management's fear of dependence on skilled workers led to the design of jobs so that little training was required and workers, like parts, could be rendered interchangeable.

Extract from M. Best, *The New Competition* (Cambridge: Polity Press, 1990), pp. 56–8.

---

support the growth of mass consumption markets in the advanced West. Christel Lane summarizes this regime as follows:

> The Fordist regime, dominant in Europe during most of the post-war period, is characterized by intense accumulation and monopolistic competition. The production paradigm has the features of mass production of standardized goods with special-purpose machinery and semi-skilled labour, subjected to a high division of labour and tight managerial control. This pattern of production organization is linked to one of mass consumption, based on high and stable wages and on high levels of welfare, secured by an interventionist state. Trade unions became accepted as legitimate negotiating partners both at the level of the firm and of the state. From the late 1960s onwards, this regime entered a period of crisis, and is being replaced by another which is as yet poorly defined. (Lane, 1995: 24)

The new competitive conditions, associated with the end of the Fordist era, have been linked with a range of factors, from the saturation of mass consumer markets to the end of the period of relatively stable international financial arrangements and the oil shocks of the 1970s (Boyer, 1988; Marglin and Schor, 1991; Piore and Sabel, 1984). Here our main concern is with the changes in the nature of competition identified from the 1970s onwards, sometimes termed the 'new competition' (Best, 1990). The slowdown in the market for standardized commodities, coupled with the growth of inter-advanced country trade which increased the variety of products on offer to consumers, is argued to have generated a system of competition based more on product differentiation, on fashion, quality, service and novelty than simply on price (Piore and Sabel, 1984). This more sophisticated market relied to a greater extent on the capacity of organizations to produce rapidly changing products in small volume, at high quality.

However, one of the consequences of the emerging debate over what system should or would replace the Fordist paradigm was an increasing recognition, based on detailed empirical comparative research, that the assumption that there was, or had been, a similar dominant production and employment regime in all advanced countries and all mass consumer goods sectors was little more than a myth. In exploring the potential alternative paradigms to the Fordist system, it became clear that in many countries and in many sectors the adoption of Fordist or Taylorist notions of work organization had been at most partial. Many societies and sectors had evolved along different trajectories, influenced but not dominated by the prevailing notions of scientific management and low discretion assembly line work (Gospel and Littler 1983; Littler 1983). As such, the available 'set' of alternative production regimes which appeared to offer the best chance of meeting the new competitive challenges had evolved alongside and in competition with the more fully developed Fordist systems. Indeed in the case of Japan, it was Japan's search to learn from and imitate the prevailing best practice systems in the West which had led it to build upon and develop the Fordist mass production system into a new production and employment paradigm (see Box 3.2).

Box 3.2 The rise of lean production

In the spring of 1950, a young Japanese engineer, Eiji Toyoda, set out on a three month pilgrimage to Ford's Rouge plant in Detroit ... Eiji was not an average engineer, either in ability or ambition. After carefully studying every inch of the vast Rouge, then the largest and most efficient manufacturing facility in the world, Eiji wrote back to headquarters that he 'thought there were some possibilities to improve the production system'.

But simply copying and improving the Rouge proved to be hard work. Back at home, Eiji and his production genius, Taiichi Ohno, soon concluded ... that mass production could never work in Japan. From this tentative beginning were born what Toyota came to call the Toyota Production System and, ultimately, lean production.

Extract from J. Womack, D. Jones and D. Roos, *The Machine That Changed the World* (New York: Rawson Associates, 1990), p. 48.

One of the reasons why the Japanese model had moved on beyond the confines of the Fordist mass production model was that it had developed a different approach to the role of labour in the production process. Instead of taking the current state of knowledge over how to organize production as the starting point for the organization of efficient production systems, the Japanese system aimed to harness not only the physical but also the intellectual or mental efforts of labour in the interests of the organization. As such the production system was oriented towards continuous improvement, based on incorporating the tacit knowledge and skills of the workforce into the production system through incremental innovation. The dominant Taylorist ideology in the US had led to a separation between planning and doing, such that 'neither the definition of work nor the flow of production would any longer be dependent upon the skill or pace imposed by the workers' (Best, 1990: 57).

This contrasts with production regimes, labelled 'the new competitors' by Best, that are characterized by the 'integration of thinking and doing within the labour process itself' (Best, 1990: 134). This integration requires different types of employment institutions and relations than those prevailing under scientific management, including, in particular, relations of high trust between managers and workers.

The Fordist system had perhaps placed too much emphasis for its long term survival on controlling labour input, and had consequently failed to find a means of harnessing the learning capacities of labour in the interest of the organization. As information technology, coupled with changes in the structure of demand, increased the speed of implementation of new products and reduced batch sizes, the importance of this learning capacity came to the fore. Yet the divergence between the production regimes prevailing in the US and Japan, for example, reflected long established trajectories of development and not new responses to changing conditions. Similarly the rise of Germany as a successful manufacturing power revealed not the successful adaptation to the post-Fordist era, but more the stance of never having embraced the doctrine of a detailed division of labour based on skill and discretion minimization. According to Robert Boyer (1988) the German system of production could be categorized as 'flex-Fordism', which according to Lane (1995: 147) is 'due to the fact that highly skilled labour and small-batch and customized production stayed dominant in some important core industries'. In contrast the UK system could be regarded as form of 'flawed-Fordism', as 'many large firms never created sufficiently large production units to get the necessary economies of scale for a fully developed Fordist system' (Lane, 1995: 148). Whether or not a country has developed a production and employment system that offers an effective competitive strategy in the post-Fordist era can be considered more an accident of a particular path of development. As we discuss further below, even the more successful systems arose out of particular historical compromises between contested interests within the economy and not from a coordinated design of an appropriate system, agreed on by the major actors.

The search for alternatives to mass production Taylorist-type production systems is no longer confined to specific countries but can be said to be a worldwide concern, affecting organizations even in those countries where the social and institutional structures are geared towards systems of low trust and low skill employment relations. However, as individual companies search for new employment 'solutions' to their competitive requirements, the question that has to be answered is whether an apparently effective employment policy in one national environment can be successfully transferred to another society where the social, institutional, cultural and economic conditions are significantly different. We need first to understand the role of the societal system in the development of relatively successful production regimes before we can assess the potential for organizations in other societies, where external support for development of a high performance production system is weak, to emulate these high-performance regimes.

Societal systems and production regimes

The distinctive historical trajectories of a number of advanced nations have provided alternative models of 'best practice' production regimes. It is to these regimes that other nations, in their search to adapt to changing markets and production conditions, may feel tempted to turn. The notion of 'alternative models' has become increasingly accepted over recent years, in contrast to the 1980s contributions to the debate, where the focus appeared to be on finding a new and single paradigm to replace that of Fordism. This latter focus was most evident in the contribution by Womack *et al.* (1990), extolling lean production as developed in Japan as the new model for the world economy, and for all sectors. Similarly Piore and Sabel's (1984) analysis of flexible specialization took the successful Italian industrial districts, sometimes known as 'The Third Italy', as their effective paradigm for the new system of competition. Germany has also appeared as a potential model economy, combining high trust industrial relations with extensive and effective skilling of the workforce.

In the 1990s most contributions to this debate recognized that there are alternative ways of meeting or matching the challenges of the post-Fordist era. For example, Boyer and Hollingsworth (1997) have suggested that there are four different types of flexible production which complement and to some extent substitute for standardized mass production. These include customized production (similar to flexible specialization or the Third Italy model as described below); diversified quality mass production (emerges out of the Fordist legacy, but responsive to quality and taste issues and associated with the car industry); flexible diversified quality production (associated with sectors where innovation is more important than for the car industry, for example — such as consumer electronics); and adaptive production (competition mainly based on continuous production of new products and/or processes) (see Table 3.1).

This range of different modes of competition provides opportunities both for countries to learn from different systems, and for different countries to specialize in different parts of the international economy. It is clear that no one model suits all countries or sectors. Best (1990) also adopts a pluralist approach, referring to the 'new competitors' as describing the range of societal production regimes which are compatible with the new production paradigm, characterized by Best as involving continuous improvement based upon a learning organization. For example, he takes the Japanese lean production model and the Italian industrial districts model as alternative means of achieving continuous improvement and learning. Lane (1995) suggests that the debate can be analysed using a spectrum from post-Fordism, associated with the flexible specialization debate and upskilling of the workforce, to neo-Fordism, where the production system is adjusted to take account of the need for greater variety, but at the cost, if anything, of even stronger managerial control over the labour process.

Table 3.1 Varieties of flexible production

Type of production	Volume	Differentiation	Innovation/ new products	Quality	Industry examples
Customized production	Low	High		High	Textiles/shoes and other fashion products
Diversified quality mass production	High (for components)	Moderate/ high		High	Car industry
Flexible diversified quality production	All volumes	Moderate	High	All quality levels	Electronic consumer goods
Adaptive production			Very high		Pharmaceuticals; software

Source: Adapted from Boyer and Hollingsworth (1997): 456–8

Appelbaum and Batt (1994) also identify four alternative production systems — the three mentioned above, namely the Japanese lean production system, the Italian flexible specialization system and the German diversified quality production systems, together with the Swedish sociotechnical system, and suggest that 'each of the main foreign alternatives ... provides a means of addressing one or another of the weaknesses of the mass production model' (p. 52). The result, at least in the US, of the discovery of a range of alternatives has, however, been to stimulate a process of piecemeal borrowing of techniques from within the various models, without necessarily a proper appreciation either of the links between the different elements of the models or of the need for these systems to be embedded within an appropriate social and institutional structure. Following Appelbaum and Batt (1994) we therefore draw upon the four alternative models to identify both the ways in which they provide a means of competing in a post-Fordist economy and the key institutional and social arrangements and social capital on which they must depend to provide a coherent and viable production regime.

Four production models explored

Japanese lean production

Japan has become synonymous in the international production system with the so-called lean production model of operation (see Box 3.3). As with Taylorism, this model has become somewhat divorced from its home base, propounded as a model

---

Box 3.3 Japanese lean production

Distinctive characteristics

New sources of competitive strength (compared to Taylorism):

- continuous improvement — *kaizen*
- quality circles
- simplification of processes
- dynamic improvement
- statistical process control
- physical not financial measures
- interprocess efficiency
- elimination of buffers
- relational subcontracting

Traditional sources of competitive strength (based on cutting capital and wage costs):

- high utilization of equipment
- high work intensity
- low wage subcontractors

Competitive strategy

- Mass production based on quality production

---

for all countries and all systems. Considered as a production system which could be applied across countries, it is possible to identify two principles in the lean production model which differentiate it from the Taylorist mass production system. First, there is the concern with continuous improvement, to go beyond the search for efficiency in the application of known techniques to incorporate new knowledge and new ways of doing things. Second, the lean production system has moved beyond the principle of minimizing production time, embedded in mass production systems, to include two further dimensions of the economies of time (Best 1990): that of minimizing time spent in process, and that of minimizing response time to new market opportunities.

The employment techniques used to effect this production system range from systems of employee involvement in the process to systems of control and monitoring. The involvement techniques include quality circles and teamworking (albeit still within an hierarchical structure) as a means by which organizations can harness employees' knowledge and skills both in the interests of continuous increases in physical effectiveness of the production system, and as a means of eliciting employee cooperation in the implementation of flexible small batch production. The control system involves the development of statistical process control to monitor the application of this new knowledge and to provide a benchmark for dynamic rather than static efficiency. The focus of the monitoring effort is directed not at financial measures, which may be distorted by price movements, but at underlying physical measurements of productivity; at improvements in interprocess efficiency through simplification of processes, modularization and better inter-departmental and inter-process systems of coordination; and at reductions in the level of buffers held within the production system, to minimize the costs of holding stocks. The attention paid to inter-departmental and inter-process connections extends to the external supply chain, leading to so-called relational subcontracting, that is, to long term and high trust relations between the core firm and the external suppliers to guarantee quality and delivery. These relationships are explained by Mari Sako, who emphasizes the pervasiveness of the norm of commitment even in parts of Japanese society where these ideals may not be met in practice:

A similar sense of community exists in a vertical *keiretsu*, a hierarchical network of core suppliers and subcontractors, headed by a patron customer company. The pervading mood in each *keiretsu* is not that of unilateral control by the patron company of its smaller suppliers. Rather, it is sustained by the ideology of co-prosperity and co-existence (*kyoei kyozon*) which emphasizes mutual dependence and common destiny among the member firms. The 'co-existence and co-prosperity' motto does not stop at the level of an ideology... Long-term commitments are made by large firms to their core suppliers and sub-contractors, in the same way that they implicitly guarantee lifetime employment to their regular employees. This enables companies to take a long-term view investing in both human resources and capital equipment... Lifetime employment is an ideal and the norm upheld by a wider section of the Japanese economy than the large companies which actually put it into practice. Similarly, the long-term mutual commitment ideal is a powerful norm embraced by non-core suppliers and subcontractors whose reality may differ substantially from the ideal. (Sako, 1992: 191–2)

These characteristics of the lean production system are considered to provide a basis for effectively reinventing the mass production system, but based this time around differentiated products and high and improving quality standards. However, the extent to which this description of the Japanese system, deliberately couched in context-neutral terms, in practice provides a blueprint for other societies depends upon how far the specific conditions and institutional structures within Japan have been critical for the relative success of the model in the world economy, at least up until the start of the 1990s.[2]

There are several ways in which the Japanese societal system can be argued to have been critical in turning the technical features of the lean production system, as described above, into a workable and relatively successful model. The problem with the technical description is that it leaves out of the discussion the macro-economic conditions, the social infrastructures and culture and the internal employment relations which are critical for determining the impact of a specific technique.

The first and critical issue is: why and under what conditions would a workforce accept and work within the type of production system so described? It has been widely argued that there are three characteristics of the Japanese employment system which can be used to 'explain' workforce compliance and active involvement:

- lifetime job guarantees;
- the opportunity for promotion through seniority;
- the presence of enterprise-based unions.

These conditions tie the interests of the workers to the interests of the organization, thereby focusing attention on the mutual benefits from continuous improvement techniques. Productivity increases cannot thereby be used to undermine the claims to a job by the existing workforce, but on the other hand the workforce have few options other than to comply with management requirements, as their opportunities on the external labour market are extremely limited. This provides a basis on which the workforce may be persuaded to share their knowledge of production techniques with management, while in other conditions this knowledge may be protected by the workforce, to increase their own control over work processes and to ensure that productivity increases are not used to undermine their own future employment prospects. These structural conditions in the Japanese social and economic system may be reinforced by cultural attitudes — the mental mapping of the Japanese workforce — although the relative importance to be accorded to culture over institutions varies according to different methodological perspectives (see Chapter Two).

The importance of worker attitudes extends to the whole principle of lean production, which can be considered a 'fragile system', in the sense that any disruption to any part of the system will have domino effects because of the absence of buffers. The cooperative work relations based around the job-for-life principle may, therefore, hold the clue as to how lean production systems can operate without significantly increasing the bargaining power of key workers to the detriment of the organization.

One question much debated by researchers is why Japan came to develop these particular employment arrangements. According to Weiss (1993), the competing accounts of how and why the job-for-life system developed have ranged from the simple cultural explanation that it suited the Japanese mentality, to the view that it was either a rational response of employers to intense labour market pressures or a political compromise induced by the emergence of radical trade unionism in the post Second World War period. Dore (1973) provides an account of Japan as a late developer that integrates these different perspectives. However, for Weiss, Dore overemphasizes the extent to which this was an initiative by employers and indeed their willingness to develop these employment practices. She provides an alternative explanation, rooted in the development of Japan's military capabilities in the inter-war period. According to Weiss, the system was imposed by the state against the wishes of the employers. Whatever the balance of the arguments, it is clear that the specific characteristics of the Japanese industrial relations system were not planned to meet particular production needs in the late 20th century, and indeed arose out of contested interests within the society.

The second contextual issue is whether there has been an exaggeration of the continuous improvement features of the lean production model in contrast with the more straightforward benefits which Japanese companies have derived from reducing capital and labour costs through a system of high utilization of both capital and labour (see Box 3.3). Thus although models of lean production emphasize opportunities to focus on *working smarter*, some studies of the Japanese system (Delbridge, 1998; Stewart, 1996) have pointed to the importance of both *working smarter and working harder* in explaining Japanese relative success. Indeed much of the 'working smarter' part of the Japanese story involves eliminating unproductive processes and unproductive time, thereby almost by definition increasing work intensity. Question marks are placed over whether other societies' workforces would be as willing to accept continuous improvement techniques if they led directly to more intense work pressures.

Japanese large corporations have also been able to utilize the extensive and more flexible and lower paid subcontracting system. While much of the focus on Japanese subcontracting relations focuses on the high trust dimension, the opportunity to lower costs as a result of very wide wage differentials between the core and peripheral sectors has been given rather less attention. Similarly the opportunities for high capital utilization have also been associated with specific conditions in the Japanese economy, namely the close relations between the state and large corporations, which until recently have resulted in a commitment to maintain a high level of demand (supported by a protectionist trade policy), which has allowed large corporations in Japan to maintain a very high level of plant utilization. This lowers capital costs and contributes to overall efficiency. The onset of recession in the 1990s, from which the economy has yet to recover, has undermined confidence in the level and stability of demand, and has led to doubts over whether the jobs-for-life model will survive even in large corporations.

German diversified quality production

The German production system has attracted almost as much attention as the Japanese one as a possible new model system to meet post-Fordist competitive conditions (see Box 3.4). As in the case of Japan, the German production system had evolved along a different trajectory to that of the standardized mass production Taylorized system. Three elements can be considered central to the German model:

- the reliance on high levels of skill within the workforce, associated with flexible working across status and skill divides (see Chapters Five and Seven);
- high trust relations between employers and unions and between management and the workforce, reinforced by national systems of collective bargaining involving the social partners and workplace systems of co-determination, not directly tied to collective bargaining (see Chapter Six);
- institutional and cultural arrangements which reinforce the emphasis on the technical over the short term financial aspects of production systems: examples include the provision of long term finance to manufacturing industry, and the favouring of the appointment of engineers over accountants as chief executives and managers of manufacturing companies.

Just as the Japanese model relies upon institutional arrangements to reinforce the commitment of the workforce to the single corporation and to provide the conditions under which companies have been able to deliver a job-for-life commitment, the German system relies upon a whole set of institutions which operate at the level of the societal system to enable the production regime to function. The importance of these societal systems is most evident in the German training system. As we discuss further in Chapter Five, the German training system is organized at a national level specifically with the objective of creating a large pool of highly trained labour which may well

---

Box 3.4 German diversified quality production

Distinctive characteristics

- high levels of skill in excess of normal requirements*
- quality of design/customization of products
- flexible deployment
- retraining and further training
- high trust based on joint labour-management institutions: works councils

Competitive strategy

- mixture of high volume, high quality and small medium-sized specialized producers

*known as redundant capacities (see Box 2.2 in Chapter Two)

---

exceed current demands for skill within the economy. This strategy has been termed that of generating 'redundant capacities' within the German economy (Streeck, 1997; see Box 2.2 in Chapter Two); that is, by providing an excess supply of skills the German economy has sought to protect itself against skill shortage standing in the way of expansion and adaptation. The workforce have skills that they may only be called upon to use occasionally, but this provides a form of built in flexibility to cope with change and adaptation. In societies where the skill of the workforce matches the average rather than the highest levels of the job demands, a skill deficit is likely to be encountered at critical stages. If, for example, a new system is implemented or a new product developed, it may be vital to be able to call upon these 'redundant capacities' among the workforce to solve such exceptional problems without undue delay and disruption. German employers have, at least until recently (see Chapter Five), been willing to 'over invest' in training as a result of strong national and regional level institutions which require 'good employers' to participate in the training programme.

Similarly, other elements of the German model are reinforced by national level institutions: the high trust relations at the workplace level have been argued to derive from a range of elements of the national system. These include the separation of wage bargaining, conducted at regional and national levels by unions and employers outside of the workplace, from intra-plant negotiations. This allows discussions over workplace organization and workplace issues to be conducted through the works council system and to be relatively independent of wage issues. This latter part of the system is reinforced by national legislation giving rights to co-determination at the workplace (see Chapter Six). High trust relations complement and reinforce the high skill base to allow for a creative, problem-solving and high quality approach to production and work organization. These high trust relations were again not forged by design but have arisen in part as a consequence of the co-determination laws, passed in response to industrial unrest in the post war period (see Chapter Six).

The focus on broad-based skills and training provides the basis for a more flexible division of labour both horizontally and vertically. One of the arguments in favour of a Taylorist narrow division of labour, from the perspective of employers, was the opportunity it provided both to economize on training costs and to remove discretion and control from the workforce. The alternative trajectory of broad-based and widespread training in Germany has rendered some of these concerns irrelevant and provided a basis, even before the emergence of post-Fordist competitive strategies, for the workforce to be involved in flexible production systems. This flexibility is, however, based on strong institutional structures. For example, promotion within the German system is strictly dependent upon both technical expertise and completion of the relevant further training. Thus foremen in Germany must complete the formal *Meister* qualification (see Box 1.3 in Chapter One). Managers will also have undergone specific formal training and further training, and will be appointed on the basis of technical expertise and not brought in as 'management' experts focused on the financial rather than the technical dimensions of the workplace.

This focus on high skill production systems has been both the result and the cause of Germany's relative success in high quality, high technology products. In contrast with Japan, the focus of the German manufacturing industry has been less on quality mass production and more on high quality, customized and high technology production, for example in machine tools. While the high skill German production system is found in both small and large firms, and extends from low technology consumer products to high technology precision engineering, it is in the latter area that Germany has particularly developed a comparative advantage in the world economy. According to Kern and Schumann (1984, 1987) the German model responded to the end of Fordism by developing new production concepts, based on an upskilled workforce. However, while there is significant evidence of upskilling in Germany, this process at the same time creates problems of skill polarization and exclusion, as not all workers are included in the process (Lane, 1995). Recent problems in Germany, related both to high unemployment and to the shocks to the German model associated with the strains of reunification, have also placed some question marks over the long term viability of the German model. Nevertheless Germany has retained its position as leader in many high quality, high technology engineering markets.

Italian flexible specialization

The industrial districts of northern and central Italy provided the 'model' for Piore and Sabel's influential discussion of flexible specialization as the alternative model to Fordism and Taylorism (see Box 3.5). As such, these regionally-specific districts have taken on a similar role to those of the Japanese lean production system or the German training system as providing a potential ideal type for the world economy. The flexible specialization model focuses on the move away from standardized mass production towards small batch flexible production based around both flexible machine tools and flexible skilled labour. Piore and Sabel's (1984) discussion focused particularly on the need for differentiated high fashion, short life products

---

Box 3.5 Italian industrial districts as an example of flexible specialization

Distinctive characteristics

- networks of small firms: industrial districts supported by municipal authorities
- small-scale production based on variety and specialization
- flexibility through collaboration: subcontracting to avoid the need for internal surplus capacity
- economies of scope through networks
- highly skilled flexible labour: subcontractors and self-employed

Competitive strategy

- specialization in design-oriented products: small batch and short product life
- networks and subcontracting used to reduce risk

---

for success within the new niche and fashion-conscious consumer markets. Because of the emphasis on quality and design as well as on flexibility, the notion of flexible specialization was developed, in which cooperative relations between firms may provide the opportunity both to become narrowly specialized in a particular area of production and to be flexible. The Italian industrial districts provided an exemplar of these cooperative relations. These industrial districts consisted of small firms located in close geographical proximity, bound together by complex inter-firm subcontracting relations, based both on differences in specialisms and as a means of adjusting to variations in the level of demand without increasing overheads. Thus firms would subcontract to each other to expand the range of possible processes and products and to offset variations in quantity of orders.

These inter-firm relations were underpinned by a range of consortia and central services, provided by regional government and local government. These central services provided the economies of scale associated normally with large organizations in areas such as access to credit, marketing and design facilities. These Northern Italian industrial districts have been particularly successful in a range of consumer products such as textiles and ceramics, but have also established themselves as leading exporters in areas such as electronics and light engineering. The skill base for the industrial districts has been generated by informal methods, mainly by training within the small family firms. This has generated a pool of skilled labour on which the district can draw. The basis for success is a peculiar mix of cooperation and competition, as Box 3.6 clarifies.

The success of these Italian districts did much to reverse standard economic and organizational thinking that had previously focused on the large bureaucratic form as the likely vehicle for all forms of economic success in the world economy, such that areas dominated mainly by small firms and by craft based skills systems should be considered examples of pre-modern industrial systems (Streeck, 1997; see Chapter Two). However, while demonstrating that small firm industrial districts could be successful, the Italian districts did not necessarily provide a model which could be easily replicated even within other parts of Italy. Again specific societal factors can be shown to have critical importance, although in this case the societal dimensions were more regional or local than national. In part the districts emerged out of a specific set of political circumstances: after the collapse of Fascism in Italy; the Communist Party became the major party of governance in the north at regional and local level, while the Christian Democrats controlled the national government and the south. As part of a strategy to prevent the rebirth of fascism in Italy, the Communist governments in the north felt that they had to win the support of small business, a group which had been critical to Mussolini's power base. This led to the development of policies at the regional and local level actively to support small business development through setting up, supporting and regulating the local industrial districts. Local government has become very much a partner in the development of support agencies and consortia, to promote the region at an international level and to provide economies of scale in access to facilities. This regulatory system has

Box 3.6 Competition and cooperation in Italian industrial districts

There is a further advantage for businesses in the districts: a very high number of operators, each one with his own market strategy and specialisation which ensures the client easy availability — within a restricted area — of products from a variety of sources and market levels ... This results in effect in a sort of 'trade fair' with the difference that this fair, contrary to traditional ones, is open during the whole buying season, or during the whole year, and it exercises on buyers a considerable promotional impact ... Despite all this, there are no signs of collusion in the districts. End suppliers ... compete in a lively way among themselves in the product market regarding price, delivery time, after sales service, intrinsic quality and quality of design ... This very lively competition is not in contradiction with the many forms of cooperation ... To start with, many entrepreneurs are related simply by friendly behaviour, as in the case when very small businesses lend each other tools, or materials not easily available on the market ... Another frequent form of cooperation among businesses is often responsible in great measure for the innovative capability of the zone. We refer to the relationship between the client and the components manufacturer. Very often a spare part or a component is not ordered on the basis of precise design with detailed specifications ... The relationship which forms the basis of the order has a strong consultancy element ... Cooperation between client and supplier can result in substantial modifications to the finished product, thus promoting technical innovations which are nearly always of an incremental type, but are still of considerable value in the market ... Other forms of co-operation ... involve many businesses and these require an agent to coordinate them. The most common cases are purchase consortia, where many businesses join up to obtain their input at a lower price; credit consortia, with several businesses bound together to guarantee each other's bank loans or to negotiate a lower bank interest rate; agencies, often represented in Italy by trade associations, which keep books and payrolls for the member businesses and compile their income return forms at a very low cost ... The objective is, therefore, to be able to take advantage of all possible economies of scale, be these concrete, as in the case of bookkeeping or the construction of physical structures, or pecuniary, as in the case of purchasing and credit consortia.

Extract from S. Brusco, 'Local productive systems and new industrial policy in Italy', in A. Bagnasco and C. Sabel (eds), *Small and Medium-Size Enterprises* (London: Pinter, 1995), pp. 55–8.

also supported more formal systems of skill and training development, thereby reinforcing the industrial district model. Much of the comparative advantage lies in the knowledge base or skill embodied in the social capital of the region. As Sebastiano Brusco (1995: 62) explains, one of the critical elements for success is the

> knowledge spread throughout the social structure of the district, which is embedded in the historical memory of men and women belonging to the district ... It is, in fact, the very rich interweaving of the relationships established among all these agents, more than the special contribution of individuals, that gives the district its competitiveness, innovative capacity, and, above all, that quick perception of opportunities for profit, the lack of which ... plays a crucial role in explaining underdevelopment.

In some cases, for example that of Benetton, the very success of the emerging organizations in the international economy has forced a change in the nature of production, away from the cooperative, small-scale industrial model. According to Harrison (1994), 'in its evolving role as a major oligopolist, rather than a "cooperative competitor", Benetton has measurably undermined at least part of the fabric of the Veneto's small firm network. It has done so by imposing an extreme form of hierarchical control on a production system which had previously been characterized by far more fluid interfirm arrangements' (1994: 92). Thus small firm industrial districts do not necessarily provide a permanent alternative to large scale oligopolistic industry.

The possibilities of transferring or replicating this Italian industrial district model to other societies have been widely discussed and debated; while other examples of industrial districts can be found, they have taken different forms, dependent upon the specific societal characteristics or the specific industrial characteristics. For example, Silicon Valley may be considered an industrial district based around software development, but its *modus operandi* varies from that of the Italian flexible specialization model (see Box 3.7). The downturn in the new economy during 2000, however, had the effect of revealing the high level of risks borne by the workers within such systems. The decline in job prospects hit not only future employment opportunities but also the value of the stocks through which many new economy workers have at least in part been remunerated. The issue of whether future high skilled employees will be so keen to share the risks with managers is not yet known.

Box 3.7 Silicon Valley

Successful careers in Silicon Valley are rarely built within the boundaries of a single firm; rather, they are defined by the ability of an individual or a team to define new markets, technologies, products, and applications. As one local semiconductor executive reportedly noted: 'Many of us wake up in the morning thinking that we work for Silicon Valley, Inc.' ... the region and its relationships, rather the firm, define opportunities for individual and collective advances in Silicon Valley. It suggests that open labour markets — and the corresponding career paths — offer important competitive advantages over traditional corporate job ladders in a volatile economic environment. The essential advantage of regional, rather than firm-based, labour markets lies in the multiple opportunities they provide for learning.

Learning occurs in Silicon Valley as individuals move between firms and industries, acquiring new skills, experiences, and know-how. It occurs as they exchange technical and market information in both formal and informal forums, and as shifting teams of entrepreneurs regroup to experiment with new technologies and applications. Learning occurs as firms of different sizes and specializations jointly solve shared problems. Above all, learning occurs through failure, which is as common as success. In short, learning in Silicon Valley is a collective process that is rarely confined within the boundaries of individual firms and ultimately draws from the resources of the region as a whole.

Extract from A. Saxenian, 'Beyond boundaries: open labor markets and learning in Silicon Valley', in M. Arthur and D. Rousseau (eds), *The Boundaryless Career* (New York: Oxford University Press, 1996), pp. 23–4.

Swedish socio-technical systems

The fourth model identified by Appelbaum and Batt (1994) as providing an alternative post-Fordist model is the Swedish socio-technical system, made famous by the so-called job enrichment experiments at Volvo. In contradiction to the detailed managerial control approach adopted within a Taylorist system, the job enrichment experiments devolved considerable power to the work team to determine the mode of work organization (Box 3.8).

For some analysts, this system reflects the particular conditions prevailing in the Swedish labour market, namely low unemployment and strong unions; it therefore represents a significant development in the democratization of work, even though it proved difficult to maintain or to generalize to other areas (Auer and Riegler, 1990; Berggren, 1994). However, some would see these experiments as part of a more general approach to employment organization — known as socio-technical systems — where the aim is to develop a highly sophisticated form of control over workers' efforts and productivity by encouraging them to believe that they are making choices and exercising discretion within the work process while management retains a high level of invisible control (Rose, 1988).

These systems of egalitarian wage structures and involvement of the workforce in the whole operation have also been argued to have been most suitable for firms operating at the luxury end of the high quality market, such as Volvo. This form of work organization has often been considered incompatible with the labour market organization of most countries, where there is wide wage and status differentiation among the workforce. Similarly it may be unsuitable for products destined for markets where production at low unit labour costs is critical. The sceptics about the Swedish model found justification for their position in the decision to close down the most experimental factories once the Swedish economy and Volvo ran into financial difficulties. However, the more optimistic analysts argued that the reason for closure was not found in the system of work organization but in problems of over capacity. Thus

---

Box 3.8   The Swedish socio-technical system

Distinctive characteristics
- experiments in autonomous teamworking
- response to demand for more humane and democratic workplaces
- responsible for process improvement and problem solving
- assembly of whole products
- highly skilled workforce

Competitive strategy
- high quality luxury markets (but recession led to closure of some of the more experimental plants)

---

to some extent the Swedish model in its fully developed form is unproven as a viable option for particular forms of production. The debates over the merits of the Swedish and the Japanese approaches to teamworking are summarized in Box 3.9.

Box 3.9 Teamworking in the car industry

The car industry has not been immune from the problems identified with the Taylorist model. One of the most prominent measures to try to overcome the deficiencies of the fragmented work system was the introduction of work teams. Piloted by the 'Human Relations' school (see for example Mayo (1933)), teamworking can be regarded 'as a modern attempt to re-align individual motivation with organizational reality' (Mueller, 1994: 386).

Two approaches

Two very different views on the most effective design of teams and organizations are competing today. The first alternative is the Japanese-inspired '*lean production*' model, originally promoted by Womack, Jones and Roos (1990). Toyota's NUMMI plant in the US, a joint venture with General Motors, is probably the most prominent 'lean production' car plant outside Japan. The plant started production in 1984 and soon after began to outperform most auto plants in the Western world in terms of productivity and quality. The second alternative is the *German–Scandinavian model* (Adler and Cole, 1993), which can be seen in the tradition of the socio-technical systems approach (see for example Emery (1976)). It is closely linked with Volvo, especially its Uddevalla site in Sweden, opened in 1990. It soon became famous for its focus on the quality of working life, offering employees many participation rights and holistic jobs in autonomous teams. The Uddevalla plant closed in May 1993 not, however, because of negative results but because of rapidly decreasing capacity utilization caused by a crisis in the auto industry. The plant has reopened in the meantime, albeit only for special production runs (Brulin and Nilsson, 1997).

Work design

Both plants, NUMMI and Uddevalla, organized production around teams. Apart from this, the organizational designs of the two plants differed greatly, revealing some of the central aspects of the 'lean production' and the 'socio-technical systems' approaches. At NUMMI, teams consist of four or five members and a hierarchical team leader. Teams work along a traditional Fordist assembly line. Job roles are narrowly defined, work standardization is very high, and at only 60 seconds, work cycles are very short. Teams are responsible for quality assurance and machine maintenance. Continuous improvement schemes play a central role, with extensive reliance on worker input and a drive for continuous, low-cost improvement. On the other hand, the production design in Uddevalla was completely different. Forty teams of around ten people built complete cars, with individual cycle times ranging from 1.5 to 3.5 hours. Work standardization was very low. Team responsibilities were far reaching, with teams organizing almost everything from the allocation of work to the employment of new team members. Team leaders rotated hourly.

Outcomes

Two years after it started operation, the NUMMI plant was almost as productive as its Toyota sister plant in Japan, and more productive than any other GM plant. According to Adler and Cole (1993), quality was equally superior. Absenteeism was low at about three per cent, and job satisfaction high. In Uddevalla, it took about double as long to produce an, admittedly more complex, car but its main strength was its ability to adjust to different capacity utilization levels and model changes (Berggren, 1994). Quality levels were similar to those at NUMMI, but absenteeism was much higher. According to employee surveys, job satisfaction

---

Box 3.9 Continued

levels were not dissimilar from other, traditionally organized, Volvo plants, a fact that might have represented workers' high expectations and constructive forms of dissatisfaction.

Interpretations

Adler and Cole (1993) argue that the 'democratic Taylorist' NUMMI system is superior, not because workers there are required to work more intensively, but because the high level of standardization provides for effective feedback and pinpointed improvements. The long work cycles at Uddevalla, they argue, made performance monitoring and improvement more difficult. The corresponding higher levels of stress at NUMMI are seen as being 'in the acceptable range' (*op. cit.*: 90). For Berggren (1994) quite the opposite is the case: the high degree of freedom for workers was one of the strongest points in the Uddevalla system. The importance placed on understanding the whole production process, practically and intellec-tually, encouraged worker morale as well as flexibility, one of the most important assets in modern competition. According to Berggren (1994: 44) lean production might show superi-or results in the short term, but in the long run, sustainable solutions will be required, char-acterized *inter alia* by the humanistic features which prevailed at Uddevalla. The high resulting skill levels of workers stimulate innovation, and, ultimately, competitive advantage. In this process, unions and governments have to play an important role.

The debate on the implications of the new systems continues. More recent work by Adler and associates (Adler *et al.*, 1997) has highlighted the importance of institutional mecha-nisms, in particular unions and safety legislation, in providing the feedback necessary to bring about continuous improvement. Initially management at the NUMMI plant did not pay much attention to the ergonomic design of the plant and was willing to tolerate a high injury rate, preferring to meet compensation claims rather than change the production system. In the 1990s a new approach was adopted, in part because the new production system relied on worker commitment and morale that was being jeopardized by the injury rate. However, more important in bringing a change in attitude was the pressure from the unions and from the Occupational Safety and Health Administration.

Borrowing and learning from other societies' production regimes?

The incentives for countries and organizations to learn from or borrow production and employment systems developed in other societal contexts depends, on the one hand, on the reasons why a country or an organization is seeking to restructure its production and employment system; and on the other hand, on the feasibility and desirability of attempting to transfer, imitate or adapt the regime found in another industrialized economy. It is clear from our discussion of the four alternative mod-els that none of these production systems was developed according to blueprints as to how a country should meet the challenge of post-Fordism. Indeed we have seen how the models have all emerged from historical processes related to wider political forces and power relations in the particular societies. These have included the relation-ship between the state and the industrial system in the context of preparations for war; the links between the local state and small business community; and the orienta-tion of the trade union movements in the countries concerned. These diverse and unplanned origins might be considered to reduce the likelihood that they represent readily transferable models.

If we turn first to the incentives for a country to seek change, we find some disagreement in views. For some societal effect theorists (for example Maurice *et al.*, 1984, 1986), there is considerable scope for societies to maintain their own individual production and employment system, which fits in with the logic of their own societal system. This scope arises from two distinct causes. First of all there is plenty of evidence that in practice it is possible to produce for similar markets, yet to adopt different production and employment regimes. All systems involve some forms of trade-off, so that while some systems score higher on one dimension of efficiency or cost than another, the opposite is true when it comes to another dimension. Countries may therefore choose whether to have a highly differentiated skill and wage structure or a more uniform wage and skill structure; both may yield similar unit production costs. In some senses different systems of organization and different principles of economic and social activity can in the international economy be regarded as functional equivalents. That is, the systems are non-identical but serve the same function of allowing nations to compete effectively in international markets.

The second reason for a country to keep to its own system is that a societal system may confer comparative advantage in particular activities, such that some societies are in a better position to specialize in some activities than others. This notion of specialization is just as compatible with the notion of globalization as that of harmonization and convergence. Indeed it can be argued that the latter only becomes a likely outcome of globalization if the knowledge, resources and institutions which confer comparative advantage in a particular activity are easily transferred from one society or one location to another. If comparative advantage depends on historical development or on specific societal institutions and culture, globalization may enhance rather than reduce differentiation. The logic of international competition under these conditions is to build upon particular strengths, not for newcomers to enter into competition with those societies whose existing favourable infrastructure and cultural and social history provide them with more than a head start. These trends towards specialization will be even stronger if the flows of foreign direct investment reflect current attributes and strengths. If low labour cost countries attract investment in assembly-line operations while the more skill-rich countries attract research and development biased activities, further polarization of production regimes may occur:

> Indeed, in so far as the international economy does continue to become more integrated, it can be argued that societies with different institutional arrangements will continue to develop and reproduce varied systems of economic organization with different economic and social capabilities in particular industries and sectors. They will, therefore, 'specialize' in distinctive ways of structuring economic activities that privilege some sectors and discourage others ... (Whitley, 1999: 3)

These possibilities for international specialization apparently provide nation states, and indeed individual organizations, with the option not only of maintaining but even of reinforcing differences, positively developing their indigenous strengths as a means of carving out their own niche market, or of meeting their economic needs in ways which fit their social and cultural preferences.

However, the interaction between societal systems and the international economy is not necessarily as permissive as this version of the societal system/business systems approach may imply. Societal systems or production regimes are not necessarily full functional equivalents, in as much as some systems prove in particular time periods and in particular sectors to be relatively more efficient and productive than others. Similarly some areas of specialization provide the basis for high productivity growth and development while others offer relatively poor prospects of achieving society-wide high standards of living or a reasonable profit rate for indigenous capital. The process of international competition does place different production regimes in competition with each other. While this competition is unable to eliminate inefficient players entirely, particularly in markets where provision is likely to remain at least partly home based, international integration does place pressure on the less efficient or competitive systems to adapt and change.

The internationalization of the world economy has resulted in wider recognition that there are alternative ways of working or alternative ways of organizing production. This knowledge may be used in a search for overall greater efficiency and productivity. In the 1980s and 1990s there was considerable interest in the adoption of the lean production or Japanese model, as a consequence both of the rising influence of Japanese transplants with the growth in Japanese foreign direct investment, and of the process of imitation of the Japanese model by domestic companies. As Box 3.10 outlines, this led to research and debate over both the extent of transfer of the

---

Box 3.10   Global Japanization?

One of the major debates over recent years has revolved around the prospects for global Japanization, by which is meant the likelihood of the adoption of the key elements of the Japanese lean production system as the new production paradigm. Elger and Smith (1994) have suggested there are three different ways in which to interpret the spread of Japanization through foreign direct investment:

- Japanization as a *whole package* approach, where all elements, or as many as possible are transferred to the host country;
- Japanization as a *dualist* strategy, where foreign direct investment is focused on the simplified process or assembly operations, thereby minimizing the need for the investment in skills and training of the foreign workforce;
- *disaggregated* Japanization, where Japanese foreign direct investment takes advantage of the resource bases of different countries, locating research and development in high skill environments and low skill assembly or processing operations in low skill, low labour cost environments.

Box 3.10 Continued

Elger and Smith point to the problems which arise out of some of the empirical investigations into the process of Japanization. Those that subscribe to the *whole package* approach tend to assume that it is possible to transfer the 'whole package' even if it is necessary to 'replace' some of the Japanese institutions with 'functional equivalents'. Thus in the UK the fact that Japanese transplants were set up in high unemployment areas was deemed to give those firms the same type of loyalty from the workforce as could be gained in Japan through the offer of a job for life (Oliver and Wilkinson, 1992). This notion that commitment under duress because of a lack of employment opportunities is equivalent to commitment based on job security has been challenged (Smith and Elger, 2000). Furthermore, there is a tendency to assume that the presence of a specific technique — whether it be teamworking or a quality circle — is sufficient to assure the transfer of the same employment practice; but the operation of teamworking or of quality circles may be entirely different, dependent upon the specific societal context.

Elger and Smith (1994) in contrast draw upon evidence both of the diversity of the nature of Japanese FDI and evidence of incomplete and partial transfer of the Japanese employment practices, to support the notion of disaggregated Japanization. They point to a number of studies that have revealed the ways in which Japanese transplants have adjusted and modified their home country practices to fit in with, and indeed take advantage of, the home country characteristics. For example, Milkman (1992) found that the Japanese transplants in California had made active use of the local immigrant population to mould an employment system based on active anti-unionism and non-core employment conditions. In the UK, the impact of the adoption of such policies as quality circles and teamworking has been shown in a whole range of studies to have been culturally or socially contingent, whether within Japanese transplants or within home-based plants aiming to imitate Japanese methods (see also Box 3.11).

Indeed, just as the Japanese themselves borrowed only selectively from the Fordist mass production system, and remoulded and reshaped Western techniques as part of the process of implementation in a different social environment, so the process of transfer and imitation of Japanese practices is necessarily selective and involves not the destruction but the continued development of nation-specific production regimes.

Japanese model, and of the efficacy of the Japanese model outside of its societal context. The conclusions of most of this research support the analytical approach that we outlined in Chapter Two. There has been considerable change within production regimes as societies indeed seek to learn from or borrow the practices of other nations. However, the impact of this learning and borrowing approach is not a simple transfer or convergence, but rather a further evolution of the specific societal system. That is, the ways in which the Japanese model have been incorporated into societal systems is different. As Edward Lorenz comments in his comparison of the emulation of Japanese methods in France and the UK:

> In view of the considerable evidence of a continuous process of emulation on the part of national producers, one might well pose the question: what remains of the notion of nationally specific production models? If we look closely at the evidence, though, we can see that while producers in all industrialized nations seek to adopt other nations' organising principles which are perceived as providing a basis for superior performance, the ways in which they do this are nationally specific ... The result will be the development of distinctive national hybrids which may differ in significant respects from the parent template.

The ... French electronics producer which experimented with quality circles and other forms of institutionalized employee involvement, only to abandon them while retaining individual employee responsibility for quality, provided a good example of this process ... Japanese producers found it advantageous to graft their system of flexible work allocation onto a careers and internal promotion structure consistent with the constraints of Germany's dual apprenticeship system. This allowed them to benefit from the ample supplies of skilled labour available on the local market ... The level of trust between labour and management and the nature of the procedures in place for resolving conflict will (also) have a significant impact on how new practices are introduced and modified. The history of the introduction of Taylorism in UK manufacturing ... provides ample evidence of the way conflict negotiation can contribute to the production of distinctive hybrid arrangements ... The conclusion to draw ... is not that we should stop talking about nationally specific models. Rather, the inference to draw is that we should be spending more time examining the dynamic processes of creative imitation that are continuously making and remaking them. (Lorenz, 2000: 255–6)

This role of international pressures in the process of making and remaking societal systems depends on how these pressures for change will be taken up and applied by local actors (see Figure 2.2 in Chapter Two). Thus the ways in which this knowledge is used to change employment systems and practices is likely to vary from one country to another. This tendency can be illustrated with respect to the ways in which the new employment practices associated with flexibilization, human resource management and Japanization have been incorporated into the traditional

---

Box 3.11   The new British flexible manufacturing firm

British arrangements for manufacture at plant level do not depend on high levels of skill or high levels of investment. Output is achieved in part by some reorganization of machinery, but more significantly by a combination of heavy dependency on the flexible use of relatively unskilled labour and a willingness to utilize external sources of production. The basic arrangement for manufacture is the use of standard technology by teams of self-regulating and formally unskilled workers. Production is organized into a number of semi-autonomous segments, which also feature as cost centres. Each of these is periodically and individually assessed in terms of its costs and benefits, and this feature shapes most aspects of management organization activity, including the control of labour.

The new flexible manufacturing firm: summary of features*

- Production is organized through the arrangement of machines and workers as cells capable of producing 'families' of components or products.
- Advanced manufacturing technology is little used, except as additions to existing configurations of equipment.
- Employed labour contributes to flexibility as teams of semi-skilled workers performing a range of specific tasks and given on-the-job training.
- Employees do not enjoy privileged status or high employment security, but compete with subcontracted labour and alternative suppliers.
- Production operations are considered as dispensable separate 'segments', about which calculations of cost are regularly made.
- Management takes the form of intensified indirect control based on the allocation of costs.

*Source: Ackroyd and Proctor (1998: 171)

UK production system, leading, according to Ackroyd and Proctor (1998), to the development of a distinctive UK flexible firm model (see Box 3.11). Here we can identify a process of both continuity and change; there have been significant changes in the standard system of work organization with the introduction of teamworking and a new emphasis on quality, but these changes have been introduced into the low trust British industrial relations model. The result has been that teamworking has led neither to new cooperative ways of working nor to new levels of skills and training. The short termist approach to UK industry is maintained through constant monitoring of the cost effectiveness of each element of the production system to determine whether activities should be outsourced or maintained in house.

Conclusions

This evidence of the continued development of distinctive societal models may be considered somewhat at odds with the increasing emphasis in management literature and business schools on the notion of best practice human resource techniques which can apparently be imported and inserted into any organization in any location, provided the organization develops a coherent 'bundle' of human resource policies consistent with the business objectives of the organization. This focus on organizational policies has in fact directed attention away from the development of an appropriate and supportive institutional and social environment within which to embed human resource policies and practices.

Organizations are not necessarily as able as the management texts would have us believe to generate either the levels of commitment, or even the levels of skill and expertise required to compete in the flexibly specialized or differentiated quality production markets. These problems arise in part because of the inconsistency between the policies of the individual organizations and the societal system in which they are located. Despite the recognition of a need for training and development in some product market environments, organizations may in practice still be wary of investing large amounts in their workforce unless either they are also willing to pay high wages to retain them (Osterman, 1995); or unless their competitors are also training, thereby providing some protection against poaching of ready trained staff (as they are able to retaliate by poaching those of their competitors). Moreover, the possibilities of engendering high levels of commitment and loyalty to the organization have been reduced by the continued downsizing even by those organizations previously publicly committed to job security — for example, IBM. This reneguing on employment commitments by high profile organizations has perhaps made it less possible in the future for organizations to use offers of job security as a means of promoting commitment and loyalty. These problems of implementation at the organization level tend to lead to a piecemeal adoption and adaptation of human resource management prescriptions. Even within societal systems that are in general more geared towards low cost and low skill production, for example the UK and the US, it may still be possible to identify a limited number of so-called high performance organizations. Nevertheless there is little evidence that this model is becoming universally adopted, even within the subset of larger organizations where most of the analysis has been focused (Cappelli *et al.*, 1997; Huselid, 1995; Osterman, 1994).

While we remain sceptical of any claim that organizations will be either able or willing unilaterally to develop high productivity employment systems based on good and secure employment opportunities for employees, we still need to recognize the increasing importance of organizations, particularly multinational corporations, in shaping employment policies and practices in the world economy. Multinationals have been influential in pressing for deregulation of labour markets and the dismantling of institutional regulations and restrictions (Streeck, 1993). As such they pose a major threat to the ability of nation states to develop and maintain strong institutionally-embedded employment systems. Multinationals may also not have a commitment towards the development of a skilled and motivated labour force within the host country, thereby raising the question of who is to pay for and provide the skill base of the world economy. These issues are returned to and discussed in detail in chapters Eight through Ten.

Notes

1   Competition on quality may be considered to be the same thing as competition on price if prices reflect relative quality; however here we identify them as separate strategies to identify the primary focus of the competitive strategy.
2   We leave to one side for the moment the equally thorny issues of whether the Japanese system, even within Japan, has been or will continue to be as successful as its international reputation might have us believe, or indeed whether any or most of the Japanese organizations have actually embraced this ideal type model as here described. These issues apply with equal force, as we discussed above, to the adoption of Taylorism.

4

The state, the family and gender: from domestic work to wage employment

Employment patterns and practices are now primarily determined not in the manufacturing but in the services sector, which accounts for 63.5 per cent of total OECD employment and close to three quarters of all employment in a number of major OECD countries (OECD, 2000: 85). Services also account for an increasing share of world trade, and a country's competitive strength in some areas of services — for example the strong reputation of the City of London in financial and related services — will affect the overall size and shape of the service economy. Yet the size of the service sector cannot be explained only by its trading strengths. An equally important issue is the extent to which service activities previously carried out in the home on an unpaid basis are now performed by people working in organizations for wages. Current variations between societies in the size and composition of the service sector can be traced to differences in the extent of transfer of activities from unpaid domestic labour to paid wage labour. Another factor leading to differences among societies is the extent to which the services outside the home are provided through public services or through a private market economy.

Differences in the way services are provided underpin many of the variations found among countries in employment structures and levels of employment. The state, as we have seen in Chapter Three, has a significant role in shaping production systems through its education and training and industrial policies. In the areas of services, the role of the state is even more significant and often more direct. The state's welfare and tax regimes shape the opportunities for the population to participate in wage work. Welfare systems are an important modern source of income support in old age, sickness or motherhood, which allows citizens to withdraw from the labour market, either temporarily or permanently. Welfare systems also provide services such as childcare and elder care, which act as substitutes for services provided by domestic labour.

This chapter explores these differences and considers their implications. We look at how welfare regimes shape the pattern of labour supply by gender, class and age.

Much of this exploration involves comparing different 'models' of welfare state development. First of all, however, we need to consider the differences between advanced countries in the share of the population in employment and to identify the major supply-side factors that may account for differences in the pattern of integration into the labour market.

Employment: how much and who does it?

Overview

Differences between employment systems of advanced societies involve even the most basic issues of who is actually in employment and how much employment is available. An increasingly popular way of comparing the volume of employment created among countries is to compute the employment rate, that is the number of people in employment divided by the working age population, (taken to be the population aged 15–64, following European Labour Force Survey conventions). Figure 4.1 shows the employment rates in major OECD countries in North America, Australasia, Japan and Europe in 2000. These data demonstrate the major differences between advanced societies in the ratio of those in employment to the eligible population. Figure 4.1 adds in, on top of the employment rate, those who are unemployed, that is actively seeking work but not able to find work. The inactive population, that is those neither seeking and available for employment nor in employment, accounts for the rest of the population, the gap between the top of the bar and the 100 per cent level. This reveals that the differences in employment levels between societies are

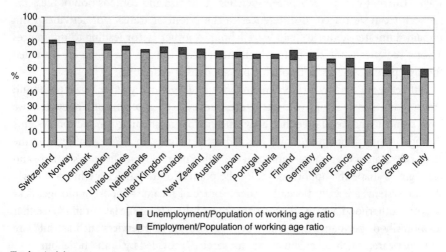

Total = Activity rate

Source: OECD 2001

Figure 4.1 Employment and activity rates in OECD countries 2000

mainly related not to differences in levels of unemployment but to differences in the share of the working age population that is inactive. This suggests that variations in employment systems relate not only to factors shaping how much work is available but also to factors that influence who considers themselves to be in the labour market or not. Differences in employment rates have been growing over time. For example the average European Union employment rate remained relatively stable at around 60 per cent between 1985 and 1997, but in the US the employment rate rose over the same time period from 69 per cent to 74 per cent (CEC 1998). Figures 4.2(a) and (b) show the employment rates of men and women separately in the same countries, ranked again by the overall employment rate. The female employment rates show wider variations than the male employment rates, suggesting that variations in the share of women in employment are one of the key factors explaining differences among countries in the overall share of the working age population in employment.

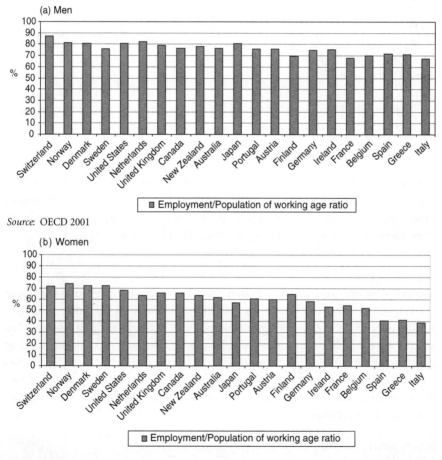

Source: OECD 2001

Figure 4.2 Employment rates for men and women in OECD countries 2000

Table 4.1 Length of transition from school to work*

Country	1984 Age at which transition begins	1984 Age at which transition ends	1994 Age at which transition begins	1994 Age at which transition ends
Belgium	18	23	19	23
Denmark	16	22	16	24
France	17	22	19	24
Germany	17	20	17	22
Greece	16	23	18	24
Ireland	17	20	18	22
Italy	16	23	17	25
Luxembourg	16	20	18	21
Netherlands	16	22	16	23
Portugal	16	22	16	23
Spain	16	26	17	27
UK	16	20	16	22

*Transition begins at the point when less than 75 per cent of the cohort are in the school system and ends when 50% are in employment.

Source: OECD (1996a)

Closer examination of who is and who is not in the labour market reveals major differences between countries relating to three stages or turning points in the lifecycle.

Age of entry into employment

First, there are differences in the age at which most of the population makes entry to the labour market, so that in some societies most young people transfer to the labour market before the age of, say, 20, while others may still retain most young people in some form of education or training to a much later age (Table 4.1).

Impact of marriage and motherhood

Second, there are major differences in the share of prime-age women in the labour market, with employment rates varying from 38 per cent to 74 per cent, even among the developed OECD countries included in Figure 4.2(b). In the past women often used to leave the labour market at the point at which they married, but the marriage effect is now relatively slight. As we will see in more detail later, differences in women's activity rate over the lifecycle are now much more related to motherhood than marriage, but the impact of motherhood on activity patterns varies significantly between advanced countries.

Retirement

Finally, the age at which older people retire from the labour market can also be seen to vary markedly. The effective retirement age of men ranges from 58.2 to 64.2 years of age

Table 4.2 Effective retirement ages of males 1970 and 1990*

Country	1970	1990
Belgium	62.7	58.2
Austria	62.2	58.5
Netherlands	64.0	59.0
Finland	62.3	59.1
France	63.1	59.4
Italy	62.0	60.3
Germany	64.5	60.6
Spain	65.0	61.4
New Zealand	64.4	61.6
Greece	65.7	61.8
Australia	64.9	61.9
Canada	65.0	62.3
Denmark	66.8	62.9
United Kingdom	65.9	62.9
Portugal	68.5	63.5
Ireland	69.5	63.7
United States	65.3	63.9
Sweden	65.3	64.2
Norway	67.2	64.4
Switzerland	67.5	64.8
Japan	69.5	67.6

*Assumes a minimum retirement age of 45

Source: Latulippe (1996), Table 2a

within the European Union and reaches a high of 67.6 years of age in Japan (Table 4.2). During the 1980s and first half of the 1990s divergence between societies in the employment rates of older male workers tended to increase as some societies moved towards new norms of very low employment rates for men in the age bracket 55 to 64 (less than 40 per cent in Belgium and France) while others maintained employment rates of 60 per cent or more (Japan, New Zealand, Norway, Sweden, Switzerland and the United States) (Figure 4.3).

Change and continuity

Distinctive societal patterns of employment can be identified, despite the fact that recent years have seen major changes in employment behaviour by age and gender in all countries. All EU countries have experienced a lengthening of the transition from school to work, even though the variations between countries have remained largely constant (see Table 4.1). Similarly, women's participation has been rising in most countries and there has only been a partial narrowing of the differences between countries (see Figure 4.4). For older workers the societal differences have been rising rather than declining for most of the past two decades (see Figure 4.3).

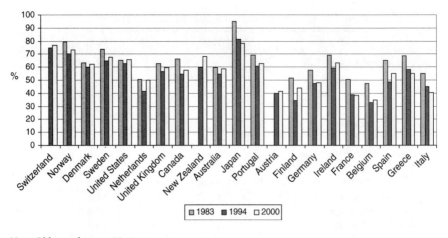

Note: Older aged men = 55–64 age group
Source: OECD (1997, 2001)

Figure 4.3 Changes in employment rates for older aged men

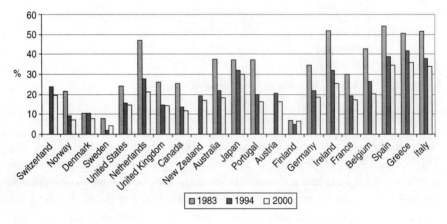

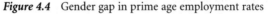

Note: Prime age = 25–54 age group
Source: OECD (1997, 2001)

Figure 4.4 Gender gap in prime age employment rates

Prime-age men show the greatest similarity in employment rates and, where there are differences, these tend to be largely accounted for by higher or lower rates of unemployment. This suggests that most prime-age men are permanent labour market participants in all advanced societies. Nevertheless, even here there has been a long term trend towards reduction in labour market participation. The higher unemployment rates and lower employment rates for prime-age men which have prevailed in most advanced countries since the end of the 1970s have resulted in some countries in an increase in the share of prime-age men who are outside of the labour force altogether. This shows up in an increase in the share who are in education or in very early retirement and in the population of long term sick or disabled. The proportions in these categories vary between societies: for example the Netherlands in the 1970s and 80s saw a very dramatic rise in the share registered as disabled, reflecting a particular form of disability benefits introduced in the Netherlands (Hartog, 1999).

In the USA there has been a huge increase in the share of prime-age men in prison, from just over 200 per 100,000 population in 1977 to 600 in 1995 (Ladipo, 2001 and Table 4.3). Freeman (1996) has argued that this large prison population may help to account for the much lower rate of long term unemployed men in the US compared to Europe. Moreover, the low wage levels on offer to the less qualified in the US, coupled with the restriction on entitlements to unemployment benefits to a maximum of six months, may lead the unemployed to turn to crime as an alternative mode of activity. However, Table 4.3 makes clear that the main difference between countries is the higher incarceration rate, not a higher crime rate. In general, all these increases in non-labour market activity have been attributed by some analysts, at least in part, to the effect of decreased employment opportunities, particularly for less skilled or less advantaged workers.

These observed differences in labour supply behaviour are not, therefore, the result of static and traditional societal systems. Instead there is evidence of changing patterns of participation within each society, but without strong evidence as yet of convergence on a standardized norm. As we will see in the following section, much of the variation among countries in both employment rates and labour supply is associated with different patterns of development of welfare state systems and institutional arrangements. Moreover, it is in changing welfare systems and institutions, as well as in changes in the structure of employment demand, that we can also trace the origins of some of the observed changes within demographic groups over recent years. It is to an explanation of both divergence and the pattern of change that we now turn.

Table 4.3 Rates of incarceration and victimization

Country	Incarceration rates per 100,000 population in 1995	Percentage of population victimized
USA	600	24
Canada	115	25
Scotland	110	26
Northern Ireland	105	17
England & Wales	100	31
France	95	25
Austria	85	19
Switzerland	80	27
Netherlands	80	32
Sweden	65	24
Finland	60	19

Source: Mayhew and van Dijk (1997), quoted in Ladipo (2001)

Differences in patterns of labour demand and supply: the role of welfare regimes?

Overview

Differences between advanced countries in their employment systems have over recent years been increasingly attributed to the impact of welfare state regimes. This interest in welfare regimes arises from two divergent sources. First, there are those who see the welfare state as a likely source of inefficiency or interference in the market, thereby associated with creating unnecessary levels of unemployment, too high levels of public expenditure and taxation, and either creating artificial barriers or artificial inducements to participation in the labour market. This argument has been deployed to explain the apparently greater employment success of the American labour market, with its weakly developed welfare system, in contrast to European economies which, it is argued, are dragged down by the high costs and institutional inertia associated with a traditional welfare state system (Krugman, 1987 and Chapter Six). These criticisms have been applied by some analysts to welfare regimes, whether or not they directly discourage labour market participation — for example by providing tax transfers to families to enable mothers to stay at home, or by generous early retirement schemes — or promote high participation by, for example, generous provision of childcare and elder care services. This care provision may free the female population to undertake wage employment but for some, such as Rosen (1995), this provision comes at too high a cost to public expenditure, resulting in high taxes apparently stifling private enterprise and initiative. From this perspective, a residual or minimal welfare state regime is seen as the only form consistent with allowing economies to develop in line with the needs of market capitalism.

An alternative perspective sees differences in welfare state regimes as part of the development of divergent forms of capitalism. Instead of welfare systems distorting the market economy, the particular path of development of 'divergent capitalisms' adds to the richness and complexities of the world economy and gives rise to different types of societies, with different strengths and weaknesses. Understanding the historical development of welfare regimes is central to an analysis of the factors influencing both the structure and level of jobs available and the level and form of labour market participation. These development paths, it is argued, show no strong tendency to convergence because of the differences in fundamental principles and practices which underpin the welfare state regimes. Varieties of capitalism are thus not limited to the varieties of production regimes, discussed and debated in Chapter Three, but extend to varieties of social and welfare regimes. The impact of welfare regimes is not only on the overall level of demand for labour in the labour market but extends to shaping the structure of jobs, the system of work organization and working time, the structure of pay differentials and the patterns of labour market activity within and between social groups. In particular, welfare regimes influence relationships between the social classes, the sexes and the generations (both within the family and within society at large). Employment arrangements are as much embedded in the social as in the production sphere; social relationships will affect attitudes towards authority relations at work and influence perceptions of the fairness of pay and promotion systems, based for example on education, age, gender or social status divisions. Thus these influences on divisions by class, age and sex not only arise out of different interrelationships between welfare regimes and employment patterns but in turn shape the development of the employment system.

Some typologies of regimes

The welfare state can be considered in a narrow sense as constituting those arrangements which act to offset or ameliorate the operation of the market, or more broadly as constituting the whole set of arrangements within a society which mediate between the state, the family and the market (Esping-Andersen, 1990). This broader definition is more appropriately considered as describing welfare state regimes and generates immediate and compelling parallels with the notion of societal systems. The focus is on the interrelationships between different spheres, and on the interdependencies between different aspects of social, economic and political life within a specific societal context. This interest in welfare state regimes was largely initiated by Esping-Andersen (1990) who argued that, instead of seeing welfare state development as taking a linear form, with countries moving over time from weak to strong welfare regimes, in practice societies can be said to cluster into three different forms of welfare state regimes based on very different principles, reflecting fundamental differences in state, family and market relations. Countries are unlikely to move from one form of welfare regime to another, because of these differences in underlying principles and different paths of historical development.

The 'three worlds' of welfare capitalism, as described by Esping-Andersen, can be labelled the *social democratic* model, the *neo-liberal* model and the *corporatist* model (see Table 4.4). In practice, these models, although couched in abstract terms to describe regime types, are taken as effectively synonymous with the three countries used by Esping-Andersen to illustrate this pattern of divergent development: namely Sweden as the ideal type for the social democratic model; the US for the neoliberal model; and Germany for the corporatist model. For Esping-Andersen the key difference between these regimes was to be found in the state-market relationships, in particular the extent to which the state welfare system provided citizens with income support that was independent of the market (Bussemaker and van Kersbergen, 1994): that is the extent to which the welfare system could be said to decommodify labour. Where labour is commodified, citizens have to sell their labour on the labour market for whatever they can get, under whatever conditions of work prevail (see Box 4.1). Only in extreme circumstances would the citizen rely on state provision as an alternative. This approach is argued to characterize the US model,

Table 4.4 The three worlds of welfare capitalism

Characteristic of welfare state	Social democratic: Sweden	Neoliberal: USA	Corporatist: Germany
Decommodification	Decommodification high. Universal citizenship rights combined with strong constraints on employers, emphasis on equality	Decommodification low. Low safety net; welfare dependent mainly on the market through private occupational welfare; emphasis on market opportunity	Decommodification medium. State takes over when family fails to provide; welfare rights linked to employment and to family position; emphasis on occupational status
Welfare principles	Welfare system based on assumption of all fit adults in employment	Residual welfare system for those unable to work; level of employment determined by market/ added worker effects	Welfare system based on income protection
Level and form of public expenditure	High public expenditure on services	Low public expenditure	High public expenditure on income transfers
Structure of employment	High public sector employment	High private services employment	High share of domestic services
Wage structure	Solidaristic wage policy, narrow wage dispersion between and within sectors and by gender	Wide wage dispersion between and within sectors and between gender and ethnic groups	Medium dispersion High wages for men, lower wages for secondary workers

Source: Based on models of welfare states provided by Esping-Andersen (1990)

Box 4.1 Commodification and de-commodification of labour

Workers are not commodities like others because they must survive and reproduce both themselves and the society they live in. It is possible to withhold washing machines from the market until the price is agreeable; but labor is unable to withhold itself for long without recourse to alternative means of subsistence.

   The politics of commodifying workers was bound to breed its opposite. As commodities, people are captive to powers beyond their control; the commodity is easily destroyed by even minor social contingencies, such as illness, and by macro-events, such as the business cycle. If workers actually do behave as discrete commodities, they will by definition compete; and the fiercer the competition, the cheaper the price. As commodities, workers are replaceable, easily redundant, and atomised. De-commodification is therefore a process with multiple routes ... It is ... a precondition for a tolerable level of individual welfare and security. Finally, without de-commodification, workers are incapable of collective action; it is, accordingly, the alpha and the omega of the unity and solidarity required for labor movement development ...

   The variability of welfare-state evolution reflects competing responses to pressures for de-commodification. To understand the concept, de-commodification should not be confused with the complete eradication of labor as a commodity; it is not an issue of all or nothing. Rather, the concept refers to the degree to which individuals, or families, can uphold a socially acceptable standard of living independently of market participation.

Extract from G. Esping-Andersen, *The Three Worlds of Welfare Capitalism* (Cambridge: Polity Press, 1990), p. 37.

---

where the neoliberal political tradition has resulted in only minimal development of welfare state benefits and entitlements.

   Under the corporatist system, the underlying principle is that of an insurance-based welfare system, whereby the State intervenes to ensure that citizens participate in insurance policies to protect themselves against loss of income through unemployment and to provide for their old age. These insurance systems largely reinforce pre-existing divisions within the labour market, providing higher benefits for those in higher status jobs. In contrast the social democratic model also provides alternative sources of support to the market, but eligibility for support is extended to all citizens on a roughly equal basis and is independent of their status as labour market participants. This provides a more complete level of decommodification — removal of the need to sell one's labour under all conditions — than under the corporatist regime.

   In order to understand the implications of the different welfare regimes for the development of the structure of the labour market and the labour market behaviour of the citizens, it is essential to place more stress on state-market-family relations than is found in Esping-Andersen's initial account. The focus on decommodification as the main principle for distinguishing welfare regimes has been argued by feminist scholars to be inappropriate from a gender or women's perspective, for in order to enjoy rights to 'decommodification' it is essential first to be a potential participant in the labour market. Some welfare regimes act to restrict women's role to the domestic or family sphere, while others encourage and promote the participation of all citizens and regard the organizations and provision of care for citizens as a public and not a purely family or private responsibility. Differences in approaches to the family, and thus to the role of women in the wage economy, in practice also link in to the three regimes based on different principles of decommodification.

The corporatist welfare system not only reinforces the differences in position of high and low status workers in the labour market but also reinforces the gender division of labour, with men taking the leading role in the labour market and women providing domestic labour in the home. This traditional division of labour was reinforced by two main dimensions of the corporatist welfare model: first through the tendency to support the care of children and the elderly by the provision of transfer payments to households rather than through the direct provision of public services; second by providing spouses with access to welfare payments through their position as dependants of their insured spouses. Thus the corporatist welfare model is based around a traditional nuclear family, with a single male breadwinner model. The increased income needs of a family are met through taxation and benefit systems, which provide transfer payments to dependants, and through insurance-based rights to welfare systems covering both men and women, provided the men are participants in the labour market and provided the women are in stable married relationships with employed men. This model was associated with a low rate of labour market participation among women in Germany, at least until the 1980s, compared to other European and advanced societies.

This pattern contrasts with experience under the social democratic model. Under this model the state provides all citizens with rights to welfare benefits, but takes action to encourage high participation in employment by all fit adults. The state thus assumes responsibility for at least part of the care requirements of the elderly and children, providing this care through direct public provision of services to which citizens have entitlement. This approach facilitates the participation of women in the wage labour market, both by providing care services and by generating a high demand for female labour in public services. A high employment rate is thus combined with a policy of high decommodification, where benefits are not dependent upon employment status and citizens can seek help with their care and family responsibilities from the state. This provides a high level of internal coherence to the system as a policy of universal rights to unemployment; and other benefits may only be sustainable if there is a relatively low take-up of these rights to benefits and a large working population is available to support those on benefits. The Swedish welfare model ran into problems in the late 1980s and early 1990s when unemployment rose after a long period of high employment and low unemployment rates, which had kept the actual costs of a generous welfare system at a low level.

The neoliberal or residual welfare state model regards the individual or the family as having the responsibility of providing care; as such it is indifferent to whether the care is provided through domestic or private market-based provision. This is identified as a private consumption choice, although dependent on the relative cost of buying services in the market compared to expected returns from wage employment. This approach is consistent with a trend towards a high level of female participation in the US, in part as a response to increased family instability and to decreasing real earnings levels among prime-age men, two factors associated with a decline in single male breadwinner households in the US. Care services are provided through a range of mechanisms, from informal childcare arrangement to the use of private daycare centres. Provision may not, however, be complete or adequate, with the result that children may be cared for in unsatisfactory conditions or left to look after themselves at older ages. Nancy Folbre has commented that the traditional system of providing for and caring for children has broken down in the US but has yet to be replaced with a coherent alternative (Folbre, 1994).

This critique of the focus on commodification has led to the proposal of an alternative classification of welfare state regimes as strong, modified or weak male breadwinner models (see Lewis, 1992 and Table 4.5). The strong male breadwinner model shows similarities to the corporatist or German system as outlined above; and the weak male breadwinner system is closer to the Swedish or social democratic model, based on universal rights and everyone being in the labour force. The modified model relates to those systems, not considered directly in the Esping-Andersen model, which could be considered to support the strong male breadwinner model on some counts but the weak male breadwinner model on others. France fits into this category, for it has a social and tax policy apparently designed to encourage women to remain in the household, yet it combines these policies with the relatively plentiful provision of public childcare assistance, which enables women to remain full-time in the labour market. This typology, however, is still not able adequately to classify the American-type residual welfare state system, as this system has been shown over recent years to provide only very weak support for a strong male breadwinner model and yet at the same time fails to provide effective state support for parenting to assist women entering the labour market.

Nor is the so-called Mediterranean model adequately represented in this typology. Here the family provides much of the system of income security and protection provided by the state in other European countries (Bettio and Villa, 1998). This has led to yet another proposed typology of welfare state regimes building upon the Esping-Andersen initial typology (Daly, 1996) and based on a fourfold classification:

- the Nordic model, based upon everyone as breadwinner;
- the continental European model, based on the male breadwinner;
- the liberal model, based on more than one breadwinner;
- the Mediterranean model based on the family as breadwinner.

As tends to be the case with typologies, the development of these approaches has led to much heated debate, both over the appropriateness of the classifications and over the extent to which they can be considered more than descriptions of ideal types, tied to single country examples, or typologies around which it is possible or appropriate to cluster all the advanced country welfare state regimes.

Table 4.5 Strong, modified, or weak male breadwinner welfare states

Characteristic of welfare state	Strong male breadwinner: Germany	Modified male breadwinner: France	Weak male breadwinner: Sweden	Residual welfare system: US
Tax system	Tax subsidies to family	Tax subsidies to family	Independent taxation	Household taxation: earned income tax credit to facilitate low wage system
Support for parents	Low provision of childcare support	High provision of childcare and unpaid leave for mothers (plus high income subsides for third child)	High provision of childcare and paid leave for both mothers and fathers	High use of private childcare
Working patterns of women and mothers	High voluntary part-time work among mothers, medium female labour force participation	High full-time work among mothers, involuntary part-time work, participation linked to number not age of children	Part-time work among mothers related to right to reduced hours; later return to full-time work	Full-time work to maintain real income of household/secure health and pension benefits/ protect against divorce
Female contribution to family income	Low contribution to family income as work part-time in lower paid jobs	High contribution as work full-time, or earnings substituted by allowance for large family	High contribution as earnings inequality low and reduced hours are compensated	High contribution to family income through long hours but large gender pay gap; wide variations between women
Gender segregation	Segregation in part-time work; female dominated sectors lower paid	Medium segregation; full-timers less segregated	High segregation in public sector employment	Desegregation of higher level occupations but gender pay gaps within occupations

Source: Based on models of welfare states provided by Lewis (1992)

In fact, the problems of finding an appropriate method of describing the rather messy social reality that we come up against once we start on any form of comparative analysis have become intensified over recent years, as there is some evidence of a reduction in the main lines of divergence between the welfare state systems. While the US or neoliberal system has remained underdeveloped and has even seen some cutting back of its already very basic welfare provisions (see Box 4.2), among countries with more developed welfare systems there is some evidence of partial convergence, associated with two developments. First, there have been rising rates of female participation and a fragmentation of traditional family systems, even in regimes usually classified as falling within the strong male breadwinner category. Second, there has been extensive pressure on the Nordic countries to cut back on what are seen as excessively generous levels of services and benefits, particularly in the context of rising unemployment; for as we have already argued, the generous welfare systems were designed around a full employment policy, designed to minimize the actual costs of full universal benefits. Whatever the arguments about convergence, these changes have not involved a wholesale rethink of the principles on which the different welfare state systems are constructed. Esping-Andersen has responded by recognizing the need to place the household or family more centre stage as the main agent in welfare provision than he did in his original formulation (Esping-Andersen, 2000). He argues, however, against multiplying the models of welfare regimes. Moreover, he calls for attempts to escape from the historical legacies of the male breadwinner model, in order to bring about a closer match between welfare regimes

---

Box 4.2 The American system of welfare — Aid to Families with Dependent Children — is reformed under Clinton

The United States is notable among advanced countries for not having a comprehensive system of welfare support. Unemployment benefits last only six months, and once they are exhausted there tends to be little in the way of State support unless the person concerned is a lone mother with dependent children. This welfare system — called Aid to Families with Dependent Children (AFDC) — was originally introduced to support primarily widows, but over time the share of non-widowed lone mothers has increased and public support for AFDC declined. In 1996 President Clinton abolished AFDC, which was a Federal system of welfare and therefore mandatory in each state, and replaced it with Temporary Aid for Needy Families (TANF). This system provides the individual states with more flexibility as to how to design their welfare systems. It also places a permanent cap on federal spending on welfare and a federal maximum time of five years for individuals to be on welfare, although states can impose shorter limits. Recipients must participate in community programmes after two months of receiving TANF, and must begin working within two years of receiving benefits; states have to meet targets of 50 per cent of single parents working at least 30 hours to receive federal aid. TANF can be denied to unwed mothers under 18, and is not available to legal immigrants for five years after entry. There are further restrictions on access for drug dealers and users, and for teen parents.

Source: J. Peck, 'Postwelfare Massachusetts', *Economic Geography*, AAG Special Issue (1998): 62–82, Table 2.

and employment systems and the new needs of both labour markets and households (Esping-Andersen, 1999).

An overhaul of the systems in some countries is indeed well overdue. Changes in lifestyles and in gender relations have undermined many of the principles on which welfare systems were founded. Indeed these changes in behaviour have been occurring often despite, rather than because of, strong institutional and social support systems, suggesting that there are limits to how far welfare regimes are able to control the pattern of behaviour of the population. Thus the identification of different historical paths of development is not an argument for maintaining mechanisms and institutions which have clearly become more outmoded in some regimes than others. Yet whatever the trends in both welfare provision and in lifestyles, welfare state regimes still continue to interact with other social and institutional arrangements in the economy to shape labour market patterns and to close down and open up options that are not found under alternative welfare state regimes. We need, therefore, to move beyond this focus on typology to discuss the actual impact of welfare regimes on the shaping of the labour market and on the shaping of labour market behaviour within advanced countries.

Employment systems and welfare regimes

Job structures

Welfare regimes have been held to affect job structures in two main ways. First and most directly, welfare regimes affect the amount of employment generated through the provision of public services. This depends not only on the size of welfare expenditure but also on its orientation; whether towards transfer payments to citizens or towards the provision of services provided through wage employment. For the most part, public services have traditionally been provided by people directly employed in the public sector. More recently many governments have been experimenting with different ways of providing public services, through cooperation with the private or the voluntary sector, through joint ventures or outsourcing. However, most differences between welfare regimes with respect to the provision of public services will show up in different levels of employment in public services.[1]

The second and more indirect way in which welfare regimes may affect the structure of employment is through the quality of jobs. Here quality refers both to the skills and tasks involved and to the level of wages. These effects are more complex and depend not only on the welfare regime *per se* but also on the associated system of collective bargaining and labour market regulation. Nevertheless, one of Esping-Andersen's main arguments was that the residual or neoliberal welfare regime had been associated with a much stronger development of so-called 'junk jobs' in the private sector than in the social democratic or corporatist regimes (see Table 4.6). The reasons for the development of so-called junk jobs were threefold.

Table 4.6 Post-industrial employment trajectories in Germany, Sweden and the US, mid-1980s

Factor	Germany	Sweden	US
Industrial activity in the mid 1980s:			
Industrial	46.9	33.7	28.2
Neutral	30.9	27.6	32.3
Post-industrial	21.3	35.6	38.1
Government employment as % of total	16.1	33.0	15.8
Government share of employed women	19.8	55.2	17.7
Women's share of public employment	39.4	67.1	46.6
Relative size of selected occupational groups:			
Managers	5.7	2.4	11.5
Professional and technicians	9.8	13.4	9.7
Nurses, social service workers, teachers	7.0	21.9	9.6
'Junk jobs': food, cleaning, waiting	5.0	4.4	7.8
Other service sector	3.8	3.8	15.7
Industrial production workers	43.9	29.4	30.5

Source: Esping-Andersen (1990), Tables 8.3, 8.4, 8.5

First, where there are low or limited unemployment benefits, workers may accept some low wage jobs that would have been rejected in more generous welfare regimes. Thus the welfare system in countries like the US, where there are effectively no unemployment or welfare benefits available after 26 weeks for those who are not single parents, has generated a labour supply available for low wage, so-called junk jobs. This supply of low paid labour is further fuelled by, for example, high rates of both legal and illegal immigration. Table 4.7 shows that the US has in fact a high risk, compared to other OECD advanced countries, of households falling into poverty even when both adults are in work.

The second factor encouraging the creation of junk jobs is that in market-driven economies high demands for services have to be met through the private rather than the public sector. Instability in both jobs and marriage has encouraged many US families to be dual earner households, but this high market activity requires high levels of personal services to sustain it. Some argue that the purchase of personal services is highly price elastic (Baumol, 1967); so that one reason for the large growth of personal services in the US could be the lack of effective labour market regulation, which allows wages and conditions in private services to be driven downwards. It is thus convenient for many dual earner households to purchase services from the market — from restaurant services to laundry and cleaning services — but these might not be demanded if there was a higher level of minimum wages than currently prevails in the US.

Thirdly, there are few subsidies to the family to facilitate the provision of services through domestic unpaid labour. Table 4.6 shows the growth of low quality jobs

Table 4.7 Poverty rates for various household types, working age population (%)

Country	All	Single adult household		Two adult household		
		In work	Not in work	Double earner	Single earner	No earner
Australia	14.5	10.1	65.6	1.1	9.0	47.5
Belgium	5.0	1.3	16.1	0.1	2.4	18.0
Canada	15.4	16.2	63.7	3.1	13.0	46.5
Denmark	6.1	8.6	20.1	0.4	2.0	7.9
Finland	7.5	12.1	30.3	1.0	1.8	8.9
France	8.4	3.8	32.5	0.2	7.8	25.6
Germany	10.4	10.5	44.2	1.5	7.0	32.4
Italy	13.3	3.2	27.1	1.2	16.3	23.5
Netherlands	8.3	12.1	27.8	0.7	3.5	17.1
Norway	7.5	10.0	28.3	0.1	4.6	11.2
Spain	12.5	8.8	28.7	4.0	10.7	27.3
Sweden	9.5	13.5	32.4	0.4	3.0	13.6
UK	17.5	7.0	57.7	1.0	12.7	52.3
United States	20.2	19.3	72.8	7.8	23.6	48.9

Source: Marx and Verbist (1998)

(junk jobs plus other service sector jobs) in the US compared to their share in Sweden and Germany in the mid 1980s. From one perspective, this table shows the US economy in an unfavourable light: a high share of low quality jobs is not a good indication of a trend either towards being a highly productive economy or a socially cohesive society in which all can share relatively equally in prosperity. However, over the years there has been declining confidence in the ability of all countries to generate sufficient high quality jobs for all their potential workforce; and the American model of a high share of junk jobs has found favour amongst some policymakers as a more productive way in which a society can utilize its human resources than parking their labour in long unemployment queues or in inactivity. Thus some societal systems have been criticized for their failure to generate low quality, low wage jobs as a means of absorbing the unemployed.

These criticisms have been directed at the two alternative paths represented by Germany and Sweden. In the case of Germany, the system is argued to rely too rigidly on the generation of high-quality jobs, mainly based in manufacturing, which can provide sufficient income, when coupled with tax subsidies from the welfare system, to enable a man to maintain himself and his family at a reasonable standard of living. This system has inhibited the development of a vibrant low wage service economy for two reasons: first it has restricted the supply of labour for low wage jobs, and secondly it has restricted the demand for services, as caring and provisioning activities have been more located in the home in Germany. This caricature of the German employment system does not capture all the complexities: for example the tax system in Germany has also generated a reasonably large share of so-called marginal part-time jobs which lie outside the normal social security system and could be considered to form part of the 'junk job' category. Also there is limited evidence that the share of services in Germany has been constrained by too high wages. The high average wage level hides quite large inter-industry wage differentials and is also based on high skill levels, which may compensate, through higher productivity, for higher wage costs (Freeman and Schettkat, 2000). Nevertheless, there has been a relatively slow growth of the service economy in Germany, a factor which has stimulated a lively debate over whether the German Government should take steps to stimulate service sector jobs by allowing the development of lower wage jobs in the German economy. Freeman and Shettkat suggest that the differences in services may be related to differences in time spent at work; it is the longer hours of work of American men and women that lead to a demand for labour intensive consumer services.

Sweden meanwhile is said to have avoided the development of a large junk job sector. Many services are provided through the public sector, where wages and conditions are set at reasonable minimum levels and protected through collective bargaining. This protection of wages extends to the private sector and involves controls both on low wages and on high wages. The relatively low degree of wage inequality in Sweden has stimulated the move towards the dual earner household, as women can make a much greater difference to family income than in countries where gender pay differentials are wider. However, in contrast with the situation in the US, the growth of dual earner households has not led to a major growth in demand for private personal services. This is first because childcare and elder care services are to a large extent available through the state sector. Another factor is the relatively high minimum wage that has to be paid in Sweden for service workers. This creates incentives for self-provisioning in some personal service areas such as cleaning. This continuation of domestic unpaid labour may also lie behind demands to keep standard working hours relatively short to facilitate the combination of work and domestic activities. This is in contrast to the US where, in many dual earner households, both partners are working long and unregulated hours. The underdevelopment of a low wage service class in Sweden again led to much debate in the 1990s as to whether it was time to end the policy of wage equality and citizenship solidarity in the interests of allowing wages to fall so as to stimulate jobs and reduce unemployment. There have been some trends in this direction but the growth of a junk job economy has still been largely resisted as against the spirit of a social democratic and inclusive societal system.

The effect of welfare regimes on the structure of jobs has repercussions for the patterns of inequality and social divisions within the broader society. The high share of public services jobs in Sweden and other Nordic countries has been associated, for example, with a higher measured level of occupational segregation by gender (Anker, 1998) than in countries with lower shares of public services. Many of the women in the Scandinavian countries who are able to work as result of the availability of care services are themselves employed by these public service providers. In the US, the wide wage disparities and the high share of low productivity jobs in the service sector reinforce income inequalities by race and educational group. There is a much higher economic 'return' to education in the US as a consequence of both the low wages at the bottom end of the labour market and the high wages at the top end. In most European countries pay differentials are much more compressed (see Chapter Six).

Care arrangements and employment

So far we have described the main macro differences in welfare regimes and their impact on job structures. More detailed analysis of actual welfare regimes indicates, however, an even wider range of institutional arrangements, with significant consequences for opportunities to combine participation in wage work with responsibility for care arrangements.

For example, up to now we have been describing welfare regimes as either providing high levels of public care provision or low levels. Table 4.8, based on a detailed analysis of welfare provision in 14 European countries, reveals that while some countries provide high levels of care for both children and the elderly, some make good provision only for the elderly and others make good provision only for children. It is child care that has the most immediate and clear impact on employment participation for a particular labour force group — namely mothers — but elder care provision is taking on increasing importance for employment in two ways. First of all, more people in work — both male and female — are likely to have responsibility for elder care in the future, as the share of the elderly population rises and fewer are likely to be able to rely on an inactive spouse to take care of their elderly relatives. Second, elder care provides a potential source of new jobs, as the number needing care rises and the number of elderly people who have family members able and willing to provide the care falls (Table 4.8).

Even if we focus only on childcare, we find that welfare regimes have very different policies and practices with respect to the provision of support to parents. The main ways in which parents or families can be supported are through leave arrangements, care arrangements and schooling. Leave arrangements may be paid or unpaid; reserved for only one parent or based on individual and non-transferable rights; flexible with respect to the age of the child and/or the extent to which it is

Table 4.8 Classification of European countries by provision of services for elderly and children

Provision	Countries
Abundant: both child and elder care	Denmark, Sweden, Finland
Abundant child/scarce elder care	Belgium, France, Italy
Abundant elder/scarce child care	Netherlands, Norway, Great Britain
Scarce: both child and elder care	Portugal, Greece, Spain, Ireland, Germany

Source: Anttonen and Sipilä (1996)

taken as full or part-time leave; and paid for by the employer or by the state. For example, in Sweden paid parental leave can be taken for 450 days or longer if taken as reduced hours, and can be taken up until a child is eight. Full-time leave or part-time leave is compensated at 80 per cent of foregone earnings. These entitlements are open to men or women, with some extra leave reserved only for fathers. In contrast, in the UK parental leave is unpaid and for three months only. From 2003, mothers may be able to take up to 52 weeks maternity leave but only the first six weeks is paid at close to foregone earnings, followed by 20 weeks at a low flat rate of pay and 26 weeks unpaid if they have been in employment for 12 months. More advantaged women in the labour market may receive more extended paid leave, courtesy of their employers or guaranteed through collective agreements.

These different arrangements can have major effects on whether women tend to have long or short breaks over the period of childbirth; whether fathers are involved as well as others in the care of children at home; and on the acceptability and use of other forms of childcare as an alternative to parental care. Fathers' involvement is critically dependent on both the existence of individual and non-transferable rights to leave and on the availability of leave paid at a relatively high level. Some countries provide good childcare when children are very small but create more problems for combining work and children when the children reach school age, due to the problems of short or discontinuous school days and lack of after-school care. In the Scandinavian countries, France and Belgium there is good provision for childcare from a young age, while in contrast Germany makes much more effective provision from the age of three. However, even more of a barrier to women working in Germany are the short school days, ending normally by lunchtime, in contrast with France where children may stay at school until five or six o'clock (Rubery *et al.*, 1998b, 1999).

Care arrangements do not, therefore, necessarily fit straightforwardly into models of good or poor support for working parents (Gornick *et al.*, 1997). Moreover, some systems tend to reinforce the role of the mother as the main carer while others at least create opportunities for changing the traditional domestic division of labour. Those that tend to reinforce the role of mother as carer include those that focus primarily on the provision of extended leave on an unpaid or low paid basis and without good alternative childcare provision. Some systems also focus primarily on opportunities to work part time, which may enable women to remain in the labour market, but as we will see below, may still have negative effects on their employment careers. Those care arrangements which provide most scope for sharing care between parents or for not disadvantaging mothers in the labour market include those that:

- focus on involving fathers in parental leave;
- provide help for women to remain in their jobs and even to continue to work full-time or close to full-time;
- provide good quality child care;
- protect full-timers against pressures to work very long hours.

While major differences remain between countries in the precise form of support for parents, there has been a general trend towards more provision and assistance in countries where the initial starting point was low. There has also been some scaling down of assistance in countries where the provision was relatively generous (for example, Sweden and Finland). In the UK, one of the countries with historically very limited provision, there have been improvements made to maternity leave, parental leave has been introduced — although on an unpaid basis — and both facilities for and financial support for childcare have been expanded. At the other end of the spectrum, the payment for leave in the Scandinavian countries has been reduced and in Norway and Finland there are new policies to provide families with funds that can either be used to support a non-working parent or to assist with childcare costs; the new policies are said by government to increase families' choice over whether to provide care themselves or to seek it outside the home (Ellingsæter, 1999). However, there are concerns in the Scandinavian countries that this could lead to a dismantling of the infrastructure of childcare provision, which in the longer term would reduce the option of seeking care outside the home.

Pension systems and employment

The declining labour market participation among older male workers which is evident in a large number of advanced countries has only been possible as a result of welfare provision in the form of pensions (old age or disability). The extent of this provision has varied between countries, affecting the rate and pattern of declining participation (see Chapter One, Box 1.9). In some cases these changes are directly linked to welfare state provision, including for example early retirement schemes or generous disability programmes; however in other cases, for example the US and the UK, there has been a relatively rapid increase in early retirement based primarily on company-specific schemes (Casey and Wood, 1993; Naschold and de Vroom, 1993). Therefore, although welfare provision is significant, and the decisions to cut back on State-funded early retirement schemes in many European countries have at least halted the decline, there are other factors at work here, including attitudes towards the acceptability of placing the burden of displacement on older workers.

Most of the explanation for why companies opt for the costly option of early retirement rather than redundancy is found in the greater acceptability of this strategy to the workforce, at least in countries where early retirement tends to be looked on favourably. In countries where perhaps age and seniority are considered with more respect, such as Japan, and where there has been a long-term emphasis on all citizens being economically active, as in Scandinavia, the early retirement option has proved less popular.

The lack of a developed welfare system is evident in the US, where there is no standard retirement age. Early retirement has been relatively commonly financed through company schemes, but many of the early retirees eventually return to the labour market as their pensions often prove inadequate. The lack of a standard retirement age, coupled with at least some legislation against age discrimination in the US, create conditions in which older workers may find it easier to find some employment than in many European countries.

Different pension systems and arrangements also impact upon gendered patterns of employment. Where pension systems are either based on the insurance principle or on company schemes, women tend to lose out because of their shorter work histories in most countries. Where company schemes are important, women tend to miss out because they tend to be employed in those companies or those job groups where there are no or only relatively weak pension schemes available. Women are often able to claim pension rights as dependent wives, and the difficulties they face in building up good pension rights through their own employment activity tend to reinforce the importance of derived rights in women's lifetime income (Davies and Joshi, 1995; Rake, 2000). This also has the perverse effect of encouraging many women to take jobs where pension rights are limited, as the chances of making good provision for themselves are in any case low, and their pension rights derived from their husbands' higher incomes may exceed even those that they may build up through returning to work on a full-time basis. Women are more likely to be available for marginal part-time jobs outside the social security provision than men, who are less likely to have a partner on whose pension entitlements they can rely. However, this reliance on a partner's pension has proved not to provide a full solution for women, even discounting the issue of implied dependence. Many more women tend to be in poverty in old age as a consequence of their lack of pension rights; and increasing numbers of women find themselves without derived rights because of marital instability, more unstable work histories among their partners, and because more women choose not to marry even if they cohabit. Women tend to fare much better under regimes where pensions are at least in part provided to citizens as rights, not based on their involvement in wage work; this applies to most of the Scandinavian countries and to some extent to the Netherlands (Ginn and Arber, 1992).

Gender regimes and employment systems

Overview

Any discussion of welfare regimes and employment necessarily also addresses the issue of the link between gender regimes and employment systems. Gender has always been central to the organization of the labour market. Even at times when the labour market was overwhelmingly dominated by men, the involvement of men in wage work was critically dependent on the gender division of labour, which allocated all or most domestic work to women, particularly at a time when the quantity of domestic work necessary for survival was even greater than today. Moreover, the increasing importance of women in the labour force in all countries means that it is impossible for policymakers or human resource managers to ignore issues of gender in today's labour market.

Gender regimes can be characterized as involving more than relationships around work; they include gender roles in culture, sexuality and politics (Connell, 1987; Mósesdóttir, 2001; O'Reilly, 2000; Pfau-Effinger, 1998). There is no simple relationship between the form of gender relations, for example, in politics or culture and gender relations at work; we will therefore for these purposes confine ourselves primarily to issues related to the gender division of labour in both paid and unpaid work. This gender division of labour is itself strongly influenced by the wider political and societal conditions which shape how women are viewed within the body politic: primarily as mothers, or as workers or as citizens. Where women are viewed first and foremost as citizens they are more likely to have equal rights to participate in wage work; where they are viewed primarily as mothers, their participation will be contingent on their primary maternal role; and where they are viewed primarily as workers, as in the 'commodified' systems, their responsibilities as mothers will have to accommodate to the needs of the employment regime. Again the three countries, Sweden, Germany and the US, provide illustrations of these three categories: for the US women are primarily workers, for Germany mothers and for Sweden citizens (Mósesdóttir, 2001). Other countries show more ambiguities: for example France has a strong policy that women should be mothers, because of concerns over its population level, but it assists women to become mothers whether they wish to stay at work (by providing childcare) or to stay at home (by providing generous benefits for women who have two or more children).[2] For men, the political regimes are likely to regard them either primarily as workers or as citizens; concern with men's reproductive role is likely to be secondary.

Gender, flexibility and part-time work

The gender regime also structures the extent to which women are regarded as a disposable, flexible or dependent labour supply. Where there is still a strong presumption that men will be the main breadwinners in the household systems, the attitude towards female workers is likely to emphasize the contingent nature of their participation in the labour market. Under these conditions women are more likely to take on the characteristics of disposable and flexible labour, whose participation depends on available job opportunities and whose labour supply price may be much lower than men's because of their access to family income to support their subsistence needs.

One of the main issues around the growth of part-time work is whether or not it is supportive of, or in opposition to, the pursuit of gender equality in the labour market. There are strong arguments expressed in both directions (O'Reilly and Fagan, 1998). For many concerned with equal opportunities, part-time work not only disadvantages women in their access to weekly or lifetime earnings but also creates conditions under which women's subordinate role in the labour market and household is reinforced. Part-time work is often organized separately from full-time work and may both be rewarded at lower hourly wage rates and be excluded from additional benefits. Moreover, part-time workers may be excluded, directly or indirectly, from promotion opportunities and training and skills development. Furthermore, part-time work, almost by definition, fails to provide sufficient earnings to meet subsistence needs, thereby reinforcing the dependence of women on the earnings of their partner. When men are involved in part-time work they are also often in receipt of additional incomes — from pensions, from student maintenance or from unemployment benefit — so that few adults meet their full subsistence costs from part-time work. Obviously the more part-time work is available throughout the job and salary spectrum the less this argument would hold, but in practice in many countries part-time work has been confined mainly to low wage segments. Part-time jobs are also often treated as more disposable by employers and more open as well to rescheduling to meet employer requirements. All these factors may lead the growth of part-time work to reinforce gender inequalities both inside and outside the labour market.

This negative assessment is not universally accepted. For others part-time work does provide increased opportunities for women to participate in wage work and moreover does not force them into having to make an unpalatable choice between work or family (Hakim, 1991). From this perspective part-time work aids equal opportunities because the alternative may be non-participation and/or the acceptance of unsuitable care arrangements. Equal opportunities here are not necessarily equated with the same or identical behaviour to that of men as workers, but instead may involve valuing differences between men and women and providing women with opportunities to be both workers and mothers. There may also need to be a parallel development towards dual roles for men, as active fathers as well as workers.

The resolution of these differences in perspective on the role of part-time work can in part be traced back to the welfare regime and the overall gender regime in which the policies of part-time work are located. Where women are in conservative male breadwinner regimes, the development of opportunities for part-time work may well be seen as providing progress towards greater gender equality; but where women already have a relatively high participation in full-time work, the promotion of part-time work as a suitable option for women may well be interpreted as a regressive step. Table 4.9 shows that although part-time work is an important form of economic activity for mothers in many countries, it is not a universal form.

However, as we will see in Chapter Six, the role of part-time work can also be influenced by the terms and conditions for part-time work secured within the collective bargaining and legal framework. Where, for example, part-time work is available in high as well as low level jobs and where part-time work is awarded full wage and benefit protection, the negative associations of part-time work with women's disadvantaged position in the labour market may well be modified (see Chapter One,

Table 4.9 Activity patterns of mothers in the EU, % of mothers*

Country	Full-time employment	Part-time employment	Unemployed	Labour market activity rate
East Germany	55.0	14.0	19.0	88.0
Denmark	49.0	25.0	10.0	84.0
Sweden	35.0	40.0	7.0	82.0
Finland	57.0	8.0	12.0	77.0
Portugal	63.0	7.0	5.0	75.0
Belgium	38.0	24.0	9.0	71.0
France	40.0	19.0	11.0	70.0
Austria	40.0	24.0	3.9	67.9
UK	18.0	35.0	6.0	59.0
Netherlands	6.0	41.0	5.0	52.0
West Germany	18.0	28.0	4.0	50.0
Greece	40.0	3.0	7.0	50.0
Italy	37.0	6.0	6.0	49.0
Spain	29.0	6.0	14.0	49.0
Luxembourg	29.0	13.0	3.0	54.0
Ireland	24.0	10.0	8.0	42.0

*Note: Most common definition of a mother is having a child aged 10 or under, but for Austria the definition is a child under 15 and for Sweden a child under 7. The unemployment rate for Austrian mothers is taken here to be the average unemployment rate for all women, as the data were not available for mothers alone.

Source: EC Childcare Network (1996)

Box 1.7). In the Netherlands there has been considerable success in negotiating new rights for part-timers within collective agreements and there is also a relatively high share of part-time jobs found among high-level managerial and professional jobs. These conditions go some way towards modifying the general criticisms of part-time work outlined above. However, the Netherlands appears to be a very special case: it has the highest part-time rate in Europe for both women and for men, and there appears to be a deep-seated preference for shorter hours among all workers, including male full-timers. Under these conditions the advances made in the Netherlands cannot necessarily be extended to other countries.

Another important example of a different notion of part-time work is provided by Sweden. Here much of the part-time work has traditionally been more a form of reduced hours working, opted for as part of the parental leave provision while children are young. This is different from working in jobs designed for part-timers and allows participants to return to full-time hours at a later date. Here there is no clear divide between the full- and the part-time labour force. Moreover, the reduced hours of work may, for at least some of the time, be subject to income compensation, if the right to paid parental leave is taken in the form of reduced hours. This means that women or men may opt to work shorter hours but receive partial compensation — up to 75 per cent of earnings — for the reduced hours. Many who opt for reduced hours may run out of entitlements to compensation before returning to full-time work, but in this system there is some direct recognition of the right of mothers to an income from full-time employment instead of the implicit assumption, still found in most welfare regimes, that mothers should automatically become dependent or semi-dependent on their partners at times when they are unable to work on a full-time basis (Rubery, 1998). Apart from the problem of assumed dependence *per se*, this approach tends to force fathers to seek much higher paid work than their female partner and to force them into overtime working instead of into shared child-care. Moreover, unpaid parental leave is unlikely to be taken up by fathers as it would have a major negative impact on the family budget. This assumption of automatic dependency thus has far reaching consequences for the continuation of the male breadwinner model, even at a time when most women are demonstrating a desire for greater economic independence.

Gender and employment: a force for convergence?

So far we have focused on the historical and still current differences in women's relative position and involvement in the labour market within the OECD part of the world. Yet one of the most striking features of recent decades has been the universality and persistence of the upward trend in women's employment in virtually all OECD countries. Moreover, the impact of the different welfare regimes on women's labour market participation and indeed on the associated size of the service economy was much more clearly evident at the beginning of the 1980s than at the end of the 20th century. The changes in gender relations over the last few decades can be considered in many senses a source of convergence between different societies, as women in all advanced countries have been exerting their desire for greater economic independence almost irrespective of the extent of support forthcoming from the state and the labour market. Figure 4.4 showed the closing gap in participation rates between men and women in prime age, the period where a large gender gap was evident in the past, just at the time of women's main responsibilities for child-care. One of the main factors bringing about this convergence is the rising educational levels among women; education has a strong upward impact on women's participation and these effects are in some countries only just beginning to be felt, such that a further long term rise in women's participation rates can be expected (Figure 4.5).

Much of the divergence in female employment rates across countries is associated with differences in employment rates for women educated to a low or medium level; among more highly educated women there is a more common pattern of relatively high participation. To some extent the rise in the share of women with higher education, coupled with the strong upward pull on participation from education, may be obscuring the continuation of low female participation outside the more highly educated group. The issues of convergence and divergence between societies

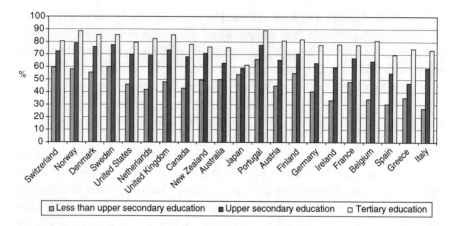

Note: Employment rates = employment/population aged 25–64
Source: OECD (2001)

Figure 4.5 Employment rates for women by level of educational attainment in OECD countries 1999

may thus have to be analysed by class and educational groups and not simply with reference to changes in overall gender gaps.

The convergence among OECD societies with respect to the gender gap in employment rates is also less strong once one takes into account hours of work. Countries still differ markedly in the significance of part-time working among women, and if employment rates are recalculated on a full-time equivalent basis the gender gap widens in almost every country. Even among more highly educated women, the societal predilection for part-time or full-time work shows through; and more highly educated women are much more likely to be in part-time work in countries where the overall part-time work ratio is high, particularly when they are mothers (Rubery and Smith, 1999). This means in fact that there is a much greater underutilization of more highly educated women within the current employment system than is evident from a simple comparison of participation rates. The importance of part-time work in female participation also reminds us that the absorption of women into the wage economy has not necessarily been based on processes which reduce discrimination. Instead women's entry into the labour market is as much associated with the maintenance of gender difference, and in particular with the continued concentration of women in female stereotypical occupations and in low paid, flexible and disposable work (Rubery *et al.*, 1999). The particular pattern of female integration has, however, varied between countries and provides a source of divergence between countries, even at a time of converging participation rates.

What we find, therefore, is that while the feminization of the labour market is a general or universal trend within OECD countries, its form and intensity vary between countries. Feminization is both a force for convergence and for divergence;

more women have entered higher level jobs as a consequence of their acquisition of higher educational standards, but more have also been employed in traditional areas of low wage and low status employment for women (Rubery *et al.*, 1999). We find that, within as well as between societies, there is evidence of both reducing and widening gender gaps. Perhaps the main difference between the situation now and that prevailing before the main expansion of welfare capitalism is that today the state is much less able either to prevent further rises in female participation or to reverse the inroads women have made over the last decades. The upward trajectory of female employment has become apparently 'relatively autonomous' from either labour market conditions or state policy (Humphries and Rubery, 1984). Nevertheless, the historical legacy of the divergent welfare, family and employment systems within the OECD area is still exerting a major influence on the current patterns of women's integration into employment and on the wider systems of gender relations in the society.

Notes

1   This is not the same as differences in public sector employment, as the latter will include also nationalized industries, and the scale of nationalized industries has also varied between countries, but in ways that are not related to the nature of public services provision.
2   This allowance was traditionally only paid to mothers of three children or more. In the 1990s it was extended to mothers on the birth of the second child and was interpreted as a move to encourage mothers to stay at home, in light of the growing problem of unemployment in France.

Skilling the labour force

Education and skills are at the forefront of the policy agenda at both national and international levels. The ability of an economy to compete at the international level has been increasingly associated with its capacity to adapt to new technologies, adopt new forms of production systems and transform systems of work organization. As we showed in Chapter Three, a range of studies suggests that these new production requirements are dependent upon the development of a broad range of skills among the workforce. This places the effectiveness of a country's national system of education and training at the centre of strategies for maintaining or improving competitiveness in the global economy. The objective is to develop a high skilled workforce compatible with the 'learning society', or the 'knowledge-based economy'. The idea is that workers ought to be trained to meet a continuous cycle of changes in job tasks, technologies and forms of work organization that are likely to occur across their working life. Phrases such as 'employability', 'adaptability' and 'flexibility' are increasingly used to set out the key objectives of new education and training programmes.

Changes are sought at both ends of the age spectrum of the workforce. For older workers, the issue is how to update or retrain those with traditional skills that are now outdated or redundant. For young people, particularly those entering the labour market without higher education qualifications, the issue is how to facilitate their development of skills to enable them to move into stable and fulfilling work.

While there appears to be a consensus among policymakers on the need for upskilling, the substance and direction of policy 'solutions' vary enormously across different countries. In general, the different approaches reflect variations in the national systems of education and training. It matters, in particular, whether the system is considered to be led by the market, where decisions are largely made by employers; by state institutions; or organized on a corporatist basis involving social partners (employers and unions) and the state. These different modes of organizing training systems — as we will see in more detail below — demand different types of policy intervention. Where training programmes are market-led, the state may seek to find means of making certain that training expenditure and training quality reach a minimum standard. In contrast, where training programmes are based on consensus agreement more emphasis is likely to be placed on negotiating changes with all the actors. The direction, and relative effectiveness, of policies to upskill the workforce are likely, therefore, to be shaped by the particular characteristics of the national system of education and training. In addition, particularly in countries marked by a highly segmented or polarized workforce, the promised benefits of upskilling may be offset by the attractiveness, at least to some employers, of providing goods and services through the medium of lower skilled 'junk jobs'.

We begin this chapter with a brief review of the relationship between education, skills and productivity. The key question is whether markets can be expected to generate appropriate quantities and qualities of skills, or whether there is a case for more active intervention by policymakers to overcome market failures. In the second section the argument is made, both at a theoretical level and with reference to actual practice, that education and skills tend to be too important to be left up to market forces. The third section identifies the main characteristics that distinguish different national approaches to education and training. The chapter then attempts to assess the relative performance of these different systems according to three criteria: the coverage of training provision and opportunity for long term skill development; the quality of the school-to-work transition; and the capacity of the education and training system to adapt to current changes in technologies, flexible working and international competition.

Education, skills and productivity

The issue of skills may be said to lie at the heart of the contradictory relations that underpin capitalist economies. For the employer, a high skilled workforce may offer opportunities to increase productivity and competitiveness, but these advantages are counterbalanced by the potentially higher training and wage costs associated with a more highly skilled workforce. For the employee, higher skills may offer opportunities for more fulfilling work; but employees may be unwilling to take on more skilled work unless offered higher wages in recognition of their skills. Conflicts between employer and employee also arise over the form and the funding of training. For example, it is typically in the interests of the employer to encourage training in skills that meet the specific requirements of the firm; whereas for the employee training in more general skills may be preferable, since it provides the broader knowledge required to adapt to future changes (in machinery or computer systems, for example) and extends the potential range of job opportunities available to employees if they move to other firms. Another area of conflict is who pays for the training: for employers there is a reluctance to pay because of the risk of employee turnover; for employees, there is the risk that the skills will not have long term market value because they are too narrow, specific, or become outdated quickly.

The 'human capital' approach to education and training found in economic theories (Becker, 1964; Mincer, 1994) tends to downplay these potential conflicts. For human capital theorists, skills are directly related to productivity and to earnings, and confer clear benefits on both employees and employers. Individual investment in education is seen as profitable for both the firm and the individual. The firm gains from an increase in productivity (achieved by the impact of higher skills on work performance) and the worker gains from a higher probability of access to work and/or increased earnings (since pay reflects the employee's contribution to overall firm output). What is held to be true at the level of the firm and the individual is also said to be mirrored at the level of the economy. Improvements in the quantity and quality of workforce skills are presumed to play an important role in shaping an economy's overall performance. There is a growing tide of opinion that it is not possible for developed countries to compete with developing countries on the basis of low wage, low skill jobs. In this context, improving the skills base becomes a key policy measure to enhance the fortunes of both workers and the economy alike. Also, economy-wide studies of the labour market show that rates of unemployment are highest among workforce groups with low skills or few qualifications. Here, policy seeks to equip workers with the appropriate knowledge and skills, both to strengthen their chances of finding work and to improve the overall employment rate (and reduce unemployment) across the economy.

If it is correct that there is a strong, straightforward and positive relationship between skills, productivity, access to work and economic performance, there remains, however, a puzzle. Why in this case have countries not achieved greater advances in training provision? (Lynch, 1994a). Some of the conventional explanations return to the contradictory and conflictual problems associated with the issue of skill, identified above. Difficulties in meeting the requirement for more skills are typically identified with the 'public good' nature of education and training, which generates problems of 'market failure'. Public goods can benefit actors in a society who have not contributed to the production of these goods. An employer may be unwilling to invest in employee training where the skills to be acquired are also valuable to competing firms, fearing the poaching of trained workers. The individual employing organization may be unable to recoup its costs of training as it is other firms that will have the benefit of the higher productivity generated by the training. Therefore, despite the potential benefits of training to the individual employer and employee, the market fails to generate an efficient solution and there is underinvestment in training.

Another problem concerns the long term nature of education and training investment; it is difficult for an employer to calculate the return on training investment — particularly in a context of rapidly changing technologies, systems of production and competitive pressures. Other, more practical problems constraining a firm's willingness to provide training are likely to be encountered by small firms. Here employers may find it difficult to provide cover for workers undertaking off-site training or to spread the costs of training across a relatively small wage bill.

There may also be a problem, under some conditions, in generating a supply of workers to meet firms' demand for higher skills. Individuals may face problems in borrowing funds to make investments in training due to the uncertainty of future returns on the investment and an inability, therefore, to secure the confidence of the creditor. These problems are exacerbated by conflicting interests between employer and employee regarding the balance of general and firm-specific skills and the issue of who pays for training. Firms may offer a low wage to trainees, with the promise of a higher wage on completion of training; but workers may be unwilling to accept such a training post if they are concerned about job security in the company or if the training does not lead to the acquisition of a certified qualification recognized by other potential employers. Where the training is of a relatively general nature, the worker may be more willing to accept a low wage during the period of training, as a form of indirect payment for the training. In this case, the skills acquired potentially enhance the person's own ability to adapt to future changes in technologies and production organization, as well as providing greater job opportunities in the wider labour market. For employers, the opposite relationship holds: they are more likely to fund training the more the training is firm-specific, as this increases the likelihood of the trained worker remaining within the firm, allowing training costs to be recouped through future improvements in productivity.

The objective of this chapter is to explore the ways different national systems of training and education approach the problem of training, and to see to what extent these constitute relatively effective 'solutions' to the problem of market failure. For most governments there appears to be too much at stake to leave it up to the market to decide the quantity and quality of training. According to a number of recent studies, it seems that the potential for conflicts and contradictions in the provision of skills development is most marked in those countries characterized by relatively decentralized and deregulated economies, such as the 'market-led' systems of the UK or the US. Indeed, there is a growing concern that the increasingly widespread adoption of a deregulatory approach to economic planning that emphasizes flexibility may be at odds with another important employment objective, that of generating a highly skilled workforce, which may require the development of a stable employment environment (see Cappelli *et al.*, 1997; Crouch, 1997; and below). State-led or corporatist national arrangements may avoid some of the conflicts and contradictions identified at the level of the individual firm in market-led systems. Nevertheless, they may present a different set of equally challenging dilemmas at the sector or national level. There is, in fact, unlikely to be a perfect or ready-made solution to any country's training problems, an issue we return to at the end of this chapter.

Occupational and internal labour markets

Differences in national systems of training can be usefully understood with the aid of two abstract models of training systems: the occupational labour market (OLM) and the internal labour market (ILM). The OLM refers to a system that provides nationally recognized occupational qualifications, usually through apprenticeship training. Typically, such training combines part-time college-based education with on-the-job training through work experience. The ILM characterizes a system where firms design either formal or informal training programmes, specific to the needs of the firm and building upon the general education that employees have acquired previously through full-time education. Table 5.1 provides a comparison of the two systems across four themes.

The four themes are all interrelated, generating a set of interlocking principles that constitute each system of vocational training. First, the two models deliver a different system of training. The OLM model provides both general vocational education and practical, on-the-job training, either in succession or side-by-side. The ILM model, in contrast, provides workplace-related training only. Moreover, whereas the employer is largely responsible for the design and implementation of training within an ILM-type system, training in the OLM model tends to be regulated by all social partners — the government, the employer associations and trade unions.

Secondly, the form of skills development varies. In the OLM case the skills are designed and certified according to broad occupational criteria; in the ILM case skills are defined in relatively narrow terms, to meet the particular needs and requirements of the individual firm, and left uncertified as they take different forms in different organizations. Thirdly, the delivery of training, whether through an OLM or an ILM-type model, shapes the social and economic status of the individual worker. In the former case, worker status is defined by possession of a broad occupational qualification that is recognized across all firms in the particular sector of economic activity or region. In the case of the ILM model, worker status hinges on their position within the firm and therefore also on the reputation of the company.

Table 5.1 Comparing occupational and internal labour market systems

Factor	OLM	ILM
System of training	General vocational education and practical training, regulated by social partners	Employer-led on-the-job training
Skills development	Certification according to broad occupational criteria	Limited to the needs of the individual firm; narrow and uncertified
Locus of employee status	Possession of recognized occupational qualification	Position within the firm
Employee mobility	Qualified workers are mobile across firms Unqualified workers may face difficulties entering the labour market	Restricted to job ladders within the firm

These differences generate distinct patterns of, and opportunities for, mobility. Trained workers in the OLM model are able to seek job opportunities across a range of firms, but in the ILM model they are constrained within the boundaries of the firm. The greater emphasis on credentials in the OLM-type system, however, may mean that unqualified workers face difficulties in entering the lower levels of a firm. Also, whether vertical job advancement in the ILM model is lower or higher than in an OLM model is contingent on the design and structure of the job ladders in place.

Typologies of country systems of training and education tend to associate certain countries with either the OLM or the ILM model. Germany is usually said to have adopted an OLM-type approach to vocational training, whereas France and Japan typically appear as countries close to an ILM-type model (Eyraud *et al.*, 1990; Marsden and Ryan, 1995). However, there are dangers associated with attempts to fit countries too neatly into one or other of the abstract models. This can be illustrated by the example of the UK, which over recent years, has tended to move away from a traditional OLM-type model based on apprenticeships towards a more hybrid approach, involving elements of the OLM model (the introduction of a national credential system — National Vocational Qualifications (NVQ) — and the expansion of apprenticeship training — the 'Modern Apprenticeship'), and of the ILM model (freedom for employers to determine the quantity and quality of training, including some influence on the content of their in-house NVQ training schemes). This combination of elements of the two systems has perhaps added to the incoherence of the reforms to the UK training system over recent years, as employers remain skeptical of the value of NVQs precisely because the employers themselves have some freedom to shape the training and qualification programmes (Marsden and Ryan, 1995). However, this incoherence may reflect the weak institutionalization of both the OLM and the ILM in the UK.

Hybrid models do not always generate incoherence: the German system might also be described as a hybrid, since it combines strong OLM-type principles with strong ILM-type principles of job ladders and in-firm mobility for skilled workers (see below). These internal structures are used as measures to retain valued staff in a context where there are opportunities, because of transferable qualifications, for inter-firm mobility (Sengenberger, 1981). These examples show that although abstract models can help us to understand some of the complexities underlying country-specific approaches to training, it is important to recognize that not only can such approaches take on elements from both types of training system, but also over time there may be moves away from one type of system towards another.

National systems of vocational training

In this section, the national systems of vocational training in five countries are selected for consideration, loosely categorized along two axes (Figure 5.1). The *y* axis

		Market-led	Consensus-led	State-led
	Occupational labour market (OLM)		Germany	
Labour market model	Features of both OLM and ILM	UK US		
	Internal labour market (ILM)		Japan	France

Form of regulation

Figure 5.1 Categorizing national systems of vocational training

shows the type of labour market, distinguishing between an occupational and an internal labour market. The *x* axis shows the form of regulation, characterizing countries according to whether they have market-led, consensus-led or state-led systems of vocational training.

The following discussion provides some details of each country's system of vocational training, along with a preliminary assessment of the outcomes of the systems reviewed from the perspective of individual workers, employers and the functioning of labour markets.

The US: a market-led, weak ILM approach

The US is the archetypal example of a decentralized, 'market-led' system of vocational training. There is very little formal structure to national training, with almost all training decisions taken by individual organizations or individual workers. In particular, there is no national system of accreditation for recognizing vocational skills, with the bulk of skills development achieved through informal workplace systems of learning-by-doing.

Lynch (1994a, 1994b) argues that the decentralized training system of the US has its roots in two sources. First, the US system of schooling is also highly decentralized, with schools enjoying a relatively high degree of local and state autonomy. Second, the US has traditionally relied on immigration to increase the supply of skilled workers, thus removing the incentive to develop a more formal national system of training and retraining institutions. Given the diversity and the lack of a transparent structure, it is only through survey evidence that one is able to construct a picture of the pattern of formal and informal training provision at the company level. Where formal training is provided, there is a great deal of variation in the way different workforce groups are targeted (see Box 5.1). Among younger workers, groups who are most likely to receive company training are managers, professional and technical employees. Workers without a university degree are very unlikely to benefit from company training (Lynch, 1994a).

Box 5.1   Who gets formal training in the US?

The 1991 National Organizations Survey (NOS) conducted in the US shows that the likelihood of a company offering formal training varies significantly by sector of economic activity, by company size, by the characteristics of the workforce and by the level of unionization. The following patterns are illustrative:

- formal training provision is more likely in the manufacturing sector and public administration than in wholesale and retail trade;
- 96 per cent of companies with 1000 or more employees offer formal training compared to 15 per cent of those with less than five employees;
- formal training is less likely in companies with a majority of part-time workers than in those with a majority of full-timers;
- 91 per cent of companies with union representation offer formal training compared to just 65 per cent of companies without a unionized workforce.

Source: Cappelli *et al.* (1997): Table 4.2

Another characteristic feature of the US training system is the tendency for companies to become increasingly reliant on external training providers, who provide packages of skills development to meet individual company needs. Companies draw upon specialist expertise from a range of external sources, including private sector consultancies, as well as non-profit organizations such as community colleges (Cappelli *et al.*, 1997: 146). As such, the training function is increasingly regulated by individual employer decisions that rely on the outside market for effective provision.

Nevertheless, there are pockets of training provision that involve joint collaboration between the company and Government or unions. The 1991 National Organizations Survey (NOS) data reveal that a third of organizations received financial assistance for formal training provision from Government agencies. Also, one in ten of all organizations received training funds for disadvantaged youths, minorities and dislocated workers as a result of the 1982 Job Training Partnership Act. Trade unions also play a significant role, despite the low overall level of union membership in the US: 15 per cent of organizations offering formal training did so because of stipulations in union contracts (Cappelli *et al.*, 1997: 144). There is also some evidence that the lack of over-arching national regulation in the US permits experimentation with training reform at the regional labour market level, and this is perhaps the level at which new training systems may emerge (see Box 5.2).

In sum, once US workers enter the labour market, skills are acquired through a combination of formal and informal training. For non-graduates, firm-specific training programmes are generally based around a narrow, traditional set of skills (partly reflecting trade union strategies of strict job control as a defence against arbitrary hiring and firing policies), which present few opportunities to prepare for a lifetime of changes in skills, technologies and production systems (Lynch, 1994a; Wever, 1995). One consequence of the informal nature of workplace-based training is that Americans tend to place considerable emphasis on investments in the more formal

Box 5.2   Local reform to the rescue? New models of US training provision

A growing number of experiments with sectoral training initiatives offer an interesting base for broader systemic reform. These initiatives organize groups of firms within regional labor markets rather than along national product lines. The firms may compete in the same local market, or operate in entirely separate industries, or form customer–supplier relationships with one another. But what they have in common with one another in each case is the convergence of their work systems and/or skills sets. Firms are brought together by a variety of independent worker organizations responding to the unique challenges encountered by the local parties in a rapidly changing business environment. The projects are designed to advance the living standards of workers by addressing the emerging skill requirements of employers beyond the boundaries of individual firms in the sector … Emerging models for organizing the new contingent workforce resemble the way that construction has traditionally been organized for generations. The union provides training, employment stability, and continuous benefits for workers who move from job to job. In effect, the union functions very much like a non-profit agency that redistributes the surplus to its members.

The Communication Workers of America (CWA) recently formed three employment centers in Cleveland, Seattle, and Southern California to supply skilled workers for high-tech jobs (Carre and Joshi, 1997). The union uses its bargaining relationships with the phone companies to convince the companies to establish agreements with contractors to hire qualified workers from its centers, and then the union negotiates an agreement with the contractors or their agents to contribute to common benefit funds. CWA has developed a newly recognized apprenticeship program to qualify dislocated workers, disadvantaged workers, and youth for various kinds of technical work in a rapidly growing field, such as the installation of fiber-optic cable networks. The hope is that a modular design of skill delivery will enable workers to build on what they already know to acquire the skills they need for new jobs in the future.

Extract from E. Parker and J. Rogers, 'Sectoral training initiatives in the US', in P. Culpepper and D. Finegold (eds), *The German Skills Machine* (New York: Berghahn Books, 1999), pp. 339–40, 346–7.

Reference in text:

F. Carre and P. Joshi, *Building Stability for Transient Workforces: Exploring the Possibilities of Intermediary Institutions Helping Workers Cope with Labor Market Instability*, Working paper No. 1 (Cambridge, MA: Radcliffe Public Policy Institute, 1997).

and credentialized education system. Importantly, while the overall US system is accurately described as predominantly market-led, institutions are not entirely absent in the determination of training provision. Government legislation has encouraged training among socially excluded groups, and the high incidence of formal training in unionized companies reflects the strong role of trade unions in many sectors.

The UK: a market-led, weak ILM/weak OLM approach

The UK is illustrative of a country that has overturned its traditional national system of training in favour of an as yet unclear hybrid approach. Until the 1960s, much of UK industry combined on-the-job training with part-time vocational education, which could be characterized as an OLM approach, having much in common with

Germany (see below), except that the UK system did not generally extend to service sector occupations. Since then, however, the apprenticeship system has been in decline, in contrast with a strengthening of the system in Germany. During the 1970s and up to the mid-1980s, the Manpower Services Commission acted as a centralized tripartite body to coordinate the activities of Industrial Training Boards, which imposed a levy on firms to finance training provision. However, these collectivist institutions were abolished and subsequently replaced by Training and Enterprise Councils, which represented a voluntarist approach to training relying on an alternative decentralized, employer-led model.

The changes during the 1980s were associated with a falling performance with regard to vocational training. By the end of the 1980s, just five per cent of the youth cohort entered apprenticeships, compared to more than 70 per cent in Germany (Marsden and Ryan, 1995). Moreover, in 1990, some 63 per cent of Britain's workforce had no vocational qualifications, compared to 26 per cent of the German workforce (Prais and Beadle, 1991). The poor comparative performance in vocational training is not solely the fault of a failure to properly regulate training. The problem is also interlocked with the short termism of the UK financial system and the low skill bias of its production system (Box 5.3). But these wider problems were exacerbated by an ad hoc approach to vocational education and training throughout the 1980s and the 1990s. Vocational education and training did not receive full attention, at least in comparison to policy commitments to invest in higher education; as a result, a high proportion of school leavers were still entering work with no vocational qualifications. Despite significant levels of Government spending in new areas of training and in subsidies for employer policies of investment in skills provision, a series of new vocational training schemes failed to provide a base for high skills development. For example, major investment during the mid-1980s to establish Youth Training Schemes (YTS) was judged to fail on three counts: the training was at a very low level; it was too firm-specific; and youth trainees tended to be exploited

---

Box 5.3 The low skill bias of UK institutions

The blame for a backward system of VET [vocational education and training] cannot be laid solely at the door of craft unions. It is in large measure attributable to a lack of leadership from management, characterised by short-termism, little interest in productive concerns and an inclination to compete on low price rather than on skill-based quality. Moreover, employers, lacking a capacity for solidarity, have tended towards skill poaching rather than sustained training effort. Both the structure and the voluntarist ethos of the state have prevented state agencies from filling the vacuum left by the representative bodies of capital, and the absence of organisations supportive of high standards of training mediating between the state and the individual firms has impeded policy implementation.

Extract from C. Lane, 'Industrial order and the transformation of industrial relations: Britain, Germany and France compared', in R. Hyman and A. Ferner (eds), *New Frontiers in European Industrial Relations* (Oxford: Blackwell, 1994), p. 172.

by employers, for whom YTS provided a convenient screening method for new recruits. All this happened despite innovation in the certification system for trainees, with the introduction of the 'standards based' rather than 'time served' National Vocational Qualifications (NVQs) in 1986. These were intended to provide national certification, with standards for each sector defined by employers. But, again, NVQs faced criticism: low entry level standards, a focus on discrete rather than flexible tasks, and variation of standards across employers have been highlighted (Senker, 1996).

The Government's introduction of the Modern Apprenticeship in 1993 and the Accelerated Modern Apprenticeship in 1996 provides some evidence of a potential revival in vocational training (see Box 5.4). By the late 1990s, over 70 sectors (covering industry and services) had Modern Apprenticeship programmes and a majority of employers surveyed said they would recommend the programme to other employers (Hasluck *et al.*, 1997). However, problems with the quantity and quality of training remain (Gospel, 1998). In particular, the decline in apprentice numbers continued during the late 1990s: it has been estimated that by the early 2000s apprentices would still only constitute around ten per cent of the 16–18 cohort — the same as in the early 1990s (Gospel, 1998: 447). The problem with quality mainly concerns the continued reliance on the NVQ framework, which still suffers from the problems described above.

Box 5.4 Modern Apprenticeships in Britain: why a revival of occupational labour markets may be prevented by market failure and missing institutional links

In an assessment of the performance and prospects of the Modern Apprenticeship, Gospel concludes that policymakers need to address problems of market failure and missing institutional links. If these are not addressed, he warns, then an important opportunity to establish an effective occupational labour market may be missed:

> One of the main problems in terms of market failure lies with employers, in that there are insufficient companies offering good-quality apprentice places ... In part ... the shortfall in places undoubtedly reflects the interrelated problems of high cost and free-riding. Even with government credits for off-the-job training, the costs of apprenticeship to the employer are not insignificant, especially in sectors such as engineering and chemicals, where apprentice wages and training costs are high (Hogarth *et al.*, 1996; Jones, 1986). They are especially high when there is pressure to make skills more transparent and transferable, as is intended with the Modern Apprenticeship, since this increases the risk of poaching ... Put another way, the problem is one of cost-sharing. Investment in general and transferable skills requires an element of cost-sharing between employers and trainees (Stevens, 1994) ... If all or most employers share the costs of training, then no one employer need fear being at a competitive disadvantage. However, in Britain the mechanisms for such cost and risk-sharing between employers are inadequate ...
>
> Crucial here are various forms of inter-firm organization and industry-wide arrangements. In Germany, local chambers of commerce and sectoral employers' organizations introduce an element of common purpose and pressure to support training and prevent free-riding ... By contrast, in Britain the influence of employers' associations and inter-firm training arrangements has declined over the last twenty-five years. Local TECs and industry

Box 5.4 Continued

ITOs (now to be called National Training Organizations) are in part an attempt to remedy this. However, their activities need to be better coordinated, and there may be a case for TECs merging with local chambers of commerce to provide a firmer foundation (Bennett, 1994; Marsden, 1995: 109) ... Employee organizations have been little involved in the Modern Apprenticeship compared with the role they have played in Germany in constructing and enforcing that country's regulatory framework. The TUC [Trades Union Congress] welcomed the Modern Apprenticeship, and some unions were involved in drawing up frameworks, especially in engineering, electrical contracting, printing, steel, and merchant shipping. Other unions, however, have felt insufficiently involved in the creation and running of the system ... In the British context, this raises the policy question for government as to whether employee representatives should have the right to participate in, and agree to, company training arrangements, perhaps based on a legal obligation on employers to inform and consult worker representatives.

Extract from H. Gospel, 'The revival of apprenticeship training in Britain?', *British Journal of Industrial Relations*, 36 (1998): 451–3.

References in text:

T. Hogarth, G. Siora, G. Briscoe and C. Hasluck, *The Net Costs of Training to Employers*, (London: Department for Education and Employment, 1996); I. Jones, 'Apprenticeship training costs in British manufacturing establishments', *British Journal of Industrial Relations*, 24 (1986): 333–62; M. Stevens, 'A theoretical model of on-the-job training with imperfect competition', Oxford *Economic Papers*, 46 (1994): 537–62; R. Bennett, 'New training institutions at the local level', in R. Layard, K. Mayhew and G. Owen (eds) *Britain's Training Deficit*, (Aldershot: Avebury, 1994); D. Marsden, 'A phoenix from the ashes of apprenticeship? Vocational training in Britain', *International Contributions to Labour Studies*, 5 (1995): 87–114.

Despite the plethora of new Government initiatives in training, the design and implementation of programmes is increasingly carried out at the company level — thus having much in common with the US model. The locus of decision-making has shifted from the collective bodies of trade unions and employer associations to the individual employer, and in some cases to the individual employee, for example through the introduction of training credits.[1]

Overall, therefore, the UK system has in recent years followed a market-driven approach to training that has dismantled many of the elements of the traditional occupational labour market system. Indeed, during the 1990s there was debate whether the UK was in fact closer to an ILM model (Marsden and Ryan, 1995). Empirical evidence suggests, however, that there are only limited opportunities for internal career progression and skills development within large firms (Grimshaw *et al.*, 2002). The UK may, therefore, perhaps be more accurately characterized as a weak hybrid of both OLM and ILM principles.

Japan: a firm-based, consensual ILM approach

Japan has acquired a strong reputation for the delivery of high quality firm level training. Like other human resource policies in the large Japanese firm, training is not an isolated strategy, but is embedded in the wider social and institutional context (Morishima, 1995). First, Japan has a well regarded basic education system, which produces high levels of literacy and numeracy among school leavers. The high levels of education achieved prior to labour market participation mean that company expenditures on training can be targeted at developing skills required by the firm. This, in part, explains why in Japan the level of training expenditures, as a share of the total firm wage bill, is significantly lower than in other countries (Dore and Sako, 1989; Lynch, 1994a). The situation contrasts markedly with the US where a sizeable share of training funds is used to teach very basic technical skills and, in some cases, remedial literacy and numeracy skills, due to the weak high school education system (Lynch, 1994a).

Secondly, accounts of the traditional approach to training in Japanese large firms place great emphasis on the presumption of lifetime employment (see below for challenges to this assumption). Combined with a pay scale that matches seniority with pay increments (see Chapter Seven), Japanese firms have traditionally established a strong internal labour market that minimizes employee turnover and provides a sheltered employment environment conducive to training provision (Box 5.5). The assumption of lifetime employment also means that frequent retraining is seen as a necessary part of a normal career. On the other side of the coin, strong social norms discourage poaching of skilled employees in Japan (Lynch, 1994a) and firms are less likely to lay off workers in periods of depressed business conditions; instead Japanese employers tend to use slack periods to undertake additional training (see Chapter Six).

Thirdly, training in the Japanese firm is delivered through a mix of formal and informal, on-the-job and off-the-job methods. Many accounts of training in the Japanese firm emphasize the superiority of their formal off-the-job training

---

Box 5.5 Lifetime commitment in the Japanese firm

In the first systematic study of a Japanese factory to be published in English, James Abegglen coined the phrase 'lifetime commitment' to describe one of the most striking characteristics of the Japanese employment system — the fact that almost the only way to get into a big Japanese firm in the elite half of the dual structure is at the beginning of one's working life, and that having got in one expects to stay until retirement ... It takes two parties to make an employment contract, and it takes certain attitudes on both sides to make for stability of employment of the Hitachi type. On the worker's side is the expectation that he *will* be able to stay with his chosen firm, and the intention to do so, an intention which is conditioned by the fact that staying is the norm of Japanese occupational life and is bolstered by the knowledge that he has a good deal financially to gain by staying on. On the employer's side is an expectation that (provided he offers 'standard' wages and conditions of employment) the workers will *wish* to stay. This expectation is combined with a sense of obligation to provide work for them as long as they do so — an obligation conditioned by the fact that it is one normally assumed by Japanese employers, and sanctioned by the employer's knowledge that he stands to meet tough union resistance and to lose a great deal in work motivation if he departs from the norm.

Extract from R. Dore, *British Factory — Japanese Factory: The Origins of National Diversity in Industrial Relations* (London: Allen and Unwin, 1973), pp. 31, 35.

---

programmes. Many large firms have training schools, which provide induction train-ing (including general instruction in the firm's business, as well as morale and loyalty building), as well as some advanced classroom-based learning. Also common is the provision of pre-promotion courses for mid-level managers and shopfloor supervisors (Dore and Sako, 1989). Of greater importance, however, is the provision of formal and informal on-the-job training (Box 5.6). This includes a range of activities: infor-mal learning from older, more experienced colleagues; formal training in new tech-nical and managerial skills; job rotation (both within and across departments); and small group participation (the well-known 'quality circles'). Dore and Sako (1989: 80) suggest that informal training practices in the large Japanese firm are especially dis-tinctive since they are relatively systematic:

> Japan's very thorough basic education system ... produces people capable of following carefully detailed and complex written instructions ... This means that a lot of learning is based on informal production of job specifications and procedure manuals meticulously written out by supervisors and used as teaching material for self-teaching by newcomers to a job. You do not just stand by Nelly; you read what Nelly has thoughtfully and metic-ulously written about what she knows.

Finally, the forms of training provision interlink with other areas of employment policy and practice within the Japanese firm. For example, the practice of job rota-tion is facilitated by the form of wage-setting arrangement. As we detail in Chapter Seven, because wages are matched with individual workers, rather than with the indi-vidual job (as is found in Western models of the internal labour market), rotation of workers around different jobs does not necessitate changes in pay. The distinctive form of payment system is a major reason, therefore, why Japanese workers experi-ence more job mobility within firms than workers in Western countries (Ohashi and Tachibaniki, 1998).[2] In addition, because workers are trained through job rotation if

---

Box 5.6   On-the-job training in the Japanese firm

On-the-job training is not solely concerned with developing specialist skills within the firm related to a particular task, nor with training people externally at specialist schools and col-leges. If it were, it is possible that specialists trained within the firm might eventually go inde-pendent on the basis of their skills or transfer to another firm. Instead, large firms in post-war Japan had their workers experience various kinds of work within the same workplace. This 'all-rounder' formula was also extended to white-collar workers, who were attached to a suc-cession of different sections and departments within the company as part of a promotion process, which resembled more a 'spiral staircase' than a 'ladder'. This method of forming a wide range of skills useful to the firm's activities is not possible except when premised on a long-term and stable employment relationship. Workers trained in this fashion acquire skills that are more or less specific to the firm, so transfer to another firm would put them at a dis-advantage.

Extract from K. Imai and R. Komiya, 'Characteristics of Japanese firms', in K. Imai and R. Komiya (eds), *Business Enterprise in Japan* (Cambridge, MA: The MIT Press, 1994), p. 24.

an occupation, or job post, becomes obsolete through new technologies, for example, they can be redeployed to other posts instead of being made redundant. This also means that Japanese workers are likely to be less resistant to the introduction of new technologies since it is not associated with a risk of dismissal, as might be the case in other countries (*op. cit.*).

This unique training system is largely applicable to full-time employees of medium and large firms. The strong dualistic character of the Japanese labour market means that many Japanese employees do not enjoy training and development within strong internal labour markets. These so-called 'peripheral workers' — female employees, casual and part-time employees, and employees of small firms — often lack any form of training opportunities (Chalmers, 1989; see below).

Germany: an economy-wide, consensual OLM approach

Where Japan is well known for high quality provision of training within individual large firms, the German system of training is internationally respected for its economy-wide, institutional regulation based on high standards and wide coverage. The design, implementation and financing of vocational training and education depend on a highly regulated system of co-determination involving all three social partners — employers, unions and government. In addition, banks play an essential role in providing long term funding arrangements.

Box 5.7 The Dual System: the lynchpin of German skill provision

Legally enshrined in the training law of 1969 but building on a much older craft training tradition, the dual system is regulated largely by institutions of private governance. The standard apprenticeship contract generally runs from three to three and a half years, depending on the particular specialty, and the content of occupational apprenticeship specialties is determined by negotiations between representatives of employers' associations and unions, with expertise also provided by the staff of the Federal Institute for Vocational Training (BiBB) (Streeck *et al.*, 1987). Responsibility for supervising training in individual companies, approving those companies to train, and testing apprentices at the end of their training falls overwhelmingly to the chambers of industry and commerce or of trades, which are para-public bodies that all employers in a given industry must join (*ibid*; Münch, 1991). Works councils have statutorily embedded rights of codetermination in questions of apprenticeship training at the firm level, although this supervisory power is *de facto* stronger as company size increases (Streeck *et al.*, 1987). Thus, the dual system rests on a legal framework that guarantees that the social partners must negotiate all changes to occupational content and have the wherewithal to monitor the operation of training at the level of the individual company. The state provides only this legal framework and a corps of experts through the BiBB.

Extract from P. Culpepper, 'Still a model for the industrialized countries?', in P. Culpepper and D. Finegold (eds), *The German Skills Machine* (New York: Berghahn Books, 1999), pp. 3–4.

References in text:
W. Streeck, J. Hilbert, K-H. van Kevalaer, F. Maier and H. Weber, *The Role of the Social Partners in Vocational Training and Further Training in the Federal Republic of Germany*, (Berlin: CEDEFOP, 1987); J. Münch, *Vocational Training in the Federal Republic of Germany*, Third edition (Berlin: CEDEFOP, 1991).

The so-called 'dual system' of apprenticeship training is the best known feature of the German training system. The dual model combines off-site general training with competence-based, on-the-job training at the workplace. Typically, apprentices spend three to four days on the job and one to two days in the classroom. Financing of the training costs is split across the tripartite coordinating structure: the Government funds the off-site schooling; the employer funds the costs of workplace training; and crucially, workers fund the period of training indirectly through acceptance of a low trainee rate of pay (typically around one third of the standard adult rate). The relatively low labour costs enhance the probability of employers participating in the formal provision of general skills, by offsetting the risks associated with worker mobility across firms. Moreover, the dual system is supported by a strong legal framework, which provides co-determination rights for the social partners (Box 5.7).

The design of training content is negotiated by the social partners. Qualifications are assured nationwide validity and recognition, and apprenticeships cover a wide range of occupations and professions, from bank clerks and hairdressers to metal workers and those in IT services (see Table 5.2). At the workplace level, works councils are active in the administration of training, as well in ensuring a balance between general and firm-specific skills development (see Chapter Seven). In addition, union representatives are active in the chambers of commerce in the negotiation of sector-wide agreements on the design and provision of training. Thus, unlike the US or the UK, German apprentices are guaranteed a strong 'voice' in ensuring that they enjoy

Table 5.2 Apprenticeships in Germany

Type of worker	Number taking certification exam	Percentage of women apprentices
Salesperson	118,049	71.1
Clerical worker	85,869	77.2
Electrician	57,230	2.0
Mechanic	48,440	1.5
Machinist	35,951	0.6
Mechanical assistant	29,672	99.2
Banking/insurance staff	24,774	53.3
Precision metal-working	22,501	0.4
Personal care	21,911	96.1
Carpenter	21,522	5.3
Mason	20,656	0.1
Technical specialist	14,752	53.4
Painter	14,115	8.7
Clothing manufacturer	13,215	96.7
Baker	12,300	16.5
Gardener	11,038	53.6

Source: Statistisches Jahrbuch für die Bundesrepublik Deutschland (Wiesbaden: Statistisches Bundesamt, 1985), cited in Witte and Kalleberg (1995)

clear advantages in the labour market (Wever, 1995), matching their skills and pay to the demands of their job and to the future prospects of skills development.

France: a state-led, ILM approach

In line with other areas of the French employment system (see Chapter Six), the state plays a strong and active role in the provision of training. As with the UK, there is a strong emphasis on general and academic education and a weak emphasis on vocational training (see Box 5.8). Workplace apprenticeships are uncommon and, where they exist, they are generally seen as an option for the less able, have a very low reputation and are treated as a cost rather than as an investment. This poor reputation has persisted despite a number of policy initiatives to raise their status.

Instead, the bulk of vocational education occurs not in apprenticeships but in full-time state education — the two-year technical lycée track (which leads to the

---

Box 5.8   Vocational training in France

One basic difference between the French and German systems is that in France large firms do not play a direct role in providing basic occupational training, which is acquired either in pubic or private schools or on the job, 98 per cent of the time in small craft shops. Thus basic occupational training, particularly in the case of industrial workers, is completely cut off from the world of big business and has not benefited either from the prestige of the large firms or from the dynamism that might have been imparted to on-the-job training programs by the industrial expansion of the 1960s. While it is true that a few large companies have set up programs to train their workers, these programs have not been integrated into national or regional efforts to train new workers. Rather they have been designed to train workers to fill the needs of a particular firm: to fill certain jobs and to meet the requirements of particular organizations ... In the French system there is a great deal of social homogeneity: more than half of all workers holding the CAP (the basic occupational certificate) are children of farmers or unskilled industrial workers. Practically none are children of fathers in intellectual professions. There is not much difference in the social background of those with low-level educational credentials and those with basic occupational certification: for example, 50 per cent of those with a CEP (elementary school certificate) are children of farmers or unskilled workers, compared with 48.5 per cent of those with a CAP (basic apprenticeship certificate). Thus acceptance in a job-training program does not constitute social selection but is rather one path that may be chosen by students whose social and academic position has already been determined as inferior ... Thus basic occupational training in France suffers from a social homogeneity whose connotations are negative, disparity of institutional support, and divergence in the educational background of entering trainees. These factors in large part account for the failure of the system to respond to social change or to develop new methods of teaching, and they tend to limit its social and educational importance. In turn the system's unresponsiveness tends to discourage trainees and reduce the effectiveness of teaching. Many drop out, and the failure rate on examinations is extremely high. The total attrition rate (ratio of number of trainees not awarded certificates to total number entering training) is nearly 60 per cent in France compared with 10 per cent in Germany.

Extract from M. Maurice, F. Sellier and J-J. Silvestre, *The Social Foundations of Industrial Power* (Cambridge, MA: MIT Press, 1986), pp. 35–6.

---

qualification known as the technical baccalaureate) — where the emphasis is placed on the theoretical aspect of vocational education. But this route towards vocational training has not acquired the level of status associated with the dual system route in Germany; far from it. Entrants to these colleges tend to come from families of lower occupational class status, and their certificates send a very different signal to employers in comparison to those of entrants to the labour market who come through one of the *grandes écoles*. The distinctiveness of these two routes is an important component underpinning the strong stratification of the French workforce by level and type of skill (Maurice *et al.*, 1986).

As in the UK, the system of production in France may act as a disincentive to firms to invest in training provision. Large French firms have failed to establish a satisfactory alternative to Fordist-type production (Boyer, 1995). Responses to changing market pressures traditionally depend on management strategy rather than on the input from a broadly skilled manual workforce. Unlike in the UK system, however, in France the state plays a stronger and arguably more creative role. A new 'training system' was established in response to longstanding concerns over the lack of firm training, as well as to evidence of employer dissatisfaction with the school-based training route which was seen as far removed from their specific needs of production. The centrepiece of the system is the 'pay-or-play' training levy, which requires firms to spend a specified fraction of their wage bill on training or pay the difference. When it was introduced in 1971, the aim was to improve the volume of firm provision of vocational training, and requirements included a specific emphasis on off-the-job general training. Over the 1980s and 1990s, the law was adapted in a number of ways: it incorporated a balance of expenditures on both general and firm-specific training; it was widened to include small and medium-sized enterprises; the levy charged was raised from its initial level of 0.8 per cent of payroll costs to 1.5 per cent in 1998; and a training tax credit was introduced (see Box 5.9). Alongside these changes, actual training expenditures as a percentage of the wage bill more than doubled during the 1970s and 1980s to almost three per cent by 1989 (Culpepper, 1999).

Nevertheless, the state-led system of encouraging firm training faces a number of criticisms. First, research evidence shows that much of the new investment targets managers and technical workers, rather than unskilled workers, and that a much higher proportion of employees in large firms benefits from training compared to those in small firms, suggesting that smaller firms prefer to pay the training levy without engaging in any training activity (Greenhalgh, 1999; Lynch, 1994a). Hence, subsidies and tax relief may need to be complemented by additional monitoring of who benefits from training provision. Second, the dominant role of the Ministry of Education has traditionally restricted the extent of decision-making power shared by the social partners. The development of qualification contracts (*contrats de qualification*) was intended to resolve this problem but in some sectors it grants greater power to employer bodies, resulting in a strong emphasis on firm-specific training without the breadth of skills required for transferability (Culpepper, 1999).

Box 5.9 'Pay-or-play': the French training levy system

The legal obligations

Firms with ten or more workers must contribute 1.5 per cent of payroll to training, broken down as:

- 0.9 per cent to the firm's training plans for any workers
- 0.4 per cent to alternating work/school training for new entrants
- 0.2 per cent to individual training (the *congé individuel de formation* or CIF programme).

Firms with ,10 workers must contribute 0.15 per cent of payroll to training.

How firms meet their legal obligations

0.9 per cent: firm's training plans

Direct provision of training for their workers: this is either supplied in-house or may be contracted from a training organization, but there are rules about what qualifies as training and which organizations qualify as providers. Providers include the employers' training associations or Associations de Formation (ASFOs).

Paying into a mutual fund or Fonds d'Assurance Formation (FAFs): these are jointly administered employer-union organizations.

0.4 per cent: alternating training

Firms pay this contribution into Organismes Mutualisateurs de l'Alternance (OMAs) which deal with youth and labour market entry training.

0.2 per cent: individual training leave

Firms pay this contribution into Organismes Paritaires Agréés au titre de Congé Individuel de Formation (OPACIFs), which deal with worker-initiated demands for training.

Additionally, a small percentage of training funds can go to designated information research organizations. A last resort is to give the funds to the Treasury; this has fallen into abeyance.

Extract from C. Greenhalgh, 'Adult vocational training and Government policy in France and Britain', *Oxford Review of Economic Policy*, 15 (1999): 101.

The performance of countries' training systems assessed

This brief review of different national approaches to education and training has illustrated the diversity and complexity of policy and practice in this area. Importantly, this diversity is associated with differences in outcomes, or 'payoffs', for the employee, the firm and the economy as a whole. In the following discussion we assess the performance of countries' training systems against different criteria. We begin with the coverage of training provision and the scope for long term employee skill development.

Training coverage and long term skill development

From our selected country examples, we find that there is a tendency for coverage of training programmes to be higher in consensus-led systems and lower in market-led systems. In the case of the market-led US system, the absence of an economy-wide or sector-wide coordinated strategy of training is associated with a polarization of the skills base. On the one hand, the highly respected system of higher education (producing the highest proportion of college and university graduates in the world), together with strong firm-based investment in management training, generates a large stock of highly educated labour. On the other hand, a large proportion of the workforce do not acquire academic or vocational qualifications, and encounter few opportunities for skills development within firms; even among those who do acquire vocational qualifications (at secondary or post-secondary school level), this investment does not always lead to higher pay or improved status in the jobs market (Wever, 1995: 100). Similarly, in the UK, despite a well regarded university sector, there are relatively large numbers of employees with few, or low level, vocational credentials. Moreover, both countries suffer from the problem of poaching (Cappelli, 1995; Crouch et al., 1999) — due, in large part, to the lack of regulation (whether state-led, or through co-determination) designed to address the public good dimension to training provision (see above). As a result, firms face considerable disincentives to cover the financing of the reproduction of a high skills base.[3]

In contrast, the consensus-led models identified with Japan and Germany are associated with a wide coverage of vocational training, resulting in a large share of highly skilled workers. In Japan, regular workers in medium sized and large firms benefit both from high levels of initial qualifications and from high levels of task-specific company training. As noted above, there is a strongly dualistic character to the provision of training for Japanese workers. However, there is some evidence that company training coverage is extended through Government subsidies to small firms' in-house training programmes (Lynch 1994a). In Germany, vocational education is the most important component of the education and training system, with a majority of all workers undertaking two to three years of vocational training. In both countries, the policy of achieving a strong skills base is interlinked with the national objective of maintaining a strong export reputation. Such a coordinated effort is clearly more likely in the German or Japanese system than in the decentralized system of the US, where it is very difficult to coordinate individual company efforts to meet national objectives.

It would appear, therefore, that it is more the form of regulation that determines the extent of training coverage, and not the distinction between OLM and ILM principles of labour market organization *per se*. For example, comparing the three countries with training systems loosely characterized by internal labour market principles, there are major differences in the extent of company-provided training. Comparative data show that a relatively small proportion of US workers receives formal company training compared to Japan and France — around 17 per cent of US workers compared to around 30 per cent in both France and Japan (Lynch, 1994a; Figure 3.1). Moreover, among workers in the US who receive training, most are technical or managerial employees who have graduated from university; very few workers who are not university graduates benefit from formal training, at around four per cent (*op. cit.*).

The distinction between the OLM and ILM systems of labour market organization has potentially more power to explain cross-national variations in opportunities for skills development over the working life. In Japan, the highly regulated internal labour markets in large firms provide a strong basis for internal advancement for all employees (see also Chapter Seven). In France, while there are strong internal labour market principles, there is a tendency towards polarization of opportunities, largely due to the gap between the high level of vocational training received by managers and the unsystematic approach to training experienced by manual workers (Maurice *et al.*, 1986). Where occupational labour market principles prevail, mobility patterns are more likely to involve inter-firm transfer. In Germany, however, there is evidence that this is not always the case, since strong OLM principles coincide with strong ILM principles within firms that provide opportunities for internal career advancement. After completion of the German apprenticeship in engineering, for example, the internal job ladder provides an internal promotion path for workers along a vertical hierarchy of skills from apprentice to skilled worker, to master-craftworker or technician, and on to professional grades. The internal opportunities for skills development provide an incentive for the employee to remain within the firm, despite the opportunities for inter-firm transfers guaranteed by acquisition of general training credentials.

The school-to-work transition

A country's system of vocational training has an important influence on the way in which young people move between school and work. In Japan, because first-job recruitment tends to be career recruitment for lifetime employment, employers tend to be more interested in general qualities of intelligence and capacity for effort, than in specific kinds of knowledge. As a result employers often build links with schools, and this both provides routes into employment and facilitates the recruitment and selection process (Dore and Sako, 1989; Ryan and Büchtemann, 1996). In Germany, a majority of school leavers enter work through the 'dual system' of apprenticeship training. The bridge from school into work is relatively transparent and accessible, but also relatively long due to the highly institutionalized form of vocational training. In countries with a market-led form of regulation, school leavers appear likely to face a short transition into paid employment. However, this transition is associated with a high degree of uncertainty over the quality and quantity of training provision. The unclear and risky nature of the transition may hinder an effective initial matching of worker characteristics with the demands of entry-level jobs, leading to 'job-hopping', interspersed with recurrent periods of unemployment.

The impact of the education and training system on the school-to-work transition takes on greater political importance in a context of high levels of youth unemployment, which has been driving policy initiatives in all countries. For all OECD countries, the rate of unemployment among young persons is typically higher than the average for all ages. There are numerous explanations for this. Some argue that the higher rate of youth unemployment is an outcome of the 'job queue effect': since young people have less experience and fewer qualifications than older people, employers may rank them at the bottom of the queue for new job positions. Another explanation suggests that youths in work are more sensitive to business cycle fluctuations, both because they are more dependent on new vacancies, which are halted during a recession, and because they are more likely to be made redundant where firm custom and practice follow the norm of 'last hired, first fired'. However, while both ideas offer possible explanations for the higher rates of youth unemployment, there is little that explains why the positive differential is high in some countries, yet low in others. A focus on the role of national systems of education and training is more useful in this respect since a high level of youth unemployment signals a breakdown in the secure transition from school to work.

Despite considerable differences in the nature of the school-to-work transition, there are some common patterns and trends across most advanced capitalist countries. In general, compulsory schooling ends at the age of 16, and since the 1970s the average length of the school-to-work transition has been prolonged due to rising participation in vocational training programmes and the expansion of higher education (see Table 4.1 in Chapter Four). It must be said, however, that attempts to measure and compare the length of transition are problematic. The OECD definition underpinning the length of transition takes the end of the transition to occur when 50 per cent of the cohort has entered employment. Consequently, countries with a low employment rate, such as Spain and Italy (where low rates of female employment pull down the average rate), appear to have relatively long school-to-work transitions. Also, a focus on the average length of transition obscures the considerable diversity of experience among the youth within a country — a problem that is greater in countries such as the UK and the US where there is a relatively high degree of polarization. This may explain why the average length of transition for both the US and Germany appears to be similar, at around five years in both cases, despite the fact that young people who opt out, or are excluded, from higher education face a much shorter transition from compulsory schooling into paid employment in the US compared to Germany.

Quantitative measures are thus of little use without a clear comparative assessment of the way different institutional arrangements shape the nature of the school-to-work transition in different countries. A focus on the differences between the US and Germany is illustrative, since they sit at opposite ends of the spectrum: for school leavers who do not enter higher education the transition into work is relatively long in Germany and short in the US. By international standards, the German system of vocational training is seen as an effective way to assist young people in the transition from school to work. A majority of German school leavers enrol in post-secondary vocational schools (one to four years) or apprenticeship training (three to four years) across a wide range of occupations (see Box 5.7). Relatively few young people enter the job market with no post-secondary qualifications, reflecting strong societal norms to the effect that participation in vocational training enhances job opportunities and that a more hurried move into low skilled employment brings only short term benefits. Overall, it seems that the system provides a stable and effective bridge into a satisfactory job with opportunities for career advancement. Nevertheless, the relatively long transition may be interpreted as a wasteful delay compared to a market-led matching process, particularly where the long period of acquiring skills may be accompanied by a fall in demand for those skills.

In the market-led system of the US, formal programmes of vocational training for new labour market entrants are the exception rather than the rule; less than two per cent of school leavers enrol in an apprenticeship (Büchtemann et al., 1993). Moreover, the short transition from a non-working student to a non-studying worker is typically associated with high job turnover, frictional unemployment and a pattern of intensive 'job shopping'. As a result young people in the US avoid the potentially wasteful delay of a long transition into paid employment, but there are problems with the market-led matching process. In particular, there may be difficulties in establishing a productive matching between job applicants and jobs, due to the absence of universally recognized vocational qualifications that would send clear signals to prospective employers. However, the US system of education and training is characterized by one notable success: more than half of a youth cohort experience an effective bridge into high skilled, high paid work though the system of higher education (either a four-year programme in a college or university, or two years at a community college). In Germany, participation in higher education is lower: around one in three school leavers there enters a higher education institution — either a university or a technical college (Fachhochschule).

These differences in institutionalized bridges between school and work directly shape patterns of post-secondary school labour market participation. A study of school leavers in the US and Germany found that twelve months after leaving school, half the US cohort were in work compared to just 11 per cent in Germany; ten per cent of US youth were unemployed compared to four per cent in Germany. In stark contrast to the US, nearly four out of five school leavers in Germany were still enrolled in some kind of post-secondary education or training (Büchtemann et al., 1993). Patterns of youth participation in the US and Germany converge only ten to 12 years after leaving compulsory schooling. Over this 12-year period, some 99 per cent of young German people had participated in some form of post-secondary education or training, compared to the situation in the US where almost one in three did not receive any form of education or training after leaving school, and nearly half (46 per cent) entered the labour market without a certificate or a degree. While young German people clearly experience a relatively long transition between school and the labour market, there is a relatively strong link between completion of vocational training and entry into paid employment in Germany: around 70 per cent of trainees entered work directly without experience of unemployment, and 80 per cent of these found work with their training firm (ibid.). At the other end of the US youth labour market, a higher proportion of young people entered higher education than in Germany (52 per cent and 16 per cent, respectively); although these high figures are offset by the high dropout rate in the US, so that the proportion of youth who actually attained a college degree was 32 per cent (*ibid.*).

Pressures for change

Whatever their current training arrangements, all countries appear to face a common set of pressures for change. These range from adjustment to the rapid proliferation of new technologies and new systems of production to global competitive pressures to implement 'best practice'. Institutional differences still matter, however, in shaping how an economy, or an individual firm, responds to the new challenges (see Figure 2.1 in Chapter Two).

The impact of these pressures for change may be to generate some unexpected outcomes. For example, even though a market-led form of institutional regulation tends to generate uneven or low levels of training provision, there is some evidence that in a period of rapid change such a system may — because of its decentralized decision-making system — allow greater company flexibility to adapt and respond. In contrast, the consensus-led form of regulation — particularly when coupled with an occupational labour market structure as in Germany — may prove an obstacle to company flexibility, since the process of negotiating change is likely to be slow. The comparison is not quite so straightforward, however, as the greater capacity of consensus-led systems to reproduce a high skills base may arguably still provide a stronger foundation for the introduction of new production systems and adaptation to new product markets and technologies (see Streeck's idea of 'redundant capacities' presented in Chapter Two). The following analysis explores these issues in more detail, in the context of a number of pressures for change faced by all advanced capitalist countries.

Technical change

The rapid pace of technical change and, in particular, the revolution in information and communication technologies (ICT) present a number of challenges to existing forms of work organization and systems of production (OECD, 1996b). First, a number of studies suggest that ICT is associated with an accelerated pace of innovation in new product and process developments (Foray and Lundvall, 1996), leading to pressures on firms to adapt or transform work practices and job categories; which, in turn, generate the problem of having to continually update training systems. Second, the recent pattern of technological change is associated with a bias in favour of job creation among the skilled workforce (Juhn *et al.*, 1993; Katz and Murphy, 1992; Krueger, 1993; OECD, 1994a, b), providing an additional incentive for firms to 'buy' rather than 'make' skills, as the potential costs of upskilling low skilled recruits rise.

For countries where training is organized through a consensus-led form of regulation, any change or adaptation in the system of training is likely to be a slow process, since it involves a complex process of negotiation between social partners. However, the price of not adapting is high since the whole system may fall into disrepute. The evidence for Germany, perhaps the clearest example of a country at the centre of such a debate, is mixed. On the one hand, a number of studies and political commentators argue that useful lessons could be learned from the US, where a spirit of entrepreneurialism fosters greater spontaneity in adapting to change; on the other hand, research points to evidence of change within the German dual system, not least in the proliferation of new occupational profiles ('ordinances') for apprenticeships (see Box 5.10).

Box 5.10 Adapt or perish: the German Dual System versus the challenge of new information technologies

Lessons for Germany from the US

With some notable exceptions — such as the rapidly growing software giant SAP — Germany has been much less successful in developing high-technology or global service firms than the US and UK ... The German culture does not appear to reward risk-taking (cf. Streeck, 1996); for example, dropping out of university to start a business is a common, often glorified route to success in the US computer industry, even if the initial company fails. In Germany, such a step would be viewed as career suicide ... Likewise, the gradual pace at which apprenticeships are changed is often out of sync with the rapidly changing skill needs of high-technology entrepreneurs. Traditional apprenticeships and *Meister*-level qualifications do provide a broad foundation of skills that help many individuals, in sectors ranging from hotels and catering to machine shops, to start their own business. Even in these cases, however, the preparation for entrepreneurs might be enhanced by emulating some of the most successful work-preparation programs in the US and UK, where young people learn by starting their own small business (Stern *et al.* 1995).

Extract from D. Finegold, 'The future of the German skill-creation system', in P. Culpepper and D. Finegold (eds), *The German Skills Machine*, (New York: Berghahn Books, 1999), pp. 425–6.

References in text:

W. Streeck, 'Lean production in the German automobile industry: a test case for convergence theory', in S. Berger and R. Dore (eds), *National Diversity and Global Capitalism*, (Ithaca, NY: Cornell University Press, 1996); D. Stern, N. Finkelstein, J. Stone, J. Latting and C. Dornsife, *School-to-Work: Research on Programs in the US* (Washington, DC: Falmer Press, 1995).

Germany ought to re-regulate

Revision processes lasting up to seven years meant that, with a training period of three years, appropriately trained skilled workers would be coming on to the labour market with a 10-year-time-lag ... In 1995, the social partners reached agreement on an accelerated procedure for issuing new ordinances. It was decided that the revision of old occupations should last no more than one year, and the creation of new occupations no more than two years. Since then, the speed with which new ordinances are issued has increased considerably. Thus between 1996 and 1999, 31 new occupations have been defined and 97 have been modernised (BiBB 1999). Critics of the German vocational training system have not yet acknowledged this 'revitalisation'.

Box 5.10 Continued

Four new occupations	Some typical fields of activity
IT electrician	Computer systems, fixed networks, radio networks, terminal and security systems
IT specialist	Commercial technical expert, mathematical and multimedia systems, computing centres, networks, client/server, fixed networks, radio networks
IT system support specialist	Industrial systems, standard systems, technical applications, commercial applications and learning systems
IT officer	Industry, commerce, banking, insurance, hospitals

Source: BMWI (1997), p. 4

These four occupations were developed by the social partners in the record time of only nine months. In 1997 and 1998, there were already 13,585 apprentices training for the new occupations, of whom about half had the *Abitur*.

Extract from G. Bosch, 'Occupational labour markets and structural change', *21st Conference of the International Working Party on Labour Market Segmentation*, Bremen, 9–11 September, 1999a, pp. 19, 21.

References in text:
BiBB (1999) *Neue und Modernisierte Ausbaildungsberufe* (Bonn and Berlin: Kurzbeschreibungen, 1999); BMWI, *Die Neuen IT-Berufe-Zukunftssicherung durch Neue Ausbildungsberufe in der Informations under Telekommunikationstechnik* (Bonn: BMWI, 1997).

For market-led forms of regulation, changes in ICT also present problems. The risk to investment in firm-specific training is raised considerably by the prospects of technologies becoming outdated prior to employers recouping the costs of training. This risk, combined with the potential need to invest in higher levels of training expenditure to meet the demands of skill-intensive work systems, may encourage firms to abandon traditional internal labour market systems. Some firms may use subcontracting or establish network relations with other firms in order to gain access to skills (Castells, 1996). Others may simply poach ready-made skills from other firms. However, as argued above, an increase in poaching generates a vicious cycle since it strengthens the disincentive to train caused by the fear of poaching. In a situation where large numbers of firms abandon training provision the consequence is a failure of the economy as a whole to reproduce the skills base of the workforce.

Consensus-led systems such as that of Germany face a potential problem of short term adjustment to new technologies, but the country's regulatory system enables the formulation of a coordinated strategy to reproduce the stock of skills among the workforce — a condition that is absent in market-led systems like those of the US or the UK.

Flexibilization of the labour market

Pressures on firms to adopt more flexible employment policies and practices are associated with the casualization of work, involving 'downsizing' programmes, greater use of temporary workers and a weakening of regulations around hiring and firing (see Chapter Six). The problem is that pressures for greater flexibility, leading to the deregulation of labour markets, may conflict with strategies of upskilling. As Crouch (1997: 369) argues:

> A deregulation approach and an enskilling one tend to embody opposing logics. In the former case all emphasis is on ease of disposal; for the latter is it important that employers regard employees as a long term investment resource, since a high rate of inter-firm mobility usually makes employers reluctant to carry out much training.

Investment in skills arguably requires a sheltered environment, yet flexibilization increases the risk of job loss considerably. Moreover, the incentive for employees to participate in a training programme is also reduced, as greater uncertainty over job security will tend to make employees more skeptical of the promise of training with deferred rewards.

The deregulation approach has gone furthest in the market-led systems of training that characterize the US and the UK. The problem appears to have been 'solved' by a growing segmentation in the labour market between insiders, with access to enskilling opportunities, and outsiders, who are either unemployed or in insecure jobs with few chances for upward mobility. However, in a context of growing use of subcontracting and franchising even so-called 'insiders' may lack the comfort of a sheltered environment; organizations are redefining and reshaping their core activities and may be unwilling to commit themselves to high training costs even for those currently at the centre of their operations. Crouch (1997: 375) again provides useful insight:

> ... it is also possible that, in the present context of intensified competitiveness, some firms are seeking to discover how far they can proceed with a policy of 'eating one's cake and having it': seeking strong but *unreciprocated* commitment and loyalty from staff. Anxieties about the constant pressure to demonstrate to shareholders adequate achievements in down-sizing and delayering lead managers to do this, these managers themselves being vulnerable to redundancy through these processes.

Unemployment

Since the 1970s, all advanced capitalist countries have experienced periods of relatively high levels of unemployment. Even among those countries, such as the US and the UK, which were relatively successful in reducing unemployment towards the end of the 1990s, past high levels may have altered the set of options available to firms and thus have had a longer term impact on policies of training provision.

In general, access to a large pool of available labour potentially allows firms to recruit skilled or experienced workers without confronting the long term question of how to develop more considered answers to their own skill needs. Under these conditions, firms are more likely to withdraw from practices of internal training provision designed to upskill inexperienced entrants to the firm, thereby reducing opportunities for new, unskilled job seekers. Once the labour market tightens, it is not clear to what extent firms will reinvest in new training provision, particularly in a context of downwards pressure on costs.

Again, the adverse impact of unemployment pressures is most obvious in countries with market-led regulatory forms of training. Where individual firms are responsible for designing and implementing training programmes that meet their own requirements, it is not clear how the collective needs of the hard-to-employ will be met where firms face a considerable incentive to reduce training provision for new entrants. High levels of unemployment, or pockets of persistent long term unemployment, may mean that governments seek to achieve two different and potentially contradictory objectives through their training policies. First they need to upskill the workforce to improve the country's international competitiveness; second, however, they may seek to use the training system as a means of integrating the unemployed into work. Training aimed at integration of often less skilled workers may lead to a downgrading of the skill content of training programmes and leave employers dissatisfied with the standards of workers provided through state-funded training schemes. This was largely the experience of the UK in the early 1980s. The Youth Training Scheme was primarily designed to integrate hard-to-employ young workers, but these schemes by and large took the place of the apprenticeship programmes which had provided a better basis for the development of a reasonably high skilled workforce.

Globalization

The growing power and size of multinational corporations (MNCs) mean that for a significant share of a country's workforce, the locus of decision-making around training provision is at a level beyond the reach of the influence of the nation state. For many MNCs, training needs are considered on a global level, irrespective of either national systems of vocational training or collective goals of upskilling. The dual problem they confront (see Chapter Eight) is how both to meet competitive pressures to reduce overheads and to improve access to a trained workforce and a sophisticated financial and communications infrastructure. Countries with consensus-led systems may offer abundant supplies of skilled labour, but opportunities to minimize labour costs may be greater in market-led systems where individual firms enjoy greater autonomy.

The international competitiveness of Germany has been called into question by its slow growth and high unemployment during the 1990s. Some observers argue that slow growth reflects a failure of existing systems of production and training to adapt in line with international 'best practice' in production, such as teamwork and continuous improvement processes. Strong craft identities among workers — intrinsic to the 'dual system' of training — are said to impede development of new forms of production that involve close cooperation and greater flexibility (Sabel, 1995; see Box 5.11). The recession also led many German manufacturing firms to lay off workers and to outsource production abroad, leading many to refrain from hiring new apprentice recruits. In fact, the sharp decrease in the supply of apprenticeship places during the 1990s has been accompanied by a decrease in demand (partly because of falling birth rates), leading some to recommend internal migration of school leavers from the former East Germany to enter apprenticeships in the former West Germany (Wagner, 1999). Finally, the training system has been under considerable strain following the decision to transfer the model to the former East Germany, despite the absence of high price, high quality markets and thus the lack of conditions for self-sustaining growth (Carlin and Soskice, 1997; Box 5.11).

Box 5.11 The German training system in crisis?

The problem of the craft-based system

The disadvantage of *Beruf*-based hierarchy and fragmentation in the German system comes to light under conditions of extremely rapid product and technological change. Each time a new product or a new technology is introduced — as opposed to an old one that is customized for a customer — the various roles that each of the categories of skill will play in the manufacture and development of the new product must be bargained out. Each will want to participate; each will have its own ideas and solutions; each will defend its turf against encroachments from the others. Electrical masters and technicians will fight with mechanical ones both on the shopfloor and in the design studios ... This is what is going on in German factories today. Jurisdictional disputes driven by the need to accelerate new product introduction at a moment when the boundaries between traditional *Berufe* are being technically eroded is driving up the cost and driving down the quality of products. Such jurisdictional conflicts do not exist in the Japanese or most advanced American systems because there are no fixed jurisdictions or occupational identities. The Japanese can combine the work of development departments and production (simultaneous engineering) and they can continually redesign their production processes to accommodate new products by utilizing U-shaped lines and group work organization.

Extract from G. Herrigel and C. Sabel, 'Craft production in crisis: industrial restructuring in Germany during the 1990s', in P. Culpepper and D. Finegold (eds), *The German Skills Machine* (New York: Berghahn Books, 1999), pp. 93–4.

The problems of unification

Since unification, an immense further training effort has been undertaken to update the quality of vocational qualifications to the more modern technology of the Western world and to the more demanding aspects of work, e.g., to enable workers to accomplish a broad range of complex tasks without guidance and to retrain those who have lost their jobs in the restructuring process (Andresen, 1992; Wagner, 1993; Grünert and Lutz, 1995). The institutions that support training in western Germany — such as the chambers, which supervise apprenticeship training (Franz and Soskice, 1995; Soskice, 1994; Streeck *et al.*, 1987) — had to be built up in the new federal states. Trade unions and employer associations moved to eastern Germany, and experts from

---

Box 5.11   Continued

the western German chambers helped to set up the new system and trained the trainers. To compensate for existing deficits in the training facilities, external training centers were instituted in eastern Germany, at a cost of 450 million DM in 1991. Despite great efforts, the number of apprenticeship places was not sufficient, even in 1991, when the Treuhand kept many companies operating: 9200 school-leavers had to be trained in external places that year. In 1992–3, the state provided 11 billion DM for retraining and further training. Large investments were made to bring vocational schools up-to-date.

Measures to ease the strain

A number of measures have been implemented designed to ease the strain on the German training system:

- designing apprenticeship occupations for new markets and updating existing qualifications; [see also Box 5.10 above]
- greater co-operation among companies to complement each other's capabilities, sharing apprenticeship and on-site training;
- external training centers set up to fill gaps in company's training capacity.

Extract from K. Wagner, 'The German apprenticeship system under strain', in P. Culpepper and D. Finegold (eds), *The German Skills Machine* (New York: Berghahn Books, 1999), p. 54.

References in text:

B·Andresen, 'Bildungsaktivitäten des Daimler-Benz-Konzerns in den neuen Bundesländern', in W. Schlaffke and R. Zedler (eds), *Wirtschaftlicher Wandel im Neuen Bundesgebiet und Strategien der Qualifizierung*, (Cologne: Deutscher Instituts-Verlag, 1992); K. Wagner, 'Qualifikationsniveau in Ostdeutschen Betrieben, Bestand — Bewertung — Anpassungsbedarf', *Zeitschrift für Betriebswirtschaft*, 63 (1993): 129–45; H. Grünert and B. Lutz (1995) 'East German labour market in transition: segmentation and increasing disparity', *Industrial Relations Journal*, 1 (1995): 19–31; W. Franz and D. Soskice (1995) 'The German apprenticeship system', in F. Buttler, W. Franz, R. Schettkat and D. Soskice (eds), *Institutional Frameworks and Labour Market Performance*, (London: Routledge, 1995); D. Soskice, 'Reconciling markets and institutions: the German apprenticeship system', in L. M. Lynch (ed.), *Training and the Private Sector: International Comparisons*, (Chicago: University of Chicago Press, 1994), pp. 25–60; W. Streeck, J. Hilbert, K-H. van Kevalaer, F. Maier and H. Weber, *The Role of the Social Partners in Vocational Training and Further Training in the Federal Republic of Germany* (Berlin: CEDEFOP, 1987).

The success of the Japanese systems of production and training has also been called into question by pressures to weaken job-for-life practices within large firms. The ongoing recession in manufacturing during the late 1990s forced many large companies to make workers redundant, throwing the tradition of lifetime commitment into disrepute. Moreover, the principle of job-for-life was called into question by an important policy drawn up by the Japan Federation of Employers' Associations (*Nikkeiren*) in 1995, recommending its modification in light of the need to adapt Japanese management styles to pressures for change (Grønning, 1998). Such changes clearly pose a threat to 'culturalist' studies of Japanese employment, which emphasize the enduring quality of its traditional value systems, in which lifetime employment and 'welfare corporatism' are seen as crucial elements. However, the extent to which large companies change their longstanding practices may depend upon how the costs of the economic slowdown are distributed among large, primary sector companies and 'peripheral' companies (small firms and subcontractors; see Box 5.12). Where employers protect job security in the large firms by using supplier firms as a buffer, there is less threat to the traditional internal labour market arrangement for organizing workplace-based training.

> **Box 5.12** Core-periphery work in the Japanese employment system
>
> In an early treatment of dualism in the Japanese employment system, Littler characterizes firms in the primary and secondary sectors as follows:
>
> > [large, primary sector firms] exercise control over the product market and help to structure the labour market itself ... training and job advancement systems are incorporated within the body of the enterprise such that an internal labour market is formed.
> > [smaller, secondary sector firms] have to face frequent instabilities in the product market and, consequently, there is considerable instability of jobs, little training or prospect of advancement, and a high turnover among the workforce. (Littler, 1983: 130)
>
> Conditions in the primary sector are linked to conditions in the secondary sector. Crawcour (1977) argues that the dual structure facilitates a 'comfortable relationship' between management and labour in the large, primary sector firm. Similarly, Kōshiro (1983) suggests that the dual structure is indispensable to the practice of lifetime commitment in large firms. In a thorough study of the 'peripheral workforce' in Japan, Chalmers argues that the interrelationship between employment conditions in the two sectors is the consequence of particular subcontracting relationships between large and small firms, and between small firms and smaller firms, and so on:
>
> > ... large firms, while retaining production control, relegate work that is labour-intensive to smaller firms. In the smaller firms, labour costs were minimized, and putting out work to sub-sub-sub contractors and contract labour was extensively practiced ... Problems such as lower wages, inferior working conditions, and unstable employment, which are not endemic in Japan's large-enterprise sector, were features of the smaller-firm environments ... any isolated eruption of dissent is not likely to affect major firms or hold them to ransom because networks of part suppliers and subcontractors are so widely cast and competitors are in such abundance. (Chalmers, 1989: 168–70)
>
> From this perspective, large Japanese firms manage fluctuations in business conditions by adjusting terms and conditions with supplier firms. This presents them with an opportunity to retain internal labour market conditions among the core workers in the primary sector and, therefore, to prevent the collapse of strong workplace-based training provision.
>
> References in text:
>
> C. Littler, 'A comparative analysis of managerial structures and strategies', in H. F. Gospel and C. Littler (eds), *Managerial Strategies and Industrial Relations: An Historical and Comparative Study* (London: Heinemann, 1983); E. S. Crawcour, *The Japanese Employment System: Past, Present and Future* (Canberra: Australia–Japan Research Centre, Australian National University, 1977); K. Kōshiro, 'The quality of working life in Japanese factories', in S. Taishiro (ed.), *Contemporary Industrial Relations in Japan* (Madison, WI: University of Wisconsin Press, 1983); N. Chalmers, *Industrial Relations in Japan: The Peripheral Workforce* (London: Routledge, 1989).

Conclusions

Drawing on the conceptual framework of internal and occupational labour markets, this chapter has compared the systems of education and training found in five countries — the US, the UK, Japan, France and Germany. These national systems provide evidence of both strong and weak forms of internal and occupational labour markets, as well as hybrid forms composed of elements of both types. Vocational training is regulated differently in each of these countries. Here, we distinguished three forms, that of market-led, consensus-led and state-led forms of regulation.

The chapter has emphasized the tensions and contradictions within national systems, as well as the external pressures for change and adaptation. New technologies and the globalization of markets and industry structure pose challenges to all systems; the form and extent of the response are likely to differ according to the way vocational training is regulated. Moreover, a challenge to the system of training may equally require adaptation in interlocking national systems of production, wage-setting arrangements or the wider regulation of employment rights. As such, the question of how countries adapt training to meet future skill needs is an issue that encompasses the wider employment and production system.

Notes

1 A number of large organizations in the UK have introduced training credits for individual workers, which take the form of a voucher to be spent on a range of accredited training programmes. In some cases, the list of training programmes may be limited to the specific needs of the organization, but in others it may include a relatively broad range of options.
2 Ohashi and Tachibaniki (1998) suggest that this compensation principle is consistent with previous traditions that the employer (like the feudal master) is responsible for the livelihood of the employee (serf).
3 Nevertheless, there is one important distinction between the UK and the US. While the workforce in both countries is relatively underskilled and undereducated, the US has been highly successful in pioneering new technology (IT and biotechnology), largely through its dedication to funding research and development.

6

Labour market flexibility and labour market regulation

The management and regulation of labour markets in the OECD economies during the 1980s and 1990s were strongly influenced by the rhetoric and realities of 'labour market flexibility'. Motivated by a concern to improve job creation, reduce unemployment and encourage innovation in new sectors of economic activity, politicians and academics have looked to the apparently deregulated and flexible labour market model of the US to transfer policy solutions to the underperforming EU countries. Publication of *The OECD Jobs Study* in 1994 underlined this view:

> Against this background, the labour market situation has become particularly worrying in Europe, where unemployment has tended to be persistent, ratcheting up in most countries with each recession, and where there is a relatively low rate of employment. This low rate of employment in Europe might perhaps be raised by stronger economic growth, but to what extent this can happen will depend on changes in institutional and other structural factors as well as choices about labour force participation. *There is a contrast with the United States where more flexible labour markets and other structural factors have allowed the creation of many new jobs.* (OECD, 1994b: 60–1, italics added)

Before the validity of this view can be assessed, it is first of all necessary to explore what is meant by the term labour market flexibility.

What is meant by labour market flexibility?

The flexibility of a labour market can be defined as the ability to adapt and respond to change. Box 6.1 identifies a range of indicators usually held to capture the extent of labour market flexibility.[1] However, as is often the case in discussions of employment issues, there are two sides to the argument. Flexibility along one dimension may be a source of rigidity and constraint on another.

The first indicator — employer freedom to hire and fire — allows for the adjustment of employment levels to fit a changing economic environment. In countries

Box 6.1   Indicators of labour market flexibility

Indicator		To adapt and respond to:	Problems
1 Employer freedom to hire and fire	⇒	changes in product markets, technologies, corporate restructuring	Encourages layoffs as short-term response; problems of uncertainty, cost to employee and firm reputation
2 Employer freedom to adjust job offers to new conditions/ employee willingness to accept new terms	⇒	changes in income and employment circumstances	Lack of subsistence income may lead to vicious cycle of precarious work and unemployment
3 Employer and employee freedom to adapt working time arrangements	⇒	non-standard time pressures in product markets and changing distribution of household responsibilities	Employer and employee interests may conflict
4 Employer freedom to adapt form of employment contract	⇒	high uncertainty of pace and direction of technological change and changing product markets	Employers often change form of employment contract to reduce costs rather than to increase efficiency
5 Employer freedom to set wage rates	⇒	changing external, 'market' wage rates and national/ local levels of unemployment	Employers may face 'leapfrogging' in tight labour markets; or difficulties recruiting or retaining staff where wages are cut in line with product markets

where employees enjoy strong employment protection, an employer may be unwilling to take the risk of hiring new labour, even in an upturn, due to the costs associated with firing in the event of unforeseen changes in economic conditions. Such constraints may slow down moves into new product markets and the adoption of new technologies.

However, freedom to hire and fire may also have some negative consequences for labour market performance. Weak employment protection may encourage layoffs during short periods of economic downturn. As well as increasing the flow into unemployment, recurrent downsizing practices may lead to the loss of skills that cannot be easily replaced in the next upturn. There may also be negative impacts on employee morale and motivation and on the firm's ability to attract good quality recruits in the upswing.

A second indicator of labour market flexibility is the ease with which unemployed workers are reabsorbed back into employment. This process is held to be easier if, on the one hand, employers are free to adjust job offers to new economic circumstances, and on the other hand unemployed job seekers are likely to adjust their expectations downwards, in line with the new set of job offers. Generous systems of unemployment benefits may prolong the period of adjustment, encouraging the unemployed to engage in a long period of job search instead of settling for one of the jobs on offer. Yet a process of rapid adjustment can also have its costs. Where unemployment benefits are low or only available for a short period of time, job seekers may be under pressure to accept jobs that do not fit their skills and which offer poor prospects of stable employment. Those who enter work under these conditions may face repeated spells of unemployment interrupted by short spells of unstable and unfulfilling work.

The third indicator shown in Box 6.1 is the flexibility to adapt working time arrangements, from both employer and employee perspectives. The employer seeks freedom to adapt working time arrangements to respond to fluctuations in product demand; to optimize use of machinery and other process technologies within the firm; or to minimize labour costs through, for example removing or avoiding additional wage premia for unsocial working hours. The employer may thus wish to organize a greater proportion of work on a part-time basis, to match peaks and troughs of product or service demand with the size of workforce. Alternatively, working time may be reorganized on a seven-day shift basis in order to consolidate unsocial hours working within the standard working week, thereby reducing wage costs. For the employee, working time flexibility is sought to balance the responsibilities of home and work, or work and personal life. The different interests of the employer and the employee often conflict. Employers seek variable and flexible hours to fit with often unpredictable demands, while employees seek hours to match their personal or family commitments, normally involving predictable or regular schedules, to enable them to plan their lives.

A fourth indicator of labour market flexibility is freedom for employers to determine the form of employment contract. Flexibility of contracts allows employers to contract for work with the self employed as opposed to employees, or to hire workers on a temporary or casual basis. This flexibility may be used where future labour demand or product market trends are uncertain, since offering employment under a standard or permanent contract for employees increases the risks borne by employers. However, this form of flexibility not only passes the burden of adjustment more on to workers, but also often involves additional costs for the workforce, in the form of lower wage costs (both lower wage levels and lower employment-related benefits) and lower opportunities for skill and career development. Economies where there is a widespread move from standard to non standard contracts may therefore suffer from inadequate development of the skill base and heightened job insecurity, resulting in low motivation and morale.

Finally, a flexible wage structure, according to economists, represents an important indicator of labour market flexibility. At the macro level, as unemployment rises real wage rates should fall, or stop rising as fast, thereby allowing the unemployed to price themselves back into work. However, this definition of a well functioning labour market is by no means uncontroversial; Keynesian economists take the opposite viewpoint, observing that falls in wages may make a bad situation worse, by undermining producer and consumer confidence. Wage flexibility is also looked for at the level of the firm. Mainstream economists call for employers to have freedom to adapt wages to market requirements. There are problems, however, in interpreting what is meant by the market: for some this flexibility is to keep wages in line with what the employer can afford, while for others efficiency considerations require employers to pay the 'market rates' associated with a particular skill or occupation. Moreover, where employers are in principle free to adapt wage structures, they may face problems of 'leapfrogging' pay settlements in sectors with a tight labour market, resulting in wage inflation and problems of macroeconomic management. Where employers try to freeze or cut wages to cope with difficulties in their product markets, in the longer term they may face problems of recruiting and retaining staff.

From this brief discussion of labour market flexibility, it is clear that whether more flexible labour markets are associated with superior labour market performance is an empirical question. Greater flexibility does not always imply greater potential to adapt and respond to change. In part, this is due to the rather complex relationship between flexibility and regulation. There are potential contradictions in the linkage between deregulated labour markets and their capacity to change that are not always identified in conventional accounts. Freedoms enjoyed by employers — for example to hire and fire at will — may remove incentives for firms to make other adjustments necessary for long term survival. These include particularly the investments necessary to develop their skill base. Nor do trends towards greater deregulation in a country necessarily enhance labour market flexibility. In fact, the opposite may well occur. For example, the growth of flexible jobs, such as part-time ones, could be expected to ease the problem of moving people from unemployment back into work. In the UK in the 1980s the exact opposite occurred; most of the new jobs available to the unemployed were low paid part-time jobs, but these did not pay sufficient wages for people to be able to afford to move from unemployment into work (Gregg and Wadsworth, 1995). Instead, most of these jobs were taken by people in households where there was already someone in full-time work — for example, by young people and by married women. Since 1997 action has been taken to make low paid jobs more attractive to the unemployed through a new system of paying in-work benefits to those in employment (the Working Families Tax Credit); but this is evidence of new forms of state intervention in the market system. In this case leaving wages to be determined apparently by market forces caused new forms of rigidity that could only be solved through the state intervening in the wages offered by the market.

This debate suggests it is necessary to examine the detailed form of regulation and deregulation and not attempt to categorize employment systems along a one dimensional spectrum, from regulated to deregulated or from flexible to rigid.

Comparing labour market performance

The debate on flexibility and deregulation in the 1980s and early 1990s emerged out of the apparent strong empirical evidence that deregulated labour markets were also the best performing labour markets. While economic growth had slowed in all advanced capitalist countries since the 1970s, the ability of the US to carry on generating jobs was far greater than that of Europe. The US created around 34 million jobs between 1980 and 1999, compared to just 20 million across the whole of the EU, even though the EU has a much larger population of working age than the US.[2] This meant that the employment rate in the US (the proportion of the working-age population in employment) was substantially higher than in the European Union during the 1980s and 1990s. As Figure 6.1 shows, the US experienced a relatively steady increase in its employment rate from the mid-1980s, with three quarters of the working-age population in employment by the end of the 1990s. Across the EU, the proportion in employment by the end of the period had returned to the same level as that in 1980.

Moreover, the US succeeded in bringing down the high levels of unemployment experienced in the early 1980s, while these persisted in Europe (Figure 6.2). During the late 1990s, unemployment rates averaged between four and six per cent in the US, but in the European Union the average was closer to ten per cent. Faced with this kind of evidence, many commentators believed there was something rotten at the heart of Europe. Institutions like the OECD, along with employer groups, acted as

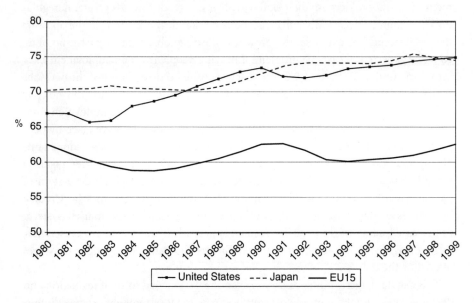

Source: OECD Labour Free Statistics

Figure 6.1 Employment in the US, Japan and the EU

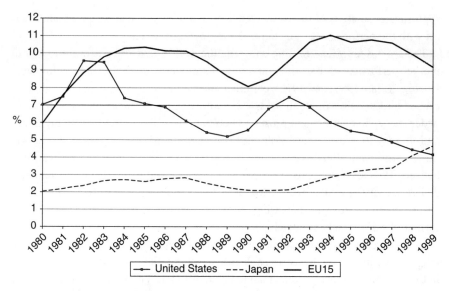

Source: OECD Labour Force Statistics

Figure 6.2 Unemployment in the US, Japan and the EU

a considerable pressure on European governments during this time to implement policies of deregulation and labour market flexibility in an attempt to mimic the US jobs miracle. The argument was that policies of flexibility would both enhance job performance and contribute to the long-term ability of economies to adapt to change. Again, *The OECD Jobs Study* provided the rationale:

> … [the central goal of employment policy should be] to improve the ability of economies and of societies both to cope with, and benefit from, change, by enhancing the ability to adjust and to adapt, and increasing the capacity to innovate and be creative. (1994a: 43)

However, although the US outperformed the European Union in creating jobs and keeping unemployment down during the 1980s and 1990s, this is not the whole picture. In particular it glosses over two important empirical findings. First, some countries within the EU outperformed the US during this same period, despite very different forms of labour market regulation. Denmark is the best example of this pattern: the share of the working-age population in employment in Denmark remained at or above the US level throughout the 1990s, and the gap in unemployment rates was closed by the end of the 1990s. Other countries stand out for their relatively high employment rates (the UK, Sweden and Portugal) (see Chapter Four, Figure 4.1). And the Netherlands is remarkable for the rapid growth in its employment rate during the 1990s — far outstripping the rate of growth in the US — combined with levels of unemployment that declined to a level lower than that in the US by the late 1990s. These patterns of labour market performance underline the need for a more sophisticated analysis of the way different forms of labour market regulation interact with the performance of a country's employment system.

The second empirical finding concerns the notion that there is more to labour market performance than the employment rate and the level of unemployment. During the late 1980s and 1990s, commentators in the US became increasingly concerned about rising inequality in wages and household incomes, as well as the widening gap in employment prospects between the well educated and highly skilled and those with a low level of skills and education (Mishel *et al.*, 1997). Workers in the US who were already on low levels of pay experienced a drop in real earnings between 1979 and 1995, and low income households suffered a decline in standards of living (Mishel *et al.*, 1997). Moreover, low pay and poor prospects for career advancement encouraged increasing numbers of young people to withdraw from the formal labour market completely.

Comparison with the experience in Europe and Japan suggests that US commentators have much cause for concern. Figure 6.3 shows that the distribution of wages in the US is much more unequal than in Japan or in Europe. Workers in the US in the highest decile of the wage distribution earn more than four times as much as those in the bottom decile.[3] In Sweden, the difference in pay is only slightly more than double, and in Japan high paid workers earn three times as much as low paid workers.

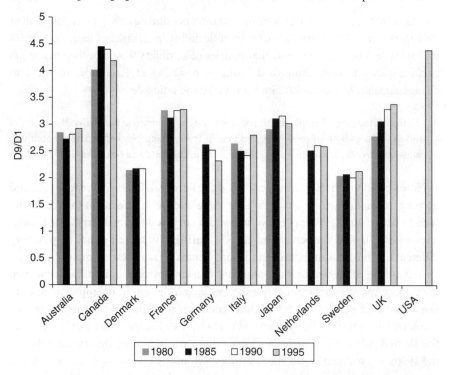

Source: OECD Employment Outlooks

Figure 6.3 Wage inequality in OECD countries 1980–1995

And it is not only a social or moral concern with equity that is at stake here. While the deregulated US model may have facilitated stronger job creation and more extensive flows out of unemployment, the growth of low wage, low productivity jobs may have been one factor acting as a brake on US economic performance compared to the EU, measured in terms of total factor productivity as well as labour productivity (Mishel *et al.*, 1997).

These kinds of issues led policy-makers on both sides of the Atlantic to turn their attention to exploring whether a policy to promote high wages and high job quality may have some advantages over a policy aimed at using low wages, and potentially low job quality, to promote a high level of employment. Indeed some have begun to question the size and the nature of the alleged trade-off between the quantity and the quality of employment (Freeman, 1994a; see Box 6.2). Also, within the US, there is growing realization that labour market flexibility may be less to do with the 'under-regulation' of labour markets, and more to do with the way it promotes worker discipline. This condition of the US labour market was famously characterized by the

---

Box 6.2 The jobs versus equality trade-off?

Recent studies have not supported the notion that there is a direct trade-off between policies to create jobs on the one hand and to promote equality in labour markets on the other. For example, the trade-off view would lead one to expect that, in the US, unemployment should fall when inequality rises; but in fact the opposite is found to be the case. Also, within European countries national unemployment rates tend to be lower in the richer and more equal countries where social welfare systems are more developed (Galbraith *et al.*, 1999). Similarly a study by Nickell (1997) shows that labour market institutions that promote equality are not generally associated with higher rates of unemployment across European countries. Based on a study of labour market data for 20 OECD countries, Nickell (*op. cit.*: 72–3) arrives at the following conclusions:

> Labour market rigidities that do not appear to have serious implications for average levels of unemployment include the following: (1) strict employment protection legislation and general legislation on labour market standards; (2) generous levels of unemployment benefit, so long as these are accompanied by pressure on the unemployed to take jobs by, for example, fixing the duration of benefit and providing resources to raise the ability/ willingness of the unemployed to take jobs; and (3) high levels of unionisation and union coverage, so long as they are offset by high levels of coordination in wage bargaining, particularly with strong employers ... It is clear that the broad-brush analysis that says that European unemployment is high because European labour markets are "rigid" is too vague and probably misleading. Many labour market institutions that conventionally come under the heading of rigidities have no observable impact on unemployment.

Scholars associated with the European Low-Wage Employment Research Network have examined differences in wage structure and employment in the US and Europe. Their analysis (Salverda *et al.*, 2001: vi) suggests several new 'stylized facts':

- It *reinforces the general picture of earnings inequality* as being much higher in the Anglo-Saxon countries compared to the Continent, as the French earnings dispersion and incidence of low pay are brought closer to the German level and British inequality and incidence closer to the American level.

Box 6.2 Continued

- It *emphasises the important role of high-wage employment* as an element of the international differences. The transatlantic employment gap is essentially two-tailed as the United States has a larger incidence of both low pay and high pay. At the intermediate levels of pay the Continental countries have an employment advantage. This, however, is much smaller for hours worked than for persons working and it is gradually decreasing over time. This is further strengthened by the finding that since 1979, on balance, American employment growth has been stronger for high-wage employment than for low-wage employment.

A third study by Stanford (2000; see also Palley (2002)) argues that the inferior employment performance of Europe is the result of deflationary macro-economic policies pursued in the name of monetary union. The level of interest rates, change in government spending and in exports and investment spending are important explanatory variables underlying labour market performance. The US enjoyed a period of relatively strong aggregate demand during the 1990s, whereas the bulk of EU member states experienced weak, contractionary demand conditions (a notable exception is Ireland). Overall, differences in aggregate demand explain more of the differences in labour market performance than do differences in labour market regulation (*op. cit.*).

Finally, a theoretical framework is put forward in the work of Conceição and Galbraith (2001), building on the work of Keynes (1964) and Kuznets (1955). Kuznets suggested that inequality increases during the early stages of industrialization but then decreases continuously after a certain threshold is reached; this became known as the inverted U-shaped relationship between inequality and growth. The experience of the US, the UK and Japan during the 1980s and 1990s seems to contradict this assertion. However, Conceição and Galbraith argue that it can be explained by recognizing that these countries are at a second stage of industrialization involving greater specialization in producing new products and machinery for production, so-called 'knowledge goods':

> ... inequality should decline with growth for most manufacturing economies, as Kuznets predicted. But it should rise for the few at the very top of the technology and investment pyramid, those that supply advanced capital goods to the rest of the world. Japan, the United States, and the United Kingdom fall into this category. (*op. cit.*: 158)

head of the US Federal Reserve Board, Alan Greenspan, in the late 1990s:

> As I see it, heightened job insecurity explains a significant part of the restraint on compensation and the consequent muted price inflation ... The continued reluctance of workers to leave their jobs to seek other employment as the labour market has tightened provides further evidence of such concern, as does the tendency toward longer labour union contracts ... The low level of work stoppages of recent years also attests to concern about job security ... Owing in part to the subdued behaviour of wages, profits and rates of return on capital have risen to high levels. (Greenspan, 1997, cited in Stanford, 2000: 11–12)

Where the goal of labour market flexibility is pursued through a policy focus on deregulation, in practice the outcome may be better characterized as a more disciplined, rather than a more flexible, labour market (Campbell, 1993). Deregulatory policies that reduce employment protection and weaken social security benefits may act as a disincentive to employees to press for wage gains or to seek more attractive employment opportunities in other organizations. The heightened discipline factor may thus generate new rigidities in the labour market. Fears for job security, despite a tighter labour market, may prevent wage rates rising in line with increased demand for labour. Also, greater use of non-standard, unregulated employment contracts may reduce the ability of employers to respond to the flexible demands of new technologies and new products, where a trained, committed workforce is seen as a competitive advantage.

Understanding labour market regulation: the role of labour market actors

Overview

Even though, as we have argued, there appears to be no universal relationship between flexibility, deregulation and labour market performance, analysis of systems of labour market regulation may still help us to understand what drives labour market performance. However, instead of asking whether deregulation aids performance we need to reformulate the question and ask: *how do different mixes of regulatory policies impact on a range of indicators of labour market performance?* This question emphasizes instead the country-specific nature of labour market regulation and the way different combinations of legislation, collective bargaining and employer decisions impact on the workings of the labour market. Here, we support the general approach of Richard Freeman:

> In Economics 1, the invisible hand of market forces sets wages, prices and quantities, aided perhaps by a Wizard of Oz 'auctioneer' who calibrates prices and wages until all markets clear. In real labour markets, however, matters are more complicated and interesting. Every country has its own labour market institutions — unions, management organizations, government agencies — and rules that help determine outcomes. Each has its own way of resolving labour-management disputes; setting wages and determining non-wage benefits; regulating hiring and firing decisions and personnel policies; and providing welfare 'safety nets' for those lacking work. Some countries rely exclusively on legal mandates to determine outcomes. Others use collective bargaining. Others give relatively free sway to management decisions and individual negotiations. All develop labour market policies intended to improve market outcomes. These differences in rules and institutions affect economic outcomes and are themselves an important element in working life. (Freeman, 1994a: 14–15)

To understand the different mixes of regulatory policies in different countries — the form of wage-setting arrangements, the level of employment protection, and so on — we need to appreciate not only the interventionary role of the state, but also that of unions and employers. Of great help in this regard is comparative work on industrial relations, which focuses explicitly on the nature and form of these three labour market actors and the differences across countries.[4] Before we proceed further, therefore, it is necessary to summarize some of the key differences in systems of industrial relations between countries, setting out the broad institutional context for a comparison of policies of labour market regulation in the following section.

What is novel about the industrial relations approach is that instead of seeing rules and institutions as a source of inertia and rigidity in labour markets, they are seen as having evolved largely in response to the need for labour markets to adapt to a range of pressures and challenges. They provide a coordinating role by setting out the rules of the game, which are necessary for management and labour each to formulate decisions in a context of stable expectations about how the other acts. But these rules of the game are by no means universal. There is considerable diversity of tradition in industrial relations across advanced countries.

This diversity is illustrated by comparative analysis of trade union behaviour from an industrial relations perspective. Hyman (2001) suggests three ideal models that can be applied to trade unionism:

- Trade unions may aim to advance the interests of the working class. Class struggle is a reference point for these unions and members are rallied around the urgent need to abolish exploitation and insecurity in the workplace.
- Trade unions may identify strongly with the ideals of the society and act to defend the social order from collapse. By achieving a recognized status within society, through social partnership, for example, the unions believe, under this model, that they are better placed to shape its development.
- Trade unions may pursue short-term economic interests, showing sensitivity to changing market conditions. This model, often called 'business unionism', is associated with the union's defence of the right to free collective bargaining in order to advance the economic interests of its members; other social and political objectives are seen as potentially detracting from these economic goals.

These models reflect contradictory tendencies at the heart of all unions; it is difficult to associate one or other model with the trade union movement in a particular country. Instead, Hyman suggests that unions in particular countries tend to be located between two points of 'the eternal triangle'. For example, British trade unionism has traditionally been located between the competing interests of class and market, due to its militant defence of the economic interests of union members and its suspicion of societal instruments of reform in favour of free collective bargaining. By contrast, Germany is located between the pressures of society and market since the notion of a 'social market economy' has been a stable reference point for most trade unions for much of the post Second World War period. For German unions, the emphasis is on the need to balance the workings of the market and state intervention in a way that delivers profits to employers; establishes the right of workers to dignity and well-being at work; and extends welfare state benefits across the population (Hyman, 2001).

Country differences in the role of trade unions are complicated by the different structures of employer associations and by the role of the state in a country's industrial relations system (see Table 6.1). As we show below, these differences interlock with both weak and strong forms of labour market regulation, helping to explain why apparently similar regulatory policies have very different effects on performance indicators in different countries. We turn now to brief summaries of industrial relations systems in six countries — the UK, Germany, France, Italy, the US and Japan.

The UK

The UK is often described as a pluralist-type model of industrial relations, with a fragmented organization of labour and management, an adversarial relationship between employers and unions, and a strong tradition of 'voluntarism'. The belief was

Table 6.1 Summary of characteristics of employer and trade union associations (1990s)

Factor	Germany	France	Italy	UK	US	Japan
Concentration of employer membership[1]	High	High	Medium	Medium	N/a	Medium
Trade union density[2]	29.1	10.0	37.7	32.1	14.9	23.8[3]
Number of national, inter-industry employer associations	1	3	10	1	0	1
Number of national, inter-industry union associations	3	5	7	1	1	3
Role of largest national-level employer association in negotiations and bargaining	Medium	Medium–Strong	Medium	Weak	N/a	Medium
Role of largest national level union association in negotiations and bargaining	Medium	Medium–Strong	Medium	Weak	None	Medium

Notes
[1] Based on percentage of employees working in firms organized by the country's largest national-level employer association (for example, 54% covered by CBI in the UK; 72% covered by BDA in Germany).
[2] Employed union members as a percentage of the labour force in dependent employment (1995).
[3] All union members (including retired and unemployed) as a percentage of the labour force in dependent employment (1995).

Source: Adapted from Traxler *et al.* (2001): Tables II.3, II.4, II.1, II.11, II.9

that unions could best defend the interests of workers, not a benevolent state; to use legislation to support what might be achievable through collective bargaining was seen as a sign of weakness (see Box 6.3). British industrial relations are often regarded as embodying strong class identities and as associated with economic strategies to defend workers' right to a job and established levels of wages (Hyman, 2001). However, the union movement has historically been fragmented in Britain, with a larger number of unions than in other European countries and members spread across a range of sectors (Edwards *et al.*, 1992). This 'multi-unionism' has created some problems of communication for union officials, complicated collective bargaining with employers and generated demarcation disputes between unions (Visser and van Ruysseveldt, 1996). Nevertheless, the union movement is not divided on political or religious grounds and there is only one national organization, the Trades Union Congress (TUC). The TUC was set up in 1868, although, along with the single national employer association (the Confederation of British Industry), it has a weak role in shaping labour market regulation (Traxler *et al.*, 2001). Since 1979, British trade unionism has faced a number of challenges. Successive waves of industrial relations legislation under the Conservative Government (1979–1997) tightened the legal regulation of unions. During the late 1990s and early 2000s, debates on union renewal have focused on social partnership, on the one hand, and on the other, on opportunities to expand membership among marginalized workers in part-time and temporary jobs (Heery, 1999; Waddington, 2000). Nevertheless, while union backing of new legislation in areas of pay and working time represents a shift towards a 'society' model of union activity, the notion of 'partnership' in Britain remains a much watered down version of the notion of 'social partnership' in many other European countries (Hyman, 2001; Marchington *et al.*, 2001).

Box 6.3 Voluntaristic traditions in British industrial relations

A succinct description and defence of voluntarism was offered, a quarter of a century ago, by the Royal Commission on Trade Unions and Employers' Associations, chaired by Lord Donovan:

> (I)t was a distinct feature of our system of industrial relations that the state remained aloof from the process of collective bargaining in private industry. It left parties free to come to their own agreement. It imposed some, but few, restrictions on the right of employees to strike or of employers to resort to a lock-out. The parties to the collective agreement themselves rarely intend that their bargain shall be a legally enforceable contract, but rather that it shall be binding in honour only. The law goes out of its way to provide that such bargains between employers' associations and trade unions shall not be directly enforceable. This abstentionist attitude has reflected a belief that it is better in the long run for the law to interfere as little as possible in the settlement of questions arising between employers and workmen over pay and conditions of work. (Donovan, 1968: 10)

Extract from Visser and van Ruysseveldt (1996: 43).

Germany

In Germany, trade unions and employer associations consider themselves as social partners who aim to achieve consensus and cooperation within a highly formalized relationship (illustrated by the 'medium rating' of the role played by the national level of employer and union associations in wider forms of labour market regulation, Table 6.1). This is an important difference from the more adversarial tradition of the UK. However, it does not mean that conflict is never present; rather because both sides agree to the rules of the game, they tend to settle their differences peaceably. As in the UK, the principle of free collective bargaining (*Tarifautonomie*) exists in Germany; but it operates in a fundamentally different way, with the state playing a strong role as guarantor and referee (see Box 6.4). The structure of unions is also unlike that in the UK. While the majority of unions are affiliated to the major Federation of German Trade Unions (the DGB), there are rival confederations, reflecting differences in political and religious beliefs. Also, in manufacturing, all employees regardless of occupation are members of the same union. Thus, demarcations between unions are clear and collective bargaining with employers less complicated. However, the rise of companies that straddle multiple sectors of economic activity has put considerable pressure on the traditional concept of industrial unionism (Streeck and Visser, 1997). This, and other pressures, have led to the possibility of a merger of public and private sector unions, establishing a 'super union' for service sector workers (Hoffmann, 2000).

Aside from voluntary membership of trade unions, the other important element in the German model is the mandatory works council system (see below). Together these two forms of representing workers' interests make up the 'dual system' of

---

Box 6.4 German industrial relations: the case of free collective bargaining through juridification

Like most other basic public policy principles in Germany, *Tarifautonomie* is enshrined in the Constitution (the Basic Law of 1949) and upheld by the Constitutional Court (*Bundesverfassungsgericht*) and the Federal Labour Court. It means that the 'social partners' (organized employers and unions) can determine wages and working conditions in independent negotiations without interference of the government. This doctrine of autonomous collective bargaining is one of the many examples of the way the labour market parties shoulder a joint responsibility. To compensate for the lack of state intervention, there is a system of legal regulations upheld by the state and enforced through the courts whose purpose it is to guarantee a fundamental balance between organized employers and trade unions, and to ensure compatibility between private collective agreements and the welfare of society as a whole. The relationships between the interest organizations, and between them and the state, are regulated by legal rules. In other words, industrial relations are subject to a high level of 'juridification' (*Verrechtlichung*). The right to strike, for instance, is subject to strict rules which must ensure that strikes are only used as a weapon of last resort, when all other means of peacefully settling differences have failed.

Extract from Visser and van Ruysseveldt (1996: 127–8).

German industrial relations, although there is considerable overlap in the operations of works councils and unions. While perhaps not as strong as in the UK, it would be wrong to say that class was not a driving force behind the evolution of German industrial relations. In particular, changes in co-determination laws in the 1970s were influenced by a resurgence of class conflict, involving unofficial strikes across Germany, leading to the 'cooption' of the grassroots revolt in the form of enhanced powers for works councils and a new law on board-level co-determination (Hyman, 2001). Unification brought a number of challenges to the former West German model, with job losses in industry and disappointed hopes among new members in the former East Germany offsetting the prospects of a strengthened union movement (Hoffmann, 2000). Future prospects depend on the balance between, on the one hand, the pressures of globalization and persistent high levels of unemployment which force unions into 'concession bargaining' with employers; and on the other, the resilience of existing statutory and cooperative structures which provide for a degree of stability against social and economic upheavals (Hoffmann, 2000).

France

The system of industrial relations in France is often described as one of étatism (or *étatisme*) with its strong Government role (frequent intervention is seen as a source of political and economic stability) and low level of trade union membership (the lowest among OECD countries, see Figure 6.4). These two characteristics may be self-reinforcing. For example, the strong role of the state provides a range of individual rights and benefits to workers, which may undermine the incentive to join a trade union: individual workers have the right to strike without the permission of unions and, as we discuss below, collective agreements on wage settlements are frequently extended to non-unionized firms. Hence, unlike in the UK, the big drop in trade union membership from around 30 per cent in the mid-1940s to ten per cent by the late 1990s (Boulin, 2000) is not the result of anti-trade union legislation. Other factors that explain the low level of French union membership include: the political strategies of unions (one of the largest unions, the CGT, has strong links with the Communist Party, see Box 6.5); the limited value placed by unions on building up a mass membership (reflecting, perhaps, a tradition of anarcho-syndicalism, as well as the lesser need for members as a source of funding, since unions are largely funded by the Government); the strong rivalry between unions (broadly speaking between those favouring reform and those favouring conflict); and active anti-union practices by employers (Boulin, 2000; van Ruysseveldt and Visser, 1996b).

At the same time, however, trade unions occupy an important place in the economic, social and political life of France (as reflected in the 'medium-strong' rating in the bottom row of Table 6.1). French unions (jointly with employer bodies) administer unemployment insurance and pension funds; they participate in policy-making bodies and have seats on the boards of nationally owned companies (which are more

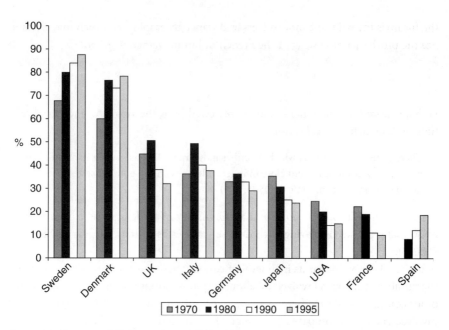

Source: Waddington and Hoffmann (2000: Table 1.7)

Figure 6.4 Trade union density 1970–1995

Box 6.5 French unions and the class struggle

In France, the division within the CGT after 1914 — when a minority supported the war effort — was followed in 1921 by a formal split and the formation of the communist-oriented CGTU. In the process, the leaders of the CGT moderated their former class rhetoric and developed a more explicit defence of reformism. As its secretary Léon Jouhaux insisted, 'We must abandon the politics of the clenched fist and involve ourselves in public affairs ... We want to be wherever workers' interests are discussed.' 'Trade unionism', he declared later, 'can develop only within an economically prosperous state' (Reynaud, 1975: 78, 80). This moderating trend was, however, interrupted by the mass struggles of 1936, with widespread strikes and factory occupations which coincided with the 'popular front' elections and resulted in substantial gains for French workers. For the next half century, '1936' remained a potent point of reference for union activists, and helped sustain a 'struggle culture' within the CGT when its counterparts elsewhere in Europe had long redefined their identities (Jeffreys, 1997: 135–6).

Extract from Hyman (2001), p. 44

---

numerous in France compared to the UK). For some (Rosenvallen, 1988), it is this strong institutionalization of the trade union movement in the functioning of the state that is in fact the reason for the crisis in the French trade union movement, and a factor that may raise doubts over its future. However, for others this role is seen as necessary for its survival, even if there is a need for some adaptation to adjust to changes in social and economic conditions (Boulin, 2000). Another factor shaping the future is the shift to a more adversarial stance by employers, which may destabilize the pro-bargaining wing of the French union movement (*op. cit.*).

Italy

Perhaps more than the other countries reviewed here, the system of industrial relations in Italy defies classification:

> There is no single formula which describes industrial relations in Italy. Ambiguity, informality, weak institutions and close interdependence with the political system are features noted by many students. (Visser, 1996: 265)

In few other European countries has the history of trade unionism been marked by so many phases displaying such diverse features as in Italy (Regini and Regalia, 2000: 365).

Italy is also notable for its high level of conflict; between 1980 and the mid-1990s, the number of workers involved in labour disputes was far higher in Italy than in the other countries reviewed here, with between 1.6 million and 13.8 million workers involved each year, compared to a range of 0.1 million to 2.1 million in adversarial Britain and less than 0.6 million each year in peaceful Germany (Visser, 1996: Appendix Table A.23). Part of the problem is the weak institutional foundation of the industrial relations system combined with a poorly defined, complex web of legal regulation. The individual employment relationship is governed by extensive legislation (see below); but in the area of collective labour law Italy follows a voluntarist tradition, like the UK, with no legislation governing collective bargaining, strikes or consultation (Ferner and Hyman, 1992). The organization of employer associations is relatively fragmented (Table 6.1); associations enjoy little control over their member firms (Treu *et al.*, 1993); as a result, their role in coordinating industrial relations is low (Visser, 1996). Trade union organization is dominated by three confederations (which all emerged out of a split within the united trade union movement after the Second World War). Relations among these main confederations are marked by dramatic swings, involving periods of conflict (1950s), cooperation (1960s), attempts at unification (early 1970s), renewed conflict (1980s) and renewed debates on unification (1990s) (Visser, 1996; Regini and Regalia, 2000). Swings in trade union membership have been equally dramatic with a sharp decline in the 1950s, a doubling of union density during the 1970s and a slow but steady retrenchment during the 1980s and 1990s (Figure 6.4). Given the challenges of privatization and increased competition in many product markets, the prospects for the Italian trade union movement depend on giving new meaning to traditional notions of solidarity:

> To some extent, the concept of solidarity offered a basis for a more concrete understanding of *sindicalismo*. In the socialist and communist traditions, solidarity was a rallying cry for working-class unity in response to a common fate and in a struggle for common interests. In the Catholic tradition, it was an appeal for the stronger and more advantaged to accept

an obligation to support the cause of the weak and disadvantaged. With the accommodation of class and society as points of reference, a synthesis of the two conceptions became possible, shared — albeit with differences of emphasis — by all three confederations. If Italian unions are to remain powerful actors in the new century, the meaning of solidarity must once more be clarified and given strategic content in response to the new challenges of the market. (Hyman, 2001: 166)

The US

In the US, the system of industrial relations is distinguished by the absence of a national employer association with member firms from more than one sector (Table 6.1), and by the business-orientated approach of the trade union movement based on the efforts of local unions to advance the economic interests of their members (Freeman, 1994a; Hyman, 2001). During the 1950s and 1960s, private sector unions were powerful actors in the US labour market, but since then trade union membership has slumped, reflecting, in part, the success of employers in establishing a 'union free' environment (Freeman, 1994a; Freeman and Rogers, 1999). As Figure 6.4 shows, union density fell from around 25 per cent in 1970 to 14 per cent in 1990, with a slight rise to 15 per cent in 1995.

The philosophy of business unionism (Box 6.6) underpinned the formation of the American Federation of Labour in the late 19th century and was captured in the slogan 'pure and simple unionism';

> This specified: a labor movement pared down to its economic essentials: its goals defined by the concrete job interests of workers; its structure determined by the industrial environment; and its strategy reliant on the exertion of economic power. (Brody, 1991, cited in Hyman, 2001: 8).

Box 6.6 Business unionism in the US: industrial relations in the margins?

The United States has a business-oriented union movement (dating back to Gompers's leadership) based largely on relatively autonomous local unions who bargain for better conditions from individual employers. American labor relations is also characterized by exclusive representation: at any given workplace workers are either represented by one union, chosen by majority vote, or they have no union. On the employer side, American businesses rarely give the right to negotiate labor contracts to employer associations; organizations like the National Association of Manufacturers or the Chamber of Commerce are primarily lobbying and information groups. Since each employer and group of workers negotiates separately, whether a work site is union or not can greatly affect the wages of the workers relative to others and enterprise profitability, producing great conflict over the existence of unions at those sites.

Extract from Freeman (1994a): 15–16.

For some, the philosophy of American business unionism is seen as a limited expression of the ideals of the labour movement, since it fails to communicate with wider social and political aims of society. But this approach has been influential, not least in the way it has influenced generations of economists in seeing unions as economic actors whose sole purpose is to raise their members' wages above the market rate. However, the problem of seeing employment primarily as an economic relationship is that politics does matter in regulating the rules of the game; in that sense, American unions may have missed an important opportunity to influence the way Government shapes labour market regulation.

Japan

As Freeman (1994) puts it, in Japan 'unions and employers are a different kettle of (raw?) fish'. Most unions are organized within individual companies, not by occupation or sector, so that there are tens of thousands of unions (around 70,000 during the

---

Box 6.7 The company union in Japan

Enterprise unions in the private sector have the following characteristics. The employees of Company A comprise Union A irrespective of occupation (salesmen, engineers, clerks, carpenters, truck drivers, and labourers), and, with few exceptions, only regular employees are eligible for membership. Workers cease to be union members if they leave Company A, if Union A is disbanded, or if Company A ceases to operate. Union A's finances must be raised by members of Union A. Officials of Union A must be regular employees of Company A and are elected by secret ballot. Union A may not take strike action without a secret ballot. No organization of workers can be a union if its objectives are confined to mutual aid or other welfare work or if its principal aim is to engage in political or social movements (Chalmers, 1989: 174).

Strengths of the company union

- high membership among management staff increases the union's knowledge of company affairs;
- protection of job security (and therefore union membership) is a strong mobilising concern;
- and union officials are elected from the company workforce.

Weaknesses

- unions are dependent on facilities provided by the company;
- the interests of members are conflated with the interests of the company;
- presence of managerial grades often causes conflict within the union;
- and the unions are indifferent to organising temporary workers, reflecting disinterest with a broader societal concern for justice.

(Cole, 1971 and Hanami, 1981, cited in Chalmers, 1989).

1990s, Kuwahara, 1998).[5] Within companies, membership is inclusive of manual and non-manual (core) workers, with relatively high levels of union density among managerial grades (see Box 6.7). As in the US, however, trends in membership have declined steadily since the 1950s (Figure 6.4), in part as a result of difficulties of organizing company unions in new firms (Katz and Darbishire, 1999). Indeed, disaggregation of union membership by company size shows that the vast majority of company union members (97 per cent) work in firms that employ more than 100 members (Kuwahara, 1998) — further evidence of the segmented structure of the Japanese employment system (Chalmers, 1989). Union activities are coordinated by industry federations (of which there are more than 100), which, in turn, are members of national confederations; *Rengo* (Japan Trade Union Confederation) is the largest, following a merger of four confederations in 1989 (Traxler *et al.*, 2001). The confederations act primarily as advisory bodies to company unions; their main activities involve political campaigns and lobbying. Employers are organized along regional or industry lines and many are members of larger employers' organizations. The main one is *Nikkeiren* (Japan Federation of Employers' Associations), which publicizes employers' opinions and provides advice to its members. It also plays a major role in coordinating wage setting (see below).

Country mixes of labour market regulation

Now that we have considered the very different roles played by unions, employers and the state in a selection of major countries, we can proceed with a comparative assessment of labour market regulation. We focus on four dimensions of labour market regulation:

- works councils
- wage setting
- employment protection
- working time regulation

These components of labour market regulation are not defined and enforced solely through state legislation. As we saw in the previous section, the extent to which the state intervenes in the area of employment varies enormously between countries, with a relatively strong role in France and a weak one in the UK. Therefore, we also need to consider the roles played by employers and unions in processes of regulation, especially through the use of collective bargaining agreements and other voluntary mechanisms. We begin our assessment with a comparison of country systems of regulation of an important form of worker representation — the works council.

Works councils

There are two forms of worker-led representation in the workplace — unions and works councils.[6] Unlike in the UK and the US, companies in most European countries are legally required to establish works councils. They date from 1945 and were designed as part of the cooperative effort of economic regeneration across Europe with the aim of providing workers with rights to information, consultation and, in some countries, co-determination in certain management decisions.

There are considerable differences in the scope and functions of works councils across countries, reflecting differences in their legal base and their relations with trade unions (see Table 6.2 and Chapter One, Box 1.10). As can be seen, compliance with the legislation requiring works councils varies. For example, the proportion of firms with councils is only 41 per cent among the medium-sized firms in the Netherlands, and only ten per cent among firms with less than ten employees in Germany. The composition of members of councils varies from parity representation (employee-management) to full employee-only representation. Intermediary forms are found in France, where councils consist of employees but are chaired by the company director. While all councils enjoy the right to company information, only in certain countries do they also have additional rights to consultation and co-decision-making. On economic (business strategy) matters, council rights never extend beyond information and consultation. However, on social affairs (personnel strategy) there is often a veto right. For example, in Germany and the Netherlands veto rights cover issues of working time, careers, dismissal, payment systems and in-house training (Slomp, 1995).

Differences in the roles and rights of works councils overlap to some extent with differences in the relationship between union delegates and works councils. In Belgium and Denmark the 100 per cent union membership among council employee members means that if councils were restricted to employees only, they would be a duplicate of the union delegation. In Germany and the Netherlands, the 'dual system' establishes a neat division of labour between councils and unions, with councils functioning mainly at the enterprise level and unions at the branch and industry levels. This division is complemented in the German case (at least in the auto industry, where most of the research has been done) by close links between unions and councils; while in the Netherlands councils enjoy greater independence. France and Spain are distinctive for the often conflictual relations between unions and councils. Strained relations may explain why councils in France are often marginalized and focus on organizing social activities, like Christmas parties (Slomp, 1995).

Works councils can be an important aspect of a country's system of labour market regulation, particularly if improved economic performance depends upon greater worker participation. The experiments with a 'partnership' approach in the UK and co-management with union officials at GM in the US can be regarded as motivated in part by the belief that such developments could help shift these economies from a low-road to a high-road or high-performance approach. However, in both countries such initiatives have been primarily employer-led, and this has led commentators to cast doubt on their ability to achieve this transformation. The establishment of works councils is not, in any case, a guarantee of cooperative and productive relations in the enterprise; their effectiveness depends on the broader industrial relations system and the ability of unions to encourage local delegates to sustain cooperative relations.

Table 6.2 Works councils in Europe

Factor	Belgium	Denmark	France	Germany	Netherlands	Spain
Minimum size enterprise covered by law (no. of employees)	100	35	50	6	35	50
Percentage of relevant enterprises with a works council	60%	80%	75%	100+: 80% 50–100: 60% 5–10: 10%	100+: 83% 35–100: 41%	—
Size and composition	6–25 Parity	4–12 Parity	3–15 Employees	1–31 Employees only	3–25 Employees only	5–75 Employees only
Chairperson	Employer	Employer	Employer	Elected by council	Elected by council	Elected by council
Unionization rate of members	Almost 100%	100%	Majority	75%	74%	90%
Information rights	Basic, economic, social and incidental info	Depends upon issues	Basic, social and incidental info	Depends upon issues	Depends upon issues	Depends upon issues
Rights in economic matters	Information	Consultation	Consultation on important decisions	Consultation on important decisions	Consultation on important decisions	Information and consultation
Rights in social affairs	Consultation; Co-determination on a few points (e.g. rules of employment, dismissal, social fund administration)	Consultation; Bargaining joint agreements about general HR policy	Consultation; veto right on flexi-time; organization of social activities	Consultation; Co-determination/ bargain joint agreement on some point (e.g. rules of employment, dismissal)	Co-determination of general rules	Information and consultation; Negotiate collective agreements

Source: Adapted from Slomp (1995), Tables 14.1 and 14.2

Wage setting

Our second dimension of regulation concerns institutional arrangements for setting wages. Despite the emphasis on market wage-setting in economics textbooks, all countries have some form of institutionalized wage regulation. Examples include minimum wage legislation; collective bargaining between unions and employers; and the use of mechanisms by governments to extend collective bargaining agreements to other firms.

As we described above, there is a widely held view that less regulated and less centralized forms of wage setting may enhance labour market flexibility and thus improve economic performance. In the real world, however, wage systems are characterized by different kinds of regulation and different mixes of centralization and coordination (formal and informal), which make universal policy prescriptions inappropriate. Table 6.3 provides a summary of characteristics of wage-setting arrangements in a number of OECD economies. If we look first at the role of collective bargaining, we find that in most countries the figures for union density and collective bargaining coverage are relatively similar. In the US, for example, 15 per cent of the workforce are unionized and 16 per cent are covered by some form of collective bargaining agreement negotiated between unions and employers. In some countries, however, there is a wide disparity between these figures. The case of France is illustrative: at just ten per cent its union density is the lowest among the countries listed, but at 95 per cent collective bargaining coverage it is second only to Belgium. This apparent paradox is explained primarily by the fact that France, in common with many other countries, such as Spain and Australia, makes widespread use of extension agreements. This practice involves the extension of collective bargaining agreements to cover non-union workers where the employer is a member of the employer association that was party to the agreement. It can also be extended by statute to third parties — such as the extension of one regional agreement to another region, or the extension of a sector-level agreement to another sector. In contrast, countries like the US and the UK have no such mechanisms in place. As a result, the level of collective bargaining coverage in a country depends not on the unionization rate *per se*, but more on what proportion of workers have an employer who belongs to an employer association, and what use if any the government makes of statutory extensions to collective agreements. The level of unionization may in fact be a better indicator of the strength of protection afforded through collective bargaining: in France, collective bargaining often does little more than replicate basic legal employment rights; the low levels of union membership make enforcement of these rights at the workplace level difficult (van Ruysseveldt and Visser, 1996b).

The third characteristic in Table 6.3 concerns the level at which bargaining takes place. Highly centralized bargaining takes place at the national level and involves the major union federations and employer associations, representing all sectors. This traditionally applied to the Nordic countries and formed part of the 'solidarity wage policy', known as the *Rehn-Meidner* model, which combined a concern for wage equality with the need for macroeconomic wage coordination (Standing, 1998).

Table 6.3 Characteristics of country systems of wage-setting

Country	Union density[1]	Collective bargaining coverage[2]	Bargaining level[3]	Bargaining coordination[4]	Extension practice[5]	Mechanism for regulating low pay
US	14.9%	16%	Company/ group specific	Weak	None	Statutory minimum wage
Japan	23.8%	17%	Company	Strong	None	Statutory minimum wage
Australia	33.1%	70%	Industry and company	Strong	High	Collective agreements[6]
Austria	43.3%	70%	Industry	Strong	High	Collective agreements
Belgium	49.7%	96%	Industry and company	Medium	High	Statutory minimum wage
Denmark	78.3%	69%	Industry/ occupation	Strong	None	Collective agreements
Finland	78.4%	83%	National/ centralized	Medium– strong	Moderate	Collective agreements
France	10.0%	95%	Industry and company	Medium	High	Statutory minimum wage
Germany	29.1%	79%	Industry	Medium– strong	Moderate	Collective agreements
Italy	37.7%	—	Industry	Medium	High	Collective agreements
Netherlands	25.7%	82%	Industry	Medium	Moderate	Statutory minimum wage
Norway	57.7%	70%	National/ centralized	Strong	None	Collective agreements
Portugal	26.8%	92%	Industry	Medium	High	Statutory minimum wage
Spain	18.6%	83%	Industry	Medium– weak	High	Statutory minimum wage
Sweden	87.6%	92%	Industry	Strong	None	Collective agreements
UK	32.1%	39%	Company and work groups	Weak	None	Statutory minimum wage

Sources: (1) 1995 data: Traxler *et al.* (2001), Table II.11; (2) 1996 data: Traxler *et al.* (2001), Table III.15; (3) 1997–98 data for the private sector: Traxler *et al.* (2001), Table III.1; (4) Adapted from Lodovici (2000), Table 2E and Traxler (1996): Table 3; (5) Traxler (1996): Table 3; (6) It is difficult to classify Australia. It does not have a national minimum wage, but a Federal minimum wage was introduced in 1997 (Safety Net Review Wages decision), which applies to employees working under Federal awards. Moreover, nearly all states apply this to workers under state awards (OECD, 1998a).

During the 1990s, however, the Nordic countries diverged, with a decentralization of bargaining in Sweden, initiated by the engineering employers acting in response to pressures of international competition (Pontusson and Swenson, 1996) and to changing political and ideological considerations (Thörnqvist, 1999).

Bargaining at the industry level generally involves unions and employer associations coming together within separate industrial sectors. Germany provides a good example of sector level bargaining (*Flächentarifvertrag*), although this generally takes place at the regional (*Länder*) level, rather than the national level. As part of Germany's dual system of industrial relations, these sector level agreements lay down minimum pay levels and requirements concerning working conditions, which are then often supplemented by a second tier of co-determination at local level. During the period of slow economic growth in the 1990s, however, this system of coordinated wage flexibility created tensions between firms in the former East and the former West Germany, and between small firms and large firms, since it allows high performing firms to top up wage rates in order to distinguish themselves from low performing firms.[7] This capacity for flexible 'wage drift' allows high performing employers to pay above agreed rates one year and freeze rates the next, yet still remain in line with the new agreed rates. In contrast, firms in low performing sectors find it difficult just to meet the minimum agreed rates each year and are therefore less able to adapt labour costs to changing economic conditions.[8]

Italy is also characterized as a country with predominantly industry level bargaining, although in practice it combines a changing mix of industry level, regional and plant level bargaining agreements across different sectors. In some sectors plant negotiations precede industry agreements; in others the main discussions take place at a regional or sub-sectoral level (Katz, 1993). The picture is further complicated by national institutional arrangements that have added a strong element of coordination in wage setting. Between 1975 and 1992, all Italian wage settlements were shaped by the *Scala Mobile* — an important symbol of trade union power in Italy. This system linked wage increases to the cost of living index through a series of tripartite agreements between unions, employers and Government. Since its abolition in 1992, bargaining has taken place at the industry and company levels under the form of 'nested' collective bargaining (Baccaro, 2000).

The main country examples of company level bargaining are Japan, the UK and the US. Japan is something of a special case since it combines company level bargaining — involving negotiation between employers and company unions — with a high level of informal coordination of wage-setting. Typically, the major iron and steel companies make identical wage offers and this sets off the *Shunto* (Spring Offensive) as other companies in other sectors follow suit.[9] The strength of influence is reinforced by the presence of *Zaibatsu* groups (conglomerates that include firms, banks and trading companies — such as *Mitsubishi*) that establish strong links between large companies between and within sectors. Public sector wage offers follow the private sector and non-unionized companies follow unionized companies. Although informal, the effect of this coordination is the same as if there were more systematic, or legal, procedures of multi-employer, centralized bargaining (Soskice, 1990). However, unlike the corporatist models, such as that of Germany, the role of unions in this informal process is secondary.

Decentralized, company level bargaining in the US and the UK lacks any system of formal or even informal wage coordination. In both countries, the last vestiges of private sector industry-wide bargaining collapsed in the 1980s: for example, the US witnessed the ending of the steel agreement in 1986, as well as a drop in the number of firms represented in the trucking and coal mining agreements (Katz, 1993); in the UK, large numbers of firms in the private sector pulled out of multi-employer agreements in favour of single-employer bargaining (Brown and Rea, 1995; Jackson *et al.*, 1993; Millward *et al.*, 1992, 2000). In both countries, the rapid decentralization of wage-setting arrangements and growing variation of inter-industry settlements signalled a disintegration of the relatively informal practices of coordination through 'pattern bargaining'. The US has also witnessed a shift away from individual company-wide agreements to plant level wage-setting, which is associated with 'concession bargaining', or 'whipsawing', as management threaten local unions with plant closure in the face of corporate restructuring (Cappelli, 1985; Parker and Slaughter, 1988). In the UK, the public sector is perhaps the last bastion of centralized wage-setting arrangements. However, in the late 1990s the Government adopted a twin-track approach of maintaining centralized pay systems, but supplemented with individualized pay systems (such as performance-related pay) for growing numbers of the public sector workforce (Grimshaw, 2000; White, 1999).

Another important difference in wage-setting arrangements concerns the way countries protect low paid workers. Again, it is difficult to characterize countries as strongly regulated or weakly regulated since approaches to regulating low pay vary enormously, from use of a statutory minimum wage to reliance on high levels of collective bargaining coverage with no direct state intervention (Bazen, 2000; OECD, 1998a). Countries in the latter group include Germany, Denmark and Italy and while there may be no national minimum wage, there is scope for other forms of intervention. For example, in Germany, sector agreements can be extended to non-signatory employers under certain conditions; and there are provisions for the state to establish a form of wages council to intervene in areas where there is no union or no collective agreement. Among those countries with minimum wage legislation, there are significant differences in the coverage of the legislation, the differentiation of rates for youth workers and in the kind of uprating mechanism (see Table 6.4). Moreover, there are dramatic differences in the level at which the minimum wage is set, ranging from 27 per cent of median male full-time earnings in Japan to 55 per cent in France, with the UK somewhere in between at 45 per cent. Also, most countries tend to set differential rates for youth workers, with up to eight different rates found in the Netherlands. In Japan there is no youth rate, presumably because of the very low standard rate. Finally, there is normally a form of indexation, or uprating, mechanism that links the rate to annual changes in inflation or wage growth. The absence of an uprating mechanism in the UK and the US presents political parties in government with the opportunity to exploit the situation for political gain — referred to in the US as 'Washington's dirty little secret' (Sachdev and Wilkinson, 1998). In the UK, this perhaps explains the rises of ten pence in the standard rate in non-election years (1999–2000, 2001–2002) and the rise of 40 pence in the election year (2000–2001).

Table 6.4 Summary of minimum wage systems in selected countries

Country	Level[1]	Employees excluded	Youth rate	Uprating mechanism
France	55.2%	Government and disabled workers (covered by separate rules)	17, 90%; under 17, 80%	Indexed to consumer prices and must rise by at least half the increase in all wages; can be raised by decree
Belgium	49.2%	Public sector workers and trainees	20–17 years, 94%–70%	Indexed to consumer prices; renegotiated regularly (usually every two years)
Netherlands	47.2%	—	22–15, 85–30%	Indexed to average growth, contingent on ratio of welfare recipients to employment
UK	41%[2]	—	18–21, 83%	None
US	33.2%	Executive, administrative and professional employees	Reduced rate for under 20 for first 90 days of work	None
Spain	30.1%	—	Under 18, 89%	Updated annually through tripartite consultation
Japan	26.5%	Some civil servants, trainees, temporary workers and short part-time workers	None	Annual consultation with local tripartite councils

Notes
[1] Level of adult minimum wage expressed as a percentage of median male full-time earnings;
[2] Own calculation (1999) based on 1999 rate; New Earnings Survey data for 1999.
Source: OECD (1998a), Tables 2.1 and 2.3; for the UK, Own calculations.

Employment protection

Perhaps more than any other area of labour market regulation, efforts to protect workers from job loss and to regulate the use of fixed-term and agency employment contracts have run up against the argument that these conflict with employers' need for flexibility. In particular, *The OECD Jobs Study* (1994) included a recommendation that governments investigate opportunities to relax employment protection. Again, wide differences in the usage and relative strictness of different components of regulation in this area defy simple policy prescriptions. Moreover, there is no evidence of a clear link between employment protection legislation and the main measures of labour market performance, employment and unemployment (OECD, 1999).

Legal rights to employment protection typically include both individual protection against unfair dismissal, and procedures that promote alternatives to mass redundancies (Buchele and Christiansen, 1999; Mosley, 1994). Particular regulations, whether legal or negotiated through collective agreements, include:

- the requirement for advance warning prior to dismissal;
- a specified minimum length of advance notice;
- a requirement for consultation with employee representatives and/or authorization from other governing bodies;
- a specified level of severance pay;
- provision for appeal for unfair dismissal.

Regulations relating to atypical work contracts may serve either to reinforce or to reduce differences in access to employment protection between those on typical or standard contracts and those on atypical or non standard contracts, particularly those on fixed-term, temporary or part-time contracts. This area of regulation has become increasingly important with the rise in the proportion of the workforce in non-standard forms of employment (Cousins, 1999; Deakin and Mückenberger, 1992). Workers on non-standard contracts may be particularly vulnerable to abuse of regulatory conditions, since the employer may be eager to avoid the costs of employment protection associated with 'standard', full-time, permanent employment. Regulations that increase differentiation include those that apply only to employees and not to workers; or include a working time threshold; or a minimum period of employment before the protection applies. Examples of regulations which reduce differentiation include restrictions on the use of temporary contracts and agency workers, and the *pro rata* extension of employment protection to part-time workers and workers on fixed-term contracts.

Table 6.5 summarizes the main characteristics of systems of employment protection for ten countries selected for comparison. The first finding is that differences within Europe are much wider than the stylized US *vs.* Europe regulation debate assumes. While the UK has an expected low measure, close to that of the US, among the remaining European countries the OECD summary index of 'strictness' of employment protection ranges from 1.5 for Denmark to 3.4 for Italy. There are major differences in statutory rights against unfair dismissal in Europe, with measures in continental Europe designed to prevent job losses, and measures in the UK and Scandinavian countries designed to support mobility through a focus on providing adequate compensation and active labour market policies (Lodovici, 2000). The US does stand apart on one issue, however, namely the absence of a requirement of justification or explanation from the employer in the case of dismissal. This is in line with the longstanding 'employment-at-will' doctrine, although there are signs of change,

Table 6.5 Characteristics of employment protection in selected countries

Country	Summary index of overall strictness	Procedures for individual dismissal for a regular worker with more than 20 years of employment			Collective dismissals: level of protection	Temporary employment: level of regulation
		Notice period	**Severance pay**	**Compensation for unfair dismissal**		
Italy	3.4	12 days (b-c) 4 months (w-c)	18 months	32.5 months	Very strong	Strong
Spain	3.1	30 days	12 months	22 months	Medium–Strong	Strong
France	2.8	2 months	2.7 months	15 months	Weak–Medium	Strong
Sweden	2.6	6 months	No legal entitlement	32 months	Very strong	Weak
Germany	2.6	7 months	No legal entitlement	18 months	Medium–Strong	Weak–Medium
Japan	2.3	30 days	4 months	26 months	Weak	Weak–Medium
Netherlands	2.2	4 months	No legal entitlement	18 months	Medium	Weak
Denmark	1.5	10 weeks (b-c) 6 months (w-c)	0.3 months 3 months	9 months	Medium–Strong	Very weak
UK	0.9	12 weeks	20 weeks (redundancy cases)	Up to £12,000 (equivalent to 8 months of average salary)	Medium	Very weak
US	0.7	No legal entitlement	No legal entitlement	Disparate rulings	Medium	Very weak

Note: (b-c) blue-collar; (w-c) white collar.

Source: Adapted from OECD (1999); Tables 2.5, 2.A.1, 2.A.3, 2.A.6

with a number of states introducing legislation in response to workers pursuing wrongful termination based on an 'implied contract' (Lodovici, 2000; OECD, 1999).

There is closer similarity among European countries in their regulation of collective dismissals, due to the adoption of a common EC Council Directive in 1975. The Directive requires member states to set up a consultation process with the aim of avoiding or alleviating redundancies, and following a 1992 amendment requires a minimum notice period of 30 days (Mosley, 1994). There is still a degree of variation. In the UK, the level of negotiation required is at a minimum; employers are required to consult with unions on selection standards and procedures for dismissal. In other countries, it is more extensive. In Germany, France and Italy, for example, consultation involves consideration of alternatives to redundancy (such as redeployment or retraining) and ways to mitigate the effects (involving a 'social plan' in Germany and France). In the US there is no legal requirement for negotiation and no special regulations covering severance pay for collective dismissal (OECD, 1999).

Regulation of fixed-term contracts and other temporary arrangements protects workers from employers attempting to avoid the costs of dismissal procedures, which are guaranteed for workers on standard employment contracts. This principle is most apparent in Italy, Spain and France, where employers have to show that the use of fixed-term contracts is designed to meet a specific situation such as seasonal work, a temporary increase in business activity or a period of training.[10] Employers are also restricted in the number of times they can renew the contract and there is a maximum to the total duration of successive contracts. By contrast, there is very weak regulation in Denmark, the US and the UK. There are currently no restrictions on the purpose of fixed-term contracts in the UK and the US, and in all three countries there are no limits to the duration of successive contracts. However, the UK and Denmark will have to adjust their legislation in line with the new European Directive providing for equal treatment between fixed-term and permanent employees, and this may lead to changes in these conditions (see Chapter Ten).

Working time regulation

Interest in regulation of working time grew exponentially in the 1990s in response to a range of concerns and pressures for change. These included interest in 'work-sharing' policies (to reduce the average working hours to increase job opportunities for the unemployed); increased flexibility for employers (to reduce costs and match operating hours to variable demand); and increased flexibility for workers (to reconcile work and family life and to promote gender equality). As with the other areas, working time may be subject to regulation through legislation and formal collective bargaining, as well as informal practices based on longstanding customary norms. In many countries, legislation sets a maximum number of hours to the working week; a maximum number of overtime hours; a premium for overtime pay; as well as a minimum holiday entitlement. Also, given the rise of part-time work and its strong role in contributing to job growth in many countries, regulations covering part-time work have received considerable attention in recent years, especially with regard to rights of part-timers compared to full-time employees.

Differences in regulation of working time help explain some of the large variation in the shares of workers working very long and very short hours in different countries. For example, as is well known, the UK has the highest share of men working long hours among OECD countries (OECD, 1999: Chart 5.2). In 1994, four out of every ten male workers in the UK worked an average of 45 hours or more each week. Japan and the US also had relatively high shares of men working long hours. But in France, Germany and Italy, long hours working is relatively uncommon, with less than one in ten men working long hours in Germany. Among women, there is less variation in the share working long hours; instead, the difference lies in the share of women working very short hours. Here it is the Netherlands that stands out, with more than three out of ten female workers working an average of 20 hours or less per week. The UK is not far behind with around a quarter of women working short hours; but in countries like Japan, the US, France and Italy such short hours working is very uncommon.

Table 6.6 sets out some of the main differences in the details of working time regulation. In some countries, such as Germany, France and Sweden, there are strict limits on weekly hours imposed by legislation or collective bargaining. Maximum limits were reduced in France in the 1990s in line with new legislation on the 35-hour week, and in Germany through changes in collective bargaining agreements in a number of sectors following the 35-hour week established in the metal industry in 1995. By contrast, in Japan and the US there are no legislative limits on maximum total working time,[11] although in these as in other countries national legislation is modified by agreements set through collective bargaining. There is also considerable variation in whether countries set limits to overtime working and the level at which they set a premium for overtime pay.

Unlike the use of fixed-term employment contracts, virtually no restrictions exist on the use of contracts for part-time work (Marullo, 1995). However, employers now have to observe the principle of equal treatment of part-time workers in comparison to full-time workers. This restricts the opportunities of employers to employ part-timers to evade regulations covering full-timers. This equal treatment principle has been established through collective agreements and as a result of cases that have established that differential treatment for part-timers may be considered to be a form of indirect discrimination by gender. More recently European labour legislation (see Chapter Ten) has provided directly for equal treatment between part-time and full-time workers. In the UK, for example, legislation had to be amended, first to extend employment protection to all part-timers working at least eight hours a week, following a decision at the European Court that exclusion of those working under 16 hours was a form of indirect discrimination; and second to take on board the recent European Directive providing *pro rata* rights for part-timers in a range of areas, including pay, benefits and training. Nevertheless, there are a number of

Table 6.6 Characteristics of working time regulation in selected countries

Country	Legal maxima			Overtime premia	Normal weekly hours set by collective agreement	Rights of part-time workers compared with full-timers
	Normal hours	Weekly overtime	Maximum total hours			
France	35	130 per annum	48	25% for first 8 hours, then 50%	35	By law equality on pay, leave, dismissals protection, severance pay
Denmark	37	None	48	50% for 1 hour, then rising to 100%	37	De facto equality on pay, leave, dismissals protection, notice periods; some excluded from pensions and unemployment benefits
Germany	48	12 (2 per day for 6-day week)	60	25%	35–39	By law equality on pay, sick pay, leave, dismissal protection; some pensions exclude part-timers; minimum hours required for welfare benefits
Italy	48	12 (2 per day for 6-day week)	60	10% plus 15% for unemployment fund	36–40	By law equality on pay, leave, dismissals protection, severance pay
Japan	40	None	None	25%	40–44	
Spain	40	2 (average 80 per annum)	47	25%	38–40	By law equality on pay; some pensions exclude part-timers
Sweden	40	12 (200 per annum)	48 or 52	No legislation	40	By law equal rights; some benefit entitlements depend on hours worked or income
UK	N/a	None	48	No legislation	34–40	By law equality on pay, leave, dismissal protection, benefits, etc.
US	40	None	None	50%	35–40	

Source: OECD (1998b), Table 5.10; Marullo (1995); details for France from Dr Phil Almond

loopholes. For example, in the UK and the Netherlands, access to overtime hours is defined according to the full-time working week, so that part-timers do not earn a premium for additional hours worked. This is not the case in France, where part-timers are entitled to premia pay once their hours exceed contracted hours or a stated threshold (Smith *et al.*, 1998). Also, entitlement to social protection (such as unemployment benefits) is restricted to people working more than a minimum number of hours (or earning a minimum level of pay) in countries such as Germany and the UK, but there are no such restrictions in France (Grimshaw and Rubery, 1997). Moreover, these differences in social protection rules provide incentives to employers to take on part-time workers in preference to full-timers, as there are often exemptions from social security contributions for employers, mirroring the exclusion of part-timers from social protection schemes.

Convergence or divergence in national regulatory systems?

In this last section, we consider the patterns of change in regulatory systems. A useful framework for assessing change is suggested by Lane (2000), which avoids the usual assumptions of a simple process of convergence towards a more deregulated model. Instead four potential scenarios are identified:

- convergence towards the deregulated model;
- divergence through accentuation/specialization of existing national systems;
- path-dependent incremental adaptation;
- hybridization within national regulatory systems.

In the first scenario, pressures for convergence towards a US-type deregulated labour market system suggest that 'thick' institutions, which provide strong employment protection and coordinate wage-setting, are vulnerable, especially as the internationalization of economies emphasizes the need for short-term adjustment to rapidly changing markets, industrial restructuring and technical change. For some commentators, convergence towards a short-termist US model is inevitable even though more regulated systems may be superior in the long run, since institutional arrangements that insulate workers from marketization are difficult to defend in a world increasingly dominated by Anglo-Saxon type capital markets which demand immediate returns (Dore, 1996).

Nevertheless, the evidence for convergence towards a deregulated model is weak. In the area of employment protection, there was very little overall change from the 1980s to the 1990s in most countries; a finding confirmed by the similarity in the OECD's own summary indicator for different countries (1999: Table 2.5). The story is complicated by the fact that within countries there are sometimes changes in both directions, reflecting changes in government as well as different approaches towards different areas of legislation. A notable example of moving towards greater regulation is Italy, with the most highly regulated system of employment protection, which actually strengthened legislation further by extending unfair dismissal regulations to small firms in 1990 (Mosley, 1994). France exhibits a relatively erratic pattern of change, with examples of deregulation (the requirement for official authorization of redundancies was abandoned in 1986) and re-regulation (in 1989 the schedule for redundancy procedures was extended and in 1993 official approval of social plans was required for collective redundancies) (Mosley, 1994). Indeed, it is France, perhaps more than any other country, where policy reflects the strong influence of changes in the political orientation and power of the Government at any one point in time. The main examples of deregulation of employment protection are Germany and Spain, which both eased restrictions on use of fixed-term employment contracts during the 1980s. In addition, Spain also extended the range of recognized objective grounds for collective redundancies in 1994, and made the procedural requirements less time consuming (OECD, 1999). Finally, in Japan revisions to the law in 1999 allowed companies to use so-called 'dispatched workers' (who numbered just over one million in 1999) for any type of work, abandoning the previous need to show the work required highly specialized skills (Japan Institute of Labour, 2001).

The case for convergence is perhaps strongest in the area of wage regulation. In many countries there is evidence of decentralization of collective bargaining, with more and more wage setting taking place at the enterprise level. Prime examples include Sweden, where central agreements first began to unravel in 1984, and where in 1990 the main employers' federation announced it would no longer participate in centralized bargaining (Katz, 1993; Thörnqvist, 1999). Also, in the UK industry-level bargaining collapsed in the mid-1980s and by the end of the 1990s only a minority of workplaces were covered by collective bargaining, with more and more employers setting pay unilaterally. However, differences in the pace of change and the form of decentralization make an overall verdict on convergence problematic.

The case of Germany is illustrative. There, the evidence points to a clear trend towards slow decentralization. Between 1990 and 1997, the number of company level agreements rose from 33,000 to 40,000 in the former West Germany and from 670 to 7000 in the former East (Hassel, 1999).[12] This 'serious tendency towards fragmentation of the previously highly centralized collective bargaining system' (*op. cit.*: 493) reflects a number of changing conditions: withdrawal of companies from employers' federations (such as the newly privatized public utilities and many multinationals); the refusal of new companies and new subsidiaries of existing companies to join employers' federations; and the more fragmented structure of bargaining in the former East Germany. However, it is a process of 'regulated decentralization'. For example, at the same time as pushing for decentralization, employer associations (most notably in the metal industry, *Gesamtmetall*) also wish to retain elements of centralized bargaining mainly because of its role in maintaining social peace (Hassel and Schulten, 1998). Thus while the US free market model may be influential at the level of ideology, talk of convergence of German and US institutions of wage setting is, as Lane puts it, 'a gross exaggeration' and 'an inadequate label' (2000: 228).

The second scenario involves divergence through increasing 'specialization' in the existing system of labour market regulation. Again, the evidence is mixed. The UK appeared to be specializing in a model of voluntarist deregulation characterized by strong employer-led flexibility throughout much of the 1980s and 1990s. However, the change in government in 1997 shifted the accent of labour market policy, which has seen re-regulation in a number of areas, such as a national minimum wage and adoption of a number of European Directives, which have strengthened employment protection in areas of working time and part-time work. Japan is another interesting example, since its phenomenal economic performance in the post-Second World War period is largely credited to its unique societal system of organizing production and employment. The strains of the long recession in the 1990s, however, have led to cracks in the traditional pillars of its employment system — lifetime employment, seniority-based wages and enterprise unionism — with some calling for radical change towards a more market-orientated approach (Iwao, 1997) and others pointing to the problems of increased use of part-time, fixed term contract and 'dispatched' workers who fall outside of core regulation (Weathers, 1999). The high level of coordination provided by the annual *Shunto* wage round weakened during the late 1990s, due to the increasing international outlook of the major companies and growing performance differentials between companies (*op. cit.*). Also, firms in certain sectors challenged the seniority principle (Lincoln and Nakata, 1997). Nevertheless, lifetime employment seems to have survived in principle, in part because employers are also wary of the alternative of having to contribute to a well-developed social welfare system and also because employers used it as a bargaining chip for more flexible payment systems (Weathers, 1999).

Our third scenario — path-dependent incremental adaptation — has wider empirical support. According to this prognosis, an understanding of the direction of change depends crucially on the different starting points and the pace of adaptation. In the US, for example, introduction of legislation on employment protection in a number of states is little more than an adaptive transformation of the existing model, designed to resolve the mounting costs of legal cases rather than a complete transformation in favour of an alternative model. Similarly, in the UK, while the late 1990s witnessed the introduction of a number of European Directives concerning employment protection, these have been implemented in conjunction with the existing peculiarities of the UK regulatory model, rather than under a new umbrella of social partnership and greater coordination of labour market activities.

In one sense, however, the notion of 'path-dependency' is a catch-all. In particular, it does not distinguish between reactive and proactive interventions driving changes in systems of labour market regulation; moreover, there are few transformations that mark a radical break from historical conditions (periods of crisis, such as the Great Depression, are obvious exceptions). As Figure 2.1 in Chapter 2 illustrates, global pressures towards transformation do not lead to automatic adjustments in societal systems but are reacted to, both positively and negatively, by the social actors shaping the societal employment system.

A more precise way of considering change in this regard is provided by our fourth scenario, that of 'hybridization'. Considering the UK again, while there were several examples of proactive intervention in employment protection and rights for atypical workers during the 1990s, decentralization of collective bargaining continued apace. By establishing a floor of rights through European legislation and allowing the system of collective bargaining to further fragment in response to employer pressures, the UK demonstrates a hybrid approach to regulation and flexibility, borrowing from both European and US labour market models. In Germany, to the extent that decentralization of collective bargaining continues within a broad framework of social partnership, then a hybrid pattern of change is also evident (Lane, 2000).

Of course the future pattern of change and the factors that will drive it are unknowable. What is clear, however, is that the old rhetoric of deregulation and flexibility has had its day. Instead, attention to different mixes of regulation with increased awareness of the different intervening roles of employers, unions and the state has led to greater appreciation of the fact that there is no 'one best way' to regulate the labour market. Ongoing processes of change within multinational firms may, in the future, mean that real pressures of globalization — in place of the rhetoric of deregulation — become an increasingly important driver of change in national regulatory systems. Whether convergence on a purified realm of global employment regulation is likely is an issue we take up in Chapter Nine. In the meantime, the next chapter furthers our investigation into the sources of diversity in national systems by looking at the many different ways work and employment are managed at the level of the workplace.

Notes

1 Here, we draw on a number of studies, for example Buchele and Christiansen (1999); Stanford (2000).
2 In 1999, the working-age population (15–64 year olds) of the US was around 180 million; that of the EU was around 251 million.
3 The highest decile refers to the ten per cent of the workforce earning the highest wages; the bottom decile refers to the ten per cent earning the lowest wages.
4 Examples of comparative studies of industrial relations include: Bamber and Lansbury (1998); Dunlop (1958); Ferner and Hyman (1992, 1998); Hyman (2001); Hyman and Ferner (1994); Ulman *et al.* (1993); van Ruysseveldt and Visser (1996a).
5 There are exceptions, such as Kaiin, the Seamen's Union, which is organized across the whole industry (Kuwahara, 1998).
6 There are other forms of worker participation which may be described as employer-led, such as quality circles, teamwork and profit-sharing.
7 It is difficult to gauge the success of attempts to transfer the dual system to the former East Germany. Many employers either left the sectoral agreement or did not join due to the more adverse economic circumstances. However, many companies signed up under

the provisions of new 'hardship clauses', which allow for deviations from agreed terms and conditions (EIRR, 1997).

8   This tension came to light during the late 1990s, with employer representatives from the German SME sector (Mittelstand) pressing for a radical overhaul of the system. However, many employers were also keen to preserve the essential principles of the system, as the determination of pay and conditions at the sectoral level allowed individual employers to devote their energies to business matters, rather than become absorbed in conflictual industrial relations issues (EIRR, 1997; Lane, 2000).

9   The primary goal of the informal coordination is to link wage claims across the economy with international competitiveness (similar to the rationale that underpins the leading role of IG Metall in Germany). Discussions with government officials focus on the assumption that if wage growth across the economy outstrips average productivity growth, this will push up inflation, which will force interest rates and the exchange rate upwards, reducing competitiveness.

10   However, in Spain, where more than one-third of the workforce is on fixed-term contracts, there is evidence that employers use these workers as a means of lowering wages, despite legislation which prohibits payment of different wage rates for permanent and fixed-term contracts (Cousins, 1999).

11   In both countries, legislation on normal hours is prescribed so that overtime premia are payable for hours worked above 40 hours per week (OECD, 1998b).

12   Survey evidence shows that the proportion of employees in Germany covered by collective bargaining dropped from 83 per cent to 75 per cent between 1995 and 1998, and that non-coverage was particularly high among SMEs and in the expanding service sectors (Hassel, 1999: Table 8).

7

Employment policy and practice: implementation at the workplace

The diversity evident in national systems of education and training, labour market regulation and welfare suggests that labour market policy in different countries can be expected to develop along quite different routes. As we have shown in the preceding chapters, these different policy trajectories are associated with a wide range of employment outcomes, including the level of investment in a skilled workforce, the degree of wage inequality and the extent, and inclusiveness, of employment protection. But a focus on national level institutions tells us little about the actual employment experiences of workers in different countries. For example, a national system of apprenticeship training may support a high skilled economy, but whether or not a highly skilled worker fully deploys their range of expertise depends on employment practices experienced within the organization. Does promotion within the organization depend upon technical expertise or supervisory skills? Is there a strict demarcation between jobs or is flexible working encouraged? Does the form of work organization encourage employee initiative and autonomy or a tight system of supervisory control? Analysis at the level of the workplace and organization can shed light on the significance of skill for the individual worker. Are jobs classified and remunerated by level of skill, or by seniority? Are highly skilled workers more likely to enjoy job security than less skilled workers?

We consider these questions in this chapter by comparing employment policies and practices at the level of the workplace across different countries, focusing on the division of labour, payment systems, job security and redundancy measures, and working time arrangements. The shift to the workplace level does not mean we are putting our knowledge of differences in national institutions to one side, to return to in some later chapter. The individual organization is embedded in its national society and is therefore shaped by wider national institutions. But these provide more than a context. The organization is a major source of tension in a societal system and may exert a powerful pressure for change where national institutions do not fit with new forms of work organization, or investments in new technologies. Thus

175

a comparative approach to employment systems is not simply a matter of identifying enduring differences in labour market institutions or ways of organizing work. It is a useful tool for understanding how change occurs within societal systems of employment, that is through the shifting dynamics of organizational behaviour and institutional adjustment (Box 7.1; and Chapter Two, Figure 2.1).

Box 7.1   The challenges of cross-national research: the contributions of 'societal analysis'

The original work of the LEST researchers in formulating 'societal analysis' as a critical and theoretical tool made an enormous contribution in thinking about the relationship between different levels of institutions and practices within society. However, in emphasizing the interdependencies and coherence between the various dimensions, it was less successful in its treatment of how societies change and adapt through processes of conflict and contradiction. Marc Maurice, in a critical reflection of earlier work by proponents of the so-called 'societal effect' approach, addresses the complexity of these two issues:

Which level of analysis?

It is indeed the process of the 'construction' of 'actors' and 'spaces', which is at the heart of societal analysis, that is reflected in the 'macro-micro' relationship ... Such an expression (used in both economics and sociology, and even in history) introduces, through metaphor, a sort of hierarchy of 'magnitudes' in the analysis of the observed phenomena that equates to different 'levels'. The 'macro' tends to encompass the 'micro', as if one was the exterior of the other or the micro was a miniaturisation of the macro. In certain cases this particular quality attributed to the 'macro' is such that it confers upon it if not the status of causality then at least a superior position in the explanation ... Societal analysis tends to reach beyond this rhetoric by giving comparability a new status. In so doing, it conceptualises the macro/micro antithesis differently, problematising it as 'sets' of interdependent relations in which 'actors' and 'spaces' are perceived in their *relationship to the wider society*. This constitutes the basic postulate of societal analysis which was given expression, originally, in the emblematic notion of 'societal effect' ... The construction of such sets of structural and relational interdependencies gives them a *'coherence'* that excludes any term-for-term comparison between their various constituent elements. (Maurice, 2000, pp. 16–17; italics in original)

Coherent but changing?

Although at its outset societal analysis highlighted 'national patterns of coherence', it does not, for all that, stick stubbornly to the construction of unique, immutable totalities. Even in its early days it was sensitive to the variability in (international) space of societal forms and arrangements; more recently it has demonstrated its ability to deal with variability over time and with the dynamic of the same phenomena. Recognition of the historical nature of the construction of actors and spaces and of the historicity of the processes involved renders the economic and social principles at work more intelligible, making it possible to take account of both their relative stability and their dynamic of change. Nevertheless this recourse to the time dimension and thus to the contingent nature of 'social constructs', does not mean that history is, in this case, the ultimate explanatory principle. In fact priority is given in our approach to the endogenisation of the explanation ... Does not the priority given to *endogenous explanation* tend to emphasise 'self-maintenance processes' and therefore *reproduction mechanisms*? And does this not give rise to a certain stability in the phenomena under investigation, thereby reinforcing the 'static' image of societal analysis already alluded to with reference to the notion of 'coherence'? In fact, any such bias is linked to an unjustified 'functionalist' interpretation of our

---

Box 7.1   Continued

approach and to a reductionist concept of the notion of structure ... The static elements reflect the relative stability of the identity of actors in their relationship to spaces, captured at a given moment ... far from being identically reproducible over time, social constructs and the processes by which they are produced have a capacity, being contingent, for both self-maintenance and 'non-identical reproduction'. (Maurice, 2000, pp. 22, 24)

The division of labour

Adam Smith's ideas on the division of labour, coupled with the widespread diffusion of Frederick Taylor's principles of 'scientific management', have exerted a strong influence on forms of work organization in all advanced capitalist countries. In the 18th century, Smith argued forcefully that efficient production depended on the firm organizing work by dividing up individual job tasks among workers with varying levels of skill. And in the late 19th century, Taylor encouraged the view that efficient production depended upon a careful separation of the conception and execution of tasks, better known as a division of labour into the hands and the brains. Given the force of these ideas one might expect to find firms in all countries organizing work on the basis of a strict demarcation of job tasks and tight supervisory control, with few opportunities for working across job boundaries and limited autonomy or discretion enjoyed by most workers.

In reality, what we know from a range of cross-national comparative research (see also Chapter Three) is that while these ideas have some relevance for firms in many countries, their application differs quite widely. For example, the Taylorist principle of separating the execution of a task from its conception is highly relevant to all capitalist enterprises, but the extent and form of division between people in supervisory managerial positions and workers in office or shopfloor posts vary considerably across countries. In this section, we illustrate this and other differences through comparison of companies in the UK, France, Germany, the US and Japan. The discussion benefits from the reviews of empirical evidence provided by Lane (1989) and Marsden (1999), as well as previous work based on the 'societal effect' approach (for example, Maurice et al., 1986; Sorge and Warner, 1986; see Chapter Two). These studies contribute to our understanding of how the links between individuals and society are shaped, on the one hand, by the division of labour and form of work organization, and on the other hand, by the educational system, the role of the company and opportunities for worker mobility (Maurice et al., 1984).

Table 7.1 summarizes differences among the five countries selected along three dimensions. The first distinguishes the general way firms in each country tend to allocate tasks to workers (drawing on Marsden (1999)). This is important as it gives an indication of how the firm links to the national system of vocational training, and also sets the context for differences in the range of worker discretion and patterns of

Table 7.1 Division of labour in manufacturing companies in five countries

Factor	US	France	UK	Germany	Japan
Principle of task allocation	Work post	Work post	Job territory	Qualification rule	Competence rank
Functional specialization (horizontal)	High	High	Medium/ High	Low	Low
Nature of job hierarchy:					
Level of technical expertise of supervisors	Low	Low	Low	High	High
Supervisory span of control	High	High	Medium	Low	Low

Source: Adapted from Marsden (1999) and Lane (1989)

worker mobility. Under the principle of 'work post', which is associated with companies in France and the US, employers divide up work into discrete tasks, assigning each to an individual worker who is then held individually responsible. In both countries, exercise of this principle reflects the greater freedom of companies in defining and organizing jobs in the context of a weakly developed system of vocational training (see Chapter Five). In France, it is typical for subordinate tasks to be separated out from managerial and planning tasks since the former are designed around very short periods of workplace-based training, reinforcing the high degree of functional specialization (Maurice *et al.*, 1984). In both countries, the strict link between discrete task and individual worker means that employers enjoy a clear range of control. But the disadvantage is that firms are less able to adapt to unforeseen events. In France, job descriptions are seen as too rigid to deal with pressures for new work systems (Crozier, 1963); in the US the focus on discrete task allocation encourages workers to focus on 'the words in the manual' (Slichter *et al.*, 1960, cited in Marsden, 1999).

The situation in the UK is somewhat similar to those in the US and France, since managers assign individuals to tasks, but here tasks are defined on the basis of some notion of job territory. Historically this has involved identifying tasks by the 'tools of the trade'. Certain tools, or the handling of particular materials, are associated with the work of an electrician, or an engineer, for example, while others are associated with the work of a printer or technician. During times when trade unions exercised greater strength in the UK, this customary form of task allocation would set the limits to management's right to direct workers to undertake one job or another. This raises a broader point regarding an important distinction from the French and American systems. Unlike the US or France, the UK principle of job territory bears a close linkage to broader notions of craft skills, or occupational skills, reflecting the stronger tradition of vocational training (in the manufacturing sector). This is also one of the reasons why the supervisory span of control is higher in the US and France than in the UK (see Table 7.1). Nevertheless, the degree of functional specialization is still relatively high in the UK, so that employers also face potential problems of adapting task allocation to changing work demands. This ought not to be taken as implying that a division of labour based on strict demarcation of tasks (work post or job territory) is necessarily negative for productivity. Stability and continuation of rules concerning who does what within an organization also play an important role in fostering worker cooperation and workplace order; rapid break up of demarcations — often claimed to be the cause of low skill problems in the UK — may in fact make the situation worse (Marsden, 1999: 43–4).

In Germany and Japan the principle of task allocation is different. Whereas in the above three countries individual tasks are identified and then assigned to individuals, in Germany and Japan companies rely on a particular procedure — known and accepted by both employers and workers — to organize workers and tasks into different categories (Marsden, 1999). A different procedure is used in each country. In Germany, the procedure is the 'qualification rule' and involves identifying workers by the type of training apprenticeship and organizing tasks according to the skills required. Job design strongly reflects the system of occupational skills and, unlike in the UK, this linkage was if anything reinforced over the 1980s and 1990s. Within each function, German firms have a large number of job categories, but importantly this provides the framework for skill enhancement as workers gain skills through job rotation. Tasks are thus organized around much more broadly defined functions, resulting in relatively low levels of functional specialization. In Japan, the weakness of the national system of vocational training means that qualifications cannot be taken as a procedural rule for organizing workers and tasks. Instead, companies adopt the internal procedure of 'competence rank', which involves ranking individual workers by status (a mix of seniority and job competence) and allocating the more demanding tasks to higher-ranking workers. Again, like Germany, there is no direct linking of workers to tasks and the degree of functional specialization in Japan is low. Japanese companies use job rotation to develop broad-based skills, although these may be less broad than in German companies (Jürgens et al., 1993, cited in Marsden, 1999).

Differences in the principles of task allocation in manufacturing companies in these five countries underline the variety of work structures inherent in levels of functional specialization and the tightness of supervisory control. Nowhere are these differences in stratification more obvious than in the nature of the dividing line between management and non-management (see Chapter One, Box 1.3). In Germany, where authority is based on technical ability and occupational skill, workers experience less authority from above and differences in status are less pronounced. Moreover, there is frequent mobility from 'skilled worker' status to technical and supervisory staff (*Meister*) through undertaking further technical training and achieving a supervisor's certificate (*Meisterbrief*). In the UK and France, supervisors have a low level of technical expertise, largely because management posts are seen as a specialist coordinating activity and, if anything, promotion to management is seen as a way out of technical work, not a way of developing further technical know-how (Lane, 1989; Lam, 1996 for the UK).

Overall, the different systems of work structures — in particular the principle of task allocation and the nature of the job hierarchy — are shaped by the way the firm is embedded in the wider system of vocational training. Moreover, the characteristics observed at the level of the workplace help explain certain features of the age composition of the workforce and patterns of worker mobility. The German–French comparison by Maurice *et al.* (1986) is the best illustration of these findings. They show that because of the weak vocational training system in France, most workers entering non-management positions possess only general schooling and expect to move into skilled positions over time through accumulating on-the-job experience. The opposite is true in Germany, where most workers complete apprenticeship training and this provides the basis for what determines whether they will enter a skilled or unskilled job; on-the-job experience is of relatively little importance. These differences shape the age composition of the workforce: in France, skilled workers tend to be older and with more years of workplace experience compared to unskilled workers, while in Germany the age composition among skilled and unskilled groups is similar. This means that, in line with the internal labour market model of France (Chapter Five), age has a greater effect on a worker's pay than in Germany. This age effect, together with the greater value attached to status in France, explains why wage differentials in French firms are always higher than in German firms. Similar findings concerning the strong role of seniority in determining internal promotions are found for the US and Japan (Lincoln and Kalleberg, 1990), again reflecting the relative importance of internal as opposed to occupational labour markets (see below).

Initial studies from the 'societal effect' school were largely concerned with explaining differences in societal structures of pay and employment. During the 1980s, this approach informed a range of studies that sought to address the equally pressing issue of the causes of productivity differences between countries. The most well known of these are the studies conducted by researchers at the National Institute of Economic and Social Research (NIESR) during the mid-to-late 1980s (such as Daly *et al.*, 1985; Prais *et al.*, 1989; Steedman and Wagner, 1989). These studies argued that differences in job hierarchies, which reflect societal forms of embeddedness in different systems of vocational training, were key to explaining the low level of labour productivity in the UK compared to Germany and France. For example, in a study of matched manufacturing plants in the UK and Germany, Daly *et al.* (1985) argued that much of the 63 per cent productivity gap was the result of limited technical skills and training provision (especially the absence of engineering skills and poor technical knowledge of foremen). Steedman and Wagner (1989) found the business of clothing manufacture in Germany more productive than in the UK and blamed this on similar problems of technical expertise and training; for example, whereas all the German supervisors in their sample of firms had completed a three-year apprenticeship and further work study, nine out of ten British supervisors had had no formal vocational training whatsoever.

Overall, the NIESR studies contribute towards an understanding of differences in economic performance, with a clear policy recommendation regarding the potential benefits to the UK of borrowing elements of the German system of vocational training. These recommendations undoubtedly had some impact in feeding through into the design and implementation of the UK's Modern Apprenticeship system, but as we discussed in Chapter Five, the extent of borrowing was limited in practice and, as we argue in Chapter Nine, strong interlinkages between the many dimensions of a country's employment system suggest that there is no straightforward process of imitation.

Payment systems

Different systems of structuring work, involving different principles of task allocation and degrees of functional specialization, are associated with variation in the way jobs are graded. For example, in the German case, we saw that jobs are typically defined by the associated vocational qualification; whereas in the UK case a more informal notion of job territory is used by employers to match workers to jobs. These different principles of task allocation set limits to the practice of job grading. The result is that in Germany, although job grading is determined by collective bargaining, this process is constrained by the strongly held notion that skill ought to be tied to vocational training requirements. In contrast, in the UK the absence of a formalized procedure for matching tasks to workers is accompanied by the absence of any industry-wide system of job grading (see Chapter One, Box 1.5). Moreover, even within a single organization in the UK there are typically several job clusters, paid and graded according to separate systems. In this section, we consider how systems of job grading and job hierarchies interact with different payment systems. Our main objective is to illustrate how different payment systems interact with other factors to shape patterns of fragmentation and mobility among workforce groups within different countries.

Payment systems may be divided into three broad categories:

- seniority (or age)-based pay
- job-based pay
- merit (or output)-based pay

Under the first type, pay is linked to the length of experience within the organization, or directly to the age of the individual employee. This payment system provides for automatic progression for all employees, typically up to some maximum limit within the job grade until further promotion. Seniority-based pay is often found in organizations with strong internal labour markets, since automatic pay advancement goes hand-in-hand with incremental acquisition of skills and steady improvement in performance as workers progress upwards through the job hierarchy. A job-based payment system links pay advancement to changes in job task, or to changes in the formal or informal training required by a particular job task. Such systems are more likely to be found in organizations where job grading relies on some form of job evaluation or a link with vocational qualifications. The third payment system ties pay to some measure of performance, either directly through a measure of output, or indirectly through appraisal of work effort. This may take the form of individual or collective performance. Unlike the first two payment systems, this system, at least in principle, may involve an addition to or subtraction from the total wage.

Seniority-based pay plays a moderate to strong role in all our selected countries except Germany, where the strong emphasis on qualifications means that payment systems pay less attention to length of service and more to jobs — classified by occupational skill. The principle of seniority is strongest in Japan (see Table 7.2) and, moreover, this applies to both blue-collar and white-collar workers. In Japan, seniority-based pay is clearly an important component of its internal labour market structure, and combines with the principle of lifetime employment to persuade employees not to quit and search for work elsewhere (McCormick and McCormick, 1996). This principle has persisted despite expectations during the 1990s that slower economic growth and ageing of the workforce would result in the dismantling of the system. Curiously, however, analysis of payment practices during the long slowdown in the late 1970s showed that age-earnings profiles actually became steeper, since demand for entry-age workers reduced and this pulled down the entry-level wage compared to that of older workers (Brown *et al.*, 1997: 106). During the slowdown of the 1990s, some studies found evidence of a flattening of the age-earnings profile, but others found evidence of its continued importance, especially in relation to other countries (Chapter One, Box 1.4; see also Marsden, 1999).

Table 7.2 Payment systems in five countries

Factor	US	France	UK	Germany	Japan
Seniority-based pay	Strong (but small increments)	Strong (declining)	Medium (declining)	Weak	Very strong (despite some decline)
Job-based pay	Strong (job evaluation important)	Strong	Medium (declining)	Strong	Weak
Merit (or output)-based pay	Medium (very strong for management)	Medium (increasing)	Strong (increasing)	Medium	Medium

Source: Adapted from Rubery *et al.* (1998b) and Marsden (1999)

Seniority-based pay is also strong in the US (Hashimoto and Raisian, 1992; Ohtake, 1998). In comparison to Japanese firms, the profile is much steeper in earlier years so that workers reach their maximum earnings at a younger age than in Japan, although the overall impact on earnings is less. Moreover, general experience (total years of work experience) counts more strongly in the US than in Japan, where the emphasis is on tenure within the firm (Hashimoto and Raisian, 1985). The comparison with the US also shows that differences in age-earnings profiles across industries in Japan are small, reflecting the stronger coordination of wage bargaining (Chapter Six). Instead, the main source of differentiation is company size, since strong internal labour markets are more likely to exist in large companies than among the small and medium-sized enterprises that make up the tiers of suppliers. In the US, there are clear lines of segmentation by level of education (with university graduates enjoying far steeper age-earnings profiles compared to workers with a high school education), and by industry. In France, seniority plays an important role in line with its strong internal labour market structures; yet even here there has been some debate about its declining effect on pay structure since the 1970s. However, the empirical evidence may reflect the changing composition of the workforce rather than a shift in the payment system. Marsden suggests that with the steep rise in youth unemployment during the 1980s, fewer workers were employed in entry level jobs, and this depresses estimates of the age-earnings profile because the greater rewards for length of service come early on (1999: 125).

The principle of job-based pay is strong in the US, reflecting the traditional practice of grading jobs using systems of job evaluation. The practice was consolidated during the bureaucratization of employment relations in the 1930s and 1940s, when the share of large firms deploying job evaluations increased from one in five to more than three in five between 1935 and 1946 (Baron *et al.*, 1986, cited in Marsden, 1999: 134; see, also, Jacoby, 1984). Job-based pay is also commonly in use in French organizations, where on-the-job training provides for progression through differently graded jobs and pay advancement. The institutionalization of the internal labour market model as the training system in France (Chapter Five) could be expected to provide employers with considerable autonomy in designing pay structures to match their internal job design. But in fact, job and pay grades within individual organizations are strongly influenced by industry classification agreements, as demonstrated by evidence that job classifications for six out of ten employees are from the respective industry agreements (Barrat *et al.*, 1996, cited in Marsden, 1999: 99). In Japan, the principle of job-based pay is weak, reaffirming the finding that the Japanese form of internal labour market is peculiar since it attaches pay to the individual worker, rather than to the job (as in the classic description of the internal labour market by Doeringer and Piore, 1971).

The importance of merit- or output-related pay in the five countries varies, but here we find some signs of convergence. In Japan, merit pay was added to the payment system in the 1950s as part of a compromise proposal by trade unions at a time when employers sought to dismantle seniority pay in favour of job-based pay.

Unions successfully blocked the use of job-based pay; the agreed payment system consisted of *nenko* (seniority pay), *shokuno-kyo* (merit pay) and a base pay component (Brown *et al.*, 1997; McCormick and McCormick, 1996). Since then, during the 1980s and 1990s there was continued resistance by unions to job-based pay, and limited diffusion of merit pay. A survey by the Japanese Ministry of Labour in 1986 showed that the proportion of payment-by-results in the total pay package was very small — just 0.5 per cent among firms in the manufacturing sector, 2.5 per cent in retail and 2.0 per cent in real estate (cited in Koike, 1994: 53). Nevertheless, merit ratings are an important determinant of promotion decisions, with supervisors conducting regular personal assessments (*satei*) of employees. As a result, Japanese workers of similar experience and education have different earnings because of different rates of promotion (Itoh, 1994). While *satei* is seen as a key contributor to improved productivity — with expectations of promotion acting as a strong incentive to increased work effort — it may also be partially responsible for a deterioration in the quality of working life. Endo (1994) argues that it has led to an increase in hidden working hours (since to finish a task in fewer hours is perceived as a sign of competence) and an increase in worker obedience to management.

In the UK, the trend since the 1980s has been one of a decline in the importance of job-based payment systems, leading to flatter grading structures, a move away from establishing links between age and pay and increased differentiation in pay through the use of performance-related pay (Rubery *et al.*, 1998a). In the absence of stronger regulation of wages, or wider coverage of collective bargaining, UK organizations enjoy a relatively free hand in designing payment systems. The problem, however, is that this has exacerbated the chaotic nature of payment structures and systems in the UK, making it difficult for prospective entrants to the labour market to make a decision on where to seek work, informed by knowledge about the jobs and pay offered by organizations. Moreover, the rise of performance-related pay raises the possibility of new forms of pay discrimination between men and women (Rubery, 1995). Performance-related pay also spread widely in France during the 1980s and 1990s, helped both by the fact that the French system of job allocation by work post facilitates measurement of individual effort, and by the encouragement to enterprise bargaining that came from the 1982 Auroux laws (Marsden, 1999: 195). In Germany, use of performance-related pay has progressed more slowly. Wage increases tend to follow expansion in jobs and development of skill. Moreover, performance management is jointly administered by management and works councils, protecting workers from manipulation of standards (Marsden, 1999), which is more of a risk in other countries like the UK, for example.

Job security and redundancy measures

Redundancies were a major news item during the 1990s in many countries, because the risk of layoffs seemed to spread to many sectors and occupations in the labour market that had previously enjoyed job security. Moreover, a new term was used to talk about redundancies — 'downsizing' — reflecting a new managerial belief that job losses were essential to improve productivity in the name of the 'lean organization'. 'Delayering' of job ladders led to the loss of middle management grades; activities were outsourced following decisions to concentrate on 'core' activities; and pressures from financial markets demanded job cuts as a signal of improved performance. In this context, fears of redundancy spiralled and captured the imagination of many media commentators. In the US, survey evidence shows that downsizing shifted the burden of redundancies from blue-collar to white-collar workers during the early 1990s, as well as from younger, less experienced workers to older and more educated workers (see Box 7.2). The wave of redundancies since September 2001 marks a break from the 1990s wave of downsizing as the traditional reasons for redundancy — including corporate crisis and a downturn in product demand — come to the fore (for earlier analysis see Massey and Meegan (1982)).

But downsizing was only one side to organizations' approach to redundancies. The other side involved attempts to develop a new, more flexible approach to

---

Box 7.2   Downsizing in the US

News accounts of the layoff of large numbers of white-collar managerial employees at companies such as General Motors, Kodak, IBM, Exxon, and Merrill Lynch illustrated [the new wave of 'downsizing']. Salaried employees had held 62.4 per cent of the jobs eliminated in 1993–1994, which is significantly larger than salaried employees' share (40 per cent) of all jobs (American Management Association, 1994). The figures in [the] [t]able ... document the recent increases in the share of job cuts borne by middle management, supervisors, and professional/technical employees.

Table   Occupational distribution of downsizing

Percentage of jobs eliminated that were:	1990–91 %	1993–94 %
Hourly	55.8	37.6
Supervisory	13.8	25.5
Middle management	17.2	18.5
Professional/technical	13.2	18.2

Source: American Management Association (1994)

Detailed statistical analysis documents that by the mid-1980s, managers were actually more vulnerable to displacement due to downsizing and plant closings than were lower-level employees after controlling for industry and individual characteristics (e.g. education, experience, race, and sex) (Cappelli, 1992).

Extract from P. Cappelli *et al.*, *Change at Work* (New York: Oxford University Press, 1997), pp. 68–9.

References in text:

American Management Association, *AMA Survey on Downsizing: Summary of Key Findings* (New York: American Management Association, 1994).

P. Cappelli, 'Examining managerial displacement', *Academy of Management Journal*, 35 (1992): 203–17.

managing employment, both to avoid making 'core' workers redundant and to minimize the costs of managing redundancies. In a review of European countries' approaches to managing redundancy Carabelli and Tronti (1999: 9) argue that the growing challenges of globalization:

> ...led employers to seek a permanent solution to the problem of creating an optimum workforce (in both qualitative and quantitative terms), by introducing flexibility into their hiring of labour (by diversifying their employment contracts) and into their deployment of that labour (adaptable skills and variable working hours) — policies that were generally combined with outsourcing and downsizing.

In all countries there is evidence of employer attempts to prevent redundancies through use of various forms of flexible employment policies and practices. The motives for and intentions of flexible policies are likely to vary from employer to employer, from country to country. Nevertheless, while each variation on the flexibility policy may allow employers to avoid the costs associated with traditional redundancies, each approach also carries with it a range of negative effects (see Table 7.3). For example, employers who offer new recruits fixed-term or temporary contracts may aim to use these workers as a buffer to protect the employment of a 'core' workforce and therefore to minimize the costs of managing redundancies. However, there are several side-effects. Workers on atypical contracts are at best only partially protected by employment protection and therefore end up shouldering the economic and social costs of redundancy. In some cases employers may be able to rely on exploiting an expanding supply of low wage labour, leading to evasion of social security contributions and failure to offer proper employment contracts, thereby increasing the costs of integrating the socially excluded into society (Carabelli and Tronti, 1999).

Of course employer policies are strongly shaped by over-arching systems of regulation of employment protection, which govern the management of temporary redundancies as well as structural redundancies. In countries where regulation over employment protection (see Chapter Six) is strong, employers' strategies to develop flexible employment policies to avoid redundancies may in fact be moving in the same direction as national labour market policy. Governments' efforts to achieve low levels of unemployment, redistribute working hours or encourage retraining and upskilling may also be stimulating the use of new forms of employment. For example, in Italy, attempts have been made to institute a flexible, uniform system to the management of redundancies. Plans outlined in 1997 under the Government of Romano Prodi envisaged a system where workers who were temporarily laid off would, in return for wage compensation, be required to engage in active retraining (paid for by employers and employees). Where structural redundancies were sought employers would be required to establish new procedures, including a notification period during which workers would receive lower pay (topped up by benefits) and be helped to find new jobs (Carabelli et al., 1999). In France, the Government provided support for the protection of workers' jobs by subsidizing retraining and

Table 7.3 Flexible employment to minimize redundancies

Factor	Employment policy	Positive outcomes	Adverse outcomes
Flexible employment contracts	Fixed term, temporary contracts	(1) Encourage job creation (2) Reduced cost of managing redundancies (3) Possible to protect 'core' workers with a buffer of 'periphery' workers	(1) Workers bear cost of redundancy (2) Workers enjoy limited employment protection (3) Encourage clandestine employment and exploitation (4) Evasion of taxes and spiral of financial crises
Flexible working hours	(1) Reduced working hours (2) Greater use of part-time work (3) Job sharing	(1) Encourages job creation (2) Redistribution of working time to minimize redundancies	(1) Employer costs of reorganizing work and production (2) Government costs of reforming social security/ pension system to remove discrimination (3) Active labour market policies needed to ensure flows between part-time and full-time jobs
Flexible pay	Performance-related pay, Profit-related pay	(1) Adaptation of pay to minimize redundancies (2) Encourages participation and commitment to organizational strategy	(1) Corporation risk shifts to the workers (2) Discriminatory appraisal of worker performance (3) Conflicts with norms regarding seniority-based pay

Source: Adapted from text in Carabelli and Tronti (1999): 5–9

programmes that encourage internal mobility (Caire and Kerschen, 1999). Also, in some European countries there have been strong national efforts (through government policies or collective bargaining agreements) to encourage the redistribution of working hours as a means of avoiding job loss. The most well known case is France, where the Robien and Aubry Acts provide employers with a series of instruments to cut working hours to prevent redundancies.

Differences in nationwide employment agendas shape policies and practices visible at the level of the organization or workplace. In particular, they shape the form and incidence of employer actions to prevent temporary and structural layoffs. As a result, while employers in some countries have taken a strong innovative approach to designing alternatives to redundancy (typically through agreements with trade unions), in other countries employers may be unable or unwilling to institutionalize creative preventive measures. In Germany, where legislation restricts employer freedom to lay off workers (see Chapter One, Box 1.8), there are clear examples of imaginative schemes being introduced at company level, the most famous of which is the Volkswagen scheme, where major reductions in working time were offered as a means of avoiding redundancies (see Box 7.3). Although Volkswagen is somewhat exceptional in the German context (it is not a member of the employers' association and bargains directly with the union, IG Metall) it does illustrate how a strong regulatory framework, particularly one that offers some compensatory support to employers, can help in formulating innovative solutions. New German legislation promoting part-time work for older people provides incentives for employers (in concert with unions) to use a form of partial early retirement; the employee also wins since an old person who halves his or her working time receives 70 per cent of previous net earnings from the employer (Heseler and Mückenberger, 1999).

Box 7.3   Innovative policies to prevent redundancy

Germany: the Volkswagen model

The Volkswagen Group had developed into the biggest European car producer and was number four worldwide with its subsidiaries Audi, Seat and Skoda. New production plants in Spain, Portugal, Eastern Europe, the new German federal states, and the recent economic decline had led to a remarkable capacity surplus within the group. Consequently Volkswagen had very serious problems. The company's 1993 annual report showed that Volkswagen had suffered a 19.2 per cent reduction in turnover, a 25.2 per cent reduction in sales, a 55.9 per cent reduction in investment and a 46.3 per cent reduction in annual results ...

Because of excess capacity and productivity improvements, in conventional terms one-third of the workforce should have been laid off between 1994 and 1995. But the company tried to avoid this solution, and the problem to solve, therefore, was how to cut down DM2 billion of labour costs, which is the equivalent of making about 30,000 workers redundant (Hartz, 1994: 10) ... Direct manpower cuts seem to be the easiest and most economical way to cut labour costs. From a legal point of view, making 30,000 workers redundant would have been a 'mass dismissal for operational reasons adjusted to production' (*Massenentlassung bei Betriebsänderung*). Consequently this would have been fairly expensive because of the co-determination rights of the works council (Rosdücher and Seifert, 1994: 4). Pursuant to paragraph 112 Betriebsverfassungsgesetz (Works Constitution Act) the works council has the right to force the company to set up a social compensation plan in order to avoid social hardship. Therefore no immediate cost saving could have been achieved, especially considering the bargaining time ... These circumstances forced Volkswagen, and especially its industrial relations director, Peter Hartz, to find alternatives in the fields of working time organization and training ...

The 28.8-hour working week

The basic idea was to save 20 per cent of the annual labour costs immediately, without lay-offs. This was possible by cutting working hours from 36 to 28.8 hours per week without wage compensation ... The key to the complicated wage package was to distribute all annual special payments over a 12-month period. In detail:

- the already-agreed increase in pay rates of 3.5 per cent was postponed from 1 November 1993 to 1 January 1994;

Box 7.3 Continued

- the 35-hour working week with full wage compensation of 2.8 per cent planned for 1 October 1995 was introduced on 1 January 1994;
- the annual special payment (96 per cent of the monthly income) and holiday bonus were transformed into monthly payments;
- the 1 per cent increase in pay rates negotiated for (1 August 1994) was brought forward to 1 January 1994;
- the remaining gap of 2 per cent of the monthly gross wage was covered by a special payment made by Volkswagen.

Source: Volkswagen A. G. (1993)
...

The part-time employment element of the model

The idea behind the part-time element is a 'contract' between the younger and the older generation. It enables younger workers, after they have finished their apprenticeship, to start working step by step to gain full employment instead of becoming unemployed. They start with a 20-hour working week for the first two years ... The part-time element for the older workers functions in the opposite way. They can reduce their working time at the age of 56 down to 24 hours and have the possibility to go down to 20 hours after their 59th birthday (Hartz, 1994: 81–7) ...

The qualification element

The qualification element of the model is based on a three- to six-month break ... During the qualification time, workers are paid 68 per cent of their last net income by the employment service. This is due to the fact that this qualification time is formally treated as short-time work in the sense of the German Employment Promotion Act (Section 63 IV Arbeitsförderungsgesetz). On top of this the workers receive an allowance from Volkswagen which can be up to 80–95 percent of their last monthly income depending on their wage group (Rosdücher and Seifert, 1994: 11).

Extract from: P. Garnjost and K. Blettner, 'Volkswagen: cutting labour costs without redundancies', in J. Storey (ed.), *Blackwell Cases in Human Resource and Change Management*, (Oxford: Blackwell, 1996), pp. 86, 87, 89–90, 91–2, 95, 96, 97.

In Japan, innovative prevention of redundancy involves a policy of transferring employees between companies, either on a temporary (*shukko oen haken*) or permanent (*tenseki*) basis (see Chapter One, Box 1.9). This policy is mainly limited to the large firms, since unionization (and therefore resistance to dismissals) is weak in small firms (Brunello, 1988). In some cases, companies may even establish 'buffer firms', through setting up a new company or a spinoff from an affiliated company, in order to absorb redundant employees. For the Japanese employer, it is not simply the direct cost of dismissal which shapes their preference for transfers. A survey of manufacturing firms in the mid-1980s found that there were three main reasons for this practice: first, the need to avoid potential damage to their reputation, especially regarding the graduate labour market, which is an important recruiting ground for the large companies; second, the difficulties of defending dismissals in court; and third, the direct and indirect costs of engaging in conflict with the union (Brunello, 1988).

Employers in many countries also practice a range of decidedly less innovative preventive measures, including the use of 'voluntary redundancy' and early retirement. The UK is a classic case. Like the US, the UK has some of the least restrictive employment protection laws among advanced capitalist countries, and in this context employers face few obstacles to a policy of declaring redundancies. A policy of 'voluntary redundancy' in the UK may not be so much a means of establishing a fairer process of selection for redundancy as a means of controlling the process of redundancies. As Turnbull and Wass (2000) comment, managers often present overly pessimistic accounts of the need for redundancy, leading to an atmosphere of resignation among workers, and communicate this news directly to individual employees rather than through trade union representatives. Unions are relatively powerless to contest management's account and are often unable to persuade members not to opt for severance payments. Importantly, in the UK context the term 'voluntary' may therefore actually be a misnomer:

> ... management will invariably announce a restructuring of work as part of, if not the occasion for, redundancy, knowing full well that this will 'persuade' certain individuals to 'volunteer' ... In some industries management have been able to target union activists, contrary to the provisions of the legislation, and ultimately derecognize the trade union through 'voluntary' severance arrangements (see Turnbull and Wass 1994). As a final pillar to managerial prerogative, if the 'wrong' employees 'volunteer' — for example those with important skills, knowledge or capabilities deemed essential to the organization — then management will typically refuse the application (see Gordon, 1984: 48). (Turnbull and Wass, 2000: 68).

The problem of management exercising too much control in the process of 'self-selection' is that older workers are usually targeted, and these are the groups most likely to face difficulties re-entering the labour market and to be responsible for dependants. Thus, despite the rhetoric of 'self-selection', management's commitment to control the process will often outweigh the worker's own independent decision in forming the final judgement (see Box 7.4). A similar situation prevails in the US, where policies of voluntary redundancies and early retirement are highly evident (Cappelli et al., 1997; see also Chapter One, Box 1.9). But the US is perhaps more illustrative of the use of contingent labour (short term and temporary contracts) as a means of providing a buffer for 'core' workers and, by simply failing to renew the temporary contract, of avoiding the costs of hiring and firing. For example, the union-employer contract negotiated at the General Motors Saturn plant (seen as an exemplar of the new high performance workplace (see also Wever, 1995)), permits GM to staff up to one in five of its workforce on a temporary basis (Cappelli et al., 1997: 77). Moreover, ambiguity over the employment rights of workers hired from a temporary work agency means that the employer escapes the risks of acting as the employer of temporary agency workers.

> **Box 7.4** Managing redundancies in the UK: the case of forced voluntary redundancy

In a study of three traditional sectors of industry in the UK, Turnbull and Wass (1997) consider the true meaning of 'voluntary' redundancy during a period of job cuts:

> The decision to 'volunteer' in each industry, however, was not simply a function of the relationship between the scale and structure of redundancy payments and the option of early retirement on the one hand, and the personal characteristics of the individual worker on the other ... coercion can play a more explicit part, most notably where management imposes changes to the labour process to 'encourage' certain groups or individuals to 'volunteer' for redundancy. Redundancies implemented under the Dock Labour Compensation Scheme aptly illustrate this process. During the national dock strike in July 1989, dockers were forced back to work on new contracts which included union de-recognition, complete flexibility, the abolition of all fixed manning scales, compulsory overtime, a requirement to work any five days in seven, and a shift 'buy-back' system under which any docker who is rostered for work but is sent home because none is available still 'owes' the company half a shift (which effectively allows the port to 'buy-back' the docker's time at half price). The 'alternative' to accepting the new contract was redundancy. As a result, redundancy fell predominantly on the older/long-service dockers, any dockers with medical restrictions which limited the range of duties they could perform (96 per cent of dockers with medical restrictions were declared redundant), and trade union activists, defined as dockers who were, or had been in the past, shop stewards or health and safety representatives (these men experienced a redundancy rate of 85 per cent, the vast majority being compulsory).

Extract from: P. Turnbull and V. Wass, 'Job insecurity and labour market lemons: the (mis)management of redundancy in steel making, coal mining and port transport', *Journal of Management Studies*, 34 (1997): 27–51.

Working time

Our final example of employment policy and practice at the level of the workplace is working time. An understanding of the way working time is managed is crucial for an explanation of the way diverse forms of new working time arrangements have sprung up in many advanced capitalist countries. While these are often described as flexible, it is important to note that time flexibility has long been practised in the form of overtime working, as well as shiftworking, nights and weekend working. What is new is the proliferation of different kinds of working time arrangements within the organization, including job-sharing schemes, compensated reduction in working hours, flexible scheduling and annualized hours, as well as intensification of traditional arrangements, such as greater use of part-time work (with short and long hours of work) and more unsocial hours working. Across the different countries, it is differences in the forms of flexibility in working time, rather than in the degree of overall flexibility, that are most striking. In countries with little regulation of working time (see Chapter Six), employers establish flexibility on their own terms. In more regulated systems, flexible arrangements tend to reflect a closer balance of interests between employers and workers.

There are a number of pressures driving change in working time arrangements, including global economic and social changes, as well as new management policies at the level of the organization (Bosch, 1999b). In countries where income inequality has increased, workers whose earnings have fallen tend to work longer hours to compensate for lost income (as is the case in the US and the UK). In other countries where income inequality has remained stable, the conditions for negotiating redistribution and reduction of working time have been more favourable (for example, in France, the Netherlands, Denmark and Germany). A second pressure for change is the transformation of household structures. There is an increasing trend for households with children to have two earners (1996 data for Europe shows that this ranges from two thirds of households in Portugal to one third in Spain) (cited in Bosch, 1999b; see Chapter Four). In countries where average working time is long (the UK, the US), men and women have less time for household activities and an increased demand for paid domestic services, which fuels an increased desire for longer working hours. A third pressure on working time involves the system of social security. For example, firms in the US pay into health and pension insurance schemes on a *per capita* basis, not on the level of earnings, which makes long working hours a more attractive option for employers than hiring new workers. Finally, changes in the way firms organize work and production shape working time policy and practice. Rather than holding large stocks of inventory, for example, firms are increasingly likely to fine-tune working time arrangements so that workers become the new buffers in the production process (see Chapter Three). Flexible systems of annualized hours arrangements may be more cost-effective than the traditional recourse to alternating between periods of overtime and short time. Other pressures at the level of the organization include the desire to adjust working hours to prevent redundancies or to facilitate job creation (see above).

Faced with these pressures, organizations in different countries have adopted a variety of flexible working time arrangements. However, reflecting in part the different regimes of working time regulation (see Chapter Six), the trends towards more flexible working take on different characteristics. In particular there are differences, first, in the extent to which they involve flexibility of full-time work or the promotion and flexibility of part-time work; and second, in the extent to which they take into account employee interests or are entirely driven by employer interests. Four examples of working time flexibility are discussed below.

Annualized hours

Annualized hours arrangements provide employers with greater scope to deploy full-time workers flexibly over the year; in return they are required to guarantee workers a certain level of annual income. Depending on the context in which the scheme is introduced, the guaranteed annual income may include compensation for workers' loss of fixed hours and for their lost earnings from overtime and unsocial hours working. In principle, such schemes could be designed to meet employee and employer interests if they allow employees some choice over their working time and provide compensation for lost overtime earnings. In practice, however, there are a number of potential difficulties. One consequence of annualization is that more workers may be required to work unsocial hours. This may have negative consequences for gender equality since women, who still tend to have prime responsibility for children, may not be able to accept jobs where such time flexibility is a requirement, thereby restricting their occupational choice. Furthermore, whereas in principle such schemes may give more leisure time and holidays, by reducing total annual hours worked as time off is given in lieu of overtime pay, in practice holiday schedules may become part of the working time schedule, reducing opportunities to choose holidays to fit with personal or family needs. Finally, the new system may extend managerial control over working time, by linking working hours to fluctuations in market demand and requiring workers to be constantly on standby to work extra hours when required.

As with all employment policies, the impact of this one depends on the context in which it is implemented. In the UK, where negotiation over working time was a major issue in bargaining among unionized workplaces during the 1990s (Millward *et al.*, 2000: 168), there has been significant 'innovation' in annualized working time arrangements (Blyton, 1994). The example described in Box 7.5 illustrates the potential pitfalls of introducing more flexible working time policies in a deregulated

---

Box 7.5 Annualized hours in the UK: problems of control and compensation

A study by Heyes (1997) of a large chemicals plant in the north of England followed the way management introduced annualized hours in order to reduce overtime costs and to replace a complicated system of shift working. Under the annualized hours scheme each employee worked three consecutive 12 hour day or night shifts, followed by a short break, over an 18 week cycle with a period of 21 days off at the end. Employees were paid for more hours than they worked so that each 'owed' the company 172 'bank' hours at the end of the year. Some of these surplus hours were allocated for training and the others could be used by the company to cover unforeseen events. However, there were a number of adverse consequences. Workers did not receive full compensation for loss of overtime earnings; on average each worker lost £4000. Workers who had not previously worked overtime felt that they were being forced to work overtime under the new system without the compensation. Also, it became more difficult to organize holidays as the demand for holidays at certain times of the year far exceeded the supply of workers willing to swap shifts. As one worker interviewed put it:

> In the 21 day break I can go on holiday, but I can't take my wife 'cos where she works she can't get the time off. The company says you can swap your shifts with your friends, but for me that's not worked out ... there's a guy on A-shift with a young daughter and a lad and he had to take 'em out of school to go on holiday. I'd be a lot happier like the way we were before (cited in Heyes, *op. cit.*).

Finally, workers felt they had to spend much of their new leisure time waiting by the phone in case they were required for short-term cover as management were able to call in their banked hours. Overall, therefore, the new annualized hours system in practice did not fully compensate the workforce and, moreover, extended the scope of managerial control (*op. cit.*).

system like that in the UK. Even where, in principle, systems like annualized hours represent an opportunity to balance employer and employee interests, the individual employer is more likely to follow a cost minimizing strategy in the absence of stronger constraints imposed through some form of regulatory mechanism.

Short-time working

Where organizations face extreme variations in demand, such that changes to overtime are an insufficient response, short-time work may be implemented as the most effective solution. For employers, it is an important means of securing labour force flexibility. For employees, it is a means of enhancing job security. Several European countries provide an additional incentive to organizations by way of various public programmes that replace earnings for hours not worked. For the government, subsidizing short-time work is a cheaper alternative than layoffs, since employers pay additional pension and health contributions whereas for the unemployed these costs are borne by the government. As a result, the example of short-time working appears to meet both employer interests for greater flexibility and employee needs for continuity of income. Interestingly, these schemes tend to apply to sectors where men work (mainly manufacturing). Few examples are found in the service sector, where women tend to work. As we show below, reduced hours schemes for women tend to take a different form, involving part-time hours without compensation for lost earnings, with some notable exceptions such as parental leave in Sweden.

Mosley and Kruppe (1996) have analysed differences in short-time work in four European countries where there are public programmes in place (France, Germany, Italy and Spain). They argue that organizational policies are strongly shaped by the national context: the incentives for employers and employees to utilize short-time work are heavily dependent not only on economic conditions but on the characteristics of national short-time work schemes, the institutional context and the availability of functional equivalents (1996: 606).

Among their four selected countries, short-time work is used most extensively in Italy and Spain. In Italy, this is explained by the stringency of employment protection (Chapter Six), which means layoffs are not a cost-effective alternative, as well as by the generosity of the Government subsidy and strong trade union activity at the organizational level (*op. cit.*). In Spain, the high level of short-time working is surprising since organizations employ a very high proportion of temporary workers, which, arguably, could provide a functional equivalent to the flexible policy of short-time working (*ibid.*). In Germany the relatively low use of short-time working is partly due to the very flexible working time arrangements already built into sector-level collective bargaining agreements. In much of German industry, a rigid weekly standard is not adhered to. Instead, organizations arrange working time so that weekly hours (say, 38.5) average out over a period of six to twelve months (in the same manner as in the EC Directive on Working Time). In this case, therefore, short-time work is much more likely to be associated with severe cyclical fluctuations, as we saw above in the case of Volkswagen. In France, use of short-time work is very low despite public programmes that offer support. However, the subsidy is less generous than that found in Germany, and moreover, short-time work is only available for shorter periods (*ibid.*).

Part-time work

In many countries, organizations have adapted working time arrangements to expand the number of part-time jobs. Employers may wish to match staffing levels more closely to fluctuations in demand for services or delivery of products, which vary on an hour-to-hour basis. Alternatively, employers may increase the use of part-timers to cut costs, especially in countries where entitlement to holidays, overtime premia or pension contributions is lower than it is for full-timers. In some countries, governments may subsidize part-time working through reductions in social security costs, particularly for jobs involving very short hours. Such schemes provide additional incentives to employers to create short part-time jobs.

Organizations have increased their use of part-timers for different reasons, but the impact on the terms and conditions of part-time employment is strongly influenced by the wider form of labour market regulation (Box 7.6). In particular, this shapes whether this form of working time flexibility leads to the integration or marginalization of part-time work (O'Reilly and Fagan, 1998). The former may be more likely where employment policies are designed to reflect a balance of employer and employee interests; the latter where employers are free to dictate strategy in their own interests. Part-time work as organized in the UK represents the archetypal example of a marginalized form of employment. The problem is not that British

---

Box 7.6 Part-time work in banking: some societal effects

In a wide-ranging study of use of part-time workers in the retail banking sector in France and the UK, O'Reilly (1994) shows that employers' use of part-timers is shaped by a range of regulatory and historical constraints and opportunities. Here, she summarizes the particular roles of education and training and the gendered construction of part-time work in the two countries:

French women tend to be better educated, with a preference for full-time continuous employment, and a stronger desire for promotion, compared to British women. In Britain there is a much higher demand for part-time work, which is linked not only to the provision of childcare, and attitudes to suitable forms of childrearing, but also to the lower levels of education attainment ... Whilst it was generally considered that part-time work was 'suitable' for women, this occurred at different periods in women's life-cycle. In Britain part-time work was generally seen as a means for women with young children to return to paid employment: a vehicle into work. In France, in the banking sector, part-time work was an option either to women with several children, those recovering from an illness, or those thinking of gradually withdrawing from paid employment. (O'Reilly, 1994: 147)

organizations pay part-timers less than full-timers for the same work. Instead, part-timers tend to be segregated into different kinds of jobs than full-timers, with a high concentration in low status and low paying sectors (Smith *et al.*, 1998; see Chapter One, Box 1.7). In the context of a highly decentralized system of wage-setting, with no coordinating mechanism for linking settlements in low status sectors with those in high status sectors, part-timers suffer a considerable wage penalty. In other countries, like Germany, there is a different form of marginalization. Part-time work is more likely than full-time work to accumulate a marginalized status over time due to limited opportunities for training and promotion within organizations. Given the importance of the training system in determining income and qualifications, part-timers accumulate disadvantage over the long term.

In some countries, part-time work is offered in a way that balances both employer and employee interests. In several European countries women have the right to reduced hours during periods of childbirth or childraising. For example, in France women in full-time work in the public sector have had the right (*temps choisi*) to reduce their hours by 20 per cent. But there is no compensation, in contrast to the arrangements for short-time working that we saw above. As such, this option for women to switch to part-time working does not impose any burden on the employer or the state. Nevertheless, people working reduced hours may still maintain rights to benefits and other entitlements as if they were full-timers, so that the short-term costs are restricted to the reduction in pay (Rubery, 1998). Sweden, in contrast to France, does provide compensation for lost earnings during parental leave, at up to 75 per cent of lost pay (see Chapter Four).

Increasing unsocial hours working

Across the European Union there was an increase in Saturday, Sunday and night working among both male and female employees in almost all member states during the 1990s (*Statistics in Focus* 2002). In countries where regulations are weak, or collective bargaining coverage is limited, the spread of unsocial hours working has occurred alongside challenges to the tradition of paying premium rates, such as time and a half for Saturdays and double time for nights and Sundays. This practice of removing the premium paid for unsocial hours and establishing a single standard rate is found in the expanding service sectors of many economies, but is also found in more unionized parts of the manufacturing sector where longstanding collective agreements on standard premium payments for working weekends and nights are being whittled away, at least in some countries such as the UK.

The trend towards expecting full-timers to work extra hours and unsocial hours without wage compensation has to some extent been set by the growth of non standard employment forms. The deployment of these workers to meet flexibility requirements has allowed employers to become used to the idea that they may be able to have flexible staffing without paying premium costs. Part-timers are often expected to work extra hours without additional compensation until their hours reach the same as full-time hours. Now full-timers in some countries are being asked to accept similar conditions, perhaps with time off in lieu as compensation. This progressive change to established ways of compensating for unsocial hours can be seen in the case of Sunday opening for shops in the UK. Full-time shop staff in post were at first offered double time for Sunday working, but both part-timers and new full-time recruits were expected to work at weekends for either a reduced or no premium (Rubery, 1998).

Conclusions

Workers across different countries do not share a similar experience of work and employment. In a manner that reflects the diversity evident in national systems of education and training, wage and working time regulation and employment protection, this chapter has demonstrated the cross-national variation in employment policies and practices found at the level of the workplace. Moreover, as the early work based on the 'societal effect' approach suggested, there is a strong interrelationship between the national and the organization and workplace levels, or 'spaces', of analysis. The division of labour within the organization — in particular, the principle of task allocation and the nature of the job hierarchy — is strongly shaped by the national system of education and training. The form of payment system adopted within the organization is interlinked with the way work is structured, and moreover, is embedded in the wider system of wage setting, involving weak or strong regulation and narrow or wide coverage of collective bargaining. Job security and redundancy measures are linked to the over-arching system of regulation of employment protection, since this imposes weak or strong constraints on employer freedom to lay off workers. And, finally, national regulations can be seen to both enable and constrain the development of new working time arrangements at the level of the organization, with public programmes encouraging policies of short-time working in some countries and relatively strong regulations discouraging the marginalization of part-time work in others.

In the next chapter, we shift our focus to consideration of the influence of multinational corporations. As a key force behind the extensive process of globalization, the structure and activities of multinationals raise important questions regarding the resilience of national systems of employment and the adoption of new ways of working in domestic organizations.

Multinationals and the organization of employment

Multinationals and the survival of nationally-specific employment regimes

The rise of the multinational corporation (MNC) poses a potential challenge to the continuation of nationally-specific employment practices. This challenge follows, first, from the simple fact that some individual multinational corporations can now be considered more powerful than many nation states, and certainly have a value in excess of the GDP of many countries. This explicit financial power is also matched by considerable political power for multinational corporations, acting both independently and collectively. For example, the pressure to establish a Single European Market, which resulted in the signing of the Single European Act in 1986 and the completion of the internal market in 1992, emanated primarily from multinational corporations, concerned about the continuation of non-tariff barriers to trade within the European Community (Ramsay, 1992; Streeck, 1993).

> ... the constitutional bargain that underlies the relaunching of European integration in the mid-1980s, (was) concluded essentially among national political elites and large European companies with organized labour excluded. At its core it involved business support for a collective effort by West European nation states to recover some measure of external sovereignty in a turbulent, deinstitutionalized world economy by pooling their individual sovereignties. In exchange, business received a commitment of the emerging European polity to a largely deregulated political economy ('a single market without a single state'), for instance, via the founding principles of mutual recognition. The social dimension of the internal market was added later, and largely remains limited to what is necessary to make the market politically and technically possible. (Streeck, 1993: 96)

Second, however, the impact of multinationals does not lie simply or mainly in their ability to lobby governments to change labour market institutions and regulations. They have a measure of direct influence on employment systems, as they may introduce new ways of managing employment in their subsidiaries at odds with the distinct and different traditions of the nation state in which the subsidiary is located. While MNCs are still liable, in principle, to meet legal regulations set down in different national economies, they may be able to negotiate relaxations of regulations or exploit loopholes, particularly if they threaten withdrawal of their investment as a bargaining tool. More significantly, they can do what indigenous employers may feel unable to do — ignore custom and practice within the country and sector, and thereby introduce novel and different ways of working and new approaches to human resource management. This power to transcend national institutions, by drawing upon different modes of organization and different corporate cultures, is part of the process of globalization. It is this influence of MNCs which may prevent or dissuade individual nation states or groups of nation states from pursuing their own system of social and economic organization.

This power is the greater the more that multinational corporations conceive of themselves, and act, as internationally integrated production systems. It is the internationally integrated corporations that are willing and able, at least in principle, to transfer production from one country to another if the restrictions placed on their ability to introduce their desired employment practices are deemed too strong. Not all multinational corporations fit into this category. As we discuss further below, many companies which operate in more than one country may be mainly seeking to develop new markets for their production and are not using international expansion to develop a new approach to the organization of production.

Our interest in multinationals does not, therefore, lie solely in the fact that they are, of themselves, extremely important parts of the international economic order. There is a further interest in that the actions of multinationals also influence the behaviour of other actors, including governments and domestic organizations. In particular, multinationals are often seen as the main agents of the diffusion of so-called best practice employment techniques, a process which could challenge the survival of alternative employment regimes and varieties of capitalism.

Multinationals as the agents of diffusion of 'best practice'

One reason why multinational corporations may be regarded as a source of convergence in employment policies is that they are expected to use their international perspective to promote diffusion of so-called best practice employment techniques, unless prevented from so doing by powerful national or pan-national governmental policies. There are two strands to the argument that multinationals are likely to promote the diffusion of practices across national boundaries. The first is an *administrative efficiency* argument, which stresses the advantages that accrue from the implementation of consistent employment policies and practices throughout a company's operations. This facilitates monitoring and measurement of performance and the development of a corporate brand name or image, at the same time easing the mobility of staff between operations. Management costs and transaction costs can also be expected to be reduced if common employment policies and practices are implemented. However, as we will see further below, there are also some hidden costs involved in attempting to administer a fully centralized system. It may be more appropriate to adopt the principle of *subsidiarity* — that is, the delegation of decision-making to the level at which it is most efficient to operate. In the area of human resource management this level may well be below that of central headquarters if the subsidiary branches are faced with employment issues that reflect different societal values, legal regulations, industrial relations systems and training and education systems.

The second strand to the debate emphasizes the technical and organizational gains for multinationals from the freedom to implement best practice techniques. However, 'best practice' can take on different meanings. As we discussed in Chapter Two it may refer to advances in technological and organizational knowledge — so-called system effects — or it may be related to practices which have come to be regarded as best practice because of their association either with the dominant country or the dominant ideology in the world economy. More parochially, 'best practice' may be defined with reference to best performance within a specific multinational, with no presumption that these practices represent a universal norm for all corporations or all sectors.

If best practice is seen as defined by current technological knowledge, multinationals can be considered well placed to speed the process of technological diffusion by using centralized control systems to overcome tendencies towards managerial inertia. MNCs may also be the main agents of diffusion of the practice and ideology associated with the so-called dominant country (see Chapter Two), particularly those MNCs whose parent companies are based in the dominant country. Many MNCs in practice may be more interested in promoting 'best practice' as defined within their own operations, based upon detailed comparison and monitoring of output and performance between MNC subsidiaries. Here the emphasis is not so much on the characteristics of the best practice itself but in the use of 'coercive comparisons' between plants in order to increase productivity or financial performance. Each individual MNC may use the concept of best practice as a means of levering up the performance in each of its subsidiaries; but the concept no longer refers to a single dominant or universal form of work and employment organization.

The concept of best practice therefore takes on many meanings. The existence of either a technologically-based best practice or even a dominant model best practice form is disputed by many, particularly when this involves implementing policies and practices in contexts dislocated from the societal environment in which the employment practice was developed. No best practice technique, in the sense of one which is 'best' in all social environments, may therefore exist. The notion that diffusion of common techniques is always in the best interests of MNCs must also be challenged (see below for discussion of reasons for local or host country influences on employment practices). Equally strong incentives may exist for MNCs to differentiate their employment policies and practices across locations to take advantage of variations in the structure of wage costs and in the skill bases of economies. There may even be problems, as again we discuss in more detail below, about the capacity of MNCs to follow through a strict programme of coercive comparison, even within their own organization. Attempts to monitor and compare productivity across different sites may not be capable of taking into account differences in technologies, products or price structures, let alone differences in social arrangements and expectations.

The apparently commonsense view that MNCs are strong sources for convergence within an increasingly globalized world economy has not therefore gone unchallenged. Nevertheless, the power of MNCs in the world economy is such that their potential ability to challenge the existence of national business systems and employment regimes requires further investigation. One starting point for a more detailed investigation is first of all to investigate differences between MNCs in their function and organization, and to identify trends in the organization of MNCs which may shed some light on whether the future patterns will be towards greater convergence.

Typologies of MNCs

Multinational corporations are as diverse as national corporations. The diversity in form and function of MNCs is expected, by most analysts, to play an important role in shaping their employment policy and practices. Considerable time and effort have been expended on classifying different types of MNCs. The classification systems that have been developed can to a large extent be considered to offer complementary and overlapping schemes, focusing on somewhat different characteristics; but essentially all aim at understanding the dominance of home country, host country or global influences on the operation and characteristics of the MNC. Initial classifications of MNCs (Stopford and Wells, 1972) focused on the relationship between strategy and structure, following the tradition in industrial economics and the work of Chandler (1962). Second generation classification systems (Bartlett and Ghoshal, 1989, 1992) moved beyond this focus on organizational structure — or the anatomy — of the organization to include the procedures and culture — the physiology and psychology of the organization — to map out the organizational flexibilities as well as structures required for different stages of internationalization. Bartlett and Ghoshal's (1989) typology of MNCs is one of the most frequently cited schemas. Here MNCs are divided into four types, as follows:

- *The multinational or multi-domestic company.* This type of company, prevalent in the expansion of multinational companies in the period between the First and Second World Wars, sets up international subsidiaries largely as a means of entering new markets. These new markets may have specific characteristics which require adaptation to local conditions; hence multi-domestic companies are organized on a decentralized federation basis.

- *The international organization*: This type of company developed in the immediate post Second World War period and was based on the international
exploitation of parent company know-how and knowledge. These organizations, based on professional management, can be classified as coordinated federations, with the parent company providing the source of innovation in
products and processes, but allowing some delegation of powers to the international subsidiaries. Within these organizations 'core competencies' are centralized and others decentralized (Leong and Tan, 1993).
- *The global corporation*: Global corporations treat the world market as an integrated whole, and organize their global production systems to reduce costs and
increase efficiency through utilizing economies of scale. These corporations
operate as centralized hubs, allowing limited delegation to local subsidiaries
and operating a tight centralized management system. Global corporations
have been associated with the growth of Japanese MNCs in the 1970s but in fact
can be found in much earlier examples of multinationals such as Ford or
Rockefeller (Paauwe and Dewe, 1995).
- *The transnational corporation*: The first three types of multinationals can be
considered, according to Bartlett and Ghoshal, to constitute first generation
multinationals. New forms of multinationals are now required to meet a more
complex environment. The transnational corporation is expected to combine
aspects of each of the three first generation forms; they need to be sensitive to
local conditions, to develop competitive strategies at a global level, to generate
knowledge and learning and to share it throughout the organization. The
transnational corporation will have multiple centres, based on both interdependency and specialization, so that national units will make distinctive and
differentiated contributions to the overall activity of the integrated transnational company. This type of organization is expected to be the most recently
developed form, and therefore still likely to be in the minority among MNCs.

This description of the evolution from first to second generation models can be
interpreted as either a description of change that has already taken place or as a prescription for a more appropriate organizational form to match the requirements of
the new world order. The empirical support for the existence of transnational corporations is still rather weak and the dominant form still tends to be that of the
multi-domestic company, even though this is associated with the first phases of
development of multinational corporations (Leong and Tan, 1993).

Bartlett and Ghoshal's classification primarily uses different historical time periods
to consider the stages of development of MNCs. Adler and Ghadar (1990) provide a
similar classification but related more to the lifecycle of a product. They utilize
Vernon's three phases of the lifecycle of a product (Vernon, 1966): from product development to growth and internationalization, based on developing and penetrating markets, to the maturity phase where the emphasis is on lowering costs. The three phases

can be related to phases of internationalization — the first phase is primarily domestic; the second corresponds to Bartlett and Ghoshal's 'international organization' category in its emphasis on both transferring knowledge from the centre and developing responsiveness to all markets. The third phase is termed multinational, but involves a global strategy to reduce costs of production. Adler and Ghadar add a fourth phase, which they label global, that involves both global integration and local responsiveness. It is thus more similar to the transnational corporation in Bartlett and Ghoshal. This fourth phases involves meeting both high targets for quality, related to specific market tastes and preferences, and strong price competition. While Vernon's famous life cycle model was based on a product life cycle of 15–20 years, Adler and Ghadar argue that the length of the product cycle has now reduced to three to five years, such that the period of time between the four phases can be considered to be shrinking. This places increasing emphasis on the fourth phase, as various elements in the product life cycle model now have to be addressed simultaneously and not consecutively. The global phase shares similarities with that of the transnational corporation: the focus is on problem solving and utilizing, rather than eliminating, the opportunities presented by cultural diversity. The two typologies are compared in Table 8.1.

The concepts of the global phase and the transnational form move the debate away from neat classifications of companies based on watertight divisions — globally-orientated or domestically-orientated — to a recognition that organizations are often more complex and contain elements of various orientations. It has also been argued that it may be inappropriate to attempt to classify a particular organization as a whole into any one category. Instead it may be more appropriate to look at different management functions and activities separately. It is possible, for example, to have an organization with a global and highly centralized marketing strategy but operating a highly differentiated and decentralized human resource management policy. This more differentiated approach follows general developments in organization theory, where it is increasingly recognized that it is inappropriate to talk about organizations as unified monolithic enterprises, with single goals, policies, orientations or cultures.

The transnational corporation concept provides, too, for more variations in the ways in which organizations function than the traditional distinction between centralized hierarchies or decentralized federations. This approach has also been taken up in the notion of the *heterarchical* organization, contrasted with the traditional *hierarchical* organization. The heterarchical organization is based around many centres. Competitive advantage in this type of organization is not associated with either one centre or one culture, such as the home country. Instead the heterarchical organization is able and willing to utilize and develop expertise in many different contexts and countries, and to exploit this knowledge on a global scale. 'Thinking' is not centralized at headquarters but pervades all operations. Centres are likely to vary in function and not conform to strict hierarchical or market divisions. Local subsidiary managers not only have greater local autonomy than in a traditional global company but also are given strategic roles to influence the direction of the company as a whole (see Box 8.1).

Table 8.1 Comparison of typologies of MNCs

Bartlett and Ghoshal (1989)		Adler and Ghadar (1990)	
Type of multinational	*Degree of centralization*	*Phase of product lifecycle and main strategy*	*Human resource policy*
MULTIDOMESTIC Entry into a range of domestic markets	Organized on a decentralized federation basis	PHASE 1: PRIMARILY DOMESTIC: Develop product	Limited or no international human resource management (IHRM) policy
INTERNATIONAL International exploitation of parent company's technology and knowledge	'Core competencies' are centralized and others decentralized	PHASE 2: INTERNATIONAL: Transferring knowledge from the centre and developing responsiveness to all markets	Development of IHRM, but focus on adaptation to local conditions provides role for host country managers
GLOBAL Focus on global product and on maximizing production efficiencies	Operate as centralized hubs allowing limited delegation to local subsidiaries and operating a tight centralized management system	PHASE 3: MULTINATIONAL: A global strategy to reduce costs of production	Focus on recruiting best international managers for post regardless of country of origin; and on developing a strong corporate culture
TRANSNATIONAL Combines global efficiency with national responsiveness and worldwide learning	Multiple centres, interdependent and specialized national units will make distinctive and differentiated contributions	PHASE 4: GLOBAL: Involves both global integration and local responsiveness	Combination of Phase 2 and Phase 3. Cultural diversity an opportunity rather than a problem; focus on flexibility and creativity

The main means of integration in a heterarchical organization is not hierarchical direct controls but the development of corporate culture as a form of 'corporate glue'. This emphasis on culture is used to create shared norms and a shared management ethos that should transcend the need for 'calculative' or 'financial' control. This emphasis on corporate culture exists alongside a liberal approach to centre-subsidiary relations: local units are free, where appropriate, to develop joint ventures with external partners and to operate independently of other parts of the group. Indeed the heterarchical organization may 'continuously create new institutional arrangements in the light of expertise concerning what works best for each specific

┌───┐

Box 8.1   Characteristics of a heterarchical firm

1   The heterarchical MNC has many centres.
2   Subsidiary managers have a strategic role, not only for the subsidiary but for the MNC
    as a whole.
3   Heterarchy implies different kinds of centres based on a mix of organizing principles:
    there is no overriding dimension superordinate to the rest.
4   A heterarchy is based on deintegration of relationships, with subsidiaries given more
    freedom to purchase components externally.
5   Integration is achieved primarily through normative control.
6   Information about the whole of the MNC is contained in each part of the MNC.
7   Thinking is not only restricted to the exclusive centre but goes on in the whole enterprise.
8   Coalitions with other companies and also other types of actors are common.
9   Its strategic approach is radical problem-orientation, that is it is not limited to strategy
    based on existing physical or human resources or on competitive positions in narrow
    fields of business.

Source: Hedlund (1986)

└───┘

purpose' (Hedlund (1986), reprinted in Ghauri and Prasad (1995): 75). This type of organization is expected to transcend narrow definitions of industries or markets and to be radical in their innovation policies and strategic thinking.

Types of MNCs and international management

The distinctions between types of MNCs are expected to have significant implications for human resource policies of companies (see Table 8.1). For the most part these consequences have been explored primarily with respect to policies relating to management. One classification of MNCs has in fact focused explicitly on issues relating to selection and recruitment of international management. Perlmutter (1969) identified three types of multinationals with respect to their attitude towards the geographic origins of the international managers:

- *ethnocentric* organizations, where the majority of international managers are recruited from the home country;
- *polycentric* organizations, where local nationals are appointed;
- *geocentric* organizations, where managers are not appointed according to their country of origin and where third country nationals often hold management positions.

Ethnocentric organizations are likely to be highly centralized, reflecting greater complexity of the organization in the home country than in subsidiaries. Polycentric organizations have a more decentralized structure, perhaps reflecting more diversity in complexity and power relations. The geocentric organization may be similar to the transnational organization which aims to transcend the limitations of a focus either on the home or the host country, and instead wishes to utilize expertise wherever it is located and from whichever nationality it is drawn. However, the need for both global and local sensitivity within the transnational approach has led to the suggestion of a refinement of this classification and the addition of a fourth category, with recruitment regionally-based in order to enhance adjustment to local conditions while at the same time ensuring a broader perspective than may be obtained if only host country nationals are appointed. 'Regional' here refers to groups of countries and continents, so that for example recruitment may be Europe-wide or South East Asia-wide (Scullion, 1995).

While these classifications may suggest that there is a neat fit between recruitment strategy and the business objectives of the organization, in practice each strategy for international human resource management also generates its own problems, even when apparently providing a 'best fit'. Where an ethnocentric policy is adopted, there are problems in maintaining the motivation of lower level host country nationals in management, because of blocked career paths. This can lead to conflicts between management levels and a failure to share information. Problems of integration are exacerbated where the home country nationals lack language skills and sensitivity to the conditions in the local markets and society. Edwards *et al.* (1999) point to the study by Broad (1994) where British managers at a Japanese transplant in Wales 'secured information from the shop floor through rumours and gossip, and kept this information from the Japanese expatriates. The British managers used this network to hinder the implementation of "high involvement management" favoured by the parent company' (1999: 289–90).

Much attention is also focused on the problem of compensation and reward packages; for the home country national there needs to be a clear financial incentive to accept an overseas placement, but the provision of a generous financial package can cause problems in two senses. First, it may be seen as inequitable by other managers within the host country plant; second, it may be difficult for the manager to reintegrate into their home country without accepting a cut in salary. Further problems arise due to the reluctance of managers to take international assignments and the relatively high likelihood of failed international placements, reflecting problems of adaptation to local culture and conditions. American expatriates have a reputation of finding greatest difficulty adapting, possibly in part because of weak language skills (Ferner, 1994: 91). According to Black *et al.* (1991), 'Between 16% and 40% of all American employees sent overseas return from their assignments early, and each premature return costs a firm roughly $100,000' (1991, reprinted in Ghauri and Prasad (1995): 327). One reason for the focus on international managers within international human resource management literature is precisely that these are considered problematic areas for personnel and company policy. Some of the reluctance to accept international assignments arises because of negative effects of some postings on individual careers (Tung, 1984). The difficulty of adaptation extends beyond the individual manager to their family, with disruptions to dual careers, interruptions to children's schooling, and problems of acculturation. Moreover, some countries face more difficulties in finding candidates for international placements due to the fact that it is common, for example in Sweden, for both partners in a marriage to have a career (Horvath *et al.*, 1981).

The alternative of appointing host country nationals presents problems, on the other hand, for developing an integrated MNC. Again language differences, plus lack of awareness of the culture and orientations of the parent company, can lead to problems of communication and lack of synergy between the different parts of the organization. Some MNCs may seek to solve problems of sensitivity both to the parent company's needs and to local conditions by recruiting host country nationals whose attitudes and expectations reveal as close a fit as possible with the cultural norms of the parent company. The success of this strategy relies on the efficacy of personality tests, and on the existence of a large enough pool of suitably qualified host country nationals to be able to identify appropriate candidates. In practice, if they are not able to rely on control through the employment of home country nationals who are trusted and known at the centre, other forms of control may be used. For example, strict output and input controls may be used; but these may have negative consequences if the performance targets are not sufficiently attuned to the context of the host country subsidiary. For example, it may be inappropriate to use targets based on minimizing staff headcount levels in a social context where employees expect stable employment contracts. Layoffs and redundancies may undermine the subsidiary's ability to hire or retain skilled staff. The control systems may also be ignored or evaded. As Laurent (1985, reprinted in Ghauri and Prasad (1995): 315) remarks, apparently simple and transferable management practices have a habit of being misunderstood or resulting in perverse effects in a different cultural context:

> In the Italian subsidiary, the introduction of a Management-by-Objectives system may be experienced as follows: 'We used to be rewarded for our accomplishments and punished for our failures. Why should we now sign our own punishment even before trying?' For the Indonesian affiliate company, the inclusion of negative feedback in performance appraisal interviews may mean 'an unhealthy pollution of harmonious hierarchical relationships'. The introduction of a matrix-type of multiple reporting relationship system may be experienced as a horrible case of divided loyalty in the Mexican subsidiary. Unlike many others, the subsidiaries of Swedish multinational corporations may complain that they do not receive enough 'help' from headquarters. Participative management may mean very different things to Scandinavians and North Americans.

The appointment of host country nationals within the management team also creates the likelihood of conflict between the apparent interests of the corporation and those of the subsidiary; the host country nationals are likely to resist attempts to scale down or close plants in their own country and thereby potentially thwart global rationalization. This will be exacerbated if the managers of subsidiaries are excluded from promotion above the national level and therefore feel no personal reason to identify with the interests of the organization as a global entity.

The geocentric approach perhaps appears to offer the best solution as it avoids the 'them and us' configuration that is the consequence of a choice between home and host country. However, this may not be a practical strategy if there are strict work permit laws in the country in question. Genuinely international managers also do not come cheap and may be relatively difficult to hire (Scullion, 1995). There are even doubts about whether the concept of a truly global manager exists, as most will eventually wish to have a stable life with a family and their preferences for global travel and mobility may then change. Previous global experience does not guarantee either knowledge or sensitivity to local conditions. The recruitment problems also mean that there is a need for longer lead times in planning management hires. Limiting international mobility to regions and country groupings could help to reduce these problems.

Employment policies and practices for non-management staff in MNCs

Human resource issues in MNCs extend far beyond the issue of recruitment of international managers. Recently an increasing interest has been shown in the factors shaping employment policy and practice for locally-based employees (Ferner, 1994), that is for almost all non-managerial staff and at least some layers of managerial or supervisory staff. This interest is reflective of three issues currently being debated in business, academic and policy circles.

The first is that MNCs may be seen as very important vehicles for the transmission of new forms of human resources policy, including models of 'best practice'. Here the interest is in whether MNCs are creating a new homogeneous approach to human resources policy which will have the ultimate effect of reducing variety in forms of employment. A second reason for interest is the increasing emphasis placed on human resources management for the overall business strategy of an organization. However, whether the business strategy is best served through a centralized and homogenized approach or by a more differentiated strategy, sensitive to local conditions, is still open to debate.

Thirdly, there are moral concerns about the employment policies adopted by MNCs. If MNCs adopt a policy of implementing local labour standards and practices, they may be seen as not only reinforcing international inequalities but also as effectively exploiting workers in less developed countries, an issue which has become of increasing concern to consumer pressure groups (see Chapter Ten). Moreover this approach may threaten jobs in developed countries, if MNCs are free to move their operations to countries where local conditions allow for much lower labour costs. MNCs may even be responsible for lowering labour standards if they instigate competition between countries for investment on the basis of low labour costs and minimum regulations. Even where MNCs apply higher than local standards there can still be moral issues, as the MNCs may then attract skilled staff and starve local companies of the best talent. For the moment, we leave these general issues of labour standards aside and will return to them in detail in Chapter Ten. For the present, we confine our discussion to the influence of local versus corporate influences on the shaping of human resource policy.

The employment policies of MNCs can be identified as shaped by two sets of influences:

- the local environment in which the establishment is located;
- the corporate environment, that is the characteristics and culture of the specific organization.

'Isomorphism' is 'the property of crystallising in the same or closely related forms' (Oxford English Dictionary). This term has been used to describe these conflicting pressures between the local and the corporate environment, described by Rosenzweig and Singh (1991) as 'rival coercive isomorphic pressures on the subsidiary' (quoted in Ferner and Quintanilla (1998): 713). However, Ferner and Quintanilla have taken the concept of rival influences further and suggested four different scenarios of isomorphic pressures. The first two conform to those postulated by Rosenzweig and Singh (1991) and Rosenzweig and Nohria (1994). The second two scenarios added by Ferner and Quintanilla (1998) take the debate further by introducing isomorphic pressure related to country of origin and to the development of a global culture.

The four sources of isomorphic pressure are presented in Figure 8.1 which builds upon the work of Ferner and Quintanilla (1998). In Figure 8.1 we seek to show how subsidiaries of organizations are embedded in social and cultural arrangements but this embeddedness takes different forms. In the case we call *local isomorphism* the subsidiary is effectively embedded directly in the host country environment as it is left to determine its own strategy by corporate headquarters. In the second case — called here *corporate isomorphism* — the influence of the host country is only indirect, as the subsidiary is embedded first within the corporate structures and the host country pressures have to be filtered though the influence of a strong corporate culture. *Cross-national isomorphism* occurs when the corporation is deeply embedded in the home country culture. In Figure 8.1 this means that the subsidiary is first embedded in the parent company culture which in turn is embedded in the home country culture. The influence of the host country is relatively weak and has to pass through the combined influence of home country and corporate culture. Home country practices are thereby introduced into the host country. In the fourth example, *global isomorphism*, the corporate culture of the MNC is itself embedded in a global corporate culture which is diffused through MNCs. This fourth type of isomorphic pressure can be considered a logical development of the diffusion of cultures if it is the case that a truly globalized economy is being constructed. MNCs could be expected to break free from the constraint of both home and host country

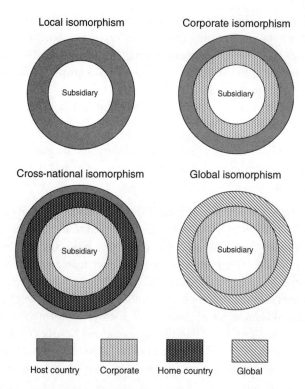

Source: Terms adopted from Ferner and Quintanilla (1998)

Figure 8.1 Varieties of isomorphism: local, corporate, cross national and global influences on subsidiaries of multinationals

institutional arrangements to develop a global corporate culture which is diffused through MNCs as a result of competition between the MNCs themselves. This diffusion process is likely to be faster the more MNCs feel that competitive threats are best met through 'mimetic' behaviour (DiMaggio and Powell, 1983), that is copying the behaviour of successful MNCs, rather than developing new systems and approaches.

These four scenarios thus set out four possible outcomes:

- MNCs which adopt primarily local policies and practices;
- MNCs which have dominant corporate cultures;
- MNCs which transmit home country influences, particularly when these are located in dominant countries;
- MNCs which transmit a global corporate culture which develops independently of home or host country influences and which results in homogeneity rather than distinctive corporate approaches.

All four elements may be found in different types of MNCs and in different sectors and countries. Even under the globalization scenario, where the end result might be expected to be more homogeneity across countries and indeed sectors, there may still be many sectors where global pressures are not sufficiently strong to break down more country- or corporate-specific ways of operating.

Three of the four scenarios are concerned with the transmission of isomorphic pressures, which may overcome local influences and shape employment in the image of the corporate culture or the home country culture, or according to a more global culture. This appears to weight the argument in favour of the diffusion of non-locally-based employment policies and practices. However, the identification of three alternative scenarios where the influence of local factors may be moderated or suppressed does not necessarily mean that the first scenario, that of adaptation to local needs, is not either the most frequently observed approach or indeed the most appropriate human resource policy for many MNCs.

Nevertheless, to explore these issues further, we first identify the various tools at the disposal of MNCs for diffusing a corporate-wide employment policy and discuss the advantages and disadvantages of their use from a corporate perspective. The obstacles that corporations may face in trying to diffuse 'best practice', even if this is their preferred objective, are also identified. We are then in a position to consider both the desirability and the likelihood of home country or corporate cultures prevailing over local cultures and practices.

Modes of diffusion of best practice

MNCs are often divided between those organizations that seek to *control outcomes or performance* and those that try to *control behaviour or process*. The former set of organizations rely primarily on financial controls and performance indicators and leave it up to local management to decide how to achieve these targets. Almost by definition, these MNCs are less likely to be involved in a specific policy of transferring best practice, although if the only way to achieve the targets is to implement one specific set of policies, the outcome of financial targets may be similar to that experienced in MNCs where more direct attention is paid to behaviour and process. Financial controls may also rule out some behaviours which may be more in line with a national employment regime: for example if the emphasis is on very short run returns on capital, policies designed to yield longer term returns, such as investment in training, may be more difficult to maintain. Moreover, it may be too simple to distinguish between behaviour and financial controls as response to the same financial controls will vary according to culture and even language. Nevertheless, in order to keep the discussion within manageable limits, we will focus here on the ways in which organizations may seek a more direct influence on behaviour and process, either because of a strong belief in the importance of a corporate culture and ethos as a means of maintaining its competitive edge, or as a means of achieving performance targets through direct influence on behavioural norms and on work and employment organization.

There are three main means by which MNCs seek to control behaviour:

- through the appointment of international managers;
- through the development of corporate culture more generally — the development and application of so-called corporate glue;
- through the use of coercive comparisons between parts of the organization to encourage the adoption of best practice.

The policies may be assisted by other strategies to reduce the influence of local norms on subsidiaries: for example, if growth is achieved through the establishment of greenfield sites rather than through acquisitions; or through the establishment of subsidiaries in areas where it is possible to recruit people who will be willing to accept different employment policies and practices than those found in the major centres of the national economy, as in areas of high unemployment and deprivation. MNCs may also aim to recruit and select local managers whose personalities and expectations are more in tune with those of the home country than those of the host country, a strategy which is likely to work best in a relatively large and open society.

While MNCs have a range of tools open to them in principle, further investigation has revealed significant limitations or downsides to each of the alternative strategies suggested above.

If we take first the case of *the appointment of international managers*, we find that although this provides in principle a means of ensuring that subsidiaries are managed by persons with a strong commitment to corporate ideals, in practice MNCs face a range of problems, not least in recruiting and maintaining a set of international managers. As already discussed above, there are limits to the mobility of any manager. Moreover, there are many problems in constructing and developing an international management career. Some of the these problems relate directly to the differences in the construction of management careers across countries. For example, German managers are expected to have high levels of technical knowledge and functional specialization, while Anglo-Saxon managers are typically generalist and advance on the basis of performance on the job, coupled with general management development (Ferner and Quintanilla, 1998). In contrast again, French managers are selected according to their participation in highly elitist education and their career progress may depend more on political factors than on direct evidence of managerial competence (*op. cit.*). The expectations of international managers with respect to their careers and training will vary between countries and moreover are likely to clash with those expectations of local mangers. An Anglo-Saxon manager may fail to command respect in Germany if they lack functional specialism and high technical competence. Nor does the appointment of an international manager automatically solve the problem of how to reconcile the competing pulls of corporate versus local influences. These problems are exacerbated if the international manager fails to establish effective communications with local managers; the result may be that top management at the subsidiary are excluded by lower management from all the internal knowledge of how the subsidiary functions.

Recognition that the superimposition of an international manager is by no means sufficient to bring about corporate consistency has led to a greater emphasis being placed on the second method of establishing conformity, that is the *development of corporate culture*. If the latter is defined as shared norms and objectives, then the aim of developing corporate culture is to change behaviour not only at top management level in subsidiaries but as far down the operation as possible. The objective is to develop shared norms rather than rely on direct bureaucratic controls. Use of corporate training programmes, visits to head office and inter-subsidiary networking are some of the means used to acquaint local management with corporate culture. However, the promotion of company-wide norms and values and a shared language can give a superficial appearance of conformity across an organization when in practice the same espoused values and the same espoused policies are still being interpreted in very different ways:

> … a French manager working in the French subsidiary of an American corporation that insists on an open-door policy may well leave his office door open — thus adjusting to the behavioural requirements of the corporate culture — without any modification whatsoever of his basic conception of managerial authority. In the French subsidiary of a Swedish firm, whose corporate values include an almost religious reliance upon informality, French shopfloor employees were recently observed as addressing their managers by their first names and using the intimate *tu* form within the boundaries of the firm. The same individuals immediately reverted to *Monsieur le Directeur* and the more formal *vous* form whenever meeting outside the firm. (Laurent, 1986, reprinted in Ghauri and Prasad (1995): 314)

Similarly, all managers of an MNC in a variety of countries may pay lip service to the norms of teamworking and empowerment, but the interpretation of these policies in practice may vary enormously; in one country this may involve fully multiskilled teams while in another it may mean simply a devolution of responsibility for output and performance targets to groups, with little or no upskilling of the workforce to facilitate more effective teamwork (see Box 3.11 in Chapter Three). Even the overt use of corporate values and corporate culture to justify policies cannot necessarily be taken as an indication that the subsidiary is acting in the interests of higher management of the MNC. Local management may be adept at using notions of corporate culture to pursue their own local objectives (Ferner, 1990, 1994; Jain *et al.*, 1998). This may be particularly the case when local managers and headquarters feel that their long term interests do not fully coincide.

The third method of pursuing common corporate objectives, the use of *coercive comparison*, may be most effective in organizations with very similar plants operating in different labour markets. It may be less appropriate where an organization has diverse business interests. Attempts to adjust for differences both in outcomes and objectives of the subsidiary or for technological differences may produce only very artificial comparisons which call into question the legitimacy of the internal productivity or performance criteria.

An understanding of the limitations on the effectiveness of these various tools in diffusing a common employment policy or so-called best practice requires first of all an appreciation of power relations and channels of influence within MNCs (Ferner and Edwards, 1995, and Box 8.2). Coercive comparison works best as a disciplinary tool, and as a means of enforcing some degree of conformity with corporate policies and objectives, when the implicit threat to the continued existence of the subsidiary has some degree of credibility. MNCs are often based around a centralized control of knowledge and of product and process innovation. This gives to the corporate centre a form of resource-based power, which may enable the imposition of practices on subsidiaries. However, according to Ferner and Edwards (1995), these types of control policies are likely to be much less effective where the subsidiary itself has some degree of independent power, based on specialized knowledge or access to markets. This will provide the subsidiary with some bargaining power, such that the outcome will depend on negotiation or exchange-based power relations, and the solution will not be simply imposed on the subsidiary. The centralization of knowledge resources does not fit so easily with new approaches to organizational growth and development as in the heterarchical companies or transnational companies discussed above. Such organizations are characterized by structures designed to exploit local knowledge and innovatory capacities and involving considerable devolution of power from the centre. Under these conditions resource-based power becomes more diffused and MNCs become more subject to exchange-based power relations between subsidiaries with independent access to valuable resources.

It is not only internal power relations or other barriers to diffusion which may encourage MNCs to adopt local employment practices. Under some conditions MNCs may have positive preferences for adopting local rather than corporate level policies; the presumption of a general process of diffusion, only hindered by institutional and organizational barriers to homogenization, must be rejected. MNCs may use

---

Box 8.2 Multinational enterprises as structures of power

According to Ferner and Edwards (1995), 'multinationals, like other organizations, can be considered to be structures of power' (231). Resource-based power is mobilized by actors to overcome resistance of other actors. 'One power resource is formal authority ... In addition ... there are informal sources of power in organizations deriving from the control of knowledge, uncertainty, financial resources and so on ... A further power resource is the ability to manipulate and mobilize symbolic elements of corporate culture in order to legitimate decision and course of action' (ibid.: 231).

Where there is overt use of power resources to influence the behaviour of other organizational actors against their potential resistance, Ferner and Edwards refer to this as 'resource-dependent power relations'. Where there is countervailing power within organizations, held by specific business units or even groups of employees or individuals, there is the potential for bargaining. This may lead to exchange relations, where 'exchange takes place because each party controls resources of value to the other side' (ibid.: 232).

their international structure not to impose uniformity but to take advantage of and exploit differences between locations. This is clearly the case in locations offering low labour costs and limited employment regulations, but it may also apply in locations offering access to high skill labour. Here deriving the full benefits from a committed and skilled labour force may be contingent upon adjusting to local custom and practice. These are factors which may encourage a devolved approach to human resource management even when the MNC has moved beyond the stage of a multi-domestic MNC and is developing a globally integrated production system.

It may, in fact, be inappropriate to seek to identify trends or to classify practices on the assumption that these will be moving in one direction and conforming to one system. We have already discussed the diversity of forms of MNCs and questioned whether we can expect an evolution towards the transnational or heterarchical organization or whether we will continue to find all types of MNCs simultaneously present. It may also be inappropriate to classify an individual MNC with respect to the multi-domestic, international, global and transnational classification, without specifying the particular aspect of policy to which the classification refers. An MNC may be multi-domestic on one dimension but global on another; moreover decisions over whether to adjust to local or corporate or global considerations may depend on the complexity of the local environment. It is in this respect that we may expect to find more evidence of multi-domestic MNCs with respect to employment policy than, for example, in areas of technology or marketing policy. Even within human resource policy, some aspects may be directed at a corporate level and others devolved to local level. And even within an individual MNC, some subsidiaries may be treated differently; some may have sufficient power and autonomy to resist coercive comparisons and continue to enjoy control over employment policy and practices, while others may be more subject to direct control by corporate headquarters.

If we turn specifically to areas of HRM policy, we can identify a range of dimensions, some of which are more likely to be determined at local level while others may be more subject to corporate level influence. For example Rosenzweig and Nohria (1994) hypothesized that one can rank HRM practices by the extent to which they can be expected to conform to local practices: from the most local — arrangements for time off — through employee benefits, gender composition, training, executive bonuses, to the least local: participation in executive decision-making (see Box 8.3). The rationale behind this ranking reflects a range of considerations, from the extent of local legal regulation (such as with time off), to the range of societal norms (with respect to women's role in the workplace), to the need to establish a consistent internal policy for reasons both of equity and strategic control (executive bonuses and participation). Lu and Bjorkman (1997) provide an alternative ranking (see Box 8.3), with recruitment and training expected to be standardized throughout MNCs due to the similarities in the technical nature of jobs, while promotion, performance appraisal and financial compensation need to be more sensitive to local needs. While this broad ranking was supported by empirical evidence, training was found empirically to be

Box 8.3 Expectations of local influence by area of employment policy

Rosenzweig and Nohria (1994) set out a ranking of local influence by area of employment policy:

Most local
- time off
- employee benefits
- gender composition
- training
- executive bonuses
- participation in executive decision-making

Least local

Rationale for ranking:

- local legal regulation (for example, time off)
- strong societal norms (with respect to women's role in the workplace)
- need for internal consistency (executive bonuses and participation)

This prior ordering of factors was largely supported by the empirical evidence.

Lu and Bjorkman (1997) provide an alternative spectrum, from most standardized to most adjusted to local needs:

Most standardized
- recruitment and training
- promotion
- performance appraisal
- financial compensation

Most adjusted to local needs

Empirical evidence supportive except that:

- training more responsive to local needs than expected
- performance appraisal more standardized than expected

more responsive to local needs, and performance appraisal more standardized by the MNC than might be expected according to this framework.

There may in fact be no universal ranking of areas of HRM policy according to the likelihood of strong host country influence. In practice this may vary not only according to the objectives and policies of the corporation but also according to the nature of the local host country environment. For example, where there is a strongly institutionalized system of training provision, there may be more difficulties in establishing a standardized MNC system of training in that particular subsidiary.

Instead of looking for such a ranking it may be more useful, following Grønhaug and Nordhaug (1992), to look at the likely influences from the host country on various aspects of HRM policy and to recognize that the extent to which these host country influences will dominate will depend on both the characteristics of the particular MNC and on the strength of these influences in a particular local environment. Grønhaug and Nordhaug (1992) divide the influences on human resource practices first into micro-environmental factors — that is, those directly associated with the organizations, such as the policies and practices of the rest of the MNC or the influence of closely related actors, including customers, suppliers, competitors and local public institutions. They then go on to discuss another level of influences on practices, which they term macro-environmental factors — that is, those conditions 'embedded in the surrounding region and country of operation' (*op. cit.*: 4). These macro-environmental factors are then broken down into socio-economic, institutional or legal and cultural influences. The institutional influences focus on the legal and regulatory constraints that have to be complied with or in some way evaded. The strength of sector and national level institutional arrangements will have major influences on the opportunities for MNCs to establish their own internal systems without encountering problems of resistance or demotivation within the workforce or problems in recruitment. The socio-economic influences refer to the state of the labour market and the economy, the patterns of social inequality and gender relations, and the level of education among the local population. The cultural influences refer to beliefs and expectations, including those relating to methods of selection for recruitment and promotion; for example recruitment may be by open, apparently meritocratic methods or according to alternative value systems, for example based on seniority, personal and family ties, or more directly political processes. Prevailing values and attitudes will also affect responses to pay and reward policies.[1] Similarly cultural and institutional factors will influence the acceptability of systems of work organization focused around individual or collective systems of organization. Political attitudes and expectations will again influence the extent to which organizations must observe or may feel able to bypass trade unions and collective agreements. Table 8.2 draws on this categorization of influences provided by Grønhaug and Nordhaug to develop some examples of how these different influences may impact on a range of areas of policy

Local versus corporate or global influences: some conclusions

As is often the case in social science research, it is easier to conclude by summarizing what we do not know than to be definite about what we might expect to find both now and in the future. Much of the above discussion of local versus corporate or global influences on employment policy and practice has been referring to possibilities or tendencies. To some extent the plausibility of the arguments over whether local, corporate or global forces will dominate depends upon empirical evidence of actual practice. However, before we turn to evidence of what we know about what happens in practice to settle the debate, we need to remember some important caveats on the use of current empirical knowledge to adjudicate on areas of difference:

- The extent of empirical information on practices in MNCs, particularly with respect to the employment of non-managerial staff, is relatively limited, so that most empirical 'facts' depend upon a limited number of studies.

Table 8.2 Macro-environmental influences on human resource practices of MNCs

Human resource management area	Socio-economic influences	Institutional/legal influences	Cultural/social norm influences
Recruitment	Availability of suitably trained labour	Legal/institutional pressure to recruit local labour	Recruitment ethics: for example meritocratic/equal opportunity principles versus personal/family recommendations
Training policy	Education and training levels of the external workforce	Institutional arrangements/ national training systems and legal requirements to train	Expectations of the role of training in career development/ job grading, and so on
Wage policy	Dispersion of earnings Inflation rate	Minimum wage laws, equal pay laws	Collective or individualized approaches to rewards for effort
Work organization	Gender division of labour Existence of occupational labour markets	Regulation of working hours Health and safety at work acts	Attitudes towards teamworking, to hierarchy
Employee/ industrial relations	Union density and collective bargaining coverage	Extension of collective agreements to non-union firms/ union recognition requirements/ employee representation laws	Attitudes towards trade unions and towards employee democracy and representation

Source: Adapted from Grønhaug and Nordhaug (1994). Note we have used some of the examples from Grønhaug and Nordhaug (1994) but we have both elaborated on the examples or changed them in some cases

- There are major problems in interpreting whether the same names or terms used to describe an employment policy or practice have the same meaning and resonance in practice in different environments.
- There is undoubtedly limited knowledge of what actually happens across international borders. Corporate headquarters may not be fully informed as to what actually happens in their international subsidiaries; similarly, subsidiary managers may have only limited knowledge and understanding of corporate

policies implemented elsewhere. This problem of limited knowledge is exacerbated where there are language and cultural divisions among managers within a subsidiary, such that the representative of headquarters may not be fully aware of what is going on even within the subsidiary they are managing.

In addition to these general problems about the nature of knowledge and the current state of collection of knowledge related to employment practices of MNCs, there are some other problems which we have already touched upon, related to attempts to classify employment policies and practices. First of all, we need to be aware that there is a range of different types of MNCs, with different objectives with respect to their international operations. Not all MNCs aim for, let alone have achieved, a globally-integrated production or operations strategy. Thus we must expect to find diversity related not only to differences in home and host country influences but also to the nature and function of international ownership. The second problem of classification is that different approaches may be made both with respect to different aspects of business policy and with respect to different dimensions of human resources policy.

Finally, there may also be major differences in strategies towards different subsidiaries, perhaps reflecting differences in the power base of the subsidiaries or differences in local environment with respect to institutional and legal regulation of human resources policies. These differences between subsidiaries may be a consequence of opportunistic responses to local conditions or may in fact be an anticipated part of the global strategy of an organization; for example, where location of different types of subsidiaries is influenced by the prevailing local conditions. Those parts of a global production system where there are particular benefits to be gained from use of relatively cheap labour will be less likely to be located in high wage, regulated systems. Those parts where a cooperative system of industrial relations and the availability of a highly skilled and committed workforce are more important may be appropriately located in environments that restrict management's rights to hire and fire or pay low wages.

Another problem that has to be faced in classifying the policies of MNCs at an empirical level is the difficulty of distinguishing between different strategies of MNCs. The initial classification systems suggested an evolution in employment policy and practice, from local or multi-domestic forms at the beginning of internationalization towards more internationally unified and coherent systems with the development of globalized companies. With development of the concept of the heterarchical organization, where the organization becomes multi-centred and focused on exploiting local differences and local knowledge, there is no longer a clear spectrum of MNCs from the domestic-focused to the globally-oriented corporation.

When we turn to the evidence of what actually appears to be happening in practice, we find quite a wide range of studies suggesting that there is a high level of responsiveness to local conditions (Jain *et al.*, 1998; Rosenzweig and Nohria, 1994; Tregaskis, 1998). The development of global corporations has led to expectations that the parent company managers would seek to impose internally consistent policies on their subsidiaries; but there are relatively few studies providing hard evidence in favour of this development. There is perhaps stronger evidence that the behaviour of MNCs varies not only according to the type of MNC but also according to its country of origin. Here the notion of the dominant country comes back into play. Some studies suggest that it is the organizations of Anglo-Saxon origin that are most likely to seek to diffuse employment policies and practices to their subsidiaries (Ferner and Quintanilla, 1998). One study goes further and suggests that the process of diffusion is not always in one direction, that is from parent company to host countries, particularly if the parent company is based in a non-dominant home country (Edwards, 1998). Under these conditions the parent company may seek to learn from its own subsidiaries, particularly those located in Anglo-Saxon countries. The process of globalization for some, therefore, is more appropriately interpreted as a process of Anglo-Saxonization.

The story with respect to Japanization is more complex, although perhaps better researched (see Box 3.10 in Chapter 3). Some studies suggest that Japanese multinationals are very responsive to local conditions (Yuen and Tak Kee, 1992), but Japanese multinationals' preference for expatriate managers in order to reinforce corporate loyalty can result in communication problems within the companies (Broad, 1994), or in attempts to integrate Japanese ways of doing things into inappropriate environments, resulting in negative outcomes or cynicism (Rinehart *et al.*, 1994). For others the focus on Anglo-Saxonization in part reflects a lack of research on the policies and practices of other MNCs. Even when the companies, say of German origin, appear to be adopting certain Anglo-Saxon practices, such as an emphasis on shareholder value or on general management skills, the ways in which these policies are implemented remain distinctly German. For example, in Ferner and Quintanilla's (1998) study of German multinationals, the notions of shareholder value and long term investment in training were not held to be in conflict but complementary, because the German MNC had taken a longer term view of the need to protect shareholder value.

Summary and conclusions

A range of possible future scenarios with respect to the influence of MNCs on employment policies and practices can be identified. On the one hand, there is the prospect of the development of a global culture, independent of home or host country influences, although perhaps rooted in the Anglo-Saxon systems. The spread of this employment culture would result in increasing homogenization and increasing challenges to distinctive employment regimes, particularly if countries felt the need to adjust to the global culture to protect flows of foreign investment.

A second scenario is the reinforcement of current divisions between countries, based around selective investment decisions by MNCs, with specialization determined by the different comparative advantages offered by different employment regimes. Here low wage and deregulated economies would be the recipients of investment designed to exploit these advantages, while research and development work would increasingly be concentrated in the more regulated economies, offering higher skills and education levels.

A third scenario sees the coexistence of different 'national employment regimes' within the same country, brought about through the influence of the home country regimes on the operations of the subsidiaries within the host country. For example, German, French, Japanese or American subsidiaries all located in one country would operate in quite different ways, influenced by the different national employment regimes of the home country. MNCs under this scenario would promote the diffusion of different varieties of capitalism. These varieties would no longer be found located in one geographical area but would coexist in the same geographical space (Ferner and Hyman, 1998; Whitley, 1999).

All three future scenarios assume homogeneity in the stage of development and function of MNCs; further diversity is also likely to emerge because MNCs will be at different stages of development of their international profiles and will have different objectives with respect to their international businesses.

Perhaps, therefore, the one thing that remains certain is that a range of different policies and practices are likely to be evident for the foreseeable future. The evolution of policy will in part depend upon political conditions, in particular the extent to which nation states and pan-national organizations establish or maintain systems of regulation in the area of employment to which MNCs must conform; or to what extent they adopt a policy of allowing MNCs to dictate the agenda with respect to employment issues. These issues are addressed further in the final two chapters of this book.

Note

1   For example, Edwards *et al.* (1993) cited in Ferner (1994) found French managers successfully resisted the introduction of a corporate-wide job evaluation scheme as this cut across the national system of pay classification.

Globalization and the future for diversity

So far in this book we have been primarily concerned with exploring the range of national employment systems. We have included in our analysis the factors that may be inducing change in those systems, and have raised the issue of whether the diversity of employment systems will be as great in the future as in the past. In this chapter we address this latter issue directly. We start by discussing what is meant by globalization and review some of the definitions on offer. We consider the consequences of these different interpretations of globalization for the scope for the survival of distinctive national employment systems and human resources policies. The second half of the chapter focuses more specifically on the forces for convergence in employment systems, and attempts to assess the balance of the argument for each of the forces that we identify. The chapter concludes by assessing the scope for and evidence of resistance to processes of globalization and convergence.

Globalization: towards the convergence of employment systems?

Globalization in many management and economic textbooks is often taken as a fact of life, an inevitable and uncontroversial feature of the late 20th century and certainly the early 21st century world order. Four major trends and developments provide evidence of the increasing international integration of the world economy. First, there is the growth of foreign trade, which may be considered a necessary if not sufficient condition for establishing a globally integrated world economy. Second, there are increasing flows of investment funds, evident in the higher rates of foreign direct investment and facilitated both by the deregulation of financial flows and by the growth of multinational companies (Table 9.1). This growth has been primarily concentrated in flows between developed countries but nevertheless has also involved significant increases for developing countries. Third, the development of

Table 9.1 Growth of foreign direct investment (FDI) ($US millions)

Area	FDI inflows by host region/economy			FDI outflows by home region/economy		
	1987–1992 average	1995	1998	1987–1992 average	1995	1998
World	173,530	328,862	643,879	198,670	358,573	648,920
Developed countries total	136,628	208,372	460,431	184,680	306,025	594,699
Western Europe	75,507	121,522	237,425	110,957	175,511	406,220
North America	52,110	68,031	209,875	35,384	103,540	159,406
United States	46,211	58,772	193,375	29,839	92,074	132,829
Other developed	9,011	18,819	13,130	38,340	26,974	29,073
Japan	911	41	3,192	33,549	22,630	24,152
Developing countries total	35,326	106,224	165,936	13,946	52,089	52,318
Africa	3,010	4,145	7,931	1,118	454	511
Latin America and Caribbean	12,400	32,921	71,652	1,309	7,510	15,455
Asia	19,613	68,126	84,880	11,495	44,060	36,182
Pacific and developing Europe	302	1,032	1,472	24	64	170
Central and Eastern Europe	1,576	14,266	17,513	44	460	1,903

FDI is defined as an investment involving a long-term relationship and reflecting a lasting interest and control of a resident entity in one economy in an enterprise resident in an economy other than that of the foreign direct investor.

Source: United Nations (1999), Annex Tables B.1 and B.2

information and communication technologies is facilitating the development of globally integrated production and distribution systems. Without the internet, integrated telecommunication and computer technologies, computerized design or programmable machines, the internationalization of production and distribution systems would be subject to much greater levels of uncertainty and time delays. Instead, centralized control is compatible with decentralized and worldwide systems of production and distribution. Fourth, the evidence for globalization is found in the presence and power of the multinational corporations themselves. The emergence of transnational or of stateless corporations adds a further dimension to the apparently open and shut case, presented within much of the economics and management literature, that we are moving into an era of globalization with profound implications for the opportunities for national governments to enact policies and practices which do not follow the dictates of the new economic order.

Interest in globalization within the academic community is by no means confined to market-orientated economists or management theorists. As it signals a major change to political and economic sovereignty, it naturally attracts interest from political science and the social sciences in general. Within these fields of enquiry, there is much less apparent consensus, not only over whether we have already entered or are about to enter a globalized world order, but also about what globalization actually means. These disagreements in practice focus on the extent to which political forces, at the national or international level, have the power to shape the development of the new world order, or whether this power lies vested in the transnational corporations or in global capital.

Is globalization here, and is its progress inevitable?

There are many and various definitions of the term globalization, and an even wider variety of contexts where the term is used loosely and without any attempt at precise definition. Those who regard use of the term globalization to describe current trends as inappropriate or a great exaggeration are more likely to insist on precise definitions and muster data and information to demonstrate that globalization has not yet happened. This group tends to see the world as facing as much continuity as change, and moreover, regards internationalization of the economic system as nothing new and certainly not to be confused with the term globalization. Those who consider globalization to be a term which captures an underlying trend towards a qualitatively new situation, which may or may not yet be fully evident in the data, are happy to use the expression in a looser way.

Hirst and Thompson (1997) are unashamed members of the first category of scholars. They provide two definitions which distinguish clearly between *a worldwide international economy and a global international economy*. The worldwide international economy:

> is one in which the principle entities are nation states and involves the process of growing interconnection between national economies. It involves the increasing integration of more and more nations and economic actors to market relationships. Trade relations as a result take on the form of national specialization and the division of labour. The importance of trade is, however, progressively replaced by the centrality of investment relations between nations, which increasingly acts as the organizing principle of the system ... international events do not directly penetrate or permeate the domestic economy but are refracted through national policies and processes. (*op. cit.*: 337)

In contrast the global international economy:

> is a distinct ideal-type from that of the worldwide economy ... In such a global system, distinct national economies are subsumed and rearticulated in the system by international processes and transactions ... the global economy raises these nationally-based interactions to a new power. The international economy becomes autonomized, as markets and production become truly global. Domestic policy makers, whether private corporations or public regulators, now have routinely to take account of the predominately international

determinants of their activities. As systemic interdependence grows, the national level is permeated and transformed by the international. (*ibid.*: 339)

For Hirst and Thompson, national political and governance structures have a continuing influence within an increasingly internationalized world economy and the degree of change has been exaggerated. Other commentators also question the degree of change but from a different perspective (for example, Hopkins and Wallerstein (1982)); the autonomy of nation states has been exaggerated in the past and their position within the world capitalist system obscured by a focus on action at the state level. In contrast, other commentators (for example, Reich (1991)) and many politicians stress discontinuity and change. This new world order is dominated by the power of multinationals. Nation states have become increasingly powerless and need to recognize these limitations on their power and adapt to these new conditions. From this perspective, the technological, market and institutional developments in the direction of global integration are an unstoppable force, equivalent to the first industrial revolution in their power to change the world economy. Whatever steps are taken to try to prevent globalization at the national or pan-national level, these forces of global capitalism will inevitably win out, largely because of the greater global efficiency the systems imply, even if the consequences may be uneven and unequal across the globe. Others, for example Gray (1998), are equally fatalistic about the spread of globalization but take issue with an interpretation of these developments as a logical or rational response to new production and technological imperatives. Instead globalization is more a political process, another form of imperialism, legitimated by the notion that the world economy must and should be persuaded to adopt a particular form of capitalism, that developed within the United States. However, for Gray, while this is the ideological objective of the globalization movement, the irony or paradox lies in the fact that the pursuit of a global free market will both generate new and competing forms of capitalism and lead to the destruction of many valuable and potentially more sustainable models of capitalism than the global model:

> Economic globalization — the worldwide spread of industrial production and new technologies that is promoted by unrestricted mobility of capital and unfettered freedom of trade — actually threatens the stability of the single global market that is being constructed by American-led transnational organizations … the central paradox of our time can be stated thus: economic globalization does not strengthen the current regime of global laissez-faire. It works to undermine it. (Gray, 1998: 6–7)

Free market ideology is, according to this analysis, likely to lead to the pursuit of a global market even if the objective can be categorized as a 'false dawn'. A different political interpretation of the current trends and developments informs Hirst and Thompson's rejection of the notion of globalization: they consider that reference to the unstoppable force of globalization should be considered as rhetoric, in the sense that governments will only use the globalization agenda to help in the legitimation of their own policy agendas. Governments will claim not to be able to do anything against the forces of globalization when they choose not to do so, but will take action when they consider it to be in their interests to do so. In short these authors reassert the continuing importance of the political in the regulation of economic and social life and see the political power as still mainly vested at the national level. Increasing internationalization has led to the emergence of regional trading groups, involving varying degrees of political integration. Even the most integrated, the EU, is still reliant on the consensus of national governments, and as Whitley (1994) points out, even the ways in which pan-national organizations such as the EU function can be traced to the influence of nation states, with the EU influenced by the French and German ways of managing governments and economies.

Even for some who predict ever greater globalization, there is still the possibility of concerted political action to offset, modify or even reverse some of these tendencies. For example, Gray recognizes the increasing questioning of the global free market idea after the Asian crises of the late 1990s, both in broad political circles and even within transnational corporations themselves. Yet for him the critical issue is the need to abandon the ideological attachment to global *laissez-faire*. There is thus both no consensus on the likely way forward or on the scope for political initiative at the national or international level capable of influencing the direction and force of change. Reich, who regards globalization as a more inevitable consequence of the exploitation of technological and market change than does Gray, is nevertheless concerned with the global distributive consequences of the change, and has argued for the need for concerted pan-national action to create a more equal world and provide more opportunities for the development of human potential. Coates (2000) too has called for a renewal of democratic institutions to take control over the path of development of the world economy. For him the debate over the continued diversity in institutional arrangements and distinctive national systems has become increasingly beside the point: 'continuity of institutions is less important than discontinuity of outcomes' (*op. cit.*: 260). He sees the social settlements for workers that were achieved under distinctive national regimes in the past as being continuously eroded, even though the institutional arrangements remain largely in place.

These wide-ranging and essentially political debates cannot be resolved here. Our purpose is twofold: first, to consider what the role is for human resources and the associated organization of employment in developing comparative advantage for organizations and nation states; and second, to explore to what extent the emerging new world order will allow for diversity in employment systems or result in a more homogenized system. Of course these questions are connected: tolerance of diversity in approach to employment is likely to be greater the more that human resources can make a positive contribution to comparative advantage. However, even if human resources policy can be linked to competitiveness, there is still no guarantee that distinctive employment regimes will survive. Short term economic pressures and broader changes in the political and economic order may fail to allow either corporations or nation states to develop their comparative advantage. Therefore, even though the questions are interconnected, we will still consider them separately.

Human resources and comparative advantage in a global market

In an age when technology and capital can flow freely across national boundaries, human resources take on a new importance as the main national asset or factor of production which is, by and large, not mobile. Despite the development of both transnational corporations and cheap and quick forms of transport, mobility of labour between nation states remains limited. Even when political barriers to mobility have been largely removed, as in the case of the EU which allows free movement of labour, the actual size of flows tends to remain small, amounting to only around 0.3 per cent of the working age population in the EU in 2000 (CEC, 2001: Table 5). In the EU region the main barrier remains one of language but the ties to the nation state or even region or local community remain strong. Even those individuals who move outside of their nation state at one stage in their lives are likely at some point either to settle permanently in a new location or return to their home country.

Labour is fundamentally different from any other factor of production in that it has its own free will and will not necessarily follow where job opportunities lead. Humans are social beings and form social relationships. The labour force cannot be treated as a collection of atomistic agents who have no stake in their social environment and social networks. In addition to these social factors which discourage mobility whatever the political conditions, outside of the integrated regional blocks mobility tends to be inhibited by ever increasing political barriers, and to be reserved only for a privileged elite or for political refugees (although the process of defining who is or is not a political refugee is itself highly politicized). More recently there have been concerns about skill shortages in the more developed countries and these economic pressures are leading to new schemes to try to recruit overseas employees to fill gaps in IT, teaching and nursing. This policy has led, however, to countries such as South Africa protesting against the loss of essential skilled staff to the South African economy (Smithers and McGreal, 2001).

Inter-country competition in a global economy is likely to result in successes and failures. However, as we also argued in Chapter Two, unlike an individual economic organization, failure for a nation state does not normally result in the breakup and disappearance of the failing country and the dispersal of the labour force to more successful countries. The citizens of the country will still need to find gainful employment even if they have become inefficient in world trade terms. Nation states have been able to support domestic industries and sectors which are not necessarily operating at 'best practice' levels of productivity or paying the lowest possible wage rates. Globalization raises the possibility that all or most capital will become mobile and all sectors subject to international competition; the result of failing the international competitiveness test may be increasing unemployment for citizens.

It is this scenario that Reich (1991) identifies as a possible outcome of global competition and which may need to be countered by imaginative pan-national political initiatives. Human resources are both the main assets of nation states, in the sense of providing the main source of comparative advantage, and the main 'liabilities' of those states. Human assets are both immobile and 'illiquid' and have to be maintained through welfare and other programmes if there are no employment opportunities. Moreover, even unemployed citizens retain some political voice and may be a source of political and social instability. Global investment decisions may reinforce and exploit pre-existing country differences, leading to ever widening inequalities between developed and less developed countries.

Reich (1991) outlined a world in which global capital will move wherever it is cost effective to move. He sees jobs as divided into three types:

- routinized jobs in production and services;
- in-person service jobs;
- jobs for symbolic analysts.

The first set, that of routinized jobs, are the most vulnerable to 'delocalization' under globalization. The notion of routinized work is that it can be carried out at a distance in space and time from the customer; and new technologies and international transport allow both manufacturing and service work to be located in very different parts of the world from the ultimate customer. Routinized work involves not only relatively low skilled service and production operators but also their supervisors and managers. This delocalization was initially confined mainly to manufacturing but new technologies enabling, for example, the setting up of call centres have allowed the delocalization to apply to services, even when direct person to person contact is required. Indeed the operation of 24 hour service provision is said to be potentially assisted by delocalization as some facilities can be located in countries where the working day begins when other people normally retire to bed. This applies also to processing operations, as these can then be done overnight before the next day's business without having to employ people on night work. Reich sees many workers in developed countries who are currently in routinized work — or who will find their work becoming routinized through technological change — facing job losses over future years because of differential wage costs.

These displaced routinized workers will largely be relatively low skilled and will compete for jobs in the in-person services sector. This set of jobs requires direct person to person contact and cannot therefore be delocalized. For example, no-one has yet found a way to have a haircut at a distance, or to have someone from India clean a house for someone in New York City without actually transporting the Indian worker to New York

City. While some jobs in in-person services are being routinized — for example the development of distance learning to replace direct teaching — there will be increasing demand for some forms of in-person services arising out of changing lifestyles, rising consumption levels and the increasing care needs of ageing populations. These jobs are only likely to be available, according to Reich (1991), at low wage levels as high wages would choke off a large part of the demand. They are, therefore, unlikely to provide an effective substitute in high wage economies for the loss of delocalized routinized jobs.

The main hope for developed economies thus apparently lies in increasing the number of symbolic analyst jobs; these are the jobs at the heart of the so-called knowledge economy and involve the application of human intelligence to problem solving. Transnational corporations will continue to be reliant on symbolic analysts for innovation, problem solving and for creating and generating markets. The corporations are likely to be attracted to locate jobs in nations where there is a plentiful supply of appropriate labour, namely highly educated labour. For Reich the main way in which nation states can attract freely floating capital to developed countries is through providing an educated labour force. As individuals, symbolic analysts will be able to look after themselves in the global world order, either by remaining in their home countries and perhaps working at a distance through the internet, or moving to where the jobs are located, as they are the group most likely to be given rights to move across boundaries. However, the interests of other citizens need to be taken into account. There is a need both for pan-national regulation of foreign investment and for governments to invest heavily in education, with the objective not simply of attracting jobs from elsewhere but also potentially of expanding the number of jobs created which require high skills and problem solving ability. The weakness of this approach has, however, been vividly summarized by Coates (2000):

> What 're-skilling labour' as a growth strategy does is leave investment as a Dutch auction in which local labour forces (and local states) bid — like whores — for the favours of mobile capital ... You cannot get off the treadmill by running faster. All you can do by that mechanism is temporarily pass others, until they respond by running faster too ... The victor in such a race is not the runner, but the treadmill. (*op. cit.*: 254)

Another influential analyst who has identified human resources as the key to future comparative advantage is Porter. For Porter (1990), human resources feed into comparative advantage in two ways: first, through their influence on a country's 'factor conditions', following the traditional model of comparative advantage in international trade theory; and second, through influencing company-specific comparative advantage. While the quality as well as the quantity of human resources influence location decisions and shape the pattern of development within countries, the organization of human resources at the firm level provides a major source of organization-specific comparative advantage. Porter argues that labour-management relationships are an important factor in the innovation process. Other labour-related factors that influence comparative advantage include attitudes towards authority; patterns or norms of interpersonal interaction; social norms with respect to individual or group behaviour; and prevailing professional standards. This extends the role of labour well beyond the simple 'investment in human capital' hypothesis and introduces dimensions to company-specific comparative advantage which cannot necessarily be easily emulated by other organizations. The interrelationships between the social environment and the company-specific comparative advantage may differ between nation states. In some cases the national cohesiveness of the social system, together with a nationally coordinated collective bargaining system, might result in relatively similar forms of company-specific comparative advantage. In other societies, where there is more company-level discretion over the system of labour-management relations or where there is a more culturally diverse population, there may be wider intra-country variations in company-specific comparative advantage, derived from specific human resource and labour-management policies and practices.

For Porter, internationalization intensifies the importance of the specific endowments of the nation state as a source of comparative advantage in a world where integration reduces the scope for sheltered domestic-based economies. For some, for example Whitley (1999), internationalization brings together national business systems into increasing competition, but does not lead to convergence or the establishment of a new global model:

> the internationalization of managerial co-ordination and of capital markets has increased competition between predominantly national business systems and their associated institutions, rather than establishing a radically new cross-national system of economic co-ordination and control. (*op. cit.*: 135)

This approach complements that found in the evolutionary economics and innovation literature, where the social embeddedness of production and innovation regimes provides the source of comparative advantage (see also Chapter Three, and Best (1990)). The new production paradigm is argued to be focused on continuous improvement, where the nature of labour-management relations, in particular the level of trust in the relationship, can be argued to play a key role. Where appropriate institutional arrangements are already in place, this argument over the enhanced role for labour in the incremental innovation/continuous improvement process provides an optimistic assessment of the capacity of economies to maintain social distinctiveness and to provide some protection against the destabilizing forces of mobile capital.

However, where there is a need for institutional arrangements to change and adapt to meet the new production paradigm requirement, the argument is less straightforward. Not only are there many obstacles to be overcome and a long gestation period before such changes are likely to bear fruit, but there is also the difficulty that the recognition of a need to change social institutions may be less likely to result in a process of re-regulation to develop new and more appropriate institutional forms. Instead there is the danger that it may simply lead to the dismantling of the old order, with no concerted effort to replace it with new forms of coordination.

Indeed, as we will elaborate in the next section, the identification of a potential role for human resource management in securing competitive and comparative advantage may not be sufficient to protect even those existing institutional arrangements which help to generate and maintain social capital in human resources relationships. There may be even fewer options to develop new innovatory institutions to build up and develop such comparative advantage. Once political factors are introduced into the picture, the possibility of perverse developments and a failure to grasp opportunities for better development paths must be entertained. Gray makes the argument that 'global markets are engines of creative destruction' (1998: 210) and will carry away in their wake the very social systems which have brought prosperity to many OECD countries in the post Second World War period. Gray, in fact, argues that global capitalism works according to Gresham's Law — that bad money drives out the good: 'worldwide mobility of capital and production triggers a "race to the bottom"' (*ibid*.: 218). His concern is primarily with the enforced cutbacks in welfare states, but the argument can also be extended to the cutting back on social institutions which sustain different forms of labour-management relations.

The central issue here is the relationship between the real economy and the financial economy. Is the future bound up with the much trumpeted knowledge economy, where the intellectual skills that humans can bring to the economy will be increasingly valued? Or does the globalization of capitalism mean that the pursuit of profit will become increasingly disconnected from the fostering of productivity improvements in the real economy? Will competition be primarily or possibly exclusively based on shareholder value (Williams, 2000), providing the basis for the maxim 'no long term', that Sennett (1998) has used to sum up the state of late 20th century capitalism? If the quick buck takes precedence over long term investments in skills and knowledge, the efforts to sustain and maintain varieties of capitalism may yet be found to be futile. It follows that in considering, as we do in the next section, the likely forces for convergence in employment systems, we will not only or mainly be concerned with the relationship between employment regimes and the productivity or efficiency of the real economy. It is changes in the social, economic and political landscape that may play the decisive role in the future for employment regimes, not their capacity to deliver a productive workforce to assist in the development of new technologies and markets.

Towards convergence in employment systems?

The issue of what is happening to employment and labour markets and whether these trends are similar across the world is a widely debated question. Yet the debate is often rather confused, particularly when, as we noted in Chapter Two, there tends to be a chronic failure to separate out the issue of change from that of convergence. All employment systems need to change and reform themselves to meet new conditions on both the demand and the supply side of the economy. All societies are adjusting to new forms of technology, to the rising share of services, to the increasing share of young people in education and the rising participation of women in the labour market. New forms of competition are requiring organizations to pay more attention to flexible production systems and to compete on the basis of the economics of time and quality. Yet convergence requires more than the direction of trends to be the same; it also requires there to be a narrower range of systems emerging.

It is important, therefore, not to confuse the process of change, and of adapting to common global pressures for change, with a convergence process. Smith and Meiksins' (1995) framework (see Chapter Two) enables these forces to be separated out at an analytical level; system imperatives — or technological and production pressures — are distinguished from convergence pressures arising out of dominant country effects and from the continued pressure for divergence associated with societal effects. If all three imperatives are present it is possible to have forces for change, for convergence and for divergence. The way in which system effects are introduced may, of course, be through the emulation of dominant country models. However, the implementation of dominant country models may not lead to precise emulation, but to selective adaptation to fit with the characteristics of the specific societal system (see Chapters Three and Eight).

As the processes of change and convergence and divergence are intertwined, it is also not necessarily appropriate or possible to identify the effects separately. Changes in the composition of employment — for example the moves towards more service sector work, more non-manual work or the growth in female employment — may in themselves involve fundamental changes in the nature of employment relations, in attitudes to work and career expectations, and in power relations, including the role for trade unions. As the dominant forms of work and the dominant labour force groups change, the impact is not simply compositional but more transformational. It may be analytically appealing to separate out these different forces and pressures for change but in practice they may not be amenable to separate measurement for methodological reasons.

Instead, therefore, we focus on the range of factors which may be considered as forces for convergence and forces for divergence. We have identified five main influences:

- the impact of the development of new production/human resource paradigms on employment systems;
- the impact of political and social change on the stability of national employment regimes;
- changes in international or pan-national governance;
- the international diffusion of ideologies and changing social and family systems;
- the prospects for forms of non-governmental resistance to forces for convergence and globalization.

Some of the issues presented here have been discussed in earlier chapters — notably Chapters Two, Three and Eight — and readers are referred back to these chapters for a more detailed specification of some of the arguments and references to the relevant literature.

The new production paradigm: towards lean production or global Japanization?

The issues related to the transmission of a new global production paradigm, sometimes called lean production, have been extensively discussed in both Chapter Three and Chapter Eight. Here we summarize the main lines of the argument. There are clear imperatives, found both in the systems of integrated competition and in the development of a common shared technology, to develop new production systems based on notions of 'best practice'. However, while there is evidence that all countries, and all types of sectors, have been striving to change their production systems to make them more flexible, more quality, delivery and design conscious and more able to harness skills and knowledge in the interest of continuous improvement and innovation, these generalities of direction hide a range of processes which may be consistent as much with divergence as with convergence. The forces for divergence can be summarized as follows:

- New forms of competition still allow for different national or sectoral business strategies — for example diversified quality mass production versus specialist flexible small scale production; low versus high value added production systems; and standardized versus customized technologies.
- The 'social system of production' can be considered a source of comparative advantage to a nation, a region or an organization. Those trying to emulate best practice may attempt to introduce systems and techniques whose success depends on the context in which they are introduced.
- The emulation of 'best practice' in reality involves a process of selection and adaptation. Even those elements that are selected for implementation may take on a different form from the 'best practice' societal model. The mode of implementation in a particular society may reflect the logic of that society's system of production or may be influenced by society-specific priorities, for example to change the balance of power in industrial relations.

The stability of national employment regimes

The stability of national employment regimes may be threatened from a range of different forces, some directly emanating from the employment and production systems as discussed above and some from more external forces.

The direct pressures on employment regimes come from the actions and policies of employers both domestic and multinational, who spurred on by the ideological climate against regulation (see the role of ideology, below) feel able to place pressure on governments and pan-national organizations to deregulate labour markets and disestablish institutional arrangements. While employers' calls for deregulation can be interpreted as a direct challenge to the prevailing employment systems, there may be other forces attacking some of the central axioms of the employment regimes but that are not the product of disenchantment with the employment regime itself. Box 9.1 provides some examples.

Of course it is also the case that we can find continuity of the institutional arrangements but, as Coates (2000) has argued, discontinuities of outcomes. Thus in assessing the stability and viability of employment systems we need to address both the continued institutionalization of the system and its ability to deliver desirable social and economic outcomes.

Pan-national governance

One of the features of the process of globalization, to the extent that it has occurred, has been the stimulation of the development of pan-national organizations at the regional level. The main examples are the EU and North American Free Trade Association (NAFTA). The impact of these pan-national organizations on the processes of globalization and convergence are disputed. Some interpret the

---

Box 9.1 Examples of developments which may be challenging or destabilizing societal systems

Germany

The increasing interest among German youth in higher education regarding apprenticeship systems may be more to do with aspirations for particular lifestyles than a rejection of the traditional German employment regime. Nevertheless a drop in the share entering apprenticeships could undermine the viability of the system. The unification of Germany has also threatened the survival of the dual system as former East German employers are less committed to the system (see Chapter Six).

Japan

In Japan lack of caution in investment decisions by Japanese banks may be forcing a move away from the jobs for life system. This is not because the system has failed to deliver highly productive, committed workers, but because the organizations are now operating in a more uncertain macro-economic environment (see Chapter Three).

Sweden

Macroeconomic conditions placed the Swedish welfare state and labour market model under pressure in the early 1990s, when unemployment rose to high levels on the back of changing international markets and problems of domestic demand management. The Swedish system combined high unemployment benefits with an active labour market policy to get people back into work; once they were unable to generate sufficient jobs for the unemployed the burden of welfare benefits increased sharply. Yet policies of cutting benefits placed the social democratic welfare state system in Sweden under threat by undermining the political consensus and the coherence of the overall system (see Chapter Four).

---

formation of the EU as a mechanism for globalization and convergence. The role of the multinationals in pressing for the formation of the Single European Market is pointed to and the developments of EU-level social institutions, such as the Social Chapter, are regarded as serving to undermine the legitimacy of the regulatory systems of individual nation states and replacing them by a form of social protection based on minimum rather than maximum or even average standards (see Chapter Eight and Chapter Ten).

The EU can also be seen as an important conduit for developing shared ideologies concerning the best ways of managing economies at the macro and micro levels. This ideological role is interpreted by commentators in different ways. Some see that the EU treaties have enshrined a conservative approach to macro-economic policy to underpin monetary union. Furthermore the EU has adopted and developed the language and rhetoric of flexibility, which may serve to undermine the case for the maintenance of distinctive employment regimes within nation states.

Others, in contrast, focus on the role of the EU in spreading its social model and the concept of working in conjunction with social partners, that is the organizations representing employers' interests and workers' interests. This ideology is seen as in conflict with the Anglo-Saxon model of employment and social organization. For supporters of the EU social model, the development of an integrated trading block is seen to provide the best chance of defending the specific European way of doing things against the dominant ideology of deregulation and flexible labour markets. To some extent these different interpretations can be explained by reference to their different points of comparison; those who see the EU as a source for convergence and global integration tend to compare the current situation to conditions prevailing before the current phase of integration. Those who see the EU as a defence against globalization tend to focus on what might happen in the future if the European countries did not act collectively to defend the European way.

Interpretations of the role of NAFTA are equally diverse. Some see it as a way to undermine what little regulation still remains in the US labour market, by allowing intensified competition from low wage countries such as Mexico. Others see the role of NAFTA as being to regulate trade with the low wage economies and to prevent trade based on even lower labour standards within Mexico, as the NAFTA agreement requires minimum wage laws and other conditions to be observed. Thus the NAFTA agreement is seen by some as a form of protectionism and by others as a means of opening up the US market to the forces of globalization (see Chapter Ten).

Global ideology and societal fragmentation?

The forces which may be most powerful in destabilizing specific societal and cultural systems may be the ones that are most difficult to control: the forces of ideas, ideology and shared transport around the world through information technology, international travel and international news and communications media. The spread of ideas and ideology is not independent of the economic forces for integration and is propagated, for example, through multinational media organizations. However, once the barriers to cultural transmission of ideas and ideologies have been broken down, there is unlikely to be a return to any notion of culturally-closed media, whatever steps may be taken to reduce the power of media companies at a global level. Exceptions to this trend towards greater openness to 'foreign' ideas and ideologies — or rather Western and in particular Anglo-Saxon ideas — can be found in the rebirth of nationalism, particularly within the ex-Communist states, and in the spread of religious fundamentalism, particularly in Muslim societies, but also echoed to some extent in the United States' intensified concern with religious issues, at least in comparison to European societies.[1]

Within most Western societies the spread of ideas and ideology can take on a momentum of its own, not directly within the control of either governments or multinationals. One example of such an ideology is that of feminism; governments are not necessarily able to enforce their particular view of appropriate female roles on all or most women, now that notions of women's economic and social independence have spread even to societies that have attempted to maintain traditional social and welfare systems.

The spread of ideas and ideologies applies at a wide range of levels. For example, the 1980s and 1990s were decades which became dominated by the notion of the supremacy of the market as the victor in the battle between Western capitalism and Eastern Communist systems of economic organization. This notion of the supremacy of the market fostered notions of consumer sovereignty, even in countries not yet able to generate supplies sufficient to meet basic needs. The establishment of the first McDonald's in Eastern Europe was seen as a great victory for Western market forces and this attracted more media attention than the continuing and worsening queues in the food shops.[2] The notion of the power of the market was also found in the new hegemony of ideas on macroeconomic management. This new hegemony denied any role for demand management at either a national or even an international level as the means of securing economic prosperity and growth. This ideology extended even to the previous socialist parties of the West, leading to the spawning of 'third way' politics in contrast to the old 'tax and spend' regimes of post Second World War leftwing governments. The new orthodoxy became the standard against which any new government had to argue. Over time these new principles have become enshrined in international institutional arrangements, from the European Monetary Union conditions, to the policies and practices of the International Monetary Fund (IMF). However, ideas and ideologies do not remain static. Towards the end of the 1990s, in the wake of Asian currency crises and continuing problems of Third World debt, there began to be increasing debate and pressure to adopt non-market solutions to world problems, for example to debt relief for Third World countries. Even more change in the global world order can be expected to be the fallout of the 11 September events, but the direction of change is as yet unclear.

This diffusion of ideology over recent decades has also probably favoured the notion of individual goals over group or collective goals and behaviour. The emphasis on individual ambition and achievement, at the level of the individual worker and the individual organization, provides an ideological climate which may be creating barriers to the development of new institutional arrangements designed to foster the collective interests of either workers or domestic capital. It also places pressure on communities and countries which have traditions based on group rather than individual achievements.

Alongside this cult of the individual, there has been a growing fragmentation of social life in many countries. This fragmentation is found in family systems and in communities. Families have been slower to form, with delayed ages of marriage and first births, and have proved to be increasingly unstable, resulting in high divorce rates and high shares of lone parent families in some countries. Moreover, as the industrial systems have restructured, communities based around traditional skills have fragmented, preventing the effective transmission of knowledge and community values. Families have become both more dispersed and more unstable, reducing the possibility of family-based rather than individual-based strategies of economic survival. Not all societies have adjusted and reacted in the same way to the pressures. For example, there are still major differences in the organization and role of the family even among, for example, EU states. These differences manifest themselves in concrete differences in, for example, the pattern and level of fertility — numbers of children, whether children are born inside or outside marriage and so on (see Table 9.2). While in all European societies a higher share of women is remaining in the labour market, in some societies this tends to involve a choice between work and family while in others there are more opportunities to combine work and family. The heterogeneity of different social and family systems is being reproduced in different modes of integration of women into wage work. There is similar divergence in how young people relate to their families; in some European societies, for example Spain, it is normal for young people to remain at home until well into their 20s or even later, while in the Scandinavian countries and the UK young people are more likely to move away from the family at a young age (see Table 9.3).

Finally, the result of greater international integration and the breaking up of local communities has perhaps led to more multiculturalism within a given geographical space. This does not necessarily mean the establishment of racial tolerance and social harmony. Nevertheless, it is increasingly possible to sample the cuisines of the world without straying outside one urban area; and these cuisines are maintained by the ethnic groups living side by side within that urban space. It has become perhaps more difficult to talk about a single or even a dominant culture in any particular geographical area; instead it is necessary to take into account ethnic, religious as well as class differences among any particular workforce and to discuss the issues of multiculturalism with respect to all organizations, not just those operating across nation states.

Table 9.2 Trends in marriage and fertility

9.2a

Country	Marriage rate (marriages per 1000 population)		Divorce rate (divorces per 1000 population)	
	1980	1995	1980	1995
Belgium	6.7	5.1	0.21	0.55
Denmark	5.2	6.6	0.40	0.41
Germany	6.3	5.3	0.25	0.33
Greece	6.5	6.1	0.10	0.17
Spain	5.9	5.0*	N/a	0.12
France	6.2	4.4*	0.22	0.38
Ireland	6.4	4.3*	N/a	N/a
Italy	5.7	4.9*	0.03	0.08
Luxembourg	5.9	5.1	0.26	0.33
Netherlands	6.4	5.3	0.25	0.37
Austria	6.2	5.3	0.26	0.38
Portugal	7.4	6.6	0.08	0.16
Finland	6.1	4.6	0.28	0.49
Sweden	4.5	3.8	0.42	0.52
United Kingdom	7.4	5.5*	0.16#	0.45*#

9.2b

Country	Mean age of mother at childbearing		% of births outside marriage		Fertility rate†	
	1980	1995	1980	1995	1980	1995
Belgium	26.6	28.5*	4.1	15.0	1.68	1.55*
Denmark	26.8	29.2	33.2	46.5	1.55	1.80
Germany	26.4	28.3	11.9	16.1	1.56	1.25
Greece	26.1	28.2	1.5	3.0	2.21	1.32
Spain	28.2	29.7**	3.9	10.8*	2.20	1.18
France	26.8	29.0*	11.4	37.2*	1.95	1.70*
Ireland	29.9	30.2*	5.0	22.7	3.25	1.86*
Italy	27.4	29.7**	4.3	8.1*	1.64	1.17
Luxembourg	27.5	28.9	6.0	13.1	1.49	1.69
Netherlands	27.7	30.0	4.1	15.5	1.60	1.53
Austria	26.3	27.7	17.8	27.4	1.62	1.40
Portugal	27.1	28.1	9.2	18.7	2.18	1.40
Finland	27.7	29.3	13.1	33.1	1.63	1.81
Sweden	27.6	29.2	39.7	53.0	1.68	1.73
United Kingdom	26.9	28.2*	11.5	33.6	1.90	1.70*

† Children per woman of childbearing age   * Provisional data   ** 1994   # Scotland and Northern Ireland are not included.

Source: Ditch *et al.* (1998)

Table 9.3 Living patterns and family status of young people aged 20–29 in Southern versus Northern European countries

Family situation	Men Southern countries: Greece, Italy, Spain	Men Northern countries: France, Germany, UK	Women Southern countries: Greece, Italy, Spain	Women Northern countries: France, Germany, UK
	%	%	%	%
Living with parents	78.0	41.1	62.7	25.1
Not living with parents, of which:	22.0	58.9	37.3	74.9
Without a partner	8.2	23.4	7.7	20.0
Couple no children	4.9	17.4	8.2	21.1
Couple with children	8.7	17.9	20.8	27.9
Lone parent	0.2	0.2	0.6	5.9
Total	100.0	100.0	100.0	100.0

Source: European Observatory on Family Matters (2000)

Resistance to globalization?

Resistance to the pressures of globalization may be located at all levels of the formal political system: that is, at the pan-national, national and regional levels. We have already discussed some of the difficulties of identifying both the existence and the effectiveness of resistance from these political bodies. Pan-national and national governments play a dual role both as agents of the process of globalization and as bulwarks against homogenization or promoters of the domestic tradition. Pressures for globalization are necessarily mediated through political bodies; this process of mediation provides a basis both for resistance and for modification and reform of the globalization process (Hirst and Thompson, 1997). As such, globalization takes its concrete form in the policies and practices actually adopted by nation states.

A prime example of the complex role that nation states have played and are playing in the globalization process is provided by the history of the Multilateral Agreement on Investment. The so-called MAI agreement was lobbied for by multinational corporations and was primarily designed to provide Western capital with protection against developing countries adopting policies which might call into question the long term viability of their investments — by favouring domestic industries, nationalizing foreign companies and the like. The Western governments responded to this lobbying by developing this agreement. Yet as the time for signing the agreement grew nearer, the impact of the agreement in limiting the freedom even for Western nation states to develop their own policy programmes became clearer; the attempt to get the agreement signed in Paris in 1999 foundered on the French Government's unwillingness to sacrifice its right to provide support to the French cinema industry.[3] The MAI may yet come back in a different form but there is still a role for national politics to halt the progress of globalization.

The process of globalization also provides a potentially new role for regions, communities or cities within nation states. This is partly the result of political developments, namely the creation of pan-national political organizations which allow regions to relate directly to the pan-national organizations rather than operating solely through the nation state. Where a region or city has a specific production and social system which provides it with comparative advantage, the development of more globally-integrated markets may provide it with access to a wider market than prevailed under the national domestic regime. However, it is not clear if the resurgence of the local and regional economy provides a means of protection for communities against the uncertainties of globalization or is itself part of the globalization process (Dunning, 2000).

Perhaps an even more interesting form of resistance to globalization comes from more informal and unorganized forces, in the form of consumer, environmental and labour pressure groups. This issue is taken up in Chapter Ten, in relation to pressure to establish international labour standards. The positions of demonstrators and protest groups vary but there is a common thread uniting the protests, namely that the development of world trade is not sufficiently in the hands of the world's citizens and that bodies such as the World Trade Organization are usurping political power. Deterministic pronouncements on the impossibility of any re-regulation of the 21st century world order are therefore premature; the development of welfare states and the associated legitimacy of labour movements in the 20th century did not emerge out of the benign authority of corporations and governments but were fought for by citizens and workers. As such, the citizens of the world in the 21st century still have the potential to change the course of world development, however many obstacles may appear to stand in their way.

Notes

1 Such concerns take on more force post the events of 11 September 2001.
2 According to the McDonald's website the first restaurant in Pushkin Square that opened at the end of January 1990 is still the busiest McDonald's in the world.
3 According to a paper produced by the French Ministry of Economy, Finance and Industry (http://www.finances.gouv.fr/pole econfin/international/ami0998/ami0998.htm), 'a satisfactory resolution of cultural issues is an essential condition of any agreement' (English translation available on website www.canadians.org).

10

Labour regulation in a global economy

'Thanks WTO, it's been a riot, said the sign opposite the hotel Bill (Clinton) stayed in during his brief, ill-fated visit to Seattle' (Larry Elliott, *The Guardian*, 6 December 1999).

Riots outside, failure to agree inside: the World Trade Organization talks were abandoned without meeting any of their objectives in November 1999. The protests outside were united only by a common feeling of mistrust of both governments and large corporations. One of the issues on which the World Trade Organization talks failed was the role of labour standards in trading arrangements. And it was over this issue that the clearest divisions among protesters could be found. On the one side, many of the groups representing organized labour argued for the inclusion of a social clause in world trade agreements, in addition to strengthened environmental protections. On the other side were groups concerned that the West's new interest in labour standards was a poorly disguised attempt to reintroduce protection and deny access to the West's lucrative markets for poor, developing economies. The riot at Seattle may suggest that it is too soon to write off the possibility of protest as a force capable of constraining and even shaping a future international economic system. Subsequent protests have descended more rapidly into violence, with less attention paid in the media to the substance of any demands. However, if protest is to be translated into any form of action, one area where there will need to be greater agreement amongst those anxious to enhance the living standards of the poor and vulnerable is that of the appropriate role of international regulation of labour standards.

International regulation takes on greater importance the more that capital is mobile and the more labour costs and labour standards influence the location of companies and subsidiaries. Without international regulation, individual nation states may be under increasing pressure to offer mobile multinational companies the lowest level of regulation at the lowest level of labour costs, just to secure investment. Attempts to bribe multinationals to enter or to stay in a particular environment may result in only partial or temporary successes, for with the global economy to play with, a better deal may always be forthcoming somewhere else. To protect against this so-called 'race to the bottom', it becomes increasingly necessary to require each nation state to respect at least a minimum set of international labour standards. However, arguments remain about how to determine that minimum set and how it should be established and enforced.

The chapter is organized as follows. First, we develop the case for and against international labour standards. Second, we consider the main international and pan-national institutions involved in setting international labour standards, including organizations that form part of the United Nations system as well as other pan-national institutions, such as the European Union and North American Free Trade Association (NAFTA). Third, we consider non-governmental or non-legislative ways of implementing labour standards in a globalized economy, for example through pressure applied by consumer groups or trade unions on multinationals to take voluntary action to improve their record on labour standards.

Why international labour standards?

The case for establishing labour standards can be made on two apparently quite separate grounds. The first argument is based on issues of social justice and indeed human rights. The second argument develops an economic case for labour standards and labour institutions, on the grounds that efficient and productive labour market systems require protection against destructive competition. Further investigation reveals that these issues are interrelated, as we outline below. However, both arguments can be deployed to make a case for the development and enforcement of international labour standards in a context of a globalizing and integrating world economy.

Where labour standards are a matter of human rights, it is argued, the case for their establishment is not dependent on the level of economic development. For example, there is fairly broad agreement that the right to be protected against forced labour should not be dependent on notions of economic affordability. The social justice argument is usually accepted as being more dependent on context or level of development; what constitutes a fair level of labour standards in one society may be regarded as unfair in another. This notion of fairness works in both directions. It may be unfair to set too low standards in a relatively rich society, such that not all citizens share in a society's prosperity. Some may argue that it is also unfair to set too high standards in a relatively poor society, if this jeopardizes the ability of the society to engage in international trade and to use this and other means to increase its wealth and expand employment opportunities. Too high levels of protection may also encourage the growth of a completely informal and unregulated sector, outside the protected sector.

In practice, there is no clear dividing line between labour standards which can be justified on grounds of human rights and those which depend on the social justice argument, defined in a specific economic and social context. For example, there are deep divisions between those who believe that the abolition of child labour is a matter of human rights and those who believe that child labour may have to be tolerated in a context where the alternative may be greater poverty or even starvation (see Lee (1997) for an overview). As social justice arguments for extending labour rights are often countered by arguments that standards conflict with economic affordability or introduce distortions to the market, the development of a case for labour standards requires an engagement with the economic case for labour institutions. This interdependency between the social justice argument and the economic case provides the framework through which much of the debate about the appropriate role for international regulation of labour standards takes place. The economic case in favour of labour standards takes the labour market and the system of human resources management as a potential source of comparative advantage. To develop the productive capacity of labour it is necessary, however, to develop labour market institutions and a floor to labour standards. The economic case against this argues that labour standards introduce rigidities and prevent adaptation to market conditions. These arguments at international level parallel debates at national level discussed in Chapter Six.

Table 10.1 summarizes these arguments. Labour standards based on human rights should be established on a universal basis. In contrast the social justice arguments for labour standards accept that the substantive level and form of labour standards, once those based on notions of human rights are in place, must reflect current wealth and living standards in the society. For example, there may be agreement that societies should establish minimum wage floors and some form of unemployment insurance. Nevertheless, the level of minimum wages and benefits payable to the unemployed must be dependent upon the societal context. The introduction of productivity arguments for international labour standards raises the possibility that

Table 10.1 Arguments for labour standards

Type of argument	Human rights	Social justice	Productivity
Dependent on level of economic development	No	Yes	Only partially dependent as labour standards can promote economic development
Universal or context-specific	Universal	Context-specific	Some universal rights may promote productivity. Higher productivity needed for more context-specific rights

labour standards can contribute to economic growth and development and not be considered solely a consumption good, to be provided out of the proceeds of economic development. Few would argue that labour standards can be set completely independently of economic development. External pressure to support existing standards or establish new standards could, under this approach, in fact be regarded as supportive of, and not a hindrance to, economic development. Moreover, as the economist Amartya Sen (1999) has argued, the objective of development is the expansion of real freedoms and the removal of 'unfreedoms': this is a broader perspective on development than the expansion of GDP and includes within it a major role for labour standards as a means towards expanding freedoms.

The effects of labour standards are contingent, dependent upon the appropriateness of the labour standards and labour institutions. Paradoxically perhaps, it is this indeterminacy in the employment relationship that provides a rationale for labour standards. If labour markets operated according to a universal model where advantages could only be gleaned through reducing labour standards and labour costs, the argument could be made that universal or international standards would hinder economic development. If labour market institutions may contribute not only to social welfare but also to productivity this argument does not hold. The basic argument for regarding labour institutions as having a positive role, at both the national economy level and the organization level, has been developed throughout this volume. It revolves around two propositions. First, that the labour contract is open-ended and indeterminate: the amount of productive labour generated by a labour contract is variable and dependent, *inter alia*, on the management of employment, including the degree of trust and security and the effectiveness of training and skill development. The second proposition is that performance under the labour contract matters for comparative advantage. The two propositions, taken together, provide the basis for arguing that labour standards can make a positive contribution to the organization and development of production systems. The notion that labour needs to be considered differently from other factors of production, and that labour markets need to be conceptualized differently from exchange markets, is fundamental to the argument for labour rights and labour standards. The International Labour Organization (see Box 10.1), which was founded to protect labour rights at an international level, has based its approach on the core assumption that labour is not a commodity.

'Labour is not a commodity.' This statement is written into the ILO's Declaration of Philadelphia and has become an axiom of ILO philosophy. It has two meanings. First, labour 'should' not be treated like a commodity; and secondly, labour 'is' not a commodity. Rather, labour is a peculiar 'resource', and the labour market a special market that functions differently from the market for television sets or the market for bananas. The peculiarity of 'labour' stems from the fact that its achievement is uncertain, because labour services are provided by human beings. The employer who hires a worker does not know beforehand what he will get: what effort the worker will make; how ready and able the worker will be to acquire skills and learn on the job; how loyal he or she will be to the firm, etc.

The employer does not buy a ready-made product, but rather a 'potential accomplishment'. (Sengenberger, 1994: 24)

To take further the division between universal and context-specific rights — the latter otherwise known as 'development-dependent' rights — Portes (1994) has proposed a fourfold distinction between basic rights, survival rights, security rights and civic rights (see Table 10.2). Basic rights are similar to the notion of universal human rights, including rights against the use of child labour, involuntary servitude and physical coercion. There is a fairly high degree of international consensus over the implementation of this set of rights. Portes suggests democratic societies are also largely willing to accept the need for civic rights, including the rights to free association, to collective representation and to free expression of grievances. The granting of these civic rights in principle provides the basis for the establishment of development-dependent survival and security rights. The survival rights include the right to a living wage, the right to accident compensation and to a limited work week, all areas where current norms in practice in a particular society may be relevant to determining minimum standards. These are also areas where rights to collective bargaining and free association improve the chances of establishing minimum standards appropriate to the level of development. Similarly security rights — rights against involuntary dismissal, rights to retirement compensation and rights to survivors' compensation — may need to be defined according to local conditions; but strong civic rights may provide the basis for negotiating security rights, to be provided either by the state or by employers.

This type of division still raises ethical dilemmas. For example, while it is uncontentious that minimum wage levels should vary between societies, it is less clear that it is ethically acceptable for health and safety standards to be lower in developing countries (Freeman, 1994b). Should equipment deemed unacceptable in the West be sold to developing countries? And should the West be able to export its polluting industries and work processes to countries not requiring investment to protect consumers and employees?

Table 10.2 Types of labour standards

Basic rights	Survival rights	Security rights	Civic rights
Rights against use of child labour	Right of living wage	Rights against arbitrary dismissal	Right to free association
Rights against involuntary servitude	Right to accident compensation	Right to retirement compensation	Right to collective representation
Rights against physical coercion	Right to a limited working week	Right to survivors' compensation	Right to free expression of grievances

Source: Adapted from Portes (1994): Table 5

Establishing international labour standards: the main actors

The International Labour Organization was founded in 1919 in response to the social upheaval and industrial unrest experienced at the end of the First World War, with the aim of building a 'social framework for peace and stability within which economic processes could generate prosperity with social justice in the life of workers and for the world of work' (Somovia, 1999). In 1919 the ILO had 42 members; by 2000 the number had risen to 175. In 1944 the general conference of the International Labour Organization adopted the Declaration of Philadelphia (see Box 10.1). This has been interpreted as giving form to the commitments of the Allied leaders during the Second World War that the post-war period would be aimed at 'securing for all (countries and peoples), improved labour standards, economic advancement and Social Security ... (as well as) freedom from fear or want' (1941 Atlantic Charter, quoted by French (1994): 19).

Box 10.1   ILO Declaration of Philadelphia, 1944

The right of all human beings 'to pursue both their material well-being and their spiritual development in conditions of freedom and dignity, of economic security and equal opportunity'.

The governance of the ILO reflects the political conditions at the time of the signing of the Declaration of Philadelphia. The trade union movement was able to secure a permanent role within the ILO, soon to be incorporated within the general United Nations system established after the Second World War. The ILO functions as a tripartite organization, that is it is governed by three constituent groups: governments, employers' associations and trade unions. The main task of the ILO is to set international labour standards. It pursues this objective through two main strategies. First, the ILO passes conventions on labour standards which its members choose whether or not to ratify: in 2000 there were a total of over 180 conventions in force. Only relatively few of the conventions have been ratified by significant numbers of member states; ratification of even some of the core labour standards, such as abolition of child labour, has only been undertaken by around two thirds of the member countries. The second strategy has been to provide a renewed push for implementing basic labour standards through a new declaration on fundamental principles and rights at work (see Box 10. 2). This declaration was agreed at the 1998 ILO conference and all member states have therefore agreed to its substance. This provides a new platform for the ILO to pursue a policy of promoting labour standards.

Box 10.2 International Labour Organization Declaration on Fundamental Principles and Rights at Work, 1998

- Freedom of association and the effective recognition of the right to collective bargaining
- The elimination of all forms of forced or compulsory labour
- The effective abolition of child labour
- The elimination of discrimination in respect of employment and occupation

However, this policy is not based on sanctions or punitive actions against non-complying states as the ILO has little power to impose international standards. There are also contrary views as to the appropriateness of a punitive stance. The policy of the ILO is to promote labour standards through technical assistance and development policies, and to work with member states on how to implement the fundamental rights included in the declaration. For protesters at the World Trade Organization, and indeed for many trade union movements, this approach is not sufficient. Over recent years there has been considerable debate about the desirability of introducing a so-called social clause into world trade agreements (see Table 10.3 for a summary of the arguments). The social clause would allow for sanctions to be taken against countries flouting these fundamental rights. The argument is made that without a mechanism of enforcement there is little likelihood of countries being willing, or indeed able, to implement basic labour standards in a context in which there is pressure, both from international trade and in the competition for international investment, not to do anything to raise labour costs or increase labour regulations. For many developing countries this debate about the social clause is a thinly disguised form of protectionism. This scepticism revealed itself at the failed World Trade Organization talks in Seattle:

> Bill Clinton personally led the US crusade to include rules on labour standards in future trade deals, something many protesters at the Battle of Seattle supported, although calling for environmental controls to be added. Clinton hoped it would turn the tide against child labour, worker oppression and trade union bans — and stamp his legacy on the talks in a bid to ease the blight of impeachment and sexual scandal that haunt him in his last 'lame-duck' year in office. But developing nations led by India and Egypt strongly protested, saying it smacked of protectionism by the wealthy economies. Their opposition hardened after Clinton talked of sanctions to punish states seen as exploiting workers. (Walters, *The Observer*, 5 December 1999)

Developing countries are particularly sceptical about the involvement of the United States in promoting the notion of the social clause, given its poor record at home in implementing basic rights and ratifying ILO conventions (Caire, 1994). It is the potential for selectivity, as much as the existence of sanctions, to which the opposers of the social clause point.

Table 10.3 Arguments for and against a social clause in world trade agreements

Arguments for the social clause	Arguments against the social clause
A means of enforcing basic labour rights	A means of reintroducing protectionism
Human rights should not be dependent on development	Aid must first be provided to enable countries to reduce the use of child labour and so on
Supports nation states against the power of multinationals to force a 'race to the bottom'	Enforcement may be used selectively against nation states for political and economic objectives
A new coordinated and integrated approach to the development of international regulation is required; free trade should not be based on exploitative labour conditions	World Trade Organisation should not be involved in setting labour standards; this is the responsibility of the ILO
The social clause campaign provides the opportunity to develop a coordinated international approach to promoting workers' interests against employers and multinationals	The social clause campaign reveals the differences in interests between trade unions and workers in the West and in the developing world
Enforcement of labour rights can promote development, not constrain it	Improvements in labour rights can only be achieved after further development and access to international markets
The social clause would only promote those labour rights that are not development-dependent but are basic human rights	The interpretation of which rights are human rights and which rights are development-dependent is subjective
This policy would protect against 'social dumping', that is the relocation to countries offering lower levels of labour regulation	The problem of social dumping has been greatly exaggerated by the West as a means of arguing for new forms of protectionism
The social clause would result in the West paying a proper price for the commodities and services it consumes	If consumers are willing to pay the price of avoiding exploitation, then a more effective weapon may be to use consumer campaigns against multinationals not respecting labour standards

From international to regional labour standards

An alternative strategy to the development of universal international labour standards is to establish pan-national regulation at a regional level. The development of globalization has brought with it a strengthening of regional trading blocks, to provide some countervailing power against unfettered markets. The most developed example of this phenomenon is the European Union; and it is in the European Union that most progress has been made towards the establishment of pan-national labour standards. It is only in Europe that the development of pan-national standards is related to partial political integration and to the notion of common citizenship rights within Europe. Within the other regional blocks, for example the North Atlantic Free Trade Association, the issue of labour standards only arises as a means of supporting the free trade arrangements. We therefore pay most attention to the development of pan-national labour standards within Europe.

Labour standards and the European Union

The European Economic Community, subsequently renamed the European Union in 1993, was established by the Treaty of Rome in 1957. All European regulations on labour standards derive from clauses in the Treaty of Rome or in the various amendments to the fundamental treaty, agreed through the Council of Ministers which consists of the prime ministers of all member states. The treaties provide the legal basis or competence of the European Commission to propose and draw up directives relating to labour standards which are then debated by the Council of Ministers. If passed by the Council, member states are then obliged to incorporate these directives into national law.

The development of labour standards in Europe has followed an uneven path, dependent both on change to the treaties and on actions to develop directives based on the Commission's competencies. For example, the principle of equal treatment for women and men was incorporated in 1957 into the original Treaty of Rome; it was this clause which was the basis for the development of European directives on equal treatment in the 1970s. The pressure to include this clause came from France, which had already passed equal treatment clauses and was concerned that it might face higher labour costs if other Community members did not have to observe the principle of equal treatment for men and women (Pillinger, 1992). This is an early example of the so-called 'social dumping' argument for labour standards.

The debate about labour standards in Europe became more intense in the late 1980s, as a consequence of the signing of the Single European Act. This established a free trade zone in Europe from 1992 but, in the period between the signing of the act in 1986 and its implementation in 1992, there was widespread concern among trade unions and some political parties over the consequences for the European social model if the development of a more open market in Europe did not provide some safeguards for citizenship and worker rights. These concerns led specifically to the signing of the Social Charter of Fundamental Rights by all member states, with the exception of the United Kingdom. This Charter had no legal status but was more a declaration of intent. At the 1992 summit meeting at Maastricht there were two key issues for the future of the European Community on the agenda: first, the development of the single currency; second, the implementation of this Charter of Fundamental Rights. The outcome was an agreement by most member states to move forward on both counts, but with the UK and Denmark claiming an opt-out of the single currency agenda, and the UK insisting on being excluded from implementation of the Social Charter, known after Maastricht as the Social Chapter or the Social Protocol. After 1997 the UK Labour Government gave up this latter opt-out and the Social Chapter is now incorporated into the fundamental treaty. The Maastricht agreement allowed for the development in principle of a wider range of labour standards. Perhaps the most novel aspect of the Social Chapter was not the extension of scope for labour standards but the introduction of a new mechanism by which European directives related to labour standards could be developed. This mechanism was that of social dialogue: representatives of European employers, organized by the European employers' associations' umbrella organization UNICE, could negotiate with representatives of European trade unions through the ETUC over new labour standards. If agreement were reached, it would be expected that the Council of Ministers would agree to the proposed new directives. These measures no longer require unanimity among member states and could be passed on the basis of qualified majority voting if necessary. In 1997 there was a new agreement at the Amsterdam summit to extend the scope for new measures in the area of discrimination, defined on a broader basis to include discrimination on the basis of gender, racial or ethnic origin, religion or belief, disability, age, or sexual orientation.

Table 10.4 summarizes the most important labour standards directives which have so far been adopted by the Council of Ministers or are in the process of being adopted (excluding the health and safety measures, as they are numerous and often apply only to specific sectors). These measures have been introduced through a variety of legislative routes and mechanisms. For example, the directives on equal treatment for women and men derive from the equal treatment requirement in the Treaty of Rome, while the regulations on working time and maternity leave were introduced under the competency for health and safety introduced into the Single European Act. These regulations were the first to provide for measures related to labour standards to be passed by qualified majority voting, that is, not requiring unanimity among member states. Since 1992 the most common method by which a directive has been developed has been the social dialogue procedure, allowed for in the Maastricht Treaty. This has been used to negotiate the European Works Council directive, the part-time workers directive, the burden of proof directive, the parental leave directive and the directive on fixed term contracts. However, recently the Commission has again been active in bringing forward directives: UNICE, the employers' organization, was not willing to participate in negotiations relating to the extension of provisions for consultation and information to all employees and a directive was brought forward by the Commission. Two new directives have also been introduced by the Commission which derive from the new rights incorporated in the Amsterdam Treaty: one directive sets a general framework on discrimination in accordance with that treaty, while the other establishes equal treatment by race and ethnic origin.

While there is now a substantive body of European law related to labour standards, it is important to note the limits to this development. First, there are large areas that are still outside the competence of the European Union and regarded as matters where the principle of subsidiarity applies; that is they are deemed to be the concern of the individual member states. These include most social security provisions and issues related to wage policy, including minimum wages and systems of collective bargaining. There is also no intention to harmonize levels of labour standards among European countries. Most directives set minimum standards on which member states are free to improve, and there is a requirement that directives should not be used as the basis for lowering existing standards in member states. Alternatively they provide for society-specific rights, for example for part-timers to be treated the same as full-timers within a particular society or member state, or for men and women to be treated the same within a member state; but there is no expectation that this will lead to the same level of standards across member states. The role of the European Union, at least at the level of regulation, has been to set a floor of rights and not to seek to replace substantive regulation at the member state level.

However, this role in setting a floor of rights has remained controversial. For countries such as the United Kingdom, where national regulation is at a low level, the controversy arises in part because the European regulations improve upon existing regulation in the UK. One reason for the UK's objections to the development of the Social Chapter in the 1980s and 1990s, and the compliance of the other member states, was that it was often only the UK that would be required to make substantial changes in national legislation to implement the corresponding directive. Similarly the UK's reluctance to embrace the social dialogue proposals under the Maastricht Treaty reflected the fact that, in the UK, social dialogue has not been used as a means of developing and regulating labour markets, in contrast to traditions in continental Europe. This opposition to the extension of social rights has been maintained even after the acceptance of the Social Chapter by the UK after 1997. At the Nice summit in December 2000 the existing European labour standards, together with other citizens' rights, were brought together in a Charter of Fundamental Rights of the European Union. Following opposition from some member states, notably the UK, this Charter did not seek to extend the competencies of the European Union in the area of labour standards, despite pressure from some other member states, such as France, which held the presidency of the Council of Ministers at the time. Nor has the Charter yet been incorporated into the treaties of the European Union, although some observers expect that this will happen eventually, thereby providing a legal consolidating framework for this rather fragmented set of employment and social standards.

While it is governments and employers that have argued that the development of labour standards in Europe has gone far enough or even too far, there are equally strong concerns among trade unions and other pressure groups, within the more regulated European societies, that the move to Europe-wide regulation will in the end weaken the European social model. The establishment of European regulations at relatively low levels is seen as a long-term threat to the ability of individual member states to maintain high levels of labour protection. European regulation is seen

Table 10.4 Labour standards established by the European Union

Area	Directive (date of publication/ deadline for implementation in national law)	Nature of rights
Employment, skills and mobility	Equal treatment of men and women (1976/1978)	Principle of equal treatment as regards access to employment, vocational training and promotion and working conditions.
	Posting of workers (1997/1999)	Protection of workers posted to work in another member state: these workers covered by minimum guarantees with respect to hours, holidays, wages, hiring out regulations, health and safety and equal opportunities in the member state where the work is carried out
Working conditions/ Protection of workers	Working time (1993/1996)	Sets maximum working week (48 hours), minimum paid holiday (4 weeks), minimum rest periods, regulates night time working etc. Many occupations exempt. Opportunities for derogations through collective agreements by social partners.
	Protection of young people at work (1994/1996)	Defines the work that young people can do and under what circumstances; requires employers not to ask young people to do work beyond their physical and mental capacities.
	Transfer of undertakings: safeguarding of employees' rights (1977/1979) (1998/2001)	Protects the terms and conditions of employees on the transfer of an undertaking.
	European Works Councils (1992/1994; (1999 UK))	Requires a European Works Council (EWC) to be established in companies with more than 1000 employees in the EU and at least 150 in each of two member states. The EWC must be consulted and informed on matters relating to the company at a Community level.
	General framework for informing and consulting employees (in process)	Extends rights to consultation and information to employees of organisations not operating on a pan-European basis.
	Part-time workers directive (1997/2000)	Part-time workers to be treated no less favourably than comparable full-time workers.

Fixed-term workers directive (1999/2000)	Fixed-term contract workers to be treated no less favourably than comparable permanent workers.
Occupational social security schemes (1986/1989); (1997/1997)	Provides for equal access to schemes and ends differences in retirement ages.
Self employed activity including agricultural work (1986/1991)	Extends protections to spouses of self employed who work in a family business.
Protection of pregnant women (including maternity leave) (1992/1994)	Adjustment to working hours and / or conditions if placed at risk; 14 weeks leave; protection against dismissal.
Parental leave and leave for family reasons 1996/1998) (1999 UK)	Leave for at least three months for male and female workers; right to time off for family emergencies.
Burden of proof in cases of discrimination based on sex (1998/2001)	Defendant has to prove that no discrimination took place if claimant establishes facts from which discrimination can be presumed to exist.
Statutory and occupational social security schemes (in progress)	Equal treatment in survivors' benefits and family benefits, retirement ages.
Equal pay (1995/1976)	Equal pay for men and women for same work or work to which equal value has been attributed.
Discrimination Equal treatment irrespective of racial or ethnic origin (2000/2003)	Right to equal treatment irrespective of racial or ethnic origin; harassment included as a form of discrimination; bodies to promote equal treatment to be established; member states to apply sanctions and report on implementation.
General framework for equal treatment in employment and occupation (2000/2003)	Framework agreement to combat discrimination on the grounds of religion or belief, disability, age or sexual orientation as regards employment and occupation; harassment included as a form of discrimination. The directive allows for some age requirements such as minimum ages or maximum recruitment ages due to training requirements.

Sources: CEC (1999); European Commission

as seeking to please all countries, such that a 'lowest common denominator' approach is adopted to the fixing of labour standards. These concerns have been particularly strong in Scandinavia, where entry into the European Union was felt by many to be a threat to the Scandinavian countries' welfare states and their traditions of labour market protection. These concerns were thought to be partly responsible for Norway's vote against joining the EU in 1994[1] and for the close vote in favour of joining in Sweden after an active campaign for a 'no' vote by many pressure groups.

For others, however, European regulation has provided an important stimulus to the maintenance and modernization of labour standards in a context where multinationals might otherwise have played a stronger role in pressurising individual member states to deregulate labour markets. The importance of establishing a universal approach to labour standards became apparent in the period when the UK was outside the provisions of the Social Chapter. Multinational companies showed themselves willing to make use of the division between those member states inside and outside the Social Chapter in negotiating with trade unions over employment rights. The case which made headlines in both the UK and France was the Hoover Corporation's relocation of business from France to Scotland and the associated closure of the French plant (Veersma, 1995: 334). The argument made by Hoover management was that the UK's opt-out from the Social Chapter was a major factor in the decision, facilitating as it had a new collective agreement. In fact the new collective agreement negotiated at the Scottish plant, which allowed for the recruitment of temporary workers on different terms and conditions, could also have been negotiated if the UK had signed up to the Social Chapter. However, the opt-out clause may have had psychological importance in pressurizing British trade unions to agree to the new terms and in persuading French unions that they were unable to protect their jobs. This example shows how multinationals may play one country off against another, or one workforce off against another, when the nation states of the EU do not adopt a common stance on what constitutes minimum acceptable standards.

North American Free Trade Association

The North American Free Trade Association (NAFTA) was set up in 1994. It involves the US, Canada and Mexico; the treaty was passed after much controversy in the US over the potential for Mexico to gain access to US markets and attract US investment because of its low labour standards. As a consequence, and as a policy directly to appease American union and other interest groups, a North American Agreement on Labour Cooperation (NAALC) was established shortly before the NAFTA agreement was passed in Congress. This allows for violations of labour standards specified in the agreement to be referred to the National Administrative Office of one of the other two countries. Violations of the Agreement fall into three categories. For those concerned with freedom of association and collective bargaining, there are no sanctions, only the prospect of a public hearing. For forced labour, equal pay, discrimination, workers' compensation and migrant labour issues, an independent Evaluation Committee of Experts may be established, but this committee can only make non-binding recommendations. Only if there are violations of child labour, minimum wages and occupational health and safety provisions is there the prospect of arbitration and possibly sanctions (Gibbons, 1998).

There is at present no suggestion, therefore, that NAFTA will develop along the lines of the EU and provide a set of minimum labour standards which must be implemented in each country; in short it remains solely a trade agreement, and one of the problems experienced in implementing the terms of the NAALC is that there are no effective mechanisms for monitoring or enforcing labour standards across the different jurisdictions.

Alternative methods of enforcing labour standards: consumer boycotts, social labelling and trade union negotiated codes of conduct

Whatever the outcome of current debates on social clauses in trade agreements, it is clear that international regulations will never be sufficient to enforce labour standards. Use of alternative methods to pressurize countries, and more particularly multinational companies, to observe basic labour standards could, some argue, provide a more effective means of ensuring compliance. The reasons are twofold. First, multinationals have a fear of adverse publicity, so that campaigns targeted on particular companies may be more successful than general international level action against all abuses of labour standards with no specific villains identified. Second, consumer campaigns may reveal an underlying willingness to pay for higher labour standards (Freeman, 1994b), a willingness that may be obscured when consumers lack information on the labour conditions under which products are produced. If labels were introduced to indicate that products had not been produced using child labour or forced labour, consumers might prove unwilling to buy products not bearing these labels, however cheap they might be.

There are a variety of alternative enforcement mechanisms, involving different groups. Trade unions have been active at company and sector level in negotiating codes of conduct and in promoting labelling campaigns. Some of these codes of conduct have been agreed at both a sector and an international level, for example the European textile agreement. The International Confederation of Free Trade Unions (1997) has drawn up a basic code of conduct of labour practices, to be considered by anyone bargaining with multinationals or protecting employees of subcontractors to multinationals. The most important part of the code could be considered the definition of the extent of the responsibility of multinationals for labour standards. The preamble starts with the assumption that the company 'recognises its responsibilities to workers for the conditions under which it products are made or its services are provided and that these responsibilities extend to all workers producing or providing products or services for the company whether or not they are employees of the company'. This places the burden of responsibility on the multinational, whether or not the company chooses to use different forms of ownership or to use contractual relations with other companies to develop its international supply chain.

The main motivation for companies to agree to negotiate codes of conduct or to issue their own independent code of conduct is to avoid bad publicity, consumer or trade union boycotts, or even court cases. Trade union boycotts have been a traditional form of union action against suppliers violating labour standards. Changes in industrial relations legislation in the UK in the 1980s placed restrictions on trade unions taking direct action to block supplies of goods of dubious origins. Other countries still permit such actions to be taken and trade union blacklisting of suppliers perhaps places the most immediate pressure on multinationals. More damage in the longer term may arise from consumer boycotts, following adverse publicity and pressure group campaigns. The sports company, Nike, has been a notable target of such campaigns (Klein, 2000). These started on American university campuses and have been supported by the strip cartoon, *Doonesbury*, which has associated Nike with labour standards abuses.

Other multinationals or international organizations have also been exposed to adverse publicity, even if not of such a sustained nature. One example of an agreement reached following adverse publicity is the code of conduct agreed between the football authorities, FIFA and the ICFTU, following revelations of the abuse of child labour employed to sew footballs. This agreement follows the basic code recommended by the ICFTU (see Box 10.3). Even when companies appear able to clear themselves of blame, they may feel obliged to take further action. A case in point was the 1996 Granada TV *World in Action* programme which showed subcontractors to

---

Box 10.3   Code of Labour Practice for Production of Goods Licensed by the Fédération Internationale de Football Associations (FIFA)

Preamble

In line with its guiding principles of fair play and ethical conduct, the Fédération Internationale de Football Associations (FIFA), recognises its responsibilities to consumers for the quality of products produced under its licensing arrangements, and to workers involved in the making of FIFA licensed products for the conditions under which these products are made.

   Each Licensee participating in the FIFA Denominations Programme must agree, as a condition of the license agreement, to ensure that the workers producing these products are provided with fair wages and decent working conditions, and that the international labour standards established by Conventions 29, 87, 98, 100, 105, 111 and 138 of the International Labour Organization are observed.

   Licensees further agree to ensure that these conditions and standards are observed by each contractor and subcontractor in the production and distribution of FIFA-licensed

---

Box 10.3 Continued

products or components of these products. Licensees should, prior to placing orders with suppliers or engaging contractors and subcontractors, assess whether the provisions of this Code can be met.

Each Licensee licensed by FIFA under the FIFA Denominations Programme, and each contractor and subcontractor engaged by the Licensee, shall compulsorily implement and respect the following principles in the production and/or distribution of products bearing the FIFA name and/or FIFA authorised marks. Furthermore, each Licensee shall warrant that these principles shall be equally imposed upon all those employed or delegated by such Licensee.

Employment is freely chosen

There shall be no use of forced or bonded labour (ILO Conventions 29 and 105).

There is no discrimination in employment

Equality of opportunity and treatment regardless of race, colour, sex, religion, political opinion, nationality, social origin or other distinguishing characteristic shall be provided (ILO Conventions 100 and 111).

Child labour is not used

There shall be no use of child labour. Only workers above the age of 15 years shall be engaged (ILO Convention 138).

Freedom of association and the right to collective bargaining are respected

The right of workers to form and join trade unions and to bargain collectively shall be recognized (ILO Conventions 87 and 98). Employers should recognize the constructive contribution of trade unions to preventing exploitation and adopt a positive approach towards the activities of trade unions and an open attitude towards their organizational activities.

Fair wages are paid

Wages and benefits paid shall meet at least legal or industry minimum standards and should be sufficient to meet basic needs and provide some discretionary income.

Hours of work are not excessive

Hours of work shall comply with applicable laws and industry standards. Workers shall not on a regular basis be required to work in excess of 48 hours per week nor more than 12 hours overtime, and shall be provided with at least one day off for every 7 day period.

Working conditions are decent

A safe and hygienic working environment shall be provided, and best occupational health and safety practice shall be promoted, bearing in mind Licensees', contractors' and subcontractors' knowledge of the industry and of any specific hazards.

The employment relationship is established

Employers should endeavour to provide regular and secure employment and refrain from the excessive use of temporary or casual labour. Obligations to employees arising from the regular employment relationship should not be avoided through the use of labour-only subcontracting arrangements, or through apprenticeship schemes where there is no real intent to impart skills or provide regular employment. Younger workers should be provided the opportunity to participate in education and training programmes.

*****

Box 10.3 Continued

Implementation and monitoring

Licensees, their contractors and subcontractors shall undertake to support and cooperate in the implementation and monitoring of this code by:

- providing FIFA or its agent with relevant information concerning their operations;
- permitting inspection at any time of their workplaces and operations by approved inspectors;
- maintaining records of the name, age, hours worked and wages paid for each worker and making these available to approved inspectors on request;
- informing, verbally and in writing, the workers concerned of the provisions of this code;
- refraining from disciplinary action, dismissal or otherwise discriminating against any worker for providing information concerning observance of this Code.

*****

Any Licensee, contractor or subcontractor found to be in breach of one or more terms of this Code of Labour Practice shall thus be subject to a range of sanctions up to and including withdrawal of the right to produce or organise production of FIFA-licensed goods. Furthermore, Licensees who fail to ensure that their contractors or subcontractors abide by the Code of Labour Practice shall be subject to the same range of sanctions.

Questions as to the interpretation of the meaning of the provisions of this Code shall be resolved according to the procedure outlined in the Memorandum of Understanding on the Code of Labour Practice between FIFA and the ICFTU/ITGLWF/FIET.

Source: India Committee on the Netherlands, *The Dark Side of Football* (ICFTU: June 2000). Website: http://www.antenna.nl/liw/iv.html

Marks and Spencer using child labour. Marks and Spencer successfully claimed that they had no knowledge of these abuses of labour rights and were awarded damages against the television company. Yet shortly afterwards they announced the negotiation of a new code of conduct for suppliers and have joined the UK ethical trading initiative.

One particular problem with codes of conduct is that of enforcement and monitoring. Many multinationals monitor their own codes of conduct or do so through subsidiaries, leading to charges that these codes are there to provide companies with the image of being a good employer, without the company having any real intention of finding out whether the standards are being adhered to in practice. Some companies do use external auditors and some labelling projects involve monitoring by separate foundations, for example the Clean Clothes Campaign and the Rugmark initiative (Gibbons, 1998). Nevertheless, it is more difficult to be sure the code of conduct is being followed than to pressure multinationals into signing up to a code if the alternative in the short to medium term is bad publicity.

Another motivation for introducing codes of conduct is to gain positive publicity for the pursuit of ethical trading policy. Individual companies have associated their business strategy with the adoption of a distinctive ethical policy — the Body Shop, for example, was founded on this basis. Others have signed up to an ethical policy initiated by consumer groups or even government departments (for example the UK Government supported an ethical trading initiative, see Gibbons (1998)).

Enthusiasm for campaigns among multinationals is directly related to consumer pressure and press coverage. Moreover, these campaigns may be just as likely to be motivated by issues of protectionism as by those of imposition of sanctions in trade agreements; trade unions tend to take up cases of abuse of labour standards in areas where domestic employees are being hit by increased international competition, for example in clothing and textile trades in the West. These pressures may still be more real and persistent than pressures from international labour regulation; but it is doubtful whether, without the example of the International Labour Organization's declaration of fundamental rights, pressure groups could so readily raise consumer consciousness on these issues. The two approaches may be best seen as complementary and not alternatives.

The way forward

Now that all ILO members have accepted the new ILO declaration on fundamental principles and rights at work, the debate on international labour standards, can, in principle at least, move forward, from a focus on whether there should be labour standards to how these should be best implemented and who should bear the cost (Lee, 1997). For example, in order for there to be an effective campaign to eliminate child labour, there would need to be a programme of compensation and aid to countries which need to make adjustments:

> Aid in the form of financial compensation for children who lose their jobs would help to safeguard against the children ending up even worse off than before. As well as being morally warranted, aid targeted in that way would also be likely to encourage recipient countries to have more effort into the elimination of child labour. (Lee, 1997: 188)

New international initiatives are needed, aimed at enabling countries to move forward on labour standards and to provide them with incentives to resist pressure from multinationals and domestic industry to lower standards. Such an approach is implicit in the ILO's new agenda. This agenda incorporates the promotion of labour standards within a more general framework to promote decent work, based around four interlocking objectives: the promotion of full employment, social dialogue, social protection, and fundamental rights at work. This approach situates the pursuit of labour standards within a more general development approach and seeks to influence the agenda of other international agencies such as the World Bank to take the issues of employment seriously. Employment is a key determinant of living standards for individuals and the wider society and a major influence on productivity, efficiency and innovation. It is central to both the economic and social dimension of policy-making and of equal and major concern to employers and workers alike. As such, it is time for employment to be considered a core issue in all international and national policy agendas.

Note

1 A speech by Professor Kristen Nygard, president of the Norwegian People's Movement, 'Nei til EU' on 16/17 January 1995 in Munich stressed the fact that the Norwegians had chosen social solidarity and the universal model of social welfare over the Bismarck model favoured by the EU, where access to social welfare depended upon employment not citizenship. See the website of the 'Nei til EU' campaign: http://www.aksess.no/nteu

QM LIBRARY
(MILE END)

Bibliography

S. Ackroyd and S. Proctor, 'British manufacturing organisation and workplace industrial relations: some attributes of the new flexible firm', *British Journal of Industrial Relations*, 36 (1998): 163–83.

P. Adler and R. Cole, 'Designed for learning: a tale of two auto plants', *Sloan Management Review*, 34 (1993): 85–94

N. Adler and F. Ghadar, 'Strategic human resource management: a global perspective', in R. Pieper (ed.), *Human Resource Management: An International Comparison* (Berlin: de Gruyter, 1990).

P. Adler, B. Goldoftas and D. Levine, 'Ergonomics, employee involvement, and the Toyota production system', *Industrial and Labour Relations Review* 50(3) (1997): 416–37.

P. Almond, *The Social Context of Human Resource Management: An Anglo-French Comparison*, doctoral thesis, Manchester School of Management, UMIST, 1999.

American Management Association, *AMA Survey on Downsizing: Summary of Key Findings* (New York: American Management Association, 1994).

B. Andresen, 'Bildungsaktivitäten des Daimler-Benz-Konzerns in den neuen Bundesländern', in W. Schlaffke and R. Zedler (eds), *Wirtschaftlicher Wandel im Neuen Bundesgebiet und Strategien der Qualifizierung* (Cologne: Deutscher Instituts-Verlag, 1992).

R. Anker, *Gender and Jobs* (Geneva: International Labour Office, 1998).

A. Anttonen and J. Sipilä, 'European social care services: is it possible to identify models?', *Journal of European Social Policy*, 6 (1996): 87–100.

E. Appelbaum and R. Batt, *The New American Workplace* (New York: ILR Press/ Cornell University Press, 1994).

D. Ashton and F. Green, *Education, Training and the Global Economy* (Cheltenham: Edward Elgar, 1996).

P. Auer and C. Riegler, *Post-Taylorism: The Enterprise as a Place of Learning Organizational Change* (Stockholm: Swedish Work Environment Fund, and Berlin: Wissenschaftszentrum Berlin, 1990).

L. Baccaro, 'Centralized collective bargaining and the problem of "compliance": lessons from the Italian experience', *Industrial and Labor Relations Review*, 53 (2000): 579–601.

G. Bamber and R. Lansbury (eds), *International and Comparative Employment Relations* (London: Sage, 1998).

J. Baron, F. Dobbin and P. Devereaux Jennings, 'War and peace: the evolution of modern personnel administration in US industry', *American Journal of Sociology*, 92 (1986): 350–83.

O. Barrat, T. Coutrot and S. Mabile, 'La négociation salariale en France: des marges de manoeuvre réduites au début des années quatre-vingt-dix', in *Données Sociales 1996* (Paris: INSEE).

C. Bartlett and S. Ghoshal, *Managing Across Borders: The Transnational Solution* (Boston, MA: Harvard Business School Press, 1989).

C. Bartlett and S. Ghoshal, *Transnational Management: Text, Cases and Readings in Cross-Border Management* (Homewood, IL: Irwin, 1992).

W. J. Baumol, 'Macroeconomics of unbalanced growth: the anatomy of urban crisis', *American Economic Review*, 57(S) (1967): 416–26.

S. Bazen, 'The impact of the regulation of low wages on inequality and labour-market adjustment: a comparative analysis', *Oxford Review of Economic Policy*, 16 (2000): 57–69.

G. Becker, *Human Capital: a Theoretical and Empirical Analysis, with Special Reference to Education* (New York: Columbia University Press, 1964).

R. Bennett, 'New training institutions at the local level', in R. Layard, K. Mayhew and G. Owen (eds), *Britain's Training Deficit* (Aldershot: Avebury, 1994).

C. Berggren, 'NUMMI vs. Uddevalla', *Sloan Management Review*, 35 (1994): 37–45.

M. Best, *The New Competition* (Cambridge: Polity Press, 1990).

F. Bettio and P. Villa, 'A Mediterranean perspective of the breakdown of the relationship between participation and fertility', *Cambridge Journal of Economics*, 22 (1998): 137–71.

BiBB (Bundesinstitut für Berufsbildung), *Neue und Modernisierte Ausbildungsberufe* (Bonn and Berlin: Kurzbeschreibungen, 1999).

J. S. Black, M. Mendenhall and G. Oddou, 'Toward a comprehensive model of international adjustment: an integration of multiple theoretical perspectives', *Academy of Management Review*, 16 (1991): 291–317. Reprinted in P. Ghauri and S.B. Prasad (eds), *International Management: A Reader* (London: The Dryden Press, 1995).

P. Blyton, 'Working hours', in K. Sisson (ed.), *Personnel Management*, Second edition (Oxford: Blackwell, 1994).

BMWI, *Die Neuen IT-Berufe — Zukunftssicherung durch Neue Ausbildungsberufe in der Informations-und Telekommunikationstechnik* (Bonn: BMWI, 1997).

G. Bosch, 'Occupational labour markets and structural change', *21st Conference of the International Working Party on Labour Market Segmentation*, Bremen, 9–11 September, 1999a.

G. Bosch, 'Working time: tendencies and emerging issues', *International Labour Review*, 138 (1999b): 131–49.

J-Y. Boulin, 'Trade unions in France: how to challenge the trend towards de-unionisation?', in J. Waddington and R. Hoffman (eds), *Trade Unions in Europe* (Brussels: ETUI, 2000).

S. Bowles, 'What markets can and cannot do', *Challenge*, July/August (1991): 11–16.

R. Boyer, *The Search for Labour Market Flexibility* (Oxford: Clarendon Press, 1988).

R. Boyer, 'Wage austerity and/or an education push: the French dilemma', *Labour*, Special issue (1995).

R. Boyer, 'The variety and unequal performance of really existing markets: farewell to Doctor Pangloss?', in J. Hollingsworth and R. Boyer (eds), *Contemporary Capitalism* (Cambridge: Cambridge University Press, 1997).

R. Boyer and J. R. Hollingsworth, 'The variety of institutional arrangements and their complementarity in modern economies', in J. R. Hollingsworth and R. Boyer (eds), *Contemporary Capitalism* (Cambridge: Cambridge University Press, 1997).

C. Brewster, A. Hegewisch and L. Mayne, 'Flexible working practices: the controversy and the evidence', in C. Brewster and A. Hegewisch (eds), *Policy and Practice in European Human Resource Management* (London: Routledge, 1994).

G. Broad, 'The managerial limits to Japanization: a manufacturing case study', *Human Resource Management Journal*, 4 (1994): 52–69.

D. Brody, 'Labor's crisis in historical perspective', in G. Strausss, D. G. Gallagher and J. Fiorito (eds), *The State of the Unions* (Madison, WI: IIRA, 1991).

C. Brown, Y. Nakata, M. Reich and L. Ulman, *Work and Pay in the United States and Japan* (New York: Oxford University Press, 1997).

W. Brown and D. Rea, 'The changing nature of the employment contract', *Scottish Journal of Political Economy*, 42 (1995): 363–77.

G. Brulin and T. Nilsson, 'Sweden: the Volvo and Saab road beyond lean production', in T.A. Kochan, R. D. Lansbury and J. P. McDuffie (eds), *After Lean Production: Evolving Employment Practices in the World Auto Industry* (Ithaca, NY: Cornell University Press, 1997).

G. Brunello, 'Transfers of employees between Japanese manufacturing enterprises: some results from an enquiry on a small sample of large firms', *British Journal of Industrial Relations*, 26 (1988): 119–32.

S. Brusco, 'Local productive systems and new industrial policy in Italy', in A. Bagnasco and C. Sabel (eds), *Small and Medium-Size Enterprises* (London: Pinter, 1995).

R. Buchele and J. Christiansen, 'Do employment and income security cause unemployment?', in J. Christiansen, P. Koistinen and A. Kovalainen (eds), *Working Europe: Reshaping European Employment Systems* (Aldershot: Ashgate, 1999).

C. F. Büchtemann, J. Schupp, and D. Soloff, 'Roads to work: school-to-work transition patterns in Germany and the US', *Industrial Relations Journal*, 24 (1993): 97–111.

B. Burchell, S.Deakin, J.Michie and J. Rubery (eds), *Systems of Production: Markets, Organisations and Performance* (London: Routledge, 2002).

J. Bussemaker and K. van Kersbergen, 'Gender and welfare states: some theoretical reflections', in D. Sainsbury (ed.), *Gendering Welfare States* (London: Sage, 1994).

G. Caire, 'Labour standards and international trade', in W. Sengenberger and D. Campbell (eds), *International Labour Standards and Economic Interdependence* (Geneva: International Institute for Labour Studies, 1994).

G. Caire and N. Kerschen, 'The management of redundancies in Europe: the case of France', *Labour*, 13 (1999): 269–325.

I. Campbell, 'Labour market flexibility in Australia: enhancing management prerogative?', *Labour and Industry*, 5 (1993): 1–32.

P. Cappelli, 'Competitive pressures and labor relations in the airline industry', *Industrial Relations*, 24 (1985): 316–38.

P. Cappelli, L. Bassi, H. Katz, D. Knoke, P. Osterman and M. Useem, *Change at Work* (New York: Oxford University Press, 1997).

U. Carabelli, A. Ceci, S. Ciucciovino and L. Tronti, 'The management of redundancies in Europe: the case of Italy', *Labour*, 13 (1999): 327–83.

U. Carabelli and L. Tronti, 'Introduction', *Labour*, 13 (1999): 3–39.

W. Carlin and D. Soskice, 'Shocks to the system: the German political economy under stress', *National Institute Economic Review*, 159 (1997): 57–76.

F. Carre and P. Joshi, *Building Stability for Transient Workforces: Exploring the Possibilities of Intermediary Institutions Helping Workers Cope with Labor Market Instability*, Working paper No. 1 (Cambridge, MA: Radcliffe Public Policy Institute, 1997).

B. Casey and S. Wood, 'Great Britain: firm policy, State policy and the employment and unemployment of older workers', in F. Naschold and B. de Vroom (eds), *Regulating Employment and Welfare* (Berlin: de Gruyter, 1993).

M. Castells, *The Information Age: Economy, Society and Culture, Volume 1: The Rise of the Network Society* (Oxford: Blackwell, 1996).

CEC, *Employment Rates Report 1998*, DG-V (Brussels: European Commission, 1996). http://europa.eu.int/comm/employment_social/empl&esf/empl99/rates_en.htm

CEC, *Employment and Social Affairs: Current Status 15 October 1999* (Luxembourg: Office for Official Publications of the European Communities, 1999).

CEC, *Employment in Europe 2001* (Brussels: European Commission, 2001).

CERC, *Les Bas Salaires dans les Pays de la CEE*. V/20024/91-FR (Brussels: European Commission, 1991).

N. Chalmers, *Industrial Relations in Japan: The Peripheral Workforce* (London: Routledge, 1989).

A. D. Chandler, *Strategy and Structure: Chapters in the History of the Industrial Enterprise* (Cambridge, MA: MIT Press, 1962).

J. Child, 'Organizational structure, environment and performance: the role of strategic choice', *Sociology*, 6 (1972): 1–22.

J. Child and M. Tayeb, 'Theoretical perspectives in cross-national organizational research', *International Studies of Management and Organization*, XII(4), Winter (1982/83): 23–70.

J. Christiansen, P. Koistinen and A. Kovalainen, *Working Europe: Reshaping European Employment Systems* (Aldershot: Ashgate, 1999).

D. Coates, *Models of Capitalism: Growth and Stagnation in the Modern Era* (Cambridge: Polity Press, 2000).

R. E. Cole, *Japanese Blue Collar: The Changing Tradition* (Berkeley, CA: University of California Press, 1971).

P. Conceição and J. Galbraith, 'Toward a new Kuznets hypothesis: theory and evidence on growth and inequality', in J. Galbraith and M. Berner (eds), *Inequality and Industrial Change* (Cambridge: Cambridge University Press, 2001).

R. W. Connell, *Gender and Power* (Cambridge: Polity Press, 1987).

C. Cousins, 'Changing regulatory frameworks and non-standard employment: a comparison of Germany, Spain, Sweden and the UK', in A. Felstead and N. Jewson (eds), *Global Trends in Flexible Labour* (Basingstoke: Macmillan (now Palgrave Macmillan), 1999).

E. S. Crawcour, *The Japanese Employment System: Past, Present and Future* (Canberra: Australia-Japan Research Centre, Australian National University, 1977).

C. Crouch, 'Skills-based full employment: the latest philosopher's stone', in *British Journal of Industrial Relations*, 35 (1997): 367–91.

C. Crouch, D. Finegold and M. Sako (eds), *Are Skills the Answer? The Political Economy of Skill Creation in Advanced Industrial Economies* (Oxford: Oxford University Press, 1999).

M. Crozier, *Le Phénomène Bureaucratique* (Paris: Seuil, 1963).

P. Culpepper, 'Still a model for the industrialized countries?', in P. Culpepper and D. Finegold (eds), *The German Skills Machine* (New York: Berghahn Books, 1999).

P. Culpepper and D. Finegold (eds), *The German Skills Machine* (New York: Berghahn Books, 1999).

A. Daly, D. Hitchens and K. Wagner, 'Productivity, machinery and skills in a sample of British and German manufacturing plants', *National Institute Economic Review*, February (1985): 48–61.

M. Daly, *Social Security, Gender and Equality in the European Union*, Working paper (Florence: European University Institute, 1996).

H. Davies and H. Joshi, 'Social and family security in the redress of unequal opportunities', in J. Humphries and J. Rubery (eds), *The Economics of Equal Opportunities* (Manchester: Equal Opportunities Commission, 1995).

S. Deakin and U. Mückenberger, 'Deregulation and European labour markets', in A. Castro, P. Méhaut and J. Rubery (eds), *International Integration and Labour Market Organisation* (London: Academic Press, 1992).

R. Delbridge, *Life on the Line in Contemporary Manufacturing: the Workplace Experience of Lean Production and the 'Japanese' Model* (Oxford: Oxford University Press, 1998).

P. DiMaggio and W. Powell, 'The iron cage revisited: institutional isomorphism and collective rationality in organizational fields', in W. Powell and P. DiMaggio (eds),

The New Institutionalism in Organizational Analysis (Chicago: University of Chicago Press, 1983).

J. Ditch, H. Barnes, J. Bradshaw and M. Kilkey, *A Synthesis of National Family Policies*, 1996 European Observatory on National Family Policies (Brussels: European Commission Employment and Social Affairs Directorate, 1998).

P. Doeringer, and M. Piore, *Internal Labour Markets and Manpower Analysis* (Lexington, MA: Heath, 1971).

Lord Donovan, *Report of the Royal Commission on Trade Unions and Employer Associations*, Cmnd. 3623 (London: HMSO, 1968).

R. Dore, *British Factory — Japanese Factory: The Origins of National Diversity in Industrial Relations* (London: Allen and Unwin, 1973).

R. Dore, 'Convergence in whose interests?', in S. Berger and R. Dore (eds), *Convergence or Diversity* (Ithaca, NY: Cornell University Press, 1996).

R. P. Dore and M. Sako, *How the Japanese Learn to Work* (London: Routledge, 1989).

J. T. Dunlop, *Industrial Relations Systems* (New York: Holt, 1957).

J. Dunning (ed.), *Regions, Globalization, and the Knowledge-Based Economy* (Oxford: Oxford University Press, 2000).

EC Childcare Network, *Review of Children's Services*, Report to the Equal Opportunities Unit of the European Commission, DG–V (Brussels: European Commission, 1996).

P. Edwards, A. Ferner and K. Sisson, 'People and the process of management in the multinational company: a review and some illustrations', *Warwick Papers in Industrial Relations*, Working paper No. 43, 1993.

P. Edwards, M. Hall, R. Hyman, P. Marginson, K. Sisson, J. Waddington and D. Winchester, 'Great Britain: still muddling through?', in A. Ferner and R. Hyman (eds), *Industrial Relations in the New Europe* (Oxford: Blackwell, 1992).

T. Edwards, 'Multinational companies and the diffusion of employment practices: a survey of the literature', *Warwick Papers in Industrial Relations*, Working paper No. 61, 1998.

T. Edwards, C. Rees and X. Coller, 'Structure, politics and the diffusion of employment practices in multinationals', *European Journal of Industrial Relations*, 5 (1999): 286–306.

EIRR, 'Flexibility, change and the future of sectoral bargaining', *European Industrial Relations Journal*, 285 (1997): 24–7.

T. Elger and C. Smith (eds), *Global Japanization?* (London: Routledge, 1994).

T. Elger and C. Smith 'Global Japanization? Convergence and Competition in the Organization of the Labour Process, in T. Elger and C. Smith (eds), *Global Japanization?* (London: Routledge, 1994).

A-L. Ellingsæter, *Gender Mainstreaming*, EC Gender and Employment Expert Group (Oslo: ISF, 1999).

L. Elliott, 'World Trade Organisation: special report', *The Guardian*, 6 December 1999.

F. Emery, 'Adaptive systems for our future governance', *National Labour Institute Bulletin* (New Delhi) (1976): 121–9. Reprinted in Emery (1981).

F. Emery, *Systems Thinking* (Harmondsworth: Penguin, 1981).

K. Endo, '*Satei* (personal assessment) and interworker competition in Japanese firms', *Industrial Relations*, 33 (1994): 70–82.

G. Esping-Andersen, *The Three Worlds of Welfare Capitalism* (Cambridge: Polity Press, 1990).

G. Esping-Andersen, *Social Foundations of Postindustrial Economies* (Oxford: Oxford University Press, 1999).

G. Esping-Andersen, 'Interview on postindustrialism and the future of the welfare state', *Work, Employment and Society*, 14 (2000): 757–69.

European Commission, *Europa website of the EURLEX, European legislation in force*, http://europa.eu.int/eur-lex/en/map.html

European Observatory on Family Matters, *Family Observer 3* (Brussels: European Commission, Employment and Social Affairs Directorate, 2000).

F. Eyraud, D. Marsden and J-J. Silvestre, 'Occupational and internal labour markets in Britain and France', *International Labour Review*, 129 (1990): 501–27.

C. Fagan, J. Plantenga and J. Rubery, 'Part-time work and inequality? Lessons from the Netherlands and the UK', in *A Time for Working, A Time for Living* (Brussels: ETUC and ETUI, 1995).

A. Ferner, 'The changing influence of the personnel function', *Human Resource Management Journal*, 1 (1990): 12–30.

A. Ferner, 'Multinational companies and human resource management: an overview of research issues', *Human Resource Management Journal*, 4 (1994): 79–102.

A. Ferner and P. Edwards, 'Power and the diffusion of organizational change within multinational enterprises', *European Journal of Industrial Relations*,1 (1995): 229–57.

A. Ferner and R. Hyman, 'Italy: between political exchange and micro-corporatism', in A. Ferner and R. Hyman (eds), *Industrial Relations in the New Europe* (Oxford: Blackwell, 1992).

A. Ferner and R. Hyman (eds), *Changing Industrial Relations in Europe*, Second edition (Oxford: Blackwell, 1998).

A. Ferner and J. Quintanilla, 'Multinationals, national systems and HRM: the enduring influence of national identity or a process of "Anglo-Saxonization?"', *The International Journal of Human Resource Management*, 9 (1998): 710–31.

D. Finegold, 'The future of the German skill-creation system', in P. Culpepper and D. Finegold (eds), *The German Skills Machine* (New York: Berghahn Books, 1999).

D. Finegold and D. Soskice, 'The failure of British training: analysis and prescription', *Oxford Review of Economic Policy*, 4(3) (1988): 21–53.

N. Folbre, *Who Pays for the Kids?: Gender and the Structures of Constraint* (London: Routledge, 1994).

D. Foray and B-A. Lundvall, 'The knowledge-based economy: from the economics of knowledge to the learning economy', in OECD (1996b).

W. Franz and D. Soskice, 'The German apprenticeship system', in F. Buttler, W. Franz, R. Schettkat and D. Soskice (eds), *Institutional Frameworks and Labor Market Performance* (London: Routledge, 1995).

R. B. Freeman, 'How labor fares in advanced countries', in R. B. Freeman (ed.), *Working Under Different Rules* (New York: Russell Sage, 1994a).

R. B. Freeman, 'A hard-headed look at labour standards', in W. Sengenberger and D. Campbell (eds), *International Labour Standards and Economic Interdependence* (Geneva: International Institute for Labour Studies, 1994b).

R. Freeman, 'Why do so many young American men commit crimes and what might we do about it?', *Journal of Economic Perspectives*, 10 (1996): 25–42.

R. B. Freeman and J. Rogers, *What Workers Want* (Ithaca, NY: Cornell University Press, 1999).

R. B. Freeman and R. Schettkat, *Differentials in Service Industry Employment Growth: Germany and the US in the Comparable German American Structural Database*, Report prepared for Directorate General of Employment and Social Affairs, Commission for the European Communities, Brussels, 2000.

J. French, 'The Declaration of Philadelphia and the Global Social Charter of the United Nations, 1944–45', in W. Sengenberger and D. Campbell (eds), *International Labour Standards and Economic Interdependence* (Geneva: International Institute for Labour Studies, 1994).

J. Galbraith, P. Conceição and P. Ferreira, 'Inequality and unemployment in Europe: the American cure', *New Left Review*, 237 (1999): 28–51.

D. Gallie, *In Search for the New Working Class: Automation and Social Integration Within the Capitalist Enterprise* (Cambridge: Cambridge University Press, 1978).

P. Garnjost and K. Blettner, 'Volkswagen: cutting labour costs without redundancies', in J. Storey (ed.), *Blackwell Cases in Human Resource and Change Management* (Oxford: Blackwell, 1996).

P. Ghauri and S.B. Prasad (eds), *International Management: A Reader* (London: The Dryden Press, 1995).

S. Gibbons, *International Labour Rights: New Methods of Enforcement* (London: Institute of Employment Rights, 1998).

H. Giersch, 'Eurosclerosis', Discussion paper 112 (October 1985), Kiel Institute for World Economics, cited in Krugman 1987.

C. Gill and H. Krieger, 'Recent survey evidence on participation in Europe: towards a European model', *European Journal of Industrial Relations*, 6 (2000): 109–32.

J. Ginn and S. Arber, 'Towards women's independence: pension systems in three contrasting European welfare states', *Journal of European Social Policy*, 4 (1992): 255–77.

A. Gordon, *Redundancy in the 1980s* (Aldershot: Gower, 1984).

J. Gornick, M. Meyers and K. Ross, 'Supporting the employment of mothers: policy variation across fourteen welfare states', *Journal of European Social Policy*, 7 (1997): 45–70.

H. Gospel, 'The revival of apprenticeship training in Britain?', *British Journal of Industrial Relations*, 36 (1998): 435–57.

H. F. Gospel and C. Littler (eds), *Managerial Strategies and Industrial Relations : An Historical and Comparative Study* (London: Heinemann, 1983).

J. Gray, *False Dawn* (London: Granta Books, 1998).

C. Greenhalgh, 'Adult vocational training and Government policy in France and Britain', *Oxford Review of Economic Policy*, 15 (1999): 97–113.

A. Greenspan, 'Testimony before the Committee on the Budget', United States Senate, 21 January 1997.

P. Gregg and J. Wadsworth, 'Gender, households and access to employment', in J. Humphries and J. Rubery (eds), *The Economics of Equal Opportunities* (Manchester: Equal Opportunities Commission, 1995).

D. Grimshaw, 'Public sector employment, wage inequality and the gender pay ratio in the UK', *International Review of Applied Economics*, 14 (2000): 427–48.

D. Grimshaw, H. Beynon, J. Rubery, and K. Ward, 'The restructuring of career paths in large service sector organisations: 'delayering, upskilling and polarisation', *Sociological Review*, 50 (2002): 89–116.

D. Grimshaw and J. Rubery, 'Workforce heterogeneity and unemployment benefits: the need for policy reassessment in the European Union', *Journal of European Social Policy*, 7 (1997): 291–318.

K. Grønhaug and O. Nordhaug, 'International human resource management: an environmental perspective', *International Journal of Human Resource Management*, 3 (1992): 1–14.

T. Grønning, 'Whither the Japanese employment system? The position of the Japan Employers' Federation', *Industrial Relations Journal*, 29 (1998): 295–303.

H. Grünert and B. Lutz, 'East German labour market in transition: segmentation and increasing disparity', *Industrial Relations Journal*, 1 (1995): 19–31.

C. Hakim, 'Grateful slaves and self-made women: fact and fantasy in women's work orientations', *European Journal of Sociology*, 7(2) (1991): 101–21.

T. Hanami, *Labor Relations in Japan Today* (Tokyo: Kodansha International, 1981).

B. Hancké, 'European Works Councils and Industrial Restructuring in the European Motor Industry', *European Journal of Industrial Relations*, 6 (2000): 35–60.

B. Harrison, *Lean and Mean: Why Large Corporations Will Continue to Dominate the Global Economy* (New York: Basic Books, 1994).

J. Hartog, 'Country employment policy reviews: The Netherlands', paper prepared for ILO Symposium on Social Dialogue and Employment Success, Geneva, 2–3 March 1999.

P. Hartz, *Jeder Arbeitsplatz Hat ein Gesicht* (Frankfurt-am-Main and New York: Campus, 1994).

A-W. Harzing, 'Internationalization and the international division of labour', in A-W. Harzing and J. van Ruysseveldt (eds), *International Human Resource Management* (London: Sage Publications, 1995).

M. Hashimoto and J. Raisian, 'Employment tenure and earnings profiles in Japan and the United States', *American Economic Review*, 75 (1985): 721–35.

M. Hashimoto and J. Raisian, 'Employment tenure and earnings profiles in Japan and the United States: reply', *American Economic Review*, 82 (1992): 346–54.

C. Hasluck, T. Hogarth, M. Maguire and J. Pitcher, *Modern Apprenticeships: A Survey of Employers* (London: Department for Education and Employment, 1997).

A. Hassel, 'The erosion of the German system of industrial relations', *British Journal of Industrial Relations*, 37 (1999): 483–506.

A. Hassel and T. Schulten, 'Globalization and the future of central collective bargaining: the example of the German metal industry', *Economy and Society*, 27 (1998): 486–522.

G. Hedlund, 'The hypermodern MNC — a heterarchy?', *Human Resource Management*, 25 (1986): 9–35. Reprinted in P. Ghauri and S. B. Prasad (eds), *International Management: A Reader* (London: The Dryden Press, 1995).

E. Heery, ' Campaigning for part-time workers', *Work, Employment and Society*, 12 (1999): 351–66.

G. Herrigel and C. Sabel, 'Craft production in crisis: industrial restructuring in Germany during the 1990s', in P. Culpepper and D. Finegold (eds), *The German Skills Machine* (New York: Berghahn Books, 1999).

H. Heseler and U. Mückenberger, 'Managing labour redundancies in Europe: the case of Germany,' *Labour*, 13 (1999): 183–236.

J. Heyes, 'Annualised hours and the "knock": the organisation of working time in a chemicals plant', *Work, Employment and Society*, 11 (1997): 65–81.

D. J. Hickson, C. L. McMillan, K. Azumi and D. Horvath, 'Grounds for comparative organization theory: quicksands or hard core?', in C. J. Lammers and D. J. Hickson (eds), *Organizations Alike and Unlike* (London: Routledge and Kegan Paul, 1979).

P. Hirst and G. Thompson, 'Globalization in question: international economic relations and forms of public governance', in J. R. Hollingsworth and R. Boyer (eds), *Contemporary Capitalism* (Cambridge: Cambridge University Press, 1997).

J. Hoffmann, 'Industrial relations and trade unions in Germany: the pressure of modernisation and globalisation', in J. Waddington and R. Hoffman (eds), *Trade Unions in Europe* (Brussels: ETUI, 2000).

G. H. Hofstede, 'Motivation, leadership and organization: do American theories apply abroad?', *Organizational Dynamics*, Summer (1980a): 42–63.

G. H. Hofstede, *Culture's Consequence: International Differences in Work-Related Values* (Beverly Hills, CA: Sage, 1980b).

G. H. Hofstede, *Cultures and Organizations: Software of the Mind* (London: McGraw-Hill, 1991).

G. H. Hofstede, 'Cultural constraints in management theories', *Academy of Management Executive*, 7(1) (1993): 81–94. Reprinted in R. M. Steers, L. W. Porter, and G.A. Bigley (eds), *Motivation and Leadership at Work* (Singapore: McGraw-Hill, 1996).

T. Hogarth, G. Siora, G. Briscoe and C. Hasluck, *The Net Costs of Training to Employers* (London: Department for Education and Employment, 1996).

J. R. Hollingsworth and R. Boyer (eds), *Contemporary Capitalism* (Cambridge: Cambridge University Press, 1997).

J. R. Hollingsworth and W. Streeck, 'Countries and sectors: performance, convergence and competitiveness', in J. R. Hollingsworth, P. Schmitter and W. Streeck (eds), *Governing Capitalist Economies* (New York: Oxford University Press, 1994).

T. Hopkins and I. Wallerstein, *World-Systems Analysis* (Beverly Hills, CA: Sage, 1982).

D. Horvath, K. Azumi, D. J. Hickson and C. J. McMillan, 'Bureaucratic structures in cross-national perspective: a study of British, Japanese and Swedish firms', in G. Dlugos, K. Weiermair and W. Dorow (eds), *Management Under Differing Value Systems* (Berlin: de Gruyter, 1981).

J. Humphries and J. Rubery, 'The reconstitution of the supply side of the labour market: the relative autonomy of social reproduction', *Cambridge Journal of Economics*, 8 (1984): 331–47.

M. Huselid, 'The impact of human resource management practices upon turnover, productivity and corporate financial performance', *Academy of Management Journal*, 38 (June 1995): 635–72.

R. Hyman, *Marxism and the Sociology of Trade Unionism* (London: Pluto Press, 1971), reprinted in T. Clarke and L. Clements (eds), *Trade Unions Under Capitalism* (Glasgow: Fontana/William Collins, 1977).

R. Hyman, *Understanding European Trade Unionism* (London: Sage, 2001).

R. Hyman and A. Ferner (eds), *New Frontiers in European Industrial Relations* (Oxford: Blackwell, 1994).

K. Imai and R. Komiya, 'Characteristics of Japanese firms', in K. Imai and R. Komiya (eds), *Business Enterprise in Japan* (Cambridge, MA: MIT Press, 1994).

India Committee on the Netherlands, *The Dark Side of Football* (ICFTU: June 2000). Website: http://www.antenna.nl/liw/iv.html

International Confederation of Free Trade Unions, *Basic Code of Conduct Covering Labour Practices* (ICFTU/ITS, 1997),
http://www.icftu.org/displaydocument.asp? Index= 990917146&Language = EN

IRS (Industrial Relations Services), *Pay and Gender in Britain* (London: Equal Opportunities Commission and IRS, 1991).

H. Itoh, 'Japanese human resource management from the viewpoint of incentive theory', in M. Aoki and R. Dore (eds), *The Japanese Firm: The Sources of Competitive Strength* (Oxford: Oxford University Press, 1994).

N. Iwao, 'A design for transforming the Japanese economy', *Journal of Japanese Studies*, 23 (1997): 399–417.

M. P. Jackson, J. W. Leopold and K. Tuck, *Decentralisation of Collective Bargaining: an Analysis of Recent Experience in the UK* (Basingstoke: Macmillan (now Palgrave Macmillan)/St. Martin's Press, 1993).

K. Jacobs and M. Rein, 'Early retirement: stability, reversal or redefinition', in F. Naschold and B. de Vroom (eds), *Regulating Employment and Welfare* (Berlin: de Gruyter, 1993).

S. Jacoby, 'The development of internal labour markets in American manufacturing firms', in P. Osterman (ed.), *Internal Labour Markets* (Cambridge, MA: MIT Press, 1984).

S. Jacoby, 'The new institutionalism: what can it learn from the old?', *Industrial Relations*, 29 (1990): 316–40.

H. Jain, J. Lawler and M. Morishima, 'Multinational corporations, human resource management and host-country nationals', *The International Journal of Human Resource Management*, 9 (1998): 553–66.

P. Jansen and L. Kissler, 'Organization of work by participation? A French–German comparison', *Economic and Industrial Democracy*, 8 (1987): 379–409.

Japan Institute of Labour (JIL), *The Labour Situation in Japan 2001/2001* (Tokyo: JIL, 2001).

S. Jeffreys, 'The exceptional centenary of the Confédération Générale du Travail, 1895–1995', *Historical Studies in Industrial Relations*, 3 (1997): 123–41.

A. Jochmann-Döll, 'Gleicher Lohn für gleichwertige Arbeit: ausländische und deutsche Konzepte und Erfahrungen', doctoral dissertation (University of Trier, 1990).

I. Jones, 'Apprenticeship training costs in British manufacturing establishments', *British Journal of Industrial Relations*, 24 (1986): 333–62.

C. Juhn, K. M. Murphy and B. Pierce, 'Wage inequality and the rise in returns to skill', *Journal of Political Economy*, 101 (1993): 410–42.

U. Jürgens, T. Malsch and K. Dohse, *Breaking from Taylorism: Changing Forms of Work in the Automobile Industry* (Cambridge: Cambridge University Press, 1993).

H. Katz 'The decentralisation of collective bargaining: a literature review and comparative analysis', *Industrial Relations and Labour Relations Review*, 47 (1993): 3–22.

H. C. Katz and O. Darbishire, *Converging Divergences: Worldwide Changes in Employment Systems* (Ithaca, NY: ILR Press, 1999).

L.F. Katz and K.M. Murphy, 'Changes in relative wages, 1963–1987: supply and demand factors', in *Quarterly Journal of Economics*, 107 (1992): 35–78.

H. Kern and M. Schumann, *Das Ende der Arbeitsteilung? Rationalisierung in der Industriellen Produktion* (Munich: C. H. Beck, 1984).

H. Kern and M. Schumann, 'Limits of the division of labour: new production concepts in West German industry', *Economic and Industrial Democracy*, 8 (1987): 151–70.

J. M. Keynes, *The General Theory of Employment, Interest and Money* (New York: Harvest/HBJ, 1964, first edition 1935).

N. Klein, *No Logo* (London: Flamingo, 2000).

K. Koike, 'Learning and incentive systems in Japanese industry', in M. Aoki and R. Dore (eds), *The Japanese Firm* (Oxford: Oxford University Press, 1994).

K. Koike and T. Inoki, *Skill Formation in Japan and Southeast Asia* (Tokyo: University of Tokyo Press, 1990).

K. Kōshiro, 'The quality of working life in Japanese factories', in S. Taishiro (ed.), *Contemporary Industrial Relations in Japan* (Madison, WI: University of Wisconsin Press, 1983).

R. B. Krueger, 'How computers have changed the wage structure: evidence from micro data, 1984–1989', *Quarterly Journal of Economics*, 108 (1993): 33–60.

P. Krugman, 'Slow growth in Europe: conceptual issues', in R. Lawrence and C. Schultze (eds), *Barriers to European Growth* (Washington, DC: The Brookings Institution, 1987).

Y. Kuwahara, 'Employment relations in Japan', in G. Bamber and R. Lansbury (eds), *International and Comparative Employment Relations* (London: Sage, 1998).

S. Kuznets, 'Economic growth and income inequality', *The American Economic Review*, 45 (1955): 1–28.

D. Ladipo, 'The rise of America's prison-industrial complex', *New Left Review*, 7 (2001): 109–23.

A. Lam, 'Work organisation, skills development and utilisation of engineers', in R. Crompton, D. Gallie and K. Purcell (eds), *Changing Forms of Employment* (London: Routledge, 1996).

C. Lane, *Management and Labour in Europe* (Aldershot: Edward Elgar, 1989).

C. Lane, 'Industrial order and the transformation of industrial relations: Britain, Germany and France compared', in R. Hyman and A. Ferner (eds), *New Frontiers in European Industrial Relations* (Oxford: Blackwell, 1994).

C. Lane, *Industry and Society in Europe* (Aldershot: Edward Elgar, 1995).

C. Lane, 'Globalization and the German model of capitalism — erosion and survival', *British Journal of Sociology*, 51 (2000): 207–234.

D. Latulippe, *Effective Retirement Age and Duration of Retirement in the Industrial Countries between 1950 and 1990* (Geneva: ILO, 1996).

A. Laurent, 'The cross-cultural puzzle of international human resource management', *Human Resource Management*, 25 (1986): 91–102. Reprinted in P. Ghauri and S. B. Prasad (eds), *International Management: A Reader* (London: The Dryden Press, 1995).

E. Lee, 'Globalization and labour standards: a review of issues', *International Labour Review*, 136 (1997): 173–89.

S. M. Leong and C. T. Tan, 'Managing across borders: an empirical test of the Bartlett and Ghoshal (1989) organizational typology', *Journal of International Business Studies*, 24 (1993): 449–64. Reprinted in P. Ghauri and S. B. Prasad (eds), *International Management: A Reader* (London: The Dryden Press, 1995).

J. Lewis, 'Gender and the development of welfare regimes', *Journal of European Social Policy*, 2 (1992): 159–73.

J. Lincoln and A. Kalleberg, *Culture, Control and Commitment: A Study of Work Organization and Work Atttitudes in the United States and Japan* (Cambridge: Cambridge University Press, 1990).

J. Lincoln and Y. Nakata, 'The transformation of the Japanese employment system', *Work and Occupations*, 24 (1997): 33–55.

C. Littler, 'A comparative analysis of managerial structures and strategies', in H. F. Gospel and C. Littler (eds), *Managerial Strategies and Industrial Relations: An Historical and Comparative Study* (London: Heinemann, 1983).

M. Lodovici, 'The dynamics of labour market reform in European countries', in G. Esping-Andersen and M. Regini (eds), *Why Deregulate Labour Markets?* (Oxford: Oxford University Press, 2000).

E. Lorenz, 'The transfer of business practices to Britain and France', in M. Maurice and A. Sorge (eds), *Embedding Organizations* (Amsterdam: John Benjamins, 2000).

Y. Lu and I. Bjorkman, 'HRM practices in China-Western joint ventures: MNC standardization versus localization', *The International Journal of Human Resource Management*, 8 (1997): 614–28.

B. Lutz, 'Education and employment: contrasting evidence from France and the Federal Republic of Germany', *European Journal of Education*, 16 (1981): 73–86.

L. M. Lynch, 'Payoffs to alternative training strategies at work', in R.B. Freeman (ed.), *Working Under Different Rules* (New York: Russell Sage, 1994a).

L. M. Lynch (ed.), *Training and the Private Sector: International Comparisons* (Chicago: University of Chicago Press, 1994b).

M. Marchington, A. Wilkinson, P. Ackers and A. Dundon, *Management Choice and Employee Voice* (London: CIPD, 2001).

P. Marginson, 'The Eurocompany and Euro industrial relations', *European Journal of Industrial Relations*, 6 (2000): 9–34.

S. Marglin and J. Schor (eds), *The Golden Age of Capitalism: Reinterpreting the Postwar Experience* (Oxford: Clarendon Press, 1991).

D. Marsden, 'A phoenix from the ashes of apprenticeship? Vocational training in Britain', *International Contributions to Labour Studies*, 5 (1995): 87–114.

D. Marsden, *A Theory of Employment Systems: Micro-Foundations of Societal Diversity* (Oxford: Oxford University Press, 1999).

D. Marsden and P. Ryan, 'Work, labour markets and vocational preparation: Anglo-German comparisons of training in intermediate skills', in L. Bash and A. Green, *Youth, Education and Work: World Yearbook of Education* (London: Kogan Page, 1995).

S. Marullo (ed.), *Comparison of Regulations on Part-Time and Temporary Employment in Europe*, Research series No. 52 (London: Department of Employment, May 1995).

I. Marx and G. Verbist, 'Low-paid work and poverty: a cross-country perspective', in S. Bazen, M. Gregory and W. Salverda (eds), *Low-Wage Employment in Europe* (Cheltenham: Edward Elgar, 1998).

D. Massey and R. Meegan, *The Anatomy of Job Loss* (London: Taylor and Francis, 1982).

M. Maurice, 'The paradoxes of societal analysis: a review of the past and prospects for the future', in M. Maurice and A. Sorge (eds), *Embedding Organizations* (Amsterdam: John Benjamins, 2000).

M. Maurice, F. Sellier and J-J. Silvestre, 'The search for a societal effect in the pro-duction of company hierarchy: a comparison of France and Germany', in P. Osterman, (ed.), *Internal Labor Markets* (Cambridge, MA: MIT Press, 1984).

M. Maurice, F. Sellier and J-J. Silvestre, *The Social Foundations of Industrial Power*, (Cambridge, MA: MIT Press, 1986).

M. Maurice and A. Sorge (eds), *Embedding Organizations* (Amsterdam: John Benjamins, 2000).

P. Mayhew and J. van Dijk, *Criminal Victimisation in Eleven Industrialised Countries* (The Netherlands; Ministry of Justice, 1997).

E. Mayo, *The Human Problems of an Industrial Civilisation* (London: Macmillan (now Palgrave Macmillan), 1933).

B. McCormick and K. McCormick, *Japanese Companies — British Factories* (Aldershot: Avebury, 1996).

B. McSweeney, 'Hofstede's model of national cultural differences and their conse-quences: a triumph of faith — a failure of analysis', *Human Relations*, 55 (2002): 89–118 .

P. Méhaut, 'Further education, vocational training and the labour market: the French and German systems compared', in A. Castro, P. Méhaut and J. Rubery (eds), *International Integration and Labour Market Organization* (London: Academic Press, 1992).

D. Metcalfe, 'The Low Pay Commission and the National Minimum Wage', *The Economic Journal*, 109 (1999): F46–66.

R. Milkman, 'The impact of foreign investment on US industrial relations: the case of California's Japanese-owned plants', *Economic and Industrial Democracy*, 13 (1992): 151–81.

N. Millward, J. Forth and A. Bryson, *All Change at Work? British Employment Relations 1980–1998*, Vol.II, WIRS (London: Routledge, 2000).

N. Millward, M. Stevens, D. Smart and W.R. Hawes, *Workplace Industrial Relations in Transition* (Aldershot: Dartmouth Press, 1992).

J. Mincer, 'Human capital: a review', in C. Kerr and P. Staudohar (eds), *Labor Economics and Industrial Relations* (Cambridge, MA: Harvard University Press, 1994).

L. Mishel, J. Berstein and J. Schmitt, *The State of Working America 1996–97* (New York: M.E. Sharpe, 1997).

G. Morgan, *Organizations in Society* (Basingstoke: Macmillan (now Palgrave Macmillan), 1990).

M. Morishima, 'Embedding HRM in a social context', *British Journal of Industrial Relations*, 33 (1995): 617–40.

L. Mósesdóttir, *The Interplay Between Gender Markets and the State in Sweden, Germany and the United States* (Aldershot: Ashgate, 2001).

H. Mosley, 'Employment protection and labor force adjustment in EC countries', in G. Schmid (ed.), *Labor Market Institutions in Europe* (New York: M.E. Sharpe, 1994).

H. Mosley and T. Kruppe, 'Employment stabilization through short-time work', in G. Schmid, J. O'Reilly and K. Schömann (eds), *International Handbook of Labour Market Policy and Evaluation* (Cheltenham: Edward Elgar, 1996).

F. Mueller, 'Teams between hierarchy and commitment: change strategies and the "internal environment"', *Journal of Management Studies*, 31 (1994): 383–403.

J. Münch, *Vocational Training in the Federal Republic of Germany*, Third edition (Berlin: CEDEFOP, 1991).

F. Naschold and B. de Vroom (eds), *Regulating Employment and Welfare* (Berlin: de Gruyter, 1993).

S. Nickell, 'Unemployment and labour market rigidities: Europe vs North America', *Journal of Economic Perspectives*, 11 (1997): 55–74.

OECD, *The OECD Jobs Study: Facts, Analysis, Strategies* (Paris: OECD, 1994a).

OECD, *The OECD Jobs Study: Evidence and Explanations, Part 1: Labour Market Trends and Underlying Forces of Change* (Paris: OECD, 1994b).

OECD, *Education at a Glance* (Paris: OECD, 1996a).

OECD, *Employment and Growth in the Knowledge-based Economy* (Paris: OECD, 1996b).

OECD, *Employment Outlook* (Paris: OECD, 1996c).

OECD, *Employment Outlook* (Paris: OECD, 1997).

OECD, 'Making the most of the minimum: statutory minimum wages, employment and poverty', in *Employment Outlook*, June (Paris: OECD, 1998a).

OECD, 'Working hours: latest trends and policy initiatives', in *Employment Outlook*, June (Paris: OECD, 1998b).

OECD. 'Employment protection and labour market performance', in *Employment Outlook* (Paris: OECD, 1999).

OECD, *Employment Outlook* (Paris: OECD, 2000).

OECD, *Employment Outlook* (Paris: OECD, 2001).

I. Ohashi and T. Tachibanaki (eds), *Internal Labour Markets, Incentives and Employment* (Basingstoke: Macmillan (now Palgrave Macmillan), 1998).

F. Ohtake, 'The United States', in T. Tachibanaki (ed.), *Wage Differentials: an International Comparison* (Basingstoke: Macmillan (now Palgrave Macmillan), 1998).

R. Olie, 'The "culture" factor in personnel and organization policies', in A.-W. Harzing and J. van Ruysseveldt (eds), *International Human Resource Management* (London: Sage, 1995).

N. Oliver and B. Wilkinson, *The Japanisation of the British Economy* (London: Blackwell, 1992).

J. O'Reilly, 'What flexibility do women offer? Comparing the use of, and attitudes to, part-time work in Britain and France in retail banking,' *Gender, Work and Organisation*, 1 (1994): 138–50.

J. O'Reilly, 'Is it time to gender the societal effect?', in M. Maurice and A. Sorge (eds), *Embedding Organizations* (Amsterdam: John Benjamins, 2000).

J. O'Reilly and C. Fagan (eds), *Part-Time Prospects: Part-Time Work in Europe, North America and the Pacific Rim* (London: Routledge, 1998).

P. Osterman, *Employment Futures* (New York: Oxford University Press, 1988).

P. Osterman, 'How common is workplace transformation and how can we explain who adopts it?', *Industrial and Labor Relations Review*, 47 (1994): 173–88.

P. Osterman, 'Skill, training and work organization in American establishments', *Industrial Relations*, 34 (1995): 125–46.

J. Paauwe and P. Dewe, 'Organizational structure of multinational corporations: theories and models', in A-W. Harzing and J. van Ruysseveldt (eds), *International Human Resource Management* (London: Sage, 1995).

T. Palley, 'The causes of high unemployment: labor market sclerosis versus macroeconomic policy', in J. Stanford and L. F. Vosko (eds), *Challenging the Market: The Struggle to Regulate Work and Income* (Montreal: McGill-Queen's University Press, 2002).

E. Parker and J. Rogers, 'Sectoral Training Initiatives in the US', in P. Culpepper and D. Finegold (eds), *The German Skills Machine* (New York: Berghahn Books, 1999).

M. Parker and J. Slaughter, *Choosing Sides: Unions and the Team Concept* (Boston: South End Press, 1988).

J. Peck, 'Postwelfare Massachusetts', *Economic Geography*, AAG Special Issue (1998): 62–82.

H.V. Perlmutter, 'The tortuous evolution of the multinational corporation', *Columbia Journal of World Business*, 4 (1969): 9–18.

B. Pfau-Effinger, 'Culture or structure as explanations for differences in part-time work in Germany, Finland and the Netherlands?', in J. O'Reilly and C. Fagan (eds), *Part-Time Prospects* (London: Routledge, 1998).

J. Pfeffer, 'Five models of behavior', in J. Pfeffer, *New Directions for Organization Theory* (New York: Oxford University Press,1997).

J. Pfeffer, *The Human Equation* (Boston, MA: Harvard Business School Press, 1998).

J. Pillinger, *Feminising the Market* (Basingstoke: Macmillan (now Palgrave Macmillan), 1992).

M. Piore and C. Sabel, *The Second Industrial Divide: Possibilities for Prosperity* (New York: Basic Books, 1984).

J. Plantenga and S. van Velzen, *Wage Determination and Sex Segregation in Employment: the Case of the Netherlands*, Report to the European Commission (DGV-Equal Opportunities Unit, Brussels, 1993).

J. Pontusson and P. Swenson, 'Labor markets, production strategies and wage bargaining institutions: the Swedish employer offensive in comparative perspective', *Comparative Political Studies*, 29 (1996): 223–50.

H. Popitz, H. P. Bahrdt, E. A. Jüres and H. Kesting, *Das Gesellschaftsbild des Arbeiters* (Tübingen: Mohr, 1957).

M. Porter, *The Competitive Advantage of Nations* (Basingstoke: Macmillan (now Palgrave Macmillan), 1990).

A. Portes, 'By-passing the rules: the dialectics of labour standards and informalization in less developed countries', in W. Sengenberger and D. Campbell (eds), *International Labour Standards and Economic Interdependence* (Geneva: International Institute for Labour Studies, 1994).

S. Prais and E. Beadle, *Pre-vocational Schooling in Europe Today* (London: NIESR, 1991).

S. Prais, V. Jarvis and K. Wagner, 'Productivity and vocational skills in services in Britain and Germany: hotels', *National Institute Economic Review*, November (1989): 52–74.

J. Purcell, 'Best practice and best fit: chimera or cul de sac?', *Human Resource Management Journal*, 9 (1999): 26–41.

K. Rake (ed.), *Women's Incomes over the Lifetime* (London: Women's Unit, Cabinet Office, 2000).

H. Ramsay, 'Whose champions? Multinationals, labour and industry policy in the European Community after 1992', *Capital and Class*, 48 (1992): 17–39.

M. Regini and I. Regalia, 'The prospects for Italian trade unions in a phase of concertation', in J. Waddington and R. Hoffman (eds), *Trade Unions in Europe* (Brussels: ETUI, 2000).

R. Reich, *The Work of Nations: Preparing Ourselves for 21st Century Capitalism* (New York: Simon and Schuster, 1991).

J-D. Reynaud, *Les Syndicats en France* (Paris: Seuil, 1975).

J. Rinehart, D. Robertson, C. Huxley and J. Wareham, 'Reunifying conception and execution of work under Japanese production management? A Canadian case study', in T. Elger and C. Smith (eds), *Global Japanization?* (London: Routledge, 1994).

J. Rosdücher and H. Seifert, *Die Einführung der '4-Tage-Woche' in der Volkswagen AG* (Berlin: Schriftenreihe der Senatsverwaltung für Arbeit und Frauen, No. 4, 1994).

M. Rose, *Industrial Behaviour*, Second edition (Harmondsworth: Penguin, 1988).

S. Rosen, *Public Employment and the Welfare State in Sweden*, Occasional paper no. 61, NBER/SNS project, 'Reforming the Welfare State' (Stockholm: Centre for Business and Policy Studies, 1995).

P. Rosenvallen, *La Question Syndicale* (Paris: Calmann-Lévy, 1988).

P. Rosenzweig and N Nohria, 'Influences on human resource management practices in multinational corporations', *Journal of International Business Studies*, 25 (1994): 229–51.

P. Rosenzweig and J. Singh, 'Organizational environments and the multinational enterprise', *Academy of Management Review*, 16 (1991): 340–61.

J. Rubery, 'Productive systems, international integration and the Single European Market', in A. Castro, P. Méhaut and J. Rubery (eds), *International Integration and Labour Market Organisation* (London: Academic Press, 1992).

J. Rubery, *Wage Determination and Sex Segregation in Employment: Report for the UK*, Report to the European Commission (Brussels: DG-V Equal Opportunities Unit, 1993).

J. Rubery, 'The British production regime: a societal-specific system?', *Economy and Society*, 23 (1994): 335–54.

J. Rubery, 'Performance-related pay and the prospects for gender pay equity', *Journal of Management Studies*, 32 (1995): 637–54.

J. Rubery, 'Part-time work: a threat to labour standards?', in J. O'Reilly and C. Fagan (eds), *Part-Time Prospects* (London: Routledge, 1998).

J. Rubery, F. Bettio, C. Fagan, F. Maier, S. Quack and P. Villa, 'Payment systems and gender pay differentials: some societal effects', in J. Rubery, with F. Bettio, M. Carroll, C. Fagan, D. Grimshaw, F. Maier, S. Quack and P. Villa (eds), *Equal Pay in Europe? Closing the Gender Wage Gap* (Basingstoke: Macmillan (now Palgrave Macmillan), 1998a).

J. Rubery and C. Fagan, *Wage Determination and Sex Segregation in Employment in the European Community*, Social Europe Supplement 4/94 (Luxembourg: Office for Official Publications of the European Communities, 1994).

J. Rubery and M. Smith, *The Future European Labour Supply*, Research paper, Employment and Social Affairs (Luxembourg: Office for Official Publications of the European Communities, 1999).

J. Rubery, M. Smith and C. Fagan, *Women's Employment in Europe: Trends and Prospects* (London : Routledge, 1999).

J. Rubery, M. Smith, C. Fagan and D. Grimshaw, *Women and European Employment* (London: Routledge, 1998b).

P. Ryan and C.F. Büchtemann, 'The school-to-work transition', in G. Schmid, J. O'Reilly and K. Schömann (eds), *International Handbook of Labour Market Policy and Evaluation* (Cheltenham: Edward Elgar, 1996).

C. Sabel, 'Bootstrapping reform: rebuilding firms, the welfare state and unions', *Politics and Society*, 23 (1995): 5–49.

S. Sachdev and F. Wilkinson, *Low Pay, the Working of the Labour Market and the Role of the Minimum Wage* (Institute of Employment Rights, 1998).

M. Sako, *Prices, Quality and Trust : Inter-Firm Relations in Britain and Japan* (Cambridge: Cambridge University Press, 1992).

W. Salverda, S. Bazen and M. Gregory, *The European–American Employment Gap, Wage Inequality, Earnings Mobility and Skill: A Study for France, Germany, the Netherlands, the United Kingdom and the United States*, Final Report from the European Low-Wage Employment Research Network (June 2001).

S. Sassen, *The Global City* (Princeton, NJ: Princeton University Press, 1991, 2001).

A. Saxenian, 'Beyond boundaries: open labor markets and learning in Silicon Valley', in M. Arthur and D. Rousseau (eds), *The Boundaryless Career* (New York: Oxford University Press, 1996).

H. Scullion, 'International human resource management', in J. Storey (ed.), *Human Resource Management: A Critical Text* (London: Routledge, 1995).

A. Sen, *Development as Freedom* (Oxford: Oxford University Press, 1999).

W. Sengenberger, 'Labour market segmentation and the business cycle', in F. Wilkinson (ed.), *The Dynamics of Labour Market Segmentation* (London: Academic Press, 1981).

W. Sengenberger, 'International labour standards in a globalized economy', in W. Sengenberger and D. Campbell (eds), *International Labour Standards and Economic Interdependence* (Geneva: International Institute for Labour Studies, 1994).

W. Sengenberger, and D. Campbell (eds), *International Labour Standards and Economic Interdependence* (Geneva: International Institute for Labour Studies, 1994).

P. Senker, 'The development and implementation of National Vocational Qualifications: an engineering case study', *New Technology, Work and Employment*, 11 (1996): 83–95.

R. Sennett, *The Corrosion of Character* (New York: Norton, 1998).

D. Silverman, *The Theory of Organizations* (London: Heinemann, 1970).

H. Simon, 'Organizations and markets', *Journal of Economic Perspectives*, 5 (1991): 30–2.

S. Slichter, J. Healy and E. Livernash, *The Impact of Collective Bargaining on Management* (Washington, DC: Brookings Institution, 1960).

H. Slomp, 'National variations in worker participation', in A-W. Harzing and J. van Ruysseveldt (eds), *International HRM* (London: Sage, 1995).

C. Smith and T. Elger, 'The societal effects school and transnational transfer: the case of Japanese investment in Britain', in M. Maurice and A. Sorge (eds), *Embedding Organizations* (Amsterdam: John Benjamins, 2000).

C. Smith and P. Meiksins, 'System, societal and dominance effects in cross-national organisational analysis', *Work, Employment and Society*, 9(2) (1995): 241–68.

M. Smith, C. Fagan and J. Rubery, ' Where and why is part-time work growing in Europe?', in J. O'Reilly and C. Fagan (eds), *Part-Time Prospects: Part-Time Work in Europe, North America and The Pacific Rim* (London: Routledge, 1998).

R. Smithers and C. McGreal, ' "Raid" on South African teachers', *The Guardian*, 16 February 2001.

J. Somovia, *Decent Work*, Report of the Director-General to the International Labour Conference 87th Session (Geneva: ILO, June 1999).

A. Sorge, 'Strategic fit and the social effect: interpreting cross-national comparisons of technology, organization and human resources', *Organization Studies*, 12 (1991): 161–90.

A. Sorge, 'Cross-national differences in personnel and organization', in A.-W. Harzing and J. van Ruysseveldt (eds), *International Human Resource Management* (London: Sage, 1995).

A. Sorge and M. Warner, 'Manpower training, manufacturing organization and workplace relations in Great Britain and West Germany', *British Journal of Industrial Relations*, 18 (1980): 318–33.

A. Sorge and M. Warner, *Comparative Factory Organization: an Anglo-German Comparison of Management and Manpower in Manufacturing* (Aldershot: Gower, 1986).

D. Soskice, 'Wage determination: the changing role of institutions in advanced industrialised countries', *Oxford Review of Economic Policy*, 6 (1990): 36–61.

D. Soskice, 'Reconciling markets and institutions: the German apprenticeship system', in L. M. Lynch (ed.), *Training and the Private Sector: International Comparisons* (Chicago: University of Chicago Press, 1994).

G. Standing, *Unemployment and Labour Market Flexibility: Sweden* (Geneva: ILO, 1998).

J. Stanford, 'Canadian labour market developments in international context: flexibility, regulation and demand', *Canadian Public Policy* 26(Supp.) (2000): S27–58.

Statistics in Focus, 'Weekend working and the family' (Luxembourg: Office for Official Publications of the European Communities, 2002).

H. Steedman and K. Wagner, 'Productivity, machinery and skills: clothing manufacture in Britain and Germany', *National Institute Economic Review*, May (1989): 40–57.

D. Stern, N. Finkelstein, J. Stone, J. Latting and C. Dornsife, *School-to-Work: Research on Programs in the US* (Washington, DC: Falmer Press, 1995).

M. Stevens, 'A theoretical model of on-the-job training with imperfect competition', *Oxford Economic Papers*, 46 (1994): 537–62.

P. Stewart (ed.), *Beyond Japanese Management: The End of Modern Times?* (London: Frank Cass, 1996).

J. Stopford and L. Wells, *Managing the Multinational Enterprise* (New York: Basic Books, 1972).

W. Streeck, 'The rise and decline of neocorporatism', in L. Ulman, B. Eichengreen and W. Dickens (eds), *Labor and an Integrated Europe* (Washington, DC: The Brookings Institution, 1993).

W. Streeck, 'Lean production in the German automobile industry: a test case for convergence theory', in S. Berger and R. Dore (eds), *National Diversity and Global Capitalism* (Ithaca, NY: Cornell University Press, 1996).

W. Streeck, 'Beneficial constraints: on the economic limits of rational voluntarism', in J. R. Hollingsworth and R. Boyer (eds), *Contemporary Capitalism* (Cambridge: Cambridge University Press, 1997).

W. Streeck, J. Hilbert, K-H. van Kevalaer, F. Maier and H. Weber, *The Role of the Social Partners in Vocational Training and Further Training in the Federal Republic of Germany* (Berlin: CEDEFOP, 1987).

W. Streeck and J. Visser, 'The rise of the conglomerate union', *European Journal of Industrial Relations*, 3 (1997): 305–32.

C. Thörnqvist, 'The decentralization of industrial relations: the Swedish case in comparative perspective', *European Journal of Industrial Relations*, 5 (1999): 71–87.

F. Traxler, 'Collective bargaining and industrial change: a case of disorganization? A comparative analysis of eighteen OECD countries', *European Sociological Review*, 12 (1996): 271–87.

F. Traxler, S. Blaschke and B. Kittel, *National Labour Relations in Internationalized Markets: A Comparative Study of Institutions, Change and Performance* (Oxford: Oxford University Press, 2001).

O. Tregaskis, 'HRD in Foreign MNEs', *International Studies of Management and Organization*, 28 (1998): 136–63.

T. Treu, G. Geroldi and M. Maiello, 'Italy: labour relations', in J. Hartog and J. Theeuwes (eds), *Labour Market Contracts and Institutions: A Cross-National Comparison* (Amsterdam: North-Holland, 1993).

R. Tung, 'Human resource planning in Japanese multinationals: a model for US firms?', *Journal of International Business Studies*, 15 (1984): 139–49. Reprinted in P. Ghauri and S. Prasad (eds), *International Management* (London: The Dryden Press, 1995).

P. Turnbull and V. Wass, 'The greatest game no more — redundant dockers and the demise of "dock work" ', *Work, Employment and Society*, 8 (1994): 487–506.

P. Turnbull and V. Wass, 'Job insecurity and labour market lemons: the (mis)management of redundancy in steel making, coal mining and port transport', *Journal of Management Studies*, 34 (1997): 27–51.

P. Turnbull and V. Wass, 'Redundancy and the paradox of job insecurity', in E. Heery and J. Salmon (eds), *The Insecure Workforce* (London: Routledge, 2000).

L. Turner, 'Prospects for worker participation in management in the Single Market', in L. Ulman, B. Eichengreen and W. Dickens (eds), *Labor and an Integrated Europe* (Washington, DC: The Brookings Institution, 1993).

L. Ulman, B. Eichengreen and W. Dickens (eds), *Labor and an Integrated Europe* (Washington, DC: The Brookings Institution, 1993).

United Nations, *World Investment Report 1999* (New York: United Nations, 1999).

J. van Ruysseveldt and J. Visser (eds), *Industrial Relations in Europe: Traditions and Transitions* (London: Sage, 1996a).

J. van Ruysseveldt and J. Visser, 'Contestation and State intervention forever? Industrial relations in France', in J. van Ruysseveldt and J. Visser (eds), *Industrial Relations in Europe: Traditions and Transitions* (London: Sage, 1996b).

U. Veersma, 'Multinational corporations and industrial relations: policy and practice', in A-W. Harzing and J. van Ruysseveldt (eds), *International Human Resource Management* (London : Sage Publications, 1995).

R.Vernon, 'International investment and international trade in the product cycle', *Quarterly Journal of Economics*, 80 (1966): 190–207.

J. Visser, 'A truly mixed case: industrial relations in Italy', in J. van Ruysseveldt and J. Visser (eds), *Industrial Relations in Europe: Traditions and Transitions* (London: Sage, 1996).

J. Visser and J. van Ruysseveldt, 'From pluralism to … where? Industrial relations in Great Britain', in J. van Ruysseveldt and J. Visser (eds), *Industrial Relations in Europe: Traditions and Transitions* (London: Sage, 1996).

Volkswagen, A. G., *Vereinbarung zur '4-Tage-Woche' (28,8 Std/Woche)* (Wolsburg, 1993).

J. Waddington, 'United Kingdom: recovering from the neo-liberal assault?', in J. Waddington and R. Hoffmann (eds), *Trade Unions in Europe: Facing Challenges and Searching for Solutions* (Brussels, European Trade Union Institute, 2000).

J. Waddington and R. Hoffmann, 'Trade unions in Europe: reform, organisation and restructuring,' in J. Waddington and R. Hoffmann (eds), *Trade Unions in Europe: Facing Challenges and Searching for Solutions* (Brussels: European Trade Union Institute, 2000).

K. Wagner, 'Qualifikationsniveau in Ostdeutschen Betrieben, Bestand — Bewertung — Anpassungsbedarf', *Zeitschrift für Betriebswirtschaft*, 63 (1993): 129–45.

K. Wagner, 'The German apprenticeship system under strain', in P. Culpepper and D. Finegold (eds), *The German Skills Machine* (New York: Berghahn Books, 1999).

J. Walters, 'What Went Wrong at the Summit? World Trade Organisation Special Report', *The Observer*, 5 December 1999.

C. Weathers, 'The 1999 *Shunto* and the restructuring of wage setting in Japan', *Osaka City University Economic Review*, 35 (1999): 71–104.

L. Weiss, 'War, the state and the origins of the Japanese employment system', *Politics and Society*, 21(3) (1993): 325–54.

K. Wever, *Negotiating Competitiveness* (Boston, MA: Harvard Business School Press, 1995).

G. White, 'The remuneration of public servants: fair pay or new pay?', in S. Corby and G. White (eds), *Employee Relations in the Public Services: Themes and Issues* (London: Routledge, 1999).

R. Whitley (ed.), *European Business Systems* (London: Sage, 1992).

R. Whitley, 'Dominant forms of economic organization in market economies', *Organization Studies*, 15 (1994): 153–82.

R. Whitley, *Divergent Capitalisms* (Oxford: Oxford University Press, 1999).

M. Whittall, 'The BMW European Works Council: A Cause for European Industrial Relations Optimism?', *European Journal of Industrial Relations*, 6 (2000): 61–84.

F. Wilkinson, 'Productive systems', *Cambridge Journal of Economics*, 7(3/4) (1983): 413–29.

K. Williams, 'Shareholder value: introduction to special issue', *Economy and Society*, 29 (2000): 1–12.

J. Wills, 'Great Expectations: three years in the life of a European works council', *European Journal of Industrial Relations*, 6 (2000): 109–118.

J. Witte and A. Kalleberg, 'Matching training and jobs: the fit between vocational education and employment in the German labour market,' *European Sociological Review*, 11 (1995): 1–25.

J. Womack, D. Jones and D. Roos, *The Machine That Changed the World* (New York: Rawson Associates, 1990).

E. Yuen and H. Tak Kee, 'Headquarters, host-culture and organizational influences on HRM policies and practices', *International Management Review*, 33 (1992): 361–83.

Index of names

Taylor, F.W. 177
Thompson, G. 225–6, 239
Thörnqvist, C. 161, 171
Toyoda, E. 55
Traxler, F. 149, 150, 157, 161
Tregaskis, O. 219
Treu, T. 154
Tronti, L. 186, 187
Tung, R. 206
Turnbull, P. 190, 191
Turner, L. 22–4

Ulman, L. 14, 24, 173
United Nations 224

Veersma, U. 254
Velzen, S. van 17
Verbist, G. 94
Vernon, R. 202, 203
Villa, P. 15–16, 89
Visser, J. 150, 151, 152, 154, 160, 173
Volkswagen A.G. 188–9
Vroom, B. de 20, 22, 98

Waddington, J. 150, 153
Wadsworth, J. 141

Wagner, K. 134–5, 180
Wallerstein, I. 30, 225
Walters, J. 247
Warner, M. 38, 177
Wass, V. 190, 191
Weathers, C. 172
Weber, H. 121, 135
Weiss, L. 41, 61
Wells, L. 201
Wever, K. 113, 122, 125, 190
White, G. 163
Whitley, R. 40, 71, 221, 226, 230
Whittall, M. 22
Wilkinson, B. 73
Wilkinson, F. 41, 46, 163
Williams, K. 231
Wills, J. 22
Witte, J. 121
Womack, J. 31, 55, 56, 69
Wood, S. 98

Yuen, E. 220

Subject index

flexibility 43–4, 138–41
  gender, part-time work and 99–103, 103–5
  and minimizing redundancies 186–7
  and labour market performance 142–7
  pressures for and training system 132–3
  see also regulation
flexible diversified quality production 57
flexible production 57
flexible specialization 57, 58, 64–7
Fordist production regimes 8–10, 54–7
foreign direct investment (FDI) 222, 223
foremen 10–12
fragmentation, social 235–38
France
  childcare 96
  deregulation and re-regulation 170
  division of labour 177–81 *passim*
  employee involvement 23; works councils
    23–4, 158, 159
  employment protection 186
  emulation of Japanese methods 72–3
  foremen 10–12
  industrial relations 150, 152–4
  payment systems 181–4 *passim*
  promotion of motherhood 100
  societal effect approach 38
  training system 110, 111, 122–3;
    performance of 124–8 *passim*
  wage setting 160
  welfare regime 88–9
  working time 195, 196
free collective bargaining 151
functional specialization 178, 179

gender pay inequality 13, 14–16
gender regimes 99–105
  employment and convergence 103–5
  flexibility and part–time work 100–3,
    103–5
General Motors (GM) 190
geocentric organizations 205–8
German MNCs 220
Germany 234
  care arrangements 96
  codetermination system 22–3, 41
  division of labour 177–81 *passim*
  employee involvement 20–4; works
    councils 22–3, 157–9
  foremen 10–12
  gender regimes 99–105
  industrial relations 148, 151–2
  job structures 92–5
  part-time work 14–16, 17
  pay 181–4 *passim*; and job grading 14,
    15–16, 181–4

production system 54–6; diversified quality
    production 58, 62–4
  regulation of layoffs 19, 20, 188–9
  social market economy 148
  societal effect approach 38
  training system 110, 111, 120–2; performance
    of 124–9 *passim*; problems due to craft
    basis 133, 134–5; technical change and
    129, 130–1
  wage setting 161–2; decentralization of
    collective bargaining 171–2, 173
  welfare regime 84–92 *passim*
  working time 167, 168, 195
global capital 48
  see also multinational corporations
global corporation 202, 203, 204
global influences 208–20
global international economy 224–7
global isomorphism 209–11
global market effects 47–8
globalization 222–40
  evidence of 222–3
  forces for convergence in employment
    systems 231–40
  global ideology and societal fragmentation
    235–39
  human resources and comparative advantage
    227–31
  inevitability of 224–7
  new production paradigm 233
  pan–national governance 234–5
  resistance to 239–40
  and specialization 71
  stability of national employment regimes
    233–4
  and training systems 133–6
government *see* state
Gresham's Law 231

heterarchical organization 203–5, 219–20
higher education 127
hire and fire, freedom to 138–9
Hoover Corporation 254
household structures 192, 237–8, 239
human capital theory 108
human resource management 31–2
  policy 215–17
human resources 227–31
human rights 242–3, 245
hybridization 111, 173

IBM 75
ideology 48–9
  global and societal fragmentation 235–9
in-person services 228–9

market
    global market effects   47–8
    state, market and family in welfare regimes
        85–92
    supremacy of   236–7
    universalist approach   27, 28–32
market-led vocational training   106–7, 111,
    111–17
    coverage   125
    labour market flexibility   132
    technical change   129–31
    unemployment   132–3
Marks & Spencer   256–8
marriage   237, 238
Marxism   29–30
masculinity vs femininity   33, 34
mass production   9–12, 53–6
McDonald's   236
Mediterranean welfare model   89–90
mental maps   33
merit (or output)-based pay   181–4
Mexico   235
micro-environmental factors   217
minimum wage systems   161, 163–4
mobility of labour   111, 227–8
Modern Apprenticeships   116–17
modified male breadwinner model   89, 90
motivation   34–6
multiculturalism   237
Multilateral Agreement on Investment (MAI)
    239–40
multi-domestic company   201, 204
multinational corporations (MNCs)   47–8, 75,
    198–221
    as agents of diffusion of best practice
        199–201
    employment policies and practices for
        non-management staff   208–210
    evidence of globalization   223
    international management recruitment and
        deployment   205–8
    local vs corporate or global influences
        217–201
    modes of diffusion of best practice   211–17
    and survival of nationally-specific employment
        regimes   198–201
    and training   133
    typologies of   201–5

nation states
    extent and inevitability of globalization
        224–7
    resistance to globalization   239–40
    role in world economy   40–2
    as unit of analysis   42

national comparative case studies   5–24
    downsizing   7, 18–22
    employee involvement   7, 22
    pay systems   7, 12–14, 16–18
    retirement   7, 18–20
    skills and work organization   7, 8–10
    working time   7, 17–18
national differences   5–6
national employment regimes
    MNCs and survival of   198–201
    production regimes   56–70; borrowing and
        learning from other societies   70–5
    stability of   233–4
National Institute of Economic and Social
    Research (NIESR)   180–1
national stereotypes   35–6
national training systems   109–24
    performance   124–9
National Vocational Qualifications
    (NVQs)   116
nationalism   236
needs, hierarchy of   34–5
neo-liberal welfare regime   85–8
Netherlands
    disability   83
    employment rate   143
    part-time work   16–18, 101
    works councils   158, 159
new production paradigm   233
    see also lean production
Nike   256
Nikkeiren (Japan Federation of Employers'
    Associations)   135, 157
Nordic countries
    centralized collective bargaining   160–2
    welfare state model   90, 91
    see also under individual countries
North American Agreement on Labour
    Cooperation (NAALC)   254
North American Free Trade Association (NAFTA)
    234–5
    labour standards   249, 254–5
Norway   96, 254

occupational labour market (OLM)   109–11
    national systems of vocational training   111,
        111–17, 120–2, 125–6
OECD countries
    gender regimes and employment systems
        99–104
    labour supply   78–83
older men: employment rates   81, 82
on-the-job training   118
organizational design   34
output (or merit)-based pay   181–4

WITHDRAWN
FROM STOCK
QMUL LIBRARY